1982

A catalogue record for this book is available from
the British Library

ISBN 978 1 84425 404 0

Library of Congress control no 2006935945

All pictures in this book are courtesy of
LAT Photographic, except where stated.

Published by Haynes Publishing,
Sparkford, Yeovil, Somerset BA22 7JJ, England
Tel: 01963 442030 Fax: 01963 440001
Int. tel: +44 1963 442030 Int. fax: +44 1963 440001
E-mail: sales@haynes.co.uk
Website: www.haynes.co.uk

Haynes North America Inc.
861 Lawrence Drive, Newbury Park,
California 91320, USA

Design and layout by Richard Parsons

Printed and bound in Great Britain by
J. H. Haynes & Co. Ltd

1982

The inside story of the sensational Grand Prix season

Christopher Hilton

Author's Acknowledgements

I am deeply grateful to Keke Rosberg (and thanks for the Foreword), John Watson, Gordon Murray, Patrick Tambay, Andrea de Cesaris, Riccardo Patrese, Alan Jenkins, Jean-Pierre Jarier, Professor Sid Watkins, Alex Hawkridge, Chris Witty, Derek Warwick, Derek Daly, Brian Henton, René Arnoux, Mario Andretti, Mauro Forghieri, Jackie Oliver, Jochen Mass and Teo Fabi. Arietto Paletti, father of Riccardo, produced a lovely, loving memorial book to his son Riccardo and sent one to Mike Earle (who ran Riccardo) and he sent it on to me. Mr Paletti very generously gave permission to use material from the book, and for that sincere thanks. I am indebted to Monica Meroni for translations. Earle also spoke touchingly about Riccardo. Renaud de Laborderie of Solar in Paris,

Christiano Chiavegato of La Stampa in Turin and Marco Ragazzoni of Autosprint in S. Lazzaro di Savena were invaluable for getting those most elusive numerals, telephone numbers.

Jeannette Green-Davies of Las Vegas Clark County Library District and Barbara Thompson of the Detroit Public Library National Automotive History Collection were enormously helpful in securing material on their respective Grands Prix.

For lending their photographs I'm indebted to Paul Truswell, David Pearson, David Hilleard, Steve Potter, Gareth Rees, Jay Gillotti, Charles J. Bough and Julian Eyres. I'm equally grateful to *Motor Sport* magazine for including a paragraph which brought these photographers to me.

ABOVE *John Player hospitality at the Lotus motorhome. From left Derick Allsop (Daily Mail), Nigel Mansell, Roger Moody (BBC), Colin Chapman, (Alan Brinton, freelance, obscured) John Blunsden (The Times), Patrick Stephenson (South African radio obscured), Nigel Roebuck (Autosport), (obscured), at far end of table Alan Henry (Motoring News). From right Malcolm Folley (Mail on Sunday), Keith Botsford (The Sunday Times). Centre, grinning, the author. For another view of this fine body of men, see Page 276.*

CONTENTS

————— 1982 —————

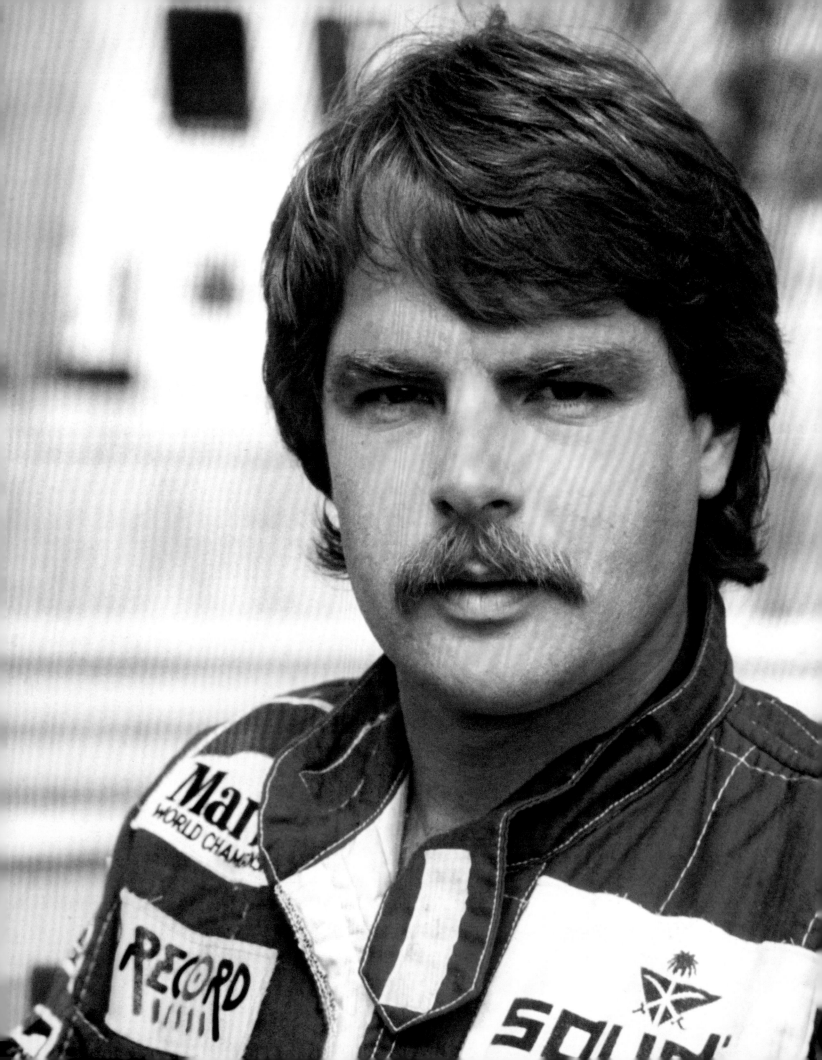

FOREWORD

BY KEKE ROSBERG

It always makes me smile when people say 'You got the World Championship in 1982 in a Williams with one win.' I say 'Oh yes, I did, but look at the record books: all the blokes who had the most wins – Alain Prost, John Watson, Didier Pironi, Niki Lauda and René Arnoux – didn't get any more than two.

I really thank Bernie Ecclestone that I was able to retire from the sport having gained a good, solid financial background for life. I don't think without Bernie it would have been possible, so I raise a glass to him every second day.

These days, I find 1982 looking me straight in the face every fortnight at the races because Frank Williams, Patrick Head and Frank Dernie are all still at the team and of course my son Nico (above) is there driving for them.

It was an amazing season, something happening all the time. We had ten more cars than now and some were forced to pre-qualify. That made a difference. There were twenty-six on the grid and a lot more depth in the whole thing. In 2006, if you looked at it, you had two cars that could really win, Renault or Ferrari. Back then – because of the unreliability of the turbos – almost anyone could win and eleven did in the sixteen races.

That's why I smile when people talk about my one.

It was enough.

KEKE ROSBERG
WORLD CHAMPION 1982

INTRODUCTION

——— 1982 ———

I was a stranger to it and no more than curious. The American Bill Bryson in his seminal *Notes From A Small Island* (Black Swan edition, London, 1997) has recorded how he reached England for the first time – Dover – and realised he was completely ignorant about all that was suddenly there before him, people, things, phrases, habits and habitats. 'I didn't know anything really, which is a strangely wonderful position to be in.'

In June 1982 I was an Englishman who'd just dropped into America – Detroit – to cover the USA-East Grand Prix. I'd never seen a Formula One car and I was all but completely ignorant of the people, the things, the phrases, the habits and habitats beyond the most obvious. I'm not at all sure I would have recognised Nigel Mansell if he'd walked past in the street.

Nor was it a strangely wonderful position to be in, because I was going to cover the Grand Prix for the *Daily Express*, and with a five-hour time gap running constantly against me: London newspaper deadlines are not arranged around Eastern Standard Time. I wasn't unduly concerned, because pretending you have a great deal of knowledge when you don't comes naturally to journalists and, anyway, any competent wordsmith knows what to do to camouflage the pretence.

The man who covered Grand Prix racing for the *Daily Express* also did tennis (a wonderful thing of itself, getting the same man to cover two sports which constantly happened at the same time in different places). He couldn't go to Detroit, or Montreal the following week, and I wanted to experience a Grand Prix in the same way that, writing about sport generally, I'd wanted to experience the Saturday of a Lord's Test, a Cup Final, the Grand National, Wimbledon, the Boat Race, the Open golf, and so on. Here was a chance.

'Get me a price and we'll see,' the Sports Editor said.

I got a price for both races and accommodation from a company which specialised in such things.

'Go,' he said.

I went.

The 'track' zigzagged in geometrical patterns round a skyscraper called the Renaissance Center which rose vast and majestic from the odd jumble of fading and faded buildings which made up downtown Detroit. From it you could see the Detroit River and Canada on the other side. The Press Room was high in the Ren-Cen (as it was called) and I didn't know a single person: motor racing journalists tend not to cover anything else. The journalists gazed, almost suspicious – who the hell's he, and where's he come from? – while I gazed down. The cars were coming out – small as models – for some sort of practice session. They were nicely coloured, nicely shaped (if that turns you on), and they made a great deal of rasping, crackling, echoing noise like a constant sequence of explosions.

Singly or in little shoals they darted, sprinted, braked, darted, sprinted, braked, going round and round and round. It all seemed to hold profound meaning for the journalists, who discussed it in a most animated way. To me it looked like still life travelling fast.

Never mind. I'd have my experience, however fleeting, and get on with the rest of my life, which certainly wouldn't involve any more long-haul flights to watch strange rituals like this.

Actually it was a wonderful ignorance.

I didn't know some journalists in that Press Room would become lifelong friends.

I didn't know that down there a fascinating tribe of lone warriors was doing the sprinting and braking, and I'd still be talking to many of them and writing about all of them these 25 years later – see Acknowledgements on page 4.

And I didn't know I'd come right into the middle of the most dramatic World Championship of all.

I was about to find out.

OPPOSITE *Yes, the cars were nicely shaped and it did turn a lot of people on. Here are the sensuous McLaren bodyshells all in a row in the Austrian pit lane.*

COMING
ROUND AGAIN

————SETTING THE SCENE————

The single paragraph had been hustled into *Autosport*'s issue of Thursday 17 September 1981 because of a rumour they'd heard as they went to press. If they'd heard sooner they'd have made a great deal more of it.

Secrecy is a most precious commodity in the incestuous world of Grand Prix racing and Ron Dennis, in the process of making himself the leading player in the McLaren team, had almost got away with a great coup.

Lauda – known affectionately throughout motor sport as The Rat, because his face was shaped like that – indeed retired in 1979 and, most logical of men, concluded that that phase of his life was over. From then on he excluded motor racing, didn't even watch the races on television. Instead he ran the airline he'd founded and which bore his name.

Dennis kept in touch, however, regularly asking 'Well, when are you coming back?' Lauda, good enough to have won the World Championship in 1975 and 1977, was only 32, no age at all for a racing driver.

He did go to the Austrian Grand Prix at the Österreichring in August to contribute some expert summarising on television with Heinz Prüller, an all-round journalist and old hand who'd commentated on Lauda's Championships. This was the first race Lauda had attended since he'd walked away in Canada two years before and, to his surprise, he experienced a sort of homecoming. He wondered. Afterwards he motored over to the well-known fitness guru Willy Dungl, who'd looked after him following an horrendous crash at the Nürburgring in 1976. Lauda made vague noises about fitness, Dungl sniffed and said 'Right, we'll see,' and after some cycling pronounced that Lauda wasn't fit for anything.

Lauda asked Dungl to put together a fitness regime, 'Just in case, you know.'

Lauda didn't go to the Dutch Grand Prix, after

Austria, but motored down to the one after that, the Italian at Monza. There the sense of homecoming deepened. He met Dennis and asked: 'Can you sort out a test for me to see if I can still handle a Formula One car?' Dennis said yes and prepared to move quickly. This was already September.

During the race McLaren driver John Watson went wide coming from one of the corners and lost control of the car. It hit the barrier and smashed into pieces, the engine and gearbox thrown back onto the track. Many, perhaps most, thought Watson must be dead and were surprised when he returned to the pits perfectly calm and still exactly as Mother Nature had created him.

This, clearly, did not inhibit Lauda or his logic. After the crash at the Nürburgring nobody could tell Lauda anything about the dangers: Lauda's Ferrari suddenly a fireball, Lauda trapped, Lauda seared, Lauda given the Last Rites. A complete mythology had grown up around his survival and it had made him in global terms not only the most famous driver but, arguably, the only driver non-followers would know instantly. The contours of his face, still seared, were iconic because they showed what a human being could survive.

The return of Niki Lauda would be global news.

Dennis picked the following Wednesday for the test and picked the Donington circuit in the Midlands. Compared to Silverstone or Brands Hatch it was more discreet in reputation and geographical position, less likely to have prying eyes roving round it.

McLaren confided in Watson. 'I knew Niki was going to be there.'

OPPOSITE *The Monaco roulette wheel is about to turn: Riccardo Patrese, Alain Prost, Didier Pironi, Andrea de Cesaris, Michele Alboreto.*

Lauda tests Brabham

Double World Champion, Niki Lauda, was due at Donington yesterday (Wednesday) to test a Brabham BT49. We hear that the test is part of serious comeback plans by the Austrian, who abruptly walked out on the Brabham team in Canada in 1979.

Lauda remembered the assembled company: Dennis, Watson, some mechanics, an ambulance and a fire engine.[1]

Autosport reported the test was 'conducted in unbelievable secrecy, with security guards everywhere, all in radio contact with each other. "No," said a Donington receptionist when we telephoned on Wednesday afternoon, "there's no-one here at all. It's funny, a lot of people have been calling about that."'[2]

Watson remembers 'in four or five laps we did the quickest time we had ever done with the car there – four days after the Monza shunt. It wasn't ostensibly to set a time. I went out and drove the car to establish a time as opposed to setting one. [Setting a time would have represented a target, establishing one was creating a yardstick Lauda could work around.] Niki got in and drove the car but he hadn't been in one for two years, he certainly wasn't race fit and he was probably unfit. His first comment was that the car had too much understeer and he didn't like a car that understeered.'

Lauda, most untypically, would say that he felt emotional about driving again but 'by the first corner I had forgotten the emotion. By then I was already a racing driver again, giving all my attention and concentration to controlling the car.'[3]

Those first few laps shocked him: how physically demanding the cars had become because of ground effects[4] – they had virtually no suspension – and how unfit he really was. He came quickly into the pits and, after that, built and built by careful degrees down the day.

As Watson says, 'Anyway, he did 15 or 18 laps.'

He got to within a whisker of Watson's yardstick and told himself 'the speed hasn't gone away'. The intrepid (and excluded) *Autosport* news hounds gleaned that by day's end Lauda had done 48 laps with a best time of 60.7 seconds compared to Watson's 59.7.

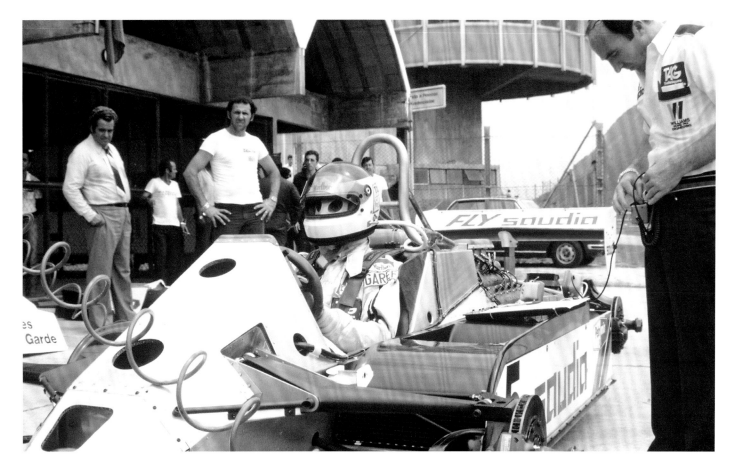

Soon enough, Lauda made his decision. He'd go to Marlboro, McLaren's title sponsors, to try and get himself more money than any racing driver had ever been paid before. He knew he was global news.

Frank Williams had two problems. He'd dropped Carlos Reutemann, who almost won the 1981 World Championship, and Alan Jones suddenly retired. Williams was looking for two drivers and made John Watson an offer. After careful consideration, because Williams was the only team apart from McLaren he'd drive for, Watson declined. Williams also contacted Lauda but that didn't lead anywhere and, worse, all the other leading drivers were staying where they were.

Williams cast his gaze over the remainder and his eye alighted upon one Keijo Rosberg, known always and only as Keke.

Let's be honest, you would not have been Frank's first choice.

'I am sure not – if Frank had been given six to eight months to consider, but I think Alan's retirement caught him by surprise. It's fair to say that.'

Rosberg, a Finn with a bristling presence and a bristling moustache, had been around. He'd raced in North America and from 1978 in Grands Prix for a variety of small teams, Theodore, ATS, Wolf, and Fittipaldi. The career spanned 36 races, one third place and one fifth. Even so, self-doubt was remote

from him and when Williams invited him to a test at the Paul Ricard circuit in the south of France he approached it with confidence.

You had to prove yourself.

'Of course I did, of course I did. I came from Fittipaldi and there was always the budget – a bit like Midland today. It was only November so Frank had the time, it wasn't a panic situation at all.'

Williams wouldn't be there in person but would listen carefully to what the team said afterwards.

'If you drove a Williams or a Theodore or you drove for Fittipaldi there wasn't that much difference. One was a bit quicker than the others but you didn't have to learn steering wheels with 27 switches, or electronic engineering until it came out of your ears. What did you have? One for drinks, one for radio and that was it. You had the same gearboxes as long as it wasn't turbo. You had the same engine, same tyres, so it was not a big deal.'

Rosberg arrived the night before the test.

'It was the Beaujolais nouveau time – it had just come out. Frank Dernie [the engineer] and me had dinner and what else are we going to do but have Beaujolais nouveau? It is not considered a criminal act in the south of Europe to have a glass of red wine. I wasn't driving until the next day.'

They turned in at 1.00 am and Rosberg reached Ricard early.

ABOVE *Waiting at Rio, Carlos Reutemann, the man who retired, didn't, and retired again: Frank Williams (right) was never far away.*

ABOVE *Keke Rosberg trapped behind Andrea de Cesaris at Dijon and getting very, very angry. Rosberg would finally find a way through for his only victory of the season.*

'They put me in the car at eight o'clock in the morning, qualifiers, cold tyres, and said "Do a time".'

This represented almost a challenge although Rosberg has said[5] that Frank Williams 'sometimes made strange decisions and this was one of them.'

Now, reflecting, he muses about 'if I hadn't done the time? It's a hypothetical question what would have happened. I don't know because it can always be taken out of context, you know. The full test would have been used to determine the capability of the driver but that lap was like the dot on the "i". Even half asleep I was quick on the lap...

'I don't think there was anybody else there except the team, Dernie and Charlie Crichton-Stuart.'[6]

Rosberg's best time on the short circuit was 1m 4.3s, quicker than Alain Prost had done in the Renault the week before (1m 4.6s) – so he could make the car perform. There was more. Williams had a fundamental conception of what a Grand Prix driver should be and that had found perfect expression in Jones, a square-shouldered Aussie who brought aspects of the outback with him: tough, rugged, self-sufficient, living hard and driving hard. 'Jones,' Williams once ruminated, 'spoiled us.'

Rosberg brought aspects of the tundra with him: tough, rugged, self-sufficient...

At a subsequent test at Ricard, Frank Williams went for a day and described Rosberg as 'bloody quick'. He signed in December.

'Getting into a big team like Williams was not harder than I expected. I never had any doubts from within the team, never had any doubts about myself, and we worked pretty well together.'

The two big names – well, Lauda already big and Rosberg about to become big – were in place. So was quiet, understated John Watson who prepared to outdrive both of them, and almost would. These three and all the rest hadn't long to wait: the season started in South Africa in January.

Every Grand Prix season is a direct descendant of all that went before and you can, if you're interested in these things, trace it back to the dawn of motoring in the 1880s. There's a direct lineage, a continuity, which is very strong. You can equally take each season in isolation because they are complete chapters unto themselves: since 1950 each has produced its own World Champion.

By 1982 the Championship had become a

FAN'S EYE VIEW

'In 1981 I started to work with Brian Jones, the circuit commentator at Brands Hatch, as a "commentator's assistant", sorting the paperwork and doing the lapcharts for him. By 1982 I attended virtually all the events that Brian did, assisting him in any way that he needed. Although this was unpaid work it allowed me access to more race meetings than I would otherwise have been able to afford to attend, and to places that I would not normally be allowed.'

**PAUL TRUSWELL,
WOKING, UK**

FROM TOP CLOCKWISE *Nelson Piquet, thinking; Patrick Tambay, waiting; Jacques Laffite, walking; Keke Rosberg, talking; Niki Lauda, listening; Alain Prost, looking.*

sophisticated place, conscious of its own image, dispensing considerable budgets and refining technology at an ever-increasing tempo. It remained, however, relatively small – in newspaper terms the most major of the minor sports – and teams did not count their employees in hundreds, nor their budgets in $100 millions.

It was still a tight-knit fraternity and small enough that everybody knew everybody.

Alan Jenkins, a leading engineer with McLaren, remembers: 'The great thing was we lived up on Winter Hill above Maidenhead. We lived in a wooden shack in the grounds of Barbro Peterson's[7] house – well, Wattie was living with her. It was idyllic. We'd walk between this huge great hedge on the morning of a race weekend, cross the lawns, tap on the window of the kitchen. Wattie would be having his breakfast. We'd grab his bag and head off to the races. Keke Rosberg was one corner round the lane, in effect the nearest door neighbour. There was a field between us and he was the next house. Tim

BELOW *Prost and the Renault, here at Monaco: the Championship would have been quite different if the car had been reliable.*

Schenken[8] and a couple of others lived up there, [Pentti] Airikkala and Ari Vatanen and every bloody mad rally driver in the place lived up there as well. It was great. When there was something going on at McLaren – a car launch or something like that – Niki would come over early and stay at Barbro's, and in fact Alain Prost even did when he joined the team.'

The moods of Grand Prix racing were changing, however. At the British Grand Prix in 1977 Renault entered a turbo-powered car, something which had not been seen before (and was regarded with curiosity). It was fiendishly fast when it worked, fiendishly unreliable, and required many, many more engineers and mechanics than the normal engines. The modern army of technicians had been born.

One problem for the driver was 'turbo lag', meaning you pressed the accelerator and nothing happened for an indeterminate time, then the power hit you like a hammer blow.

'The throttle lag was such an issue,' Jenkins says. 'It wasn't the power, it was this hesitancy, and it

affected some drivers worse than others. Desperate, yes! For example, when we first started with Porsche[9] they thought they were the kingpins about throttle lag and understood it more than anybody else – but they weren't running engines with the same boost and the same horsepower as a Formula One car. What they thought was reasonable horsepower ended up 50 per cent more.

'It was so difficult to judge because you couldn't really time it: there was just this delay. You couldn't feather it, you couldn't balance it. Alain had come to us used to it a bit from the Renault, Niki found it desperate. We could dick around with the car all week but if somebody could tweak it just to reduce the delay we'd go a second quicker, two seconds quicker just by reducing the delay a bit.'

By 1981 Renault had been joined by Ferrari in using turbos, although Nelson Piquet, a slender Brazilian with a nasal way of speaking English, won the Championship in a Brabham from Reutemann and Jones in the Williamses. All three had the traditional, affordable Cosworth engines which you bought off the shelf from the factory at Northampton, as teams had been doing for a generation. In the final race of 1981, where Piquet won the Championship, a young Briton, Derek Warwick, managed to qualify. He drove for the small and underfinanced team called Toleman, and he had a turbo engine propelling him. In 1982 Brabham would have them too, made by BMW.

That made the season very unusual, because different teams were deploying these two utterly different kinds of engine.

The moods were changing in other ways. FOCA (Formula One Constructors' Association) had been established and, led by Bernie Ecclestone and Max Mosley, was flexing its muscles over the running of the sport. That brought them into direct conflict with FISA (Fédération Internationale du Sport Automobile) led by an autocratic Frenchman, Jean-Marie Balestre. The split cut into the teams: most British-based teams sided with Ecclestone; Ferrari and Renault – the so-called grandee teams – with Balestre. The two would engage in a trial of strength which wrecked one Grand Prix and threatened the structure of the whole thing.

The cars were becoming more sophisticated. 'I did some tests in 1982,' Jenkins says. 'We were just starting to be able to put some numbers to the aerodynamics in those days and just starting to be able to discuss aerodynamic balance in terms of numbers which related not just to settings on the car but to ride height. You battled away in a wind tunnel not really knowing much about where everybody

ABOVE *Nelson Piquet and Gordon Murray ...discussing the revolutionary Pit Stop Ploy?*

LEFT *Grand Prix racing prepared to tread where it had never been before (courtesy Detroit Public Library National Automotive History Collection).*

FROM: Mark Giannotta
Carl Byoir & Associates, Inc.
100 Renaissance Center
Suite 2002
Detroit, Michigan 48243-1048
(313) 259-1363

FOR: DETROIT RENAISSANCE

FOR RELEASE

DETROIT TO HOST 1982
U.S. GRAND PRIX RACE

Henry Ford II, newly-elected Chairman of Detroit Renaissance, today announced an agreement with Bernard Ecclestone, Chairman of Formula One Constructors Association, that will bring Grand Prix racing to downtown Detroit in 1982. The Grand Prix is run on two other U.S. courses each year; Long Beach, California and Las Vegas. The Detroit race is scheduled to take place on Sunday, June 6.

The successful drive to land the 1982 Grand Prix Formula One race was spearheaded by Detroit Renaissance. Robert E. McCabe, President of Detroit Renaissance, said he is optimistic about the future of Formula One racing in Detroit. "Our intention is to begin in 1982 and have a world championship race here every year.

McCabe estimated that the Grand Prix will draw some $3 to $4-million in tourist dollars to Detroit annually.

The 2.5-mile race course will begin south of Renaissance Center and proceed east along the river to Rivard. It will then go north to Atwater, west on Atwater to St. Antoine, north to Woodbridge and then east making a transition to East Jefferson. A hairpin turn brings the course west on Jefferson to the Chrysler Service Drive where it runs north to Congress.

(more)

DETROIT TO HOST--2/

The course then proceeds west on Congress to Beaubien, south to Larned, west to Woodward, south to Jefferson and west to Washington Boulevard. The cars will then turn south in front of Cobo Hall and east and south on Civic Center Drive to Atwater. A sharp turn to the east brings the course through the Atwater tunnel to Renaissance Center where it turns south to the river's edge, then east to the pit area and start line.

Commenting on Federation Internationale de Sport Automobile's selection of Detroit for the race, McCabe said, "We were able to show them an exciting downtown riverfront course, a 1,400-room hotel at the Renaissance Center, and a ready-made complex of garages within the circuit. In addition, the fact that we are Detroit interested them in terms of their own visibility on a worldwide scale.

"Add this in with the overwhelming support of the Detroit auto manufacturers and the City and State, and you come up with the kind of backing necessary to make this thing happen."

- 0 -

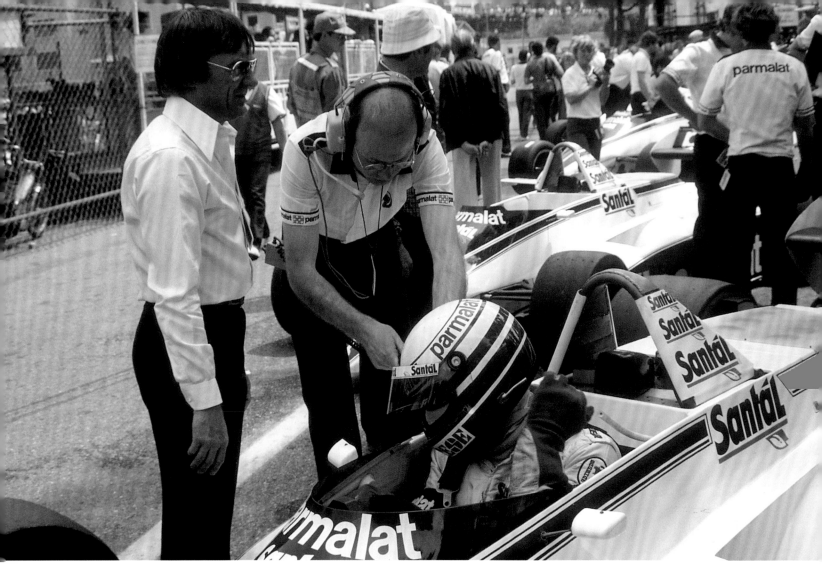

else was because people weren't really moving around much in those days. Race engineers and designers weren't commodities or celebrities. We were the guys that drew the car during the week.

'In 1982 you still had the team managers like Teddy Mayers and the Tyler Alexanders running the cars themselves at McLaren. Peter Warr did it at Lotus. That's the way it was in the pit lane. I was one of the first of the designer people to be handed the headset [to talk to the driver] – not because I was necessarily good at it but I probably knew more about why the car was the way it was. We are almost out the other end of that now, where there are race engineers who just sit and look at numbers all day long. They have no idea how the car is built, all they see is what it does. But there was this middle period where John Barnard [of McLaren] was prominent, Gordon [Murray of Brabham] was prominent, Patrick Head [of Williams] was prominent – and their right-hand men, the Frank Dernies and the like, me and others. The entire pit lane was full of design engineers of one sort or another. We didn't call ourselves aerodynamicists, we just did it!'

The depth in quality of the drivers spiced the season's prospects and an astonishing fact confirms

it: the 16 Grands Prix would have 11 different winners. To make a direct comparison with the current era, 2003 had seven, 2004, 2005 and 2006 only five. Nor is it so simple because, circa 2003–6, a couple of drivers tended to dominate and the others sneaked a win or two when the dominators faltered. In 1982 nobody dominated and when you glance at the drivers you see why.

Ferrari fielded Gilles Villeneuve and Didier Pironi. Of Villeneuve, Watson says: 'He drove in a manner which was 100 per cent commitment and he stood out among his contemporaries for this fighting spirit.' Villeneuve had a touching innocence people still treasure. Pironi, handsome Parisian with a taste for gorgeous women, was anything but innocent. During the season's traumas Patrick Tambay, a softly-spoken and urbane Frenchman, came in.

Brabham fielded Piquet and Riccardo Patrese, an Italian who'd had a tempestuous start to his career – at one stage the other drivers wanted him banned – but was now a natural, reliable and rather amiable No 2.

Williams, of course, fielded Rosberg and Reutemann, who – initially – changed his mind about retiring. The team had Cosworth engines and, reflecting, Rosberg says 'I had no idea where we were' in relation to the main opposition. 'It was the turbo era, don't forget, and basically that shed a dark light on everything. They had 250 horsepower more and we were in the same race! It was a confusing era. By that time the turbo's response time was OK but they were still a little bit unreliable. That was the only way that a Williams could compete.'

Revealingly, during the Long Beach Grand Prix, Frank Williams would set out his priorities. 'The Formula One world constructors' cup is only a $50 trophy but it means more to me than winning the driving Championship. To me, it means that Frank Williams beat Ferrari and Renault. That's what it's all about.'[10]

To drivers, of course, their Championship is what counts and that is amplified because it's what the public and media care about: the human, personalised, gladiatorial aspect. Teams see it a different way because they make the cars and measure themselves against the cars the other teams have made. The fact that that Championship excites neither public nor media is – to the largely anonymous, hardworking and very dedicated people who constitute a team – largely irrelevant.

McLaren fielded Lauda and Watson, who could be surprisingly aggressive and assertive in a racing car, and precisely the opposite of that when he levered himself out. All racing drivers are interesting, but, in terms of this contradiction, few were more interesting than he.

Lotus fielded Elio de Angelis, moneyed Roman and handsome in the Pironi way, effortlessly accomplished in surprising fields (we shall see) – and fast. He was partnered by Nigel Mansell, preparing for his second full season and much admired by Lotus founder Colin Chapman.

Renault, virtually a French state team, fielded Prost and René Arnoux. Prost, son of a cabinetmaker in a place nobody had heard of, brought logic and intellect to his driving. He was called The Professor because he made the track a laboratory. Arnoux was more earthy, feisty, impish, and looked as if he'd never been in a laboratory in his life.

These were the major teams and of the 11 winners they would provide ten. The 11th was a delightful Italian, Michele Alboreto, then passing through the Ken Tyrrell school of driving before ascending to the major teams. Alboreto's eyes always danced with pleasure, he was generous by nature and you knew he lived to be in a racing car although, if crossed, he could become Vesuvius.

Then there were the minor teams, Alfa Romeo among them. Andrea de Cesaris, who'd drive for them, says 'the Alfa was quite a good car but unreliable. Today it would have been a winning car: they'd have put a driver in, let him drive for three days and fix all the problems, but at that stage we didn't have test drivers, we didn't have a test team and we didn't have enough time. Having a good car

BELOW *Nigel Mansell at Long Beach, where he'd be seventh. A quarter of a century later, the JPS livery remains one of the most striking of all.*

FAN'S EYE VIEW

Julian Eyres was a schoolboy who, in his own words, 'sneaked' into Brands Hatch and bid to be near the cars and drivers. What he took, as you can see, has a delightful informality – and a striking authenticity as a result. Nobody posed, or did any posing! You'll be meeting him and more of his work at the British Grand Prix.

JULIAN EYRES
HIGH WYCOMBE, UK

FROM TOP CLOCKWISE
René Arnoux, drinking; Frank Williams pondering; Bruno Giacomelli, signing; Derek Warwick, smiling (just); Andrea de Cesaris, bowing; Derek Daly, preparing.

like that and not having the results it deserved was really bad.'

Osella, an Italian team, usually ran one car at the races but this season they'd run two, for Frenchman Jean-Pierre Jarier and Italian rookie Riccardo Paletti. 'When we were discovering the wing cars and ground effects we truly had problems with the cars,' remembers Jarier, 'because the suspensions remained the old suspensions and, with the ground effects, you had one tonne more weight bearing down. The cars were very dangerous and it was becoming terrible for the drivers.

'We asked for the ground effects to be limited and we had a war against the FISA several years before. Balestre gave FOCA great liberty in deciding a lot of things. Before he had been at war with Bernie, now he was at his side.'

Not for long (again as we shall see).

Toleman – founded by Ted Toleman, who made a fortune transporting production cars from British ports to dealers – was small, very British (the headquarters were off Brentwood High Street) and very ambitious. They had Rory Byrne, who'd go on to design Schumacher's Ferraris, and Pat Symonds, who'd go on to become a master tactician with Renault and Fernando Alonso. Toleman's turbo

engines came from Brian Hart, himself running a small operation in nearby Harlow.

Alex Hawkridge was team manager, and if I tell you that he, Byrne and Symonds were all softly spoken, all approachable and all had a warming sense of humour you'll catch the flavour of the whole team.

Chris Witty handled the publicity. The previous year, 'our debut, had been a disaster. We ran on Pirelli tyres and the amazing thing was that for a British team we were able to go out and get all Italian sponsors. We had Candy, we had Saima – a transport company – and Diarvia. There used to be a guy working for Pirelli called Nigel Wollheim – he did the PR for them – and he could speak 93 languages all at the same time. He conversed with the Italian press and consequently I got to know all those guys very well. Where we scored was that we were very open about things.

'At the end of 1981 we'd had Henton and Warwick. Henton was replaced by Teo Fabi and he brought other sponsors. Italian companies are very loyal to their drivers. Fabi had shown speed – he'd always shown speed: the first guy to do a 200mph lap at Indy. Remember, nobody came into the team unless Rory had given them the seal of approval.

ABOVE The most unusual aspect of Grand Prix racing is that your team-mate is your real rival because he has the same equipment. Manfred Winkelbock and Eliseo Salazar, here proving it.

ABOVE *Gilles Villeneuve only felt really alive in a racing car and died in one – this one – too.*

Rory was never high-handed in any shape or form but he and Alex had a strong bond they still have to this day.

'From our point of view, Warwick was always going to stay because he wasn't anywhere near as volatile as Henton who, bless him, certainly called a spade a spade. Brian is one of those wonderful characters who I always look back on and smile. You know the day he laid one on Warwick? We were doing Formula 2 in 1980, we were at Enna and we had the two Tolemans. John Gentry was Warwick's engineer, Rory looking after Henton, and Gentry and Warwick pulled a flanker and just pipped Henton to the pole. That evening we were walking off to the restaurant and the drivers were lagging behind and...'

'I didn't hit Warwick, I hit John Gentry!' Henton says, chuckling. 'He didn't hit me back. I think he was too shocked. And I still won the Championship...'

Anyway, Witty is adamant: 'In fairness to Henton I must add that he proved when he had the equipment that he could do it.'

Warwick says that 'the team decided they wanted to stay with me so they dropped Henton and signed Fabi. It was a big moment because their loyalty stayed with me. The car was no better because we didn't have the money to build a new one. The engine was – but not a lot. At least we started qualifying and the team improved.'

Jackie Oliver, running the Arrows team, had hired Tambay – who'd been in Grand Prix racing from 1977 but was now making a new life in America, preparing to drive in CanAm and Champcar. He was living in Hawaii and when Oliver rang they had a heartfelt conversation about Tambay's travel arrangements to South Africa. There was no direct flight from Hawaii so Tambay would have to come to London and change planes for Johannesburg, a combined journey of some 30 hours. He said he wanted first class not 'coach' and Oliver, like Toleman constantly having to husband his resources, said he'd pay coach and Tambay could pay the difference to upgrade himself.

Urbane, perceptive, popular Patrick Tambay was about to embark on one of the most expensive weekends of his life when he boarded the plane in Hawaii.

To the modern follower of Grand Prix racing, nurtured on grids of 22 cars, 1982 is a teeming, crowded, slightly incomprehensible place: 39 drivers from 17 countries contested the races in 17 different makes of cars. Some races needed pre-qualifying and a guillotine in qualifying itself to prune the number to the (then statutory) grid of 26. Monaco was the traditional exception at 20 because the narrow streets supposedly couldn't cope with the full cavalry charge.

Arranged by the numbers the cars bore, these are the 39. Several drove for more than one team:

To put Formula One drivers into groups is hazardous because they don't fit. They tend to be self-centred, nakedly ambitious and necessarily bullet-proof. Events in South Africa would challenge that in a breathtaking and unique way but, overall, it held true. All 39 needed to win to justify (to themselves as well as everybody else) why they had been put on the earth – but every race could only ever have one winner. Each of the 39, drawn from so many different backgrounds and mentalities, faced the 16-hurdle marathon in their own way and viewed from different perspectives.

A paternal eye prepared to watch over them. Professor Sid Watkins was now established as Formula One's resident doctor. 'The fitness of the drivers is decided by the national doctors of their Associations, so they have a medical certificate which clears them for racing which is issued by their own country,' he says. 'What I did was to collect their blood groups, allergies, previous history, previous fractures, that sort of thing, and have a dossier on each of them. That was usually done in the few days when they all assemble at the beginning of the season. That was one of my tasks at the first race. Thereafter I kept an eye on them. I didn't know the new chaps when they came in but I soon did get to know them. Mostly they were at the back of the grid just in front of me in the medical car – a lot nearer me than Keke or Niki or whoever at the front.'

Prof Watkins would be busy in South Africa and at subsequent races because Moreno, Boesel, Baldi, Paletti, Byrne and Fabi were newcomers.

You might imagine all this was just like every season but 1982 was already very different.

The Rat, you see, had smelt a rat.

Footnote: To Hell And Back, Niki Lauda, Stanley Paul, London 1986; 2. Autosport, 24 September 1981; 3. Ibid; 4. 'Ground effects' was once a major buzz word in Grand Prix racing. Simply put, the idea was to funnel air into the narrow area under the car, creating low pressure. The higher pressure over the car then forces the car down – giving it a huge amount of grip; 5. Frank Williams, Maurice Hamilton, Macmillan, London 1998; 6. Charlie Crichton-Stuart had aristocratic connections (although you'd never have known), was a long-time friend of Frank Williams and worked on sponsorship for the Williams Grand Prix team. He died in 2001. Not to be confused with Creighton Brown, who might have stepped straight from the British Foreign Office – he was in fact a moving force in McLaren's dominance from 1980. He died in 2006. Keke Rosberg told me, sadness in his voice: 'The two nicest people in my Formula One days were Creighton Brown and Charlie, and both of them are gone'; 7. Barbro Peterson, widow of Lotus driver Ronnie, who died after a crash at Monza in 1978; 8. Tim Schenken, a promising young Australian driver; 9. McLaren had Porsche engines (badged 'TAG') from 1983 to 1987; 10. Las Vegas Review.

DRIVER/TEAM LINE UP

Team	Driver No.	Driver
Brabham	1	Nelson Piquet (Brazil)
	2	Riccardo Patrese (Italy)
Tyrrell	3	Michele Alboreto (Italy)
	4	Slim Borgudd (Sweden)
	4	Brian Henton (Great Britain)
Williams	5	Carlos Reutemann (Argentina)
	5	Mario Andretti (USA)
	5	Derek Daly (Ireland)
	6	Keke Rosberg (Finland)
McLaren	7	John Watson (Great Britain)
	8	Niki Lauda (Austria)
ATS	9	Manfred Winkelhock (West Germany)
	10	Eliseo Salazar (Chile)
Lotus	11	Elio de Angelis (Italy)
	12	Nigel Mansell (Britain)
	12	Roberto Moreno (Brazil)
	12	Geoff Lees (Great Britain)
(NO NUMBER 13, CONSIDERED BAD LUCK)		
Ensign	14	Roberto Guerrero (Colombia)
Renault	15	Alain Prost (France)
	16	René Arnoux (France)
March	17	Jochen Mass (West Germany)
	17	Rupert Keegan (Great Britain)
	18	Raul Boesel (Brazil)
	19	Emilio de Villota (Spain)
Fittipaldi	20	Chico Serra (Brazil)
(NO NUMBER 21)		
Alfa Romeo	22	Andrea de Cesaris (Italy)
	23	Bruno Giacomelli (Italy)
(NO NUMBER 24)		
Talbot Ligier	25	Eddie Cheever (USA)
	26	Jacques Laffite (France)
Ferrari	27	Gilles Villeneuve (Canada)
	27	Patrick Tambay (France)
	28	Didier Pironi (France)
	28	Andretti
Arrows	29	Henton
	29	Marc Surer (Switzerland)
	30	Mauro Baldi (Italy)
Osella	31	Jean-Pierre Jarier (France)
	32	Riccardo Paletti (Italy)
Theodore	33	Tommy Byrne (Ireland)
	33	Jan Lammers (Holland)
	34	Daly
Toleman	35	Derek Warwick (Great Britain)
	36	Teo Fabi (Italy)

23 JANUARY

STRIKING OUT

——— SOUTH AFRICA, KYALAMI

Herr Andreas Nikolaus Lauda of Vienna had furtive eyes which didn't miss much and a suspicious mind. On 24 December 1981 he sniffed the form from Paris the postman had just delivered and didn't like it at all. The form was accompanied by a letter from the governing body of motor sport, FISA, instructing him to complete the form or forget about the opening round of the marathon at Kyalami. He liked that even less.

The form, a single sheet written in plain language, was the application for a 'super licence', a device to ensure that drivers were properly qualified to compete in Grand Prix racing. This involved showing ability to a specified level in the lesser formulae to keep out the inexperienced and the incompetent. FISA were making an exception for Lauda on the strength of his accomplishments before his two-year retirement.

The furtive eyes scanned down the first four clauses of the single page. The first couple presented no problem and ordinarily 3 and 4 would have presented no problem either:

'3. A super licence will only be issued when a driver has entered into a commitment to drive for a particular team and signed the super licence form issued by FISA.'

'4. The licence issued to the driver will name the team with which he has a commitment to drive.'

RIGHT *The start of the season down Kyalami's majestic sweep. The Renault of René Arnoux leads and team-mate Alain Prost is already behind him from the third row.*

South Africa
Kyalami

RACE DATE January 23rd

CIRCUIT LENGTH 4.10km/2.55 miles

NO. OF LAPS 77

RACE DISTANCE
316.00km/196.35 miles

WEATHER Hot, Dry

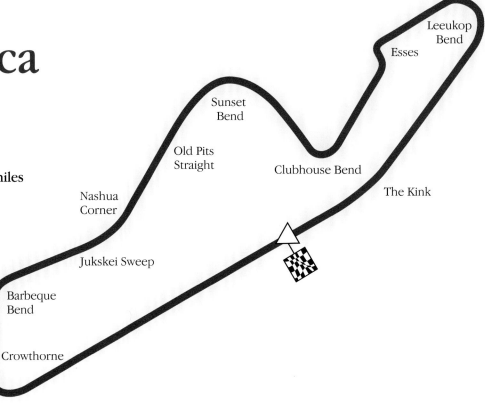

Leeukop
Bend

Esses

Sunset
Bend

Old Pits
Straight

Clubhouse Bend

The Kink

Nashua
Corner

Jukskei Sweep

Barbeque
Bend

Crowthorne

DRIVER'S VIEW

'The circuit was always very peculiar in certain ways, very high – 6,000 feet – and the performance varied. You sometimes started testing on the Monday and you could do a good time but struggle all the week to repeat it – sand blowing, climactic conditions, wind changes and so on. It was a lovely circuit, fast, sweeping corners and the long pit lane straight flat out. That was fearsome but what the heck? You could see cars slipstreaming, out-braking each other at the end. Great! Even the other corners were very challenging. To get on to the straight you went up to the right-handed Leeukop – Lion's Head – bend. After Crowthorne you went into a right then the left, Jukskei – Hippo – sweep. There was a little river at the bottom and hippos had been there a few years earlier. Many attempts at improving safety killed a lot of good, characterful circuits.'

———— *Jochen Mass*

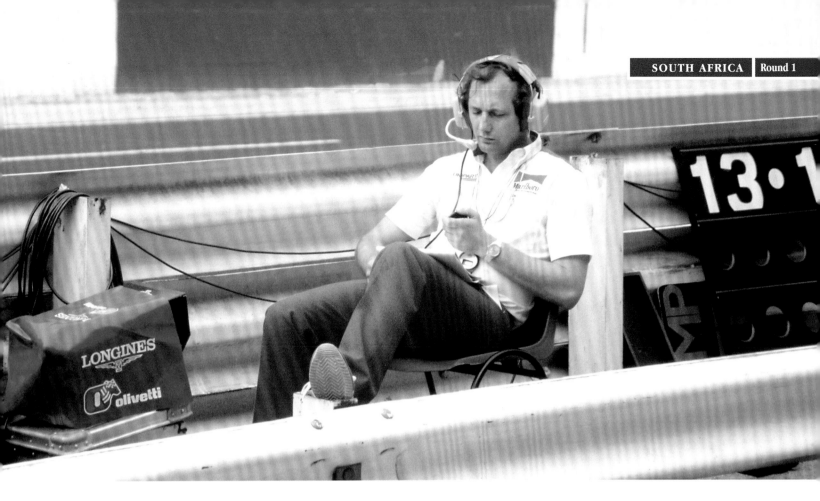

ABOVE *Simpler days. Ron Dennis, running McLaren, stays plugged in.*

Everybody has to drive for somebody, and what can be the harm in putting that on a form? In no sense did it commit the driver to stay with that team. The furtive eyes scanned down again:

'FIA FORMULA ONE WORLD CHAMPIONSHIP 1982 APPLICATION FOR A FISA SUPER LICENCE

'I .... (the driver) OF .... HOLDER OF INTERNATIONAL LICENCE N° .... ISSUED BY .... HEREBY APPLY FOR A FISA SUPER LICENCE TO DRIVE FOR ....(the team) IN THE 1982 FIA FORMULA ONE WORLD CHAMPIONSHIP.

'In consideration of the issue of this licence I undertake and agree as follows:

1 – I am committed to the above team to drive exclusively for them in the FIA Formula One World championship(s) until the .... 19...'

The Rat summoned his formidable logic. Drivers, he concluded, were not being offered a super licence for themselves: the super licences were being granted to the driver and team – in his case, Lauda/McLaren. That would prevent drivers leaving one team to join another because, if they did, their super licence would no longer be valid. That in turn meant they would no longer be able to race.

The logic moved to the next conclusion: drivers, he saw, would be 'at the mercy of third parties',[1] and he glimpsed transfer fees, 'horse trading and contract buy-outs', deals between one team and another – and the drivers standing beside the feast hoping for crumbs.

The furtive eyes scanned down again.

'5. I will do nothing which might harm the moral or material interests or image of International Motorsport or the FIA Formula One World championship.'

Who would decide this? What might constitute harm? Who would define that? Paragraphs 6 and 7 obliged the drivers to take no action in the event of a dispute 'other than the procedures set out in the International Sporting Code.' They were being invited to bind their arms behind their own backs.

Lauda rang Pironi, President of the Grand Prix Drivers' Association, and Pironi explained that it had all been discussed at their last meeting. It had also been agreed at the Formula 1 Commission[2] in early December. Lauda deployed his arguments and he convinced Pironi.

The form was the product of events in 1981 when Prost, making his debut in Grand Prix racing with McLaren, became convinced the car was not safe and refused to drive for the team again regardless of the fact that he had a contract to do so. Prost told Teddy

ABOVE *The pit lane was narrow, as the two ATS cars found out. And the pits were basic, as everyone found out.*

Mayer that, if necessary, he would simply walk away from motor sport altogether. Renault approached Prost, he joined them, and Mayer (by training a lawyer) discovered how problematic the law was if you tried to prevent someone from gaining their livelihood. The super licence form represented an attempt to prevent such a situation recurring.

John Watson wasn't happy about the implications of the form and, as he said, he was not alone. He received his form 'just before New Year – we all got it at different times because we were all over the world.' Laffite got his between Christmas and New Year, read it and rang FISA 'immediately' but there was nobody there. He asked that Balestre should phone him because he saw trouble coming in South Africa.

Lauda claims Pironi made phone calls and was able to prevent 'most of the other drivers' from signing, but in fact 24 did, leaving six refuseniks: Pironi himself, Lauda of course, Villeneuve – who had seen something similar in Canadian ice hockey and didn't like it[3] – Arnoux, Giacomelli, and de Cesaris.

Watson talked it over with McLaren and signed because he had only a one-year contract, so signing

could not be 'detrimental' to him, but he sympathised with drivers who had longer contracts and 'would have to go to FISA to get permission to leave a team.'

And they all went to South Africa for testing the week before the Grand Prix, the testing continuing on the Monday and Tuesday of Grand Prix week.

A curiosity here: apartheid was in full force and sporting connections between South Africa and the rest of the world (rugby, soccer, cricket, Olympic Games) long since severed. Motor racing continued to make an annual pilgrimage there from 1970 to 1985 (with the exception of 1981, for reasons we shall see – but nothing to do with apartheid). That it was able to go annually and provoke virtually no controversy (or even comment, never mind soul searching) remains inexplicable unless you postulate that externally it was not regarded as a sport at all but something existing entirely within its own world and of no interest to the black population.[4]

The country to which the drivers came, the country they were so familiar with, was a curious place, part America – Johannesburg's centre looked like any US city – part Europe and part Africa. People

in 1980. (The 1981 race, a victim of the FOCA–FISA power struggle – only FOCA teams went – was non-Championship.) Marc Surer, driving an Arrows, crashed and broke both his feet. Henton was invited to replace him and accepted, but the team's sponsors wanted Tambay. Henton would go to South Africa anyway, to spectate and fish for another drive.

The Grand Prix was traditionally on a Saturday, the qualifying therefore on Thursday and Friday. It meant Wednesday was a free day between the testing and the start of the Grand Prix meeting. The F1 Commission met and immediately the temperature started rising. Pironi formally objected to drivers having to state which team they were driving for, the length of their contract and the moral harm paragraph.

'I was just listening because Didier Pironi did all the talking,' Lauda would say.[5] 'Didier was diplomatic but firm, he was polite and completely unemotional. The important thing was to keep on talking.'

Someone pointed out that any alterations would have to go through the FISA Executive, which presumably meant nothing could be done until they were all back in Europe after the Grand Prix. Pironi said that without the alterations the Grand Prix Drivers' Association members would not practice.

Balestre took this as a direct challenge and reportedly told Pironi where he could go, adding that the drivers who had not signed for super licences were excluded from practice the next day because their cars could not be scrutineered without the proper licence.

Overnight the resolve of the drivers hardened.

BELOW *The contracts dispute – Niki Lauda explains the drivers' side. F1 had never seen industrial action before.*

living like animals in the cardboard and corrugated iron shantytowns could see the cluster of moneyed skyscrapers. The white middle class lived in detached houses with lush gardens, behind high fences and shoot-to-kill guards. If you'd seen a pride of lions wandering over a cricket pitch you wouldn't have been surprised, and perhaps the players wouldn't have been either. You felt that here, amidst so many cultures, architectural styles and accents – the aggressive Afrikaners chewing words, the Portuguese refugees from Angola, the African tongues – a country was feeling for an identity and might never find one. The Grand Prix represented more than a precious contact with the outside world, it was just one of the 16 World Championship rounds. In other words, this extreme activity in this extreme country represented normality in the same way it would in Rio, Long Beach, Imola and everywhere else it went.

Kyalami, surrounded by parched veldt, was functional in its infrastructure as so many circuits were in 1982.

During the testing Prost did a 1m 05.71s, destroying the lap record of 1m 13.15s set by Arnoux

ABOVE *Taken for a ride or going for a ride? The drivers board the bus and in a moment Niki Lauda will spirit them to Johannesburg and a strike.*

Pironi and Lauda pressed for mutual contracts: the driver couldn't leave a team while his contract lasted, the team couldn't fire him.

At 7.00 on the Thursday morning a bus, arranged by GPDA secretary Trevor Rowe, drew up not far from the paddock entrance with Pironi and Lauda in it. Most of the drivers stayed at the nearby Kyalami Ranch Hotel and they'd be arriving early for a GPDA meeting before the hour-long practice session at 10.20. As each arrived they were invited to park their cars and get onto the bus. Mass didn't show up ('He's always late,' someone said) and Ickx refused. In fact, Mass had been staying with friends of his South African-born wife and so had been out of touch. He knew nothing about the bus but it wouldn't have made any difference.

Jean-Pierre Jarier got on. 'Everything was explained to me and I knew exactly what was going on. You have two subjects: a bad atmosphere because Bernie Ecclestone tried to introduce the system of transfers like in football to Formula 1 and therefore the drivers were against it. Second there had been a drama at one of the races in 1981 because the track broke up into small pieces in a

corner and people went off.' The drivers asked for the track to be 're-made' but this was refused.

Jarier sensed that whatever power the drivers held was being taken from them. He was old enough to have driven in 1973. 'I remember Jackie Stewart and Peter Revson going to see the organisers at Buenos Aires on the Wednesday of the Argentinean Grand Prix and saying "The morning practice is impossible, it's too hot – you do the practice at 4.00 in the afternoon." The organisers said "Yes, yes," and they changed the timetable so the session would be run with less sun. It was a world where things were very different.'

Keke Rosberg 'arrived at the circuit and there was a bus on the gate. I don't remember who was outside – was it Pironi or was it Lauda? Anyway, "Here's a bus, let's get in the bus, we need to have a meeting".' Rosberg clambered aboard.

Derek Warwick reached the circuit 'and I was still completely star-struck to be among all these great drivers. We got on the bus and I thought "Now where are we going?"

'The trouble is as a driver you were under peer pressure: when you've people like Piquet,

Reutemann, Lauda, Villeneuve, Pironi, Arnoux, the pressure to strike with them and create a united front was massive. Not that they put me under any pressure. I just felt that my allegiance should be with the drivers because it was a case of numbers: 95 per cent of the drivers were striking. Jochen Mass didn't because he's always been his own man and I think Jacky Ickx was going to stand in for Marc Surer, who was injured.'

Everybody else clambered aboard in their turn.

The drivers were, as Lauda recounts it, going for a drive.

With Lauda hanging out of the back waving, the bus set off, but as it left the bottom gate of the circuit John McDonald of the March team tried to block it. Laffite and some other drivers got out and pushed McDonald's car clear. Then the bus proceeded on the scenic route to Johannesburg some 15 miles away pursued by 'a whole convoy' of TV cameras, journalists and photographers. The bus went to the Sunnyside Park Hotel in the suburbs. It offered full amenities including a swimming pool.

The drivers were boycotting Thursday practice and, unless a settlement was reached, first qualifying in the afternoon. Grand Prix racing had never seen industrial action before, nor imagined it.

'We never had the meeting: the bus drove straight to the hotel and that was it,' Rosberg says. 'I did not feel that we were doing the right thing as highly paid sportsmen going on strike. No. I thought it could be more intelligent than that and, honestly, we could find other ways to reach our goal. So I didn't agree

with it. It was an awful beginning of the year for me because obviously I was getting excited about the prospect with Williams.

'Once we were at the hotel it was too late. You wouldn't walk out but if I had wanted to go I would have said "Listen, guys, I'm going," and just walked out of the door. I stayed. At those moments there has to be also loyalty towards the other drivers so the Pironi-Lauda speculation was absolutely correct: once we get them together they will hold together. First of all I never was a GPDA member, never attended the meetings because it was a waste of time – 25 racing drivers discussing issues, you know. And I always felt motives behind the South African strike were not as they were being told to us. Maybe unconsciously. I don't think Niki would have been conscious of it, but I strongly believe that the whole energy that Niki had for this matter came from the fact that he had just returned after retirement, and who was he? He was just one of the guys, you know, and he needed to get his head above the rest again. So this gave him a good opportunity, Pironi was grateful because he had the support of somebody and that's how it went.

'I had the personal pressure of not having raced for Williams yet. The sack? I didn't really consider it at that moment because Carlos was with me. To be completely truthful, I felt that as long as Carlos was there as well then we'd be OK. That Frank wouldn't like it was clear, that it wouldn't improve my relationship with the team was clear, but by that time I didn't have a choice any more. It was too late – and

BELOW *There really was confusion round the bus, with the drivers inside and the world media outside.*

he wasn't going to fire both of us. However, given the choice I would not have been there. The whole thing was ridiculous.'

Pironi remained at the circuit to negotiate with Balestre and Bobby Hartslief, Managing Director of Kyalami Entertainment Enterprises and the circuit owner.

At 10.19 the track opened for practice.

The race organisers threatened to impound the cars if the race didn't happen and Ecclestone threatened the drivers that they would be sued for recompense if the cars were impounded.

Throughout, Ecclestone adopted a hard line and at one point, in a remarkable interview,[6] questioned the value of drivers. 'Nobody came up to me at Kyalami and asked where Jones or Andretti were. Already they're not missed. Why should any of the rest of them be missed? If it had suited Carlos not to come back, he wouldn't have given a stuff about F1 now, or whether the crowds came now or didn't. He couldn't give a damn if it suited him not to turn up. In the same way it suited Scheckter to stop when he did and suited Niki to walk out in the middle of a race. I think he said at the time "I'm leaving because of the politics, I just want to be a racing driver." If you analyse it, the drivers just don't make sense.'

Henton had no drive but decided to 'hold out and all the others went on strike. I didn't go on the bus to Johannesburg.'

BELOW *Political shadows were everywhere: Didier Pironi (right) marches towards another meeting during the strike.*

Toleman, Osella and March were informed that, because they had not taken part in pre-qualifying, they'd broken their agreement to the Grand Prix organisers, were removed from the event and might have their entire assets seized.

Negotiations went on at the track through 1.20, when the first qualifying session should have begun and the 'cars silently lined the pit lane'.[7] Pironi kept in touch with Lauda by telephone and the drivers settled into a day enjoying what the hotel had to offer. They were beginning to show industrial-strength solidarity, itself an amazing thing although not that amazing. It functioned at two levels, one replacing the other: the loners' natural reluctance to act collectively melting into strong-willed (and frequently bloody-minded) men refusing to be pushed around.

Pironi arrived from the circuit and explained that if they didn't return and drive immediately they faced life bans. There seems to have been a distinctive mood at the hotel with very real concerns about what they were doing 'camouflaged by high jinks and laughter.' Lauda knew that the older drivers understood what the consequences might be – Ecclestone had already fired Piquet and Patrese. Lauda realised how difficult it was for the younger drivers, facing a nightmare of broken contracts, being sued, missing the first race and facing the reaction of their sponsors. Lauda concluded that maintaining solidarity was crucial. Each driver had a great deal to lose. Rosberg faced his own nightmare. He had toiled in no-hope teams for years and now here he was in a plum drive for a leading team and he might lose it before he'd driven the car in anger if Frank did fire both his drivers.

Lauda understood that if drivers began wavering, or external forces made them waver, they'd be picked off one by one.

At 3.40 the Stewards issued a long statement saying the Grand Prix had been postponed for a week and the drivers were immediately suspended. Hartslief said 'FOCA lodged 4m Rand [£2.2m] in trust to cover our losses. We had a Supreme Court application drawn up for lodging on Friday to impound all the cars at the circuit if the drivers did not compromise their complaints. Bernie Ecclestone was happy about this arrangement and he would have recovered the money from the drivers.'

At 4.14 a spokesman for Hartslief said at the circuit 'none of the drivers whose licences have been withdrawn will ever be eligible for the World Championship again.' He added that 'there are 150 super licences in the world so a very wide selection is available to choose from' for the Grand Prix.

Fifteen minutes after that the team managers held a meeting.

Pironi met the F1 Commission and Balestre offered to write a letter to the drivers to clarify the position on licences and, equally, on the moral harm clause, reassuring drivers it did not mean they'd face penalties if they arrived unshaven or passed wind in public. Pironi telephoned Lauda and they discussed it, rejected it.

At 5.45 the Stewards said the team managers had unanimously requested the drivers be allowed to compete 'to save the Grand Prix' and they now could: 'the Stewards have decided to allow the drivers wishing to participate in the Grand Prix on 23rd January to come and present their appeal on 22nd January between 8am and 9am exactly.'

What appeal?

This Thursday evening Balestre refused to speak to Pironi and Lauda, who said: 'He represents FISA, the official body, so I can understand in a way why he didn't want to talk to us. When he said he wasn't prepared to negotiate with the drivers who refused to take part in practice, that was because he wanted to support his own organisation. But you can always find a way to talk to someone...'[8]

At the Kyalami Ranch, during dinner, drivers' wives and girlfriends threw bread rolls and plates at Balestre.

The Super Licence form represented the feudal mentality of Grand Prix racing with its strict hierarchy and its take-it-or-leave-it attitude to both insiders and outsiders. Part of the subsequent rage by Balestre, simmering anger from Ecclestone, and vocal displeasure from other team managers centred on the fact that, suddenly and completely, their hierarchy was under direct, public challenge and the only weapon they had – threats – was counter-productive.

The drivers in Johannesburg inhabited the conference room. 'We ended up barricaded in it,' Warwick says. 'You know what was fantastic? I got to know my colleagues for the first time because, being a non-qualifier at the back of the grid, you don't get a chance to speak to the guys at the front. That was good. The other things that were massive when we were in that compound – we were there for 24 hours – was Bruno Giacomelli standing up with a chart and dissecting an AK47 machine gun. He drew these magnificent drawings of how to take the gun to bits and so on. It was very, very funny because in the normal Bruno Giacomelli way he was very, very funny anyway. I think it was a big shock for everybody in authority because they thought they could control the drivers but, to be quite honest, I

ABOVE *The potentates debate tactics: (from left) Daniel Audetto of Ferrari, Jackie Oliver, Ken Tyrrell, Bernie Ecclestone (back to camera), Peter Warr and Colin Chapman.*

don't know that half of them in the room knew what we were striking for.'

Lauda kept their spirits up by telling jokes and, a piano brought, Villeneuve played light music and de Angelis classical pieces.

'What really blew me away,' Warwick says, 'was that we had a piano in the room and Elio de Angelis started playing it. Apparently he could have been a concert pianist and it astonished me – the other talents that some of these guys had. Then Gilles played Scott Joplin.'

Many remember the performance by de Angelis. 'Believe it or not,' Derek Daly says, 'the most vivid memory I have of being stuck in the hotel room was Elio de Angelis playing the piano like a concert pianist. Remarkable. Definitely, definitely that was a gift, a talent, of his.'

Jarier points out that 'it was a big room and Elio de Angelis played classical music and Gilles played. Very sympa. In that era virtually all the drivers stayed in the same hotels – Kyalami Ranch in South Africa, the Glen Motorhome in Watkins Glen and so on. A Formula One team was 15, 20 people. There were far fewer journalists, far fewer television people and everybody knew each other.' In other words, many of the drivers in the big room were not strangers to each other, however much those at the back of the grid had to be.

Alex Hawkridge arrived to try to reach Fabi and Warwick. Fabi was easy to reach because, as it seems, he was already staying in the hotel and had his own room. 'Teo we didn't threaten as such, we told him he was contracted to drive. He came out and I was able to speak to him. We reminded him he had signed a contract to drive, and the idea of solidarity wouldn't help him if he was without a drive and to think where his best interests lay. Elio was playing the piano – astonishing – and I could hear him. He was a proper concert pianist.'

Publicity man Witty went with Hawkridge. 'The drivers' strike? I remember thinking "How stupid". I remember going down there and hanging around outside. Alex had obviously talked to Fabi to get him to escape. Fabi was very quiet.'

Food was sent in and drink was sent out to the reporters hovering outside.

Jackie Oliver arrived. 'You go down there to see if you can reason with people and try and prevent a disaster commercially for the team and the drivers that I had hired. You say "Look, this is not going to lead anywhere." I was thinking to try and explain to Patrick and to Mauro that they were joining a campaign that was going to damage them and bring no advantage – especially Patrick – and also damage the team, because there were Italian sponsors involved. They were going to deduct money so I went down there to try and persuade them.

'The room was barricaded. An associate of mine pushed the door open and shouted out their names: "Come and talk to us and we'll resolve this." Of course, as happens when you do that, someone pushed the other way and there was a bit of a pushing and shoving session – by a friend of mine called Douglas Norden, who is known to be a little aggressive when challenged. He was nothing to do with the team, just a friend along trying to help and it turned into a bit of a scuffle. Then the door shut.

'Niki and others saw it as a further restriction on the drivers' power and they wanted to stop it, and that is always the difficulty with change, isn't it? We were to have another example at Imola when the FOCA went on strike against the FIA. Through the history of human struggle there have been the instances involving union.'

Lauda made sure the piano blocked the door so there would be no further scuffles, giving the police reason to enter.

Mo Nunn at Ensign tried to get Guerrero to come out by taking his girlfriend. When they saw each other they dissolved into tears and Lauda allowed him out to see her providing he – Lauda – came, too.

Jean Sage of Renault tried to get to Prost and Arnoux but was beaten off.

The drivers ordered a room big enough to put 30 mattresses onto the carpet – that provoked prolonged ribaldry. At 11.00 pm they moved from the conference room to this dormitory and settled down for the night, having worked out an elaborate way of getting to the toilet across the hallway. It was conducted on the honour system with a key on a plate in the middle of the room.

Lauda would remember: 'I was sharing a bed with Patrese, someone next to Rosberg was snoring until Villeneuve put a blanket over him in the middle of the night, but all the time we stood together.'

Warwick would remember: 'The drivers spent time with me and we spent a lot of time together – I was sleeping with them, exactly, yes! I haven't slept on the same mattress as Carlos Reutemann ever since, mind you...'

To which Derek Daly says: 'The funny thing is I think I was on the other side because I have a picture of me beside Reutemann. I don't know if he snored. I do think he was still dressed in his driver's suit.'

Pironi said at the time: 'We will see it through. FISA has too much to lose to let the Grand Prix be called off. I'm confident they will relent.'

'We'd had a lot of pressure because you had people like Jackie Oliver and Alex Hawkridge coming to the hotel,' Warwick says. 'We were threatened with our jobs if you don't get back there and that, of course, is why Fabi crawled out of the toilet window. He was

FAN'S EYE VIEW

'I have had an interest in motor racing since watching a sprint meeting with MG TCs, Nortons and so on in 1948. In 1982 I was 41 and working as an inventory controller for a forklift company.

'Through the 1970s the Sports Car Club of SA ran the Press Room at Kyalami and I helped out there. I saw few races but had the privilege of free run of the pits and circuit during practice. By the 1980s, with the rise of the ever more omnipotent Bernie Ecclestone, amateurs were no longer required. So for 1982, after checking the radio for updates on the drivers' strike, I bought a ticket and went as a paying spectator, hoping for a race. The Barbeque and Jukskei section of Kyalami is a daunting place. The cars were very close, very fast and very much on the limit. I felt exposed and uncomfortable on the outside of the corner – the accidents to Villeneuve, Pironi and Paletti later in that season brought home how unforgiving this business can be.

'Some of the pictures taken that day show the flimsy nature of the catch fencing.'

DAVID PEARSON,
EDENGLEN, SOUTH AFRICA

FROM TOP CLOCKWISE *Gilles Villeneuve retired after six laps with a turbo failure – he would be gone from South Africa forever; Elio de Angelis (Lotus) comes up to lap Derek Daly in the Theodore; Prost catches Didier Pironi after the pit stop and clearly doesn't intend to be behind him for long; Keke Rosberg, driving hard for fifth place and proving that, given the car, he could keep pace with the front-runners.*

the only one who broke ranks. He did the dirty on me. Everybody said to me they understood if I had to go back – I was explaining to people like Lauda "It's OK for you guys, you're going to have a job, you're some of the best drivers around but I'm the new kid on the block, my team-mate's just jumped ship and I am very vulnerable." And every one of them said "We guarantee you that you will not be fired." In other words, if one is fired everybody goes. That gave me a little bit more confidence to stay there.'

'No,' Fabi says, 'I did not get out of a toilet window! That was my first race in Formula One – or my first attempt to race in Formula One – and it was my first contract in Formula One. Alex Hawkridge was very clear with me. He told me "Teo, if you want to keep racing with Toleman you must not strike." So I never got with the other drivers. I always stayed in my room – the drivers were meeting at my hotel. I remember Laffite coming into my room and maybe another driver. It was a very difficult position to be in at the first race because I might have lost my career before it had begun. My decision caused a lot of problems in my relations with the other drivers for at least one year or even longer but it was the only decision I could take.

'When Alex said "Teo, decide what you want to do," I said "Well, I'm going to drive." Sorry for you if it spoils a good story that I didn't get out of the window! I never got into the toilet! Previously I had had an offer from Alex Hawkridge to race in Formula 2 and I turned the offer down because I decided to stay with March. When he took me on board in Formula One it was against his will. He didn't want me because I'd turned down that Formula 2 drive. I was only able to get the Toleman Formula One drive because of Candy, an Italian company and the Toleman sponsor. So my position really was very difficult even before the strike.'

Daly feels the strike 'was completely driven by Lauda, Villeneuve and Pironi. I was caught in the middle. I did not want to strike, I wanted to race. I was almost forced to get involved in the strike. Remember I was so new to the whole thing. I didn't have the horsepower to stand up to those in authority, I was afraid it was going to lose me the drive that I had.'

Pironi was up early on the Friday, journeying to the Kyalami Ranch to put the drivers' views to Balestre. That was by 6.00. Pironi spoke to Lauda on the telephone. Lauda, unshaven, called a press conference to say that the situation remained unchanged.

Balestre and Pironi returned to the circuit and the F1 Commission met. The personnel: Pironi, Balestre, Colin Chapman, Hartslief, David Waldron (FISA), Sage, Marco Piccinini of Ferrari, Gerard Larrousse of Renault, Nunn, Ecclestone and Max Mosley.

'The FISA was not prepared to back down over this, but I think the drivers were as long as they received assurances that no sanctions would be taken against them. We were just going on and on and on. Talk, talk, talk. Getting nowhere,' Chapman said. Balestre, however, gave Pironi to understand there would be negotiations.

Hartslief said that if the drivers refused to sign their forms by 10.30 the Grand Prix was off; if they agreed, practice would start at 11.00.

Pironi rang Lauda with that news just after 10.00. The content of what was happening remains disputed: Lauda was sure the drivers had 'won' and Pironi was too, but Ecclestone said nothing had changed and Colin Chapman insisted it was only a 'truce': 'Nobody has won anything. We're in a state of suspended animation. The fight starts again after the race, as far as I can see.' Villeneuve, on the other hand, felt that Pironi had 'achieved guarantees that things will be modified. He says it's fine.'

At 9.30 Fabi arrived at the circuit, ready to practice. 'I agree with the aims of the strikers but I feel the South African Grand Prix should go on,' he said.

Hawkridge had 'no idea how Teo got back to the track, no idea. Maybe he got a cab. He was quite determined, he definitely didn't want to sit out the race. I think he just thought it through and felt that this drivers' solidarity thing hadn't helped him get into Formula One and it wasn't going to help him stay there. Derek? It didn't affect our relationship in the long term at all but we did have some words with him. We told him exactly what we had told Teo, that in our view he was aligning himself with people who wouldn't help him when the chips were down.'

'Fabi slipped back, slipped behind enemy lines,' Witty says. 'No great fanfare or anything. Lauda & Co were very anti him for breaking ranks but I don't think it had any long-term ramifications. You just get back in a race car and race, don't you? I do remember Lauda's assurance to Warwick.'

Formula One had not lost its sense of humour, or what passes for it. At 10.07 as Mass took his March out he was applauded all down the pit lane and as he completed his first flying lap all the teams held out pit boards. Next time round they held out a wide variety of times for the flying lap. After three laps he was black-flagged because, evidently, the track wasn't clear when, circulating alone, it could hardly have been more clear. Black humour, in fact. He said that 'the whole disagreement has been an embarrassment to motor sport.'

Reflecting today, he adds this: 'I did not take part in the strike as a matter of principle although I knew something was in the pipeline. I thought it was a lot of rubbish to strike, bullshit, never work. You have to find a better solution than that. So they went to the

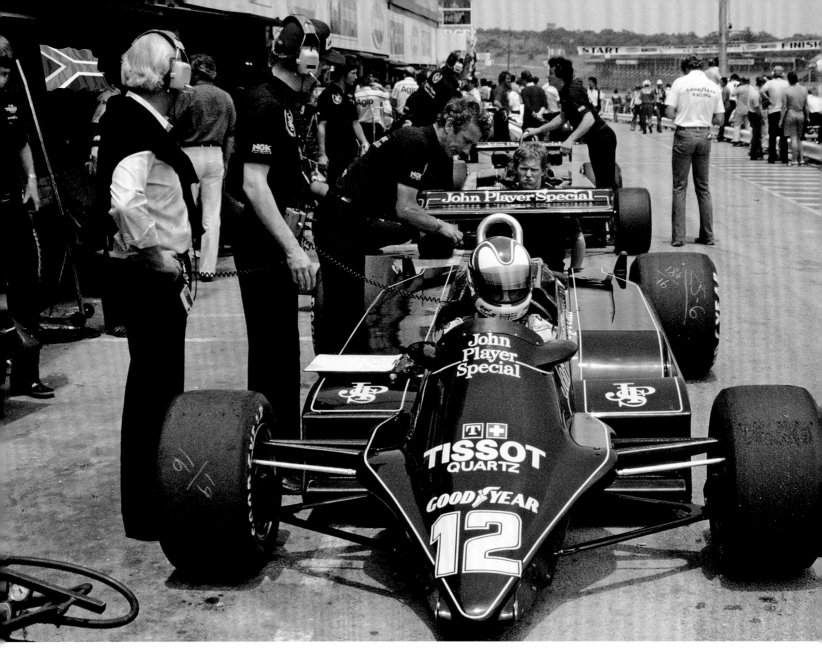

ABOVE *Nigel Mansell prepares to go out, Colin Chapman (left) never very far away.*

hotel and slept on camp beds and God knows what to be away from their teams and the pressure. Right? Next morning I got to the circuit and heard they were on strike. I thought "This is crap, I'm going to go out anyway." I knew they would not be able to maintain this strike in any case. That was clear to me: they would achieve nothing. I did a few laps on my own and suddenly they all chickened out. Yes, people were applauding me going down the pit lane. Not that I felt heroic or smart about it, but my conviction was this strike doesn't work so I may as well drive. I thought that if I drove they would all drive – because basically they all wanted to drive. They did come back and race, of course, yes.'

At 11.00 the drivers arrived at the circuit and prepared for two sessions, one of 90 minutes' practice in the morning and an hour in the afternoon for the grid. Lauda was quoted as saying: 'We have got what we wanted and we are now going to practice.' That did nothing to improve the strained

atmosphere down the pit lane. Mo Nunn, clearly still incensed, withdrew the Ensign car, leaving Guerrero marooned. Guerrero claimed Nunn said he – Guerrero – was in no state physically or mentally to drive the car, Guerrero persuaded him he was but it was too late to reinstate the car.

Tambay, repelled by the politics and cars which had no suspensions ('virtually undriveable'), spoke quietly to Jackie Oliver and said he was retiring from Formula 1.

'It wasn't the strike which made me say I don't want Formula One,' Tambay says. 'I enjoyed the strike! It was the best time I ever had with all my friends although it was a very, very costly reunion with them. [We'll come to the cost in a moment.] What I didn't like was Teo Fabi sneaking out behind our backs to try and get back into the car, and what I didn't like was that I knew we had been screwed – they [Balestre & Co] had said "Come back out to the circuit and everything's going to be sorted and

STARTING GRID

1 1:06.35 **R. Arnoux**	**2** 1:06.62 **N. Piquet**
3 1:07.10 **G. Villeneuve**	**4** 1:07.39 **R. Patrese**
5 1:08.13 **A. Prost**	**6** 1:08.36 **D. Pironi**
7 1:08.89 **K. Rosberg**	**8** 1:09.30 **C. Reutemann**
9 1:09.73 **J. Watson**	**10** 1:10.03 **M. Alboreto**
11 1:10.24 **J. Laffite**	**12** 1:10.62 **E. Salazar**
13 1:10.68 **N. Lauda**	**14** 1:10.68 **D. Warwick**
15 1:10.68 **E. de Angelis**	**16** 1:10.95 **A. de Cesaris**
17 1:11.00 **E. Cheever**	**18** 1:11.22 **N. Mansell**
19 1:11.28 **B. Giacomelli**	**20** 1:11.80 **M. Winkelhock**
21 1:12.07 **R. Boesel**	**22** 1:12.10 **J. Mass**
23 1:12.36 **S. Borgudd**	**24** 1:13.41 **D. Daly**
25 1:13.46 **C. Serra**	**26** 1:13.83 **J.-P. Jarier**

everything's going to be all right," and I knew we were screwed.'

Tambay had seen what Chapman had seen: nothing had really changed (and the drivers were subsequently fined). Tambay expressed it as a 'done deal between our representatives and the other side so I thought "OK, I am going away." I still have the clipping from *L'Equipe* of what I said: "Maybe I'll come back to Formula One one day if it's to drive for Ferrari or Renault."'

Oliver says 'Patrick didn't want to do the race because he hadn't had a chance to practice and he got fed up with it. That story's quite funny.' Yes, and we've touched on the airfare negotiations already. Here's the whole story, beginning when Oliver originally approached him to drive in South Africa: 'I'd called Tambay and said "Would you do it for me?" and there was an argument over his fee. We agreed his fee for that race as a leader into maybe doing other races for us, and he said "Well, I want a first class air ticket." I said I am not paying first class airfare from the States. We agreed on an economy ticket and he said he would pay the difference. And of course because he joined the strike and then didn't race he didn't get his fee. It cost him dearly and we joke about that now. I see him at the Goodwood revival meeting and every time he reminds me how much that race cost him.'

Tambay remembers the episode in detail. 'Not only the air fare from Hawaii but I got fined $5,000 like everybody else for striking by the FIA and on top of it I didn't get paid what Jackie Oliver was going to pay me because I didn't want to drive. I was fed up with Formula One and its politics. So I made a big loss on the airfare, the fine and the retainer. The

BELOW *Some spectators found their own perches although Peter Dyke (in yellow), who looked after the JPS sponsorship, often saw things from a different angle.*

whole thing was a shame. I think I stood straight in my boots and if he had been a gentleman he would have paid my expenses! I was in Hawaii and it was a flight from Hawaii to London and London to Johannesburg – because there was nothing direct – and I was not about to fly for 30-something hours in coach class.'

And there, grinning broadly (he usually did), stood the strong, square figure of Brian Henton – available for selection as of this second, Jackie. Oliver gave Henton the Tambay drive but, that morning, Henton became embroiled in a tug-of-war between the Arrows management and Herr Lauda.

Arrows 'were bollocking me saying "Get in the car" and all the rest of it,' Henton remembers. 'The other drivers all came back and I am just about to go out for practice and they needed my signature on their petition. I'd got the team shouting in one ear "Get in that car and get out there" and, just as I'm sitting, Niki Lauda – who'd been massaging me all the time and I'd been saying "No, no, no" – rushes up with this petition. He "hit" me at the right time. "Just sign this, sign it, sign it." I thought I only want to get out onto the track, so I signed it and never

saw him again – but he'd got all the signatures.

'Was I unpopular? No, no, at the end of the day everybody is looking after themselves, simple as that. It was quite funny. Everybody talked about camaraderie and all that in motor racing but it boiled down to this: you were in that seat and you wanted a better seat if you could get it, and, even if you got a better seat and were leading the Championship, you were trying to keep your arse in the seat because everybody was after it.'

Ecclestone had all three Brabham cars liveried with the number 2 and, claiming Piquet had had hardly any sleep 'and might not be fit to drive,' refused to let him take part in the first session. Nor would Piquet be allowed into the qualifying until he had had a medical.

Reflecting, John Watson says the strike happened 'essentially because Formula One teams were trying to introduce football-style contracts, which led to the drivers saying "No, we don't want this," which in turn led to the stand-off and the drivers went off. I didn't feel a driver should lose control – or relinquish – his own rights to negotiate. In other words, while the football contract is applicable to footballers it didn't have to be applicable to us, and that it should be introduced without any conversation or discussion was unfortunate.

'The drivers' unity held except for a couple of drivers. Roberto Guerrero was bullied by Mo Nunn but there was a lot of bullying and pressure, and some of the things that were done were very unpleasant by teams on drivers.

'I always felt Pironi was the principle of the whole thing, not Niki. Niki was, if you like, more a spokesman and negotiator. He had more acceptance, more gravitas as a negotiator than Pironi. Remember also that Pironi was driving in a grandee team and we also had this bloody war going on between FISA and FOCA, so I think Niki was a much more suitable intermediary than Pironi.'

In the practice session Prost had a puncture and spun into a safety wall.

Heavy, dark cloud threatened qualifying and rain brought it to an end 25 minutes early. By then Arnoux had pole from Piquet, Villeneuve third and Patrese fourth, Prost fifth and Pironi sixth. That seemed to be shaping the season already: all had turbo-powered cars.

'The turbos had the advantage everywhere,' Watson says. 'What they didn't have was the reliability. They were in the process of learning how to make a turbocharged engine run – and reliably – but essentially they had the advantage everywhere, even street circuits like Detroit and Monaco.'

The extra power of the turbos forced the normally-aspirated teams to install water tanks in their wings, fill them before the race (to make the minimum weight), drain them for the race and fill them up again afterwards. Prost found this 'blatant cheating' and 'distasteful'[9] but, as Rosberg pointed out, it was the only way they could get near parity.

Arnoux averaged 138.3mph [222.67kmh], Rosberg – fastest of the non-turbo runners – 133.3mph [214.45kmh]. If you multiply that difference by the race distance, 196 miles across 77 laps, you have a chasm. Emphasising that, the turbos were doing more than 200mph at the end of the long, main straight and the non-turbos 20mph less.

Professor Watkins sat in the passenger seat of the medical car directly behind the grid and it would set off when the racing cars set off so that it could reach any accident – the moments after the grid is launched are fraught – quickly. As with so much else, Watkins brought professionalism and improvement to all that he did, and in this case it concerned who should drive the medical car. 'In the old days, after I'd had some frightening experiences with the local hero, Bernie said "Well, what we'll do is one of the chaps who hasn't qualified for the race will drive you on the first lap." So when we'd finished qualification on the Saturday he'd pick the guy to be my personal conductor for the first lap. One time I got Derek Daly – I got most of them! There was a bang. I said "What's that?" He said "Reverse!" Another was Rupert Keegan. He actually put it in reverse on the grid, so when the racing cars set off we set off the other

BELOW Once he'd thought it through, Niki Lauda set out to prove that he could still drive a Grand Prix car competitively. Here he is, heading into the points.

way. Just as well they weren't doing anything else with their lives – like brain surgery...'

Who sat poised in the driving seat next to The Prof as the racers waited for the green light on this particular occasion has vanished into the mists of time – but Baldi, Paletti, Henton and Fabi hadn't qualified...

On a hot afternoon Arnoux made a swift getaway. Piquet, who hadn't started in a Grand Prix with a turbo engine before, hesitated and cars went past him, including Prost who was behind Arnoux when they reached Crowthorne Corner. The order completing lap 1: Arnoux, Prost, Villeneuve, Pironi, Rosberg, Patrese.

In fact Arnoux led to lap 13 and by then five drivers were out, including Piquet (accident) and Villeneuve (broken turbo). Rosberg was struggling with the Williams because, from lap 5, 'as I went into a corner and changed down the gear knob came off in my hand and I missed a gear, over-revving the engine. I also dropped the knob and it rolled around getting in the way of my feet and the pedals for the rest of the race.'

On lap 14 Arnoux was baulked by a slower car and Prost went by into the lead. 'By then I was driving under no pressure at all. I knew that if I did not have any mechanical problems the race would be an easy one for me.' It was, until lap 41 when he went into the Jukskei sweep and 'the car suddenly went sideways. I was only just able to catch it and maintain control. Another few metres into the corner I would have run out of road and had a big accident.' The left rear tyre had punctured. 'The next hardest thing was to drive back to the pits at a sensible speed so that it wouldn't damage the car too much.' The pits were three-quarters of a lap away but he made it and sat motionless as four news tyres were fitted.

He emerged eighth and a lap down, which seems normal enough.

Without knowing it, he was about to prove something so simple that it changed Grand Prix racing.

Arnoux led from Reutemann, who had been making steady progress since the start, Rosberg third, Watson fourth. Before the puncture Prost

OPPOSITE *One of the most popular drivers of his era, Jacques Laffite, brings his Talbot Ligier into the pits. He'd have an unhappy race – fuel vaporisation.*

BELOW *Historic puncture. Prost comes in, gets a new wheel and wins – opening up a whole new strategy.*

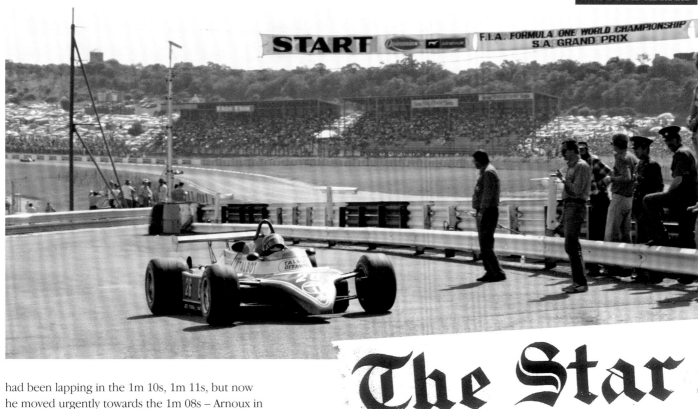

had been lapping in the 1m 10s, 1m 11s, but now he moved urgently towards the 1m 08s – Arnoux in the 1m 12s. Prost caught and overtook Alboreto in four laps, unlapped himself a lap later, caught and overtook Lauda on lap 51, swept past Watson on lap 54 and Rosberg on lap 55.

Pironi had taken second place from Reutemann, and Prost needed only six laps to catch and despatch him, one more lap to despatch Pironi. That left only Arnoux, struggling with tyres. Prost has described his own driving as aggressive.

	Arnoux	Prost
Lap 62	1:12.9	1:10.3
Lap 63	1:12.7	1:08.7
Lap 64	1:13.1	1:09.8
Lap 65	1:12.5	1:11.1
Lap 66	1:14.1	1:10.0
Lap 67	1:14.0	1:09.5

Now Prost swept past Arnoux, whose tyres were causing so much vibration that he could barely hold the car. Before the end Reutemann got past Arnoux, too, Lauda fourth and proving he could still drive a Grand Prix, Rosberg fifth and delighted. The two points were twice as many as he scored in the whole of 1981.

Lauda records how, throughout the weekend, there had been rumours that once the drivers reached the airport to fly home they would be arrested,[10] although on what grounds it is difficult to say. What happened was quite different: during the race the Stewards issued a statement, given to

The Star

Fans pour in as clouds lift over GP

By John Bentley

Thousands of spectators streamed into Kyalami for today's Quindrink/Pointerware South African Grand Prix.

Race promoter, Mr Robert Binckes said advance bookings amounted to R265 000. This was 30 percent up on last year despite booking having been closed between the start of business on Thursday and noon Friday because of the main

GP crisis as drivers stall Fisa

By Geoff Dalglish and John Bentley

The South African Tshirano PGA faced an 11th hour crisis today with a continued deadlock between the drivers and Fisa, the world governing body.

Negotiations continued as the 1 pm start neared.

According to spokesman Niki Lauda, the drivers object to several provisions of the contract, including a requirement that the drivers agree not to criticise Fisa.

Lauda also said the drivers objected to licence provisions requiring them to give details of their earnings.

The race is on — drivers settle contract row

By John Bentley

Striking Formula One drivers ended their dispute with the world motor sport controlling body Fisa this morning and said tomorrow's South African Grand Prix would take place.

The drivers returned to the circuit this morning from their "siege" hotel in Johannesburg where they have been barricaded since yesterday.

ABOVE A world in headlines, and in Johannesburg the strike was big news.

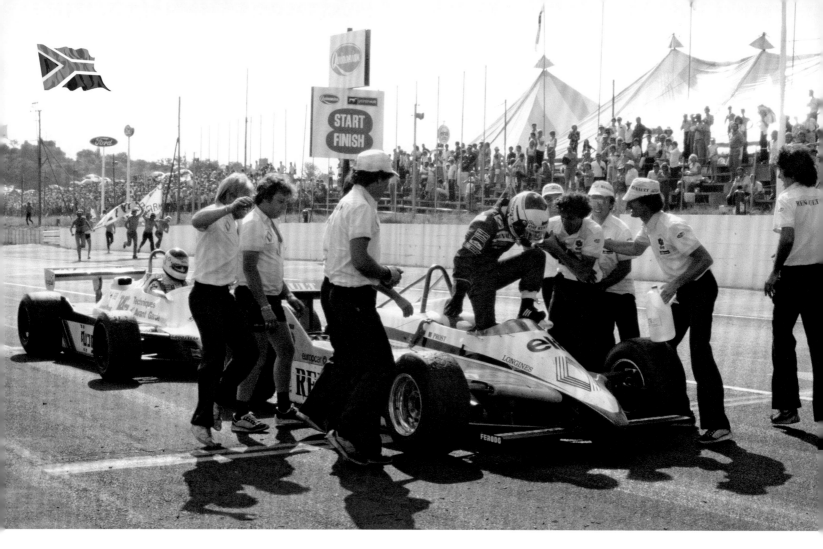

ABOVE *Historic moment – Prost has won despite the puncture. There's a sense of incredulity rather than jubilation among the Renault team members.*

OPPOSITE *Prost sprays the sweetest taste, victory, while Reutemann looks on.*

each team, saying that the drivers' Super Licences were being suspended. Three drivers – Fabi, Mass and Henton – were spared: Fabi because he'd gone to the track prepared to drive, Mass because he had driven, and Henton because he got the Arrows drive after Tambay withdrew following the strike.

Francis Tucker, Steward of the South African Grand Prix, said: 'For the purpose of running a race, a temporary truce was called in the disagreement between the drivers and officials. The truce lasted until the end of the race. At the end of the race, the truce agreement was terminated. This means that the position which existed prior to the agreement is effectively reinstated.' The drivers were suspended immediately and each paid 300 Rand to appeal the decision. FISA said they supported the suspensions and an Executive Committee would meet in Paris on the following Thursday, January 27.

Jean-Pierre Jarier sums it up. 'In 1982 it really was Ecclestone who had the power and he tried to impose the contracts and the struggle for the control of Formula One began. The GPDA was conquered [battu], we went on strike and we obtained something all the same – not much, but a little. In the end Ecclestone won completely – well, he lost in South Africa because the contracts were not implemented, but we had proof that he wanted

to control motor sport. It was the last time that the drivers resisted Ecclestone's power. After that it was finished. That weekend at Kyalami was the end of the weight of the drivers.'

A cynic (and you don't have to look far to find one of those) summed up the drivers' plight perfectly when he said this: 'You should never take "yes" for an answer in Grand Prix racing.'[11]

Championship: Prost 9 points, Reutemann 6, Arnoux 4, Lauda 3, Rosberg 2, Watson 1.

Footnote: 1. To Hell And Back; 2. The F1 Commission comprised three members of FOCA, three manufacturers, two European organisers, two non-European organisers, two sponsors' representatives, one member of FISA, and the reigning World Champion (non-voting); 3. Chasing The Title, Nigel Roebuck, Haynes, Sparkford 1999; 4. In fact, and perhaps not surprisingly, when Grand Prix racing reached Detroit for the first time in June of this 1982 there were strong feelings. Something called the African Liberation Week Support Committee said it would use the week before the race to protest against the 'involvement of South Africans'. A spokesman for the Grand Prix countered that 'we have nothing to do with South Africa' and pointed out that there were no South African drivers or sponsors. 'No nothing.' The Liberation Committee were undaunted by this, pointing out that the South African Grand Prix was part of the Championship and consequently got 'propaganda publicity value' from the Detroit race. A spokesman was quoted as saying: 'How many blacks can afford $75 to go watch the rich man's slot cars? [toy models!] We'll all need a ticket and a pass just to walk around our own city's downtown area '; 5. Grand Prix International magazine; 6. Autosport; 7. The Star, Johannesburg; 8. Grand Prix International; 9. Life In The Fast Lane, Prost; 10. To Hell And Back, Lauda; 11. Grand Prix International.

Race Result

WINNING SPEED 205.77kmh/127.86mph

FASTEST LAP 216.38kmh/134.45mph
(Prost 1m 8.27s on lap 49)

LAP LEADERS Arnoux 1–13, 41–67 (40);
Prost 14–40, 68–77 (37)

RACE

	Driver	Team	Engine	Laps	Time
1	A. Prost	Renault RE30B	Renault V6t	77	1h 32m 08.40s
2	C. Reutemann	Williams FW07C	Cosworth V8	77	1h 32m 23.34s
3	R. Arnoux	Renault RE30B	Renault V6t	77	1h 32m 36.30s
4	N. Lauda	McLaren MP4	Cosworth V8	77	1h 32m 40.514s
5	K. Rosberg	Williams FW07C	Cosworth V8	77	1h 32m 54.54s
6	J. Watson	McLaren MP4B	Cosworth V8	77	1h 32m 59.39s
7	M. Alboreto	Tyrrell 011	Cosworth V8	76	
8	E. de Angelis	Lotus 87B	Cosworth V8	76	
9	E. Salazar	ATS D5	Cosworth V8	75	
10	M. Winkelhock	ATS D5	Cosworth V8	75	
11	B. Giacomelli	Alfa Romeo 179D	Alfa RomV12	74	
12	J. Mass	March 821	Cosworth V8	74	
13	A. de Cesaris	Alfa Romeo 179D	Alfa Rom V12	73	
14	D. Daly	Theodore TY01	Cosworth V8	73	
15	R. Boesel	March 821	Cosworth V8	72	
16	S. Borgudd	Tyrrell 011	Cosworth V8	72	
17	C. Serra	Fittipaldi F8D	Cosworth V8	72	
18	D. Pironi	Ferrari 126C2	Ferrari V6t	71	
r	J. Laffite	Talbot Ligier JS17	Matra V12	54	Fuel vaporisation
r	D. Warwick	Toleman TG181C	Hart 4t	44	Accident
r	R. Patrese	Brabham BT50	BMW 4t	18	Oil loss/turbo bearing
r	E. Cheever	Talbot Ligier JS17	Matra V12	11	Fuel vaporisation
r	G. Villeneuve	Ferrari 126C2	Ferrari V6t	6	Turbo
r	N. Piquet	Brabham BT50	BMW 4t	3	Accident
r	N. Mansell	Lotus 87B	Cosworth V8	0	Electrics
r	J.-P. Jarier	Osella FA1C	Cosworth V8	0	Accident
nq	M. Baldi	Arrows A4	CosworthV8		
nq	R. Paletti	Osella FA1C	Cosworth V8		
nq	B. Henton	Arrows A4	Cosworth V8		
nq	T. Fabi	Toleman TG181B	Hart 4t		

nq = did not qualify; r = retired

CHAMPIONSHIP

	Driver	Points
1	A. Prost	9
2	C. Reutemann	6
3	R. Arnoux	4
4	N. Lauda	3
5	K. Rosberg	2
6	J. Watson	1

	Team	Points
1	Renault	13
2	Williams	8
3	McLaren	4

21 MARCH

BOILING WATERS

BRAZIL, RIO DE JANEIRO

The politics festered. FISA fined the drivers between $10,000 and $5,000, the drivers appealed and the FIA Court of Appeal met in Paris to pass judgement on all of it. The Court criticised FISA, Balestre and the drivers, and reduced the fines to $5,000. It calmed everything. The drivers paid and, as Lauda said cryptically,[1] the drivers appealed that, but many years later he still had no idea if he'd got his money back. Pironi praised the Court of Appeal, and the Super Licence in its provocative form died into that most final of sounds: silence.

There ought to have been an Argentinean Grand Prix but financial problems ruled it out, so Brazil followed South Africa and many, many thousands headed to Jacarepagua, the circuit reclaimed from marshland some 20 miles south of Rio de Janeiro, to crown Nelson Piquet their World Champion.

On the Friday, however, some barriers were declared unsafe before the morning session, something regarded with amazement by the Formula One fraternity because the track had been used for testing and there had been plenty of time to rectify problems. The session was delayed three times and Lauda said: 'We are expected to pay a $5,000 fine when we are late or don't practice. Who pays the bill for this?'

Mist seeped round the majestic mountains which formed a backdrop to the circuit.

Several factors converged to suggest a very, very physical race. The weather – searing hot, overcast and humid – threatened to boil the drivers, and

RIGHT *The Rio heat takes its toll of Nelson Piquet, who's just spent one hour 43 minutes and 53 seconds winning the race – only to be disqualified because his Brabham car was underweight. That's why you still never see his time in any of the records.*

Brazil
Rio de Janeiro

RACE DATE March 21st

CIRCUIT LENGTH 5.03km/3.12 miles

NO. OF LAPS 63

RACE DISTANCE
316.95km/196.94 miles

WEATHER Hot, dry

Carlos Pace

Lagoa
(Lake)

Morette

Girao

Cheirinho

Box

Molykote

Vitoria

Nonato

Norte
(North)

Sul
(South)

Juncao

DRIVER'S VIEW

'The two Brazilian circuits – Rio and Interlagos at São Paulo – were completely different. The old, big Interlagos was a fantastic racetrack with big, big corners. Rio was flat as a kipper, not totally featureless but like a precursor to the modern layout: largely constant radius corners. There was no feel. Ironically it wasn't a bad circuit. The corners were good and it had no chicane although I think latterly they have put one in. You had a lot of third and fourth gear corners and a reasonable length straight with a slow corner on to it which was good for overtaking – but the corner at the other end was very fast, so if you were going to do any overtaking there you had to be alongside the other car. Otherwise you couldn't: no slipping down the inside of somebody who is committed. That corner was tough because it had a difficult entry and then it kept going and going and going.'

— John Watson

the track surface, notoriously bumpy, threatened to batter them (no suspensions to absorb the bumping, of course).

Arnoux, who qualified fourth, said 'it's just crazy. In places your vision goes blurred with the vibration and you can hardly see the road. After a few laps it seems impossible to carry on.'

Warwick remarked that the Toleman was 'terrible over the bumps'.

Pironi, who'd had a crash testing at Paul Ricard, said 'at qualifying speeds you are exhausted after eight or ten laps. No one could do more. It is really not at all pleasant.'

Noticeably the drivers were doing as few laps as possible, governed by the conditions but also the realisation that tyres were only good for one flying lap, and with two sets for each session qualifying compressed itself into four laps. The Renaults did some serious running – Prost 11 laps, Arnoux 13, though in batches rather than constant running. Lauda was at the other extreme, out after 35 minutes for a 1:39 working down to 1:31, into the pits, out nine minutes later for a 1:30, his best.

Rosberg, second fastest to Prost on this opening day, threatened to boil some of the turbo cars.

LEFT AND BELOW *The bodyshells, almost sculptures, which can transform the Ferrari into an instant work of art. It didn't help Villeneuve, who had an accident after 29 laps.*

1		**1** 1:28.80 **A. Prost**
	2 1:29.17 **G. Villeneuve**	
2		**3** 1:29.35 **K. Rosberg**
	4 1:30.12 **R. Arnoux**	
3		**5** 1:30.15 **N. Lauda**
	6 1:30.18 **C. Reutemann**	
4		**7** 1:30.28 **N. Piquet**
	8 1:30.65 **D. Pironi**	
5		**9** 1:30.96 **R. Patrese**
	10 1:31.22 **A. de Cesaris**	
6		**11** 1:31.79 **E. de Angelis**
	12 1:31.90 **J. Watson**	
7		**13** 1:31.99 **M. Alboreto**
	14 1:32.22 **N. Mansell**	
8		**15** 1:32.52 **M. Winkelhock**
	16 1:32.76 **B. Giacomelli**	
9		**17** 1:34.05 **R. Boesel**
	18 1:34.26 **E. Salazar**	
10		**19** 1:34.38 **M. Baldi**
	20 1:34.41 **D. Daly**	
11		**21** 1:35.02 **S. Borgudd**
	22 1:35.03 **J. Mass**	
12		**23** 1:35.08 **J.-P. Jarier**
	24 1:35.08 **J. Laffite**	
13		**25** 1:35.24 **C. Serra**
	26 1:35.28 **E. Cheever**	

Prost consolidated on the second day, Villeneuve joining him on the front row. Villeneuve made a 'mighty charge that left his Ferrari's rear tyres in shreds as he pushed himself, car and tyres to the limit, smoke pouring off the rear tyres under acceleration and lumps of rubber, too.'[2] Rosberg lined up on the second row beside Arnoux.

The heat remained but the humidity went as the clouds departed and the sun shone. Piquet on the fourth row did not deter the locals, who poured into the circuit preparing to make a lot of noise. Villeneuve, meanwhile, fully intended to lead the race in its early stages for reasons of personal morale and did so from the green light, Rosberg tracking him and the two Renaults tracking him. They rounded the Norte horseshoe feeding on to the straight and immediately the turbo power came into play, Villeneuve stretching away from Rosberg and the Renaults flooding past him. Rosberg settled, Patrese behind him. He knew it was going to be a long race.

ABOVE *A majestic study of Jacarepagua: ferocious foreground, brooding background. This is the parade lap and the leaders have already gone. Carlos Reutemann is No 5, Lauda obscured behind him.*

On lap 3 Patrese swept past Rosberg, and so, two laps later, to an explosion of celebration, did Piquet. A lap after that Piquet took Prost, and the crowd created its own ticker-tape of thousands of torn newspapers and programmes. On lap 9 he moved past team-mate Patrese.

Order at lap 10: Villeneuve, Arnoux, Piquet, Patrese, Prost – who had a misfire – and Rosberg.

Arnoux was suffering tyre problems and fell back into Piquet's grasp. Rosberg retook Patrese and the order tilted to: Villeneuve moving away, Piquet, Rosberg, Patrese, Arnoux, Lauda. That lasted only a moment because Reutemann banged wheels with Lauda, forcing him to retire, and further round the lap Reutemann hit Arnoux, who was spinning. Both retired.

On lap 27 the crowd was silenced when Rosberg took Piquet, erupted when Piquet took him back, fell silent again when Rosberg retook him – and both of them were catching Villeneuve, who was

clearly struggling. Then on lap 30 Villeneuve went wide into the hairpin onto the back straight and the Ferrari was on the marbles – some say it had two wheels on the grass. 'The car wouldn't put its power down, which let Nelson get alongside – on the outside – into the hairpin. I had a choice, hit him or go off. And I chose to go off, the car snapped round and that was that. Some people thought that Nelson had hit me but that wasn't true.'[3]

With Piquet in the lead the crowd abandoned any restraint they might have had and made Jacarepagua rock.

On lap 34 Patrese retired, officially 'unable to continue'. He'd later explain that he'd blacked out, the Brabham spinning before he recovered enough to limp to the pits, utterly exhausted. He had to be lifted from the car and laid down in the pit, where he received medical attention. He needed an hour to recover.

Piquet was not to be caught, Rosberg following him home, then Prost, Watson, Mansell, and young Alboreto. On the podium Piquet all but passed out but Rosberg, himself exhausted, found the strength to hold him up.

Prost 13, Piquet 9, Rosberg 8, Reutemann 6, Arnoux and Watson 4.

After the race Reutemann told Frank Williams that he was thinking of retiring. Williams asked him to make a final decision by the Friday, which would give the team just over a week to find a replacement for Long Beach. Williams returned home and, as a precaution, on the Tuesday reached for his telephone and dialled a number in Nazareth, Pennsylvania. A soft-spoken American answered. He was called Mario Andretti and although contracted to drive in the CART series there was no clash of fixtures with Long Beach. Sure he'd like to drive there.

Frank Williams settled down to wait until Friday and the deadline he had given Reutemann.

Ferrari and Renault launched protests about the water tanks on the Brabham and Williams but the Stewards rejected them. They appealed to the Brazilian ASN and that went to FISA in Paris, which gave Rosberg a queasy feeling. It was entirely justified but he wouldn't know that until after Long Beach.

By way of explanation, he says 'the water tank at the beginning of the season was the one that gave

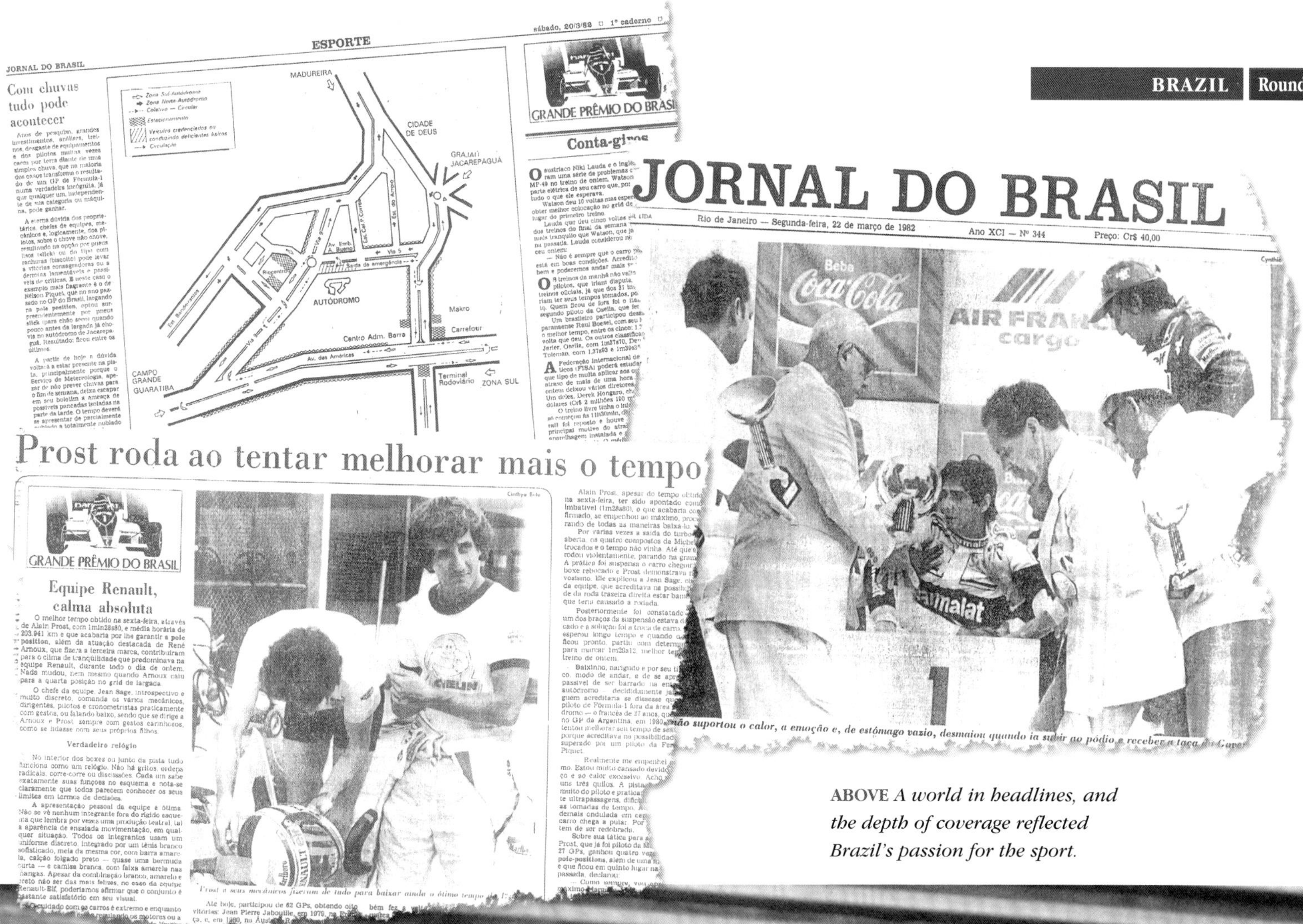

ESPORTE

sábado, 20/3/82 □ 1º caderno □

JORNAL DO BRASIL

Com chuvas tudo pode acontecer

GRANDE PRÊMIO DO BRASIL

Conta-giros

JORNAL DO BRASIL

Rio de Janeiro — Segunda-feira, 22 de março de 1982   Ano XCI — Nº 344   Preço: Cr$ 40,00

Prost roda ao tentar melhorar mais o tempo

GRANDE PRÊMIO DO BRASIL

Equipe Renault, calma absoluta

ABOVE *A world in headlines, and the depth of coverage reflected Brazil's passion for the sport.*

us at least a theoretical chance to compete with the turbos. Without the water tank we were finished.'

Nor was Balestre idle. At Rio he made an enigmatic announcement – personal but on FISA headed notepaper – about what he saw as immediately necessary to resolve the problems of the Grand Prix car. He spelled them out: putting suspensions back ... reducing cornering speeds ... hold engine power before reducing it ... reduce tyre sizes ... study the wings ... give drivers greater protection.

This was all common sense but vested interests govern Formula One, not common sense. There was the matter of how much Renault, Ferrari, BMW and others had spent on developing turbo engines and how they would react to a reduction of power, hauling them back towards the dear old Cosworth DFV, still available off the shelf in Northampton.

Whatever Balestre wanted, or stipulated was necessary, would be subject to the Concorde Agreement signed the previous March and designed to achieve harmony. No major rule changes were to be implemented without unanimous agreement. Ferrari and Renault had been two of the main 'architects' of this.[4]

Balestre said he intended to present his idea to the FIA Congress in Casablanca the following month.

Footnote: 1. To Hell And Back; 2. Grand Prix International; 3. Autosport; 4. Ibid.

Race Result

WINNING SPEED 181.89 kmh/113.02 mph

FASTEST LAP 186.68kmh/116.00mph
(Prost 1m 37.01s on lap 36)

LAP LEADERS Villeneuve 1–29 (29);
Piquet 30–63 (34)

Note: Piquet finished first in 1h 43m 53.76s (183.04kmh/
113.73mph), and recorded the fastest lap in 1m 36.58s
(187.52kmh/116.52 mph). Rosberg finished second in 1h 44m 05.73s.

RACE

	Driver	Team	Engine	Laps	Time
dq	N. Piquet	Brabham BT49D	Cosworth V8	63	Car underweight
dq	K. Rosberg	Williams FW07C	Cosworth V8	63	Car underweight
1	A. Prost	Renault RE30B	Renault V6t	63	1h 44m 33.13s
2	J. Watson	McLaren MP4B	Cosworth V8	63	1h 44m 36.12s
3	N. Mansell	Lotus 91	Cosworth V8	63	1h 45m 09.99s
4	M. Alboreto	Tyrrell 011	Cosworth V8	63	1h 45m 23.89s
5	M. Winkelhock	ATS D5	Cosworth V8	62	
6	D. Pironi	Ferrari 126C2	Ferrari V6t	62	
7	S. Borgudd	Tyrrell 011	Cosworth V8	61	
8	J. Mass	March 821	Cosworth V8	61	
9	J.-P. Jarier	Osella FA1C	Cosworth V8	60	
10	M. Baldi	Arrows A4	Cosworth V8	57	
r	E. Salazar	ATS D5	Cosworth V8	37	Engine
r	C. Serra	Fittipaldi F8D	Cosworth V8	36	Accident
r	R. Patrese	Brabham BT49D	Cosworth V8	34	Driver exhausted
r	G. Villeneuve	Ferrari 126C2	Ferrari V6t	29	Accident
r	N. Lauda	McLaren MP4B	Cosworth V8	21	Accident
r	R. Arnoux	Renault RE30B	Renault V6t	21	Accident
r	C. Reutemann	Williams FW07C	Cosworth V8	21	Accident
r	E. de Angelis	Lotus 91	Cosworth V8	21	Accident
r	E. Cheever	Talbot Ligier JS17	Matra V12	19	Water leak
r	B. Giacomelli	Alfa Romeo 182	Alfa V12	16	Engine
r	J. Laffite	Talbot Ligier JS17	Matra V12	15	Misfire/skirt
r	A. de Cesaris	Alfa Romeo 182	Alfa V12	14	Undertray
r	D. Daly	Theodore TY02	Cosworth V8	12	Accident
r	R. Boesel	March 821	Cosworth V8	11	Rear suspension
nq	T. Fabi	Toleman TG181B	Hart 4t		
nq	R. Guerrero	Ensign N181	Cosworth V8		
nq	B. Henton	Arrows A4	Cosworth V8		
nq	D. Warwick	Toleman TG181C	Hart 4t		
npq	R. Paletti	Osella FA1C	Cosworth V8		

dq = disqualified; npq = did not pre-qualify; nq = did not qualify; r = retired

CHAMPIONSHIP

	Driver	Points
1	A. Prost	18
2	J. Watson	7
3	C. Reutemann	6
4	R. Arnoux	4
	N. Mansell	4
6	N. Lauda	3
	M. Alboreto	3
8	K. Rosberg	2
	M. Winkelhock	2
10	D. Pironi	1

	Team	Points
1	Renault	22
2	McLaren	10
3	Williams	8
4	Lotus	4
5	Tyrrell	3
6	ATS	2
7	Ferrari	1

4 APRIL

BACK IN CONTROL

—— USA WEST, LONG BEACH

California was then arguably the English-speaking community in all the world most remote from Anglo-Saxon norms and normalities (no matter that it might qualify as a Spanish-speaking community now). Long Beach, despite the presence of the *Queen Mary* moored as a tourist attraction and a red British telephone box on the quay, looked very California: that disconcerting mingle of aggressive neon, so many sun-kissed ladies with l-o-n-g legs and perfect blonde hair that they all seemed to have been made in a factory, skyscrapers and shopping malls, skateboarders and freeways, hippies and preachers, Chinese laundries, every conceivable kind of restaurant (except English, of course), historic pubs which were several weeks old and a lot of cars.

You might think it was equally remote from Grand Prix racing but in fact it had been on the calendar every year since 1976 and offered every appearance of Formula One having found a settled home there: a nice place to go each spring.

Niki Lauda knew his way round – he'd finished second in 1976, again in 1977, driven there in the 1978 and 1979 races – and therefore knew how to apply his logic. He did. It gave him deep satisfaction at both the physical and intellectual level (he claims he was whistling for joy inside the cockpit), and in the race only Rosberg could live with him.

What the Californians made of all this is problematical, not least because Hollywood wasn't far away and, if you are in proximity to that, putting on a show – any show – ain't gonna be easy,

RIGHT *The poignant podium. Lauda proves he can still win Grands Prix and nobody would ever see Villeneuve smiling like this again.*

56

USA West Long Beach

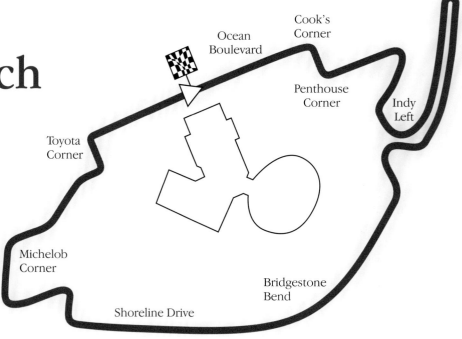

RACE DATE April 4th

CIRCUIT LENGTH
3.42km/2.13 miles

NO. OF LAPS 75.5

RACE DISTANCE
258.80km/160.81 miles

WEATHER Hot, dry

Le Gasomet

Cook's Corner

Ocean Boulevard

Penthouse Corner

Indy Left

Toyota Corner

Michelob Corner

Bridgestone Bend

Shoreline Drive

DRIVER'S VIEW

'All street circuits are very demanding. Long Beach was a very, very good one – it had a dangerous zone but a lot of spectacular corners. It was quite fast and a couple of corners were very fast. And walls everywhere! You couldn't compare it to Monaco because it was different, it was not even the same as Detroit – Detroit was all sharp bends. Long Beach was more similar to a normal circuit, more open. Monaco and Detroit were very closed. I liked street circuits because of the demands on the driver. You had to be on the limit all the time but you always knew one mistake and you would have to pay. Normally in Grand Prix racing a little mistake is OK – but at a place like Long Beach you paid.'

—Andrea de Cesaris

buddy. Nor are the local papers likely to ignore the homespun angles, which cuts the whole thing into its true perspective. Before the Grand Prix meeting, the *San Franciso Chronicle* wrote of the Toyota Pro-Celebrity race: 'Autograph hunters were abandoning the world's top international Grand Prix drivers in droves yesterday as they swarmed around their Super Bowl heroes Joe Montana and Jack (Hacksaw) Reynolds.'

You don't know Mr Montana and The Hacksaw?

That's just the point. Every American knew them and virtually no American knew The Rat or The Flying Finn (as he was inevitably and tediously dubbed). Perhaps this is a bit harsh because, after all these years, Formula One did have a following and plenty of Long Beach aficionados had seen the Grand Prix cars before – but nationwide in the continental US of A?

Rosberg was big here and Reynolds big there – but Rosberg was there.

The *Los Angeles Times* provided a profound journalistic lesson in how to give an international story a local angle, too. A piece on Piquet began:

'The trophy case at Acalanea High School in Lafayette, Calif., near Berkeley, displays trophies won by football's Norm Van Brooklin, Olympic swimming gold medallist Donna de Varona and world figure skating champion Charlie Tucker.

'There should also be a place in the same for Nelson Souto Maior, the No 3 man on Acalane boys' tennis team in 1968.

'Today, that tennis player is known as Nelson Piquet – the World Formula 1 driving champion from Brazil who Sunday will compete in the Long Beach Grand Prix.'

Ah, but California could be a good place to be. Witty remembers 'when we were at Long Beach, Teo said "Let's go to Disneyworld," and I said "OK." He and I went on our own like two kids and all he wanted to do was go on Space Mountain and I went with him on it. It's like a rollercoaster ride but in the dark. It has high G-forces and all those things. I'm thinking "Here's a guy who wouldn't say boo to a goose," but he had this desire inside. He said "That kind of G is sort of what you get in a car." Teo was not outwardly flamboyant in any shape or form but he was very polite and came from a family business – big talcum powder manufacturer, as they were.'

You could argue that a race is a self-contained entity, entire unto itself, and it doesn't matter where it's run. The most efficient and cost-effective way to implement that philosophy would be to build a track as near Heathrow Airport as possible and run them all there, only altering the title of each race. Instead, the Grand Prix people gathered on Shoreline Drive with its fringing of palm trees and concrete blocks, and the l-o-n-g legs travelled languidly by.

Reutemann would be absent. On the deadline Friday, as Williams had stipulated, Reutemann rang him and said 'Frank, I'm out of it, I'm retiring.' And that, concluded Williams, was that.

ABOVE *The Ferarri was glamorous, the background wasn't always.*

ABOVE *The true nature of Long Beach as the race unfolds – sharp turns, concrete blocks. De Cesaris leads Arnoux and Lauda.*

There was a lively and provocative question within the Formula One fraternity and it centred on Lauda's motivation for his return. A rumour claimed that his airline was in trouble and the comeback was helping to finance it. Like trying to prove a negative, if Lauda denied this ('Well, he would, wouldn't he?') the rumour persisted. A question flowed from this: how serious was Lauda about the comeback? Anyone who had even the most passing acquaintance with the man knew the question to be absurd. Lauda was serious about everything he did, particularly getting back to something which had nearly killed him. If he wanted to know what he had put at risk again he received the most direct, graphic evidence every time he looked in a mirror.

There'd been Kyalami, the strike and 'that Lauda back to foment trouble'. He'd qualified halfway down the grid and finished a distant fourth. He judged his performance 'reasonable' but he had had to take the 'incredible physical demands' of a car with wings. He'd taken it.[1] There'd been Rio, qualifying higher up the grid and running sixth when Reutemann hit him. This was not million-dollar stuff.

By the Saturday in Long Beach, Lauda had banished all doubts regarding his presence.

Reutemann of course was gone, temporarily replaced by Mario Andretti. 'At that point I had decided to be out of Formula One and I'd already come back to the States,' Andretti says. 'If the odd drive came up, however, even in circumstances you don't want to see, I could take it. It was always the love of driving with me and that was generally known, so sometimes, if there was an opportunity to fill a gap, they could call me and I was going to be likely to accept.

'I didn't like the Williams at Long Beach at all and then I found out later that Keke Rosberg had a totally different set-up, much, much softer. I tried to tell them but I wasn't a permanent member of the team. I talked to Frank Dernie. When we tested at Willow [one day at the Willow Springs Raceway, California], which is high speed, I said "Look, this very stiff set-up may be OK for here but Long Beach is a totally different animal. You don't have the downforce." My car was like being on a pogo stick. It was jumping around as if I had no feel of it. I found out later that

STARTING GRID

Pos		
1	**2** 1:27.43 N. Lauda	**1** 1:27.31 A. de Cesaris
2	**4** 1:28.97 A. Prost	**3** 1:27.76 R. Arnoux
3	**6** 1:28.27 N. Piquet	**5** 1:28.08 B. Giacomelli
4	**8** 1:28.57 K. Rosberg	**7** 1:28.47 G. Villeneuve
5	**10** 1:28.70 J.-P. Jarier	**9** 1:28.68 D. Pironi
6	**12** 1:29.02 M. Alboreto	**11** 1:28.88 J. Watson
7	**14** 1:29.46 M. Andretti	**13** 1:29.33 E. Cheever
8	**16** 1:29.69 E. de Angelis	**15** 1:29.58 J. Laffite
9	**18** 1:29.94 R. Patrese	**17** 1:29.75 N. Mansell
10	**20** 1:30.47 B. Henton	**19** 1:30.18 R. Guerrero
11	**22** 1:30.91 D. Daly	**21** 1:30.47 J. Mass
12	**24** 1:31.03 S. Borgudd	**23** 1:30.97 R. Boesel
13	**26** 1:31.82 E. Salazar	**25** 1:31.59 M. Winkelhock

Keke had exactly 50 per cent of the stiffness that I did. I don't know why they stuck me with a really heavy go-kart-like set-up.'

At Williams, Rosberg became the Number 1 driver, something which gave him pleasure and reassurance. He translated that to provisional pole on the Friday – from Lauda. Andretti came 14th and spoke in something approaching awe of the G-forces.

The Saturday produced genuine drama. Lauda waited 24 minutes before making a run on race tyres. He did six laps, climaxing at 1:27.4, a time seemingly ample for pole. He brought the car to the pits, got out and spectated. As the flag signalled the end of the session, Lauda grinned and set off for the debrief. Under the rules, cars which had begun their final lap before the flag were entitled to finish them and one estimate says at least 20 cars were doing this. Among them was de Cesaris and he seized pole from Lauda by an eye-blink, 1:27.316 against Lauda's 1:27.436. The two men could not have been more different and their reactions demonstrated it: Lauda expending minimum effort on his lap and returning from it perfectly composed, no drop of sweat; de Cesaris returning 'in a very emotional state, weeping and shaking in the enormity of the moment.'[2]

By then his brother Emilio in the Alfa Romeo pit was weeping, too, while mechanics embraced each other and a crowd gathered. De Cesaris sat in the car, hauled his helmet and balaclava off. He had been sweating profusely and yes, there were the tears...

BELOW By now, Mario Andretti was in the No 5 Williams but the rear suspension failed.

FAN'S EYE VIEW

'I was born in Wyoming but I grew up and went to school in Los Angeles. My interest in motor sport began with listening to the Indy 500 on the radio, starting in 1956. It continues today in my retirement on the central coast of California.

'In 1982 I was a 39-year-old film editor working in the television and film industry. At Long Beach I went on the Friday practice day. The shots of people and static cars were taken in the pits – on Ocean Boulevard at that time – and just a chainlink fence separated us from cars and drivers. Derek Warwick signed my program as he sat outside the garage area. I remember him not being a very happy camper. Frank Williams walked by in a hurry with no time for autographs.

'The sights and sounds were very spectacular because the spectators were so close to the track. I can remember Villeneuve "throwing" his car off of Ocean Boulevard down Linden Avenue. It was something to behold!'

**STEVE POTTER,
LOS OSOS, CALIFORNIA**

FROM TOP CLOCKWISE *Jacques Laffite, genial and serious; Colin Chapman and Nigel Mansell had a close rapport; Prost and Arnoux, when they were still talking; seen through the wire, de Angelis. Villeneuve deep in conversation with Rob Walker, a doyen of motorsport who once ran his own team.*

De Cesaris had his reasons and, as he says, 'Yes, pole was good.' He'd spent 1981 at McLaren and felt 'betrayed' by what had happened there. 'The McLaren people were saying all kinds of things and you English journalists wrote a lot of bullshit about those things – de Crasheris and stuff like that. In Formula One today it would be unacceptable for a driver to be treated like I was with McLaren. Niki Lauda signed up and I was put in a very bad light. I had many failures with the car and still they said it was my fault. I was looking over my shoulder all the time.

'So Long Beach was really good. You know why? Because Lauda was in pole position and they were already partying beside the pits – just minutes to go before the end of the session – and they didn't even see me going round. They heard on the loudspeaker "de Cesaris on pole!" and they already had champagne in their hands, so I destroyed their party. It was like a kind of revenge.'

Rosberg qualified on the fourth row.

De Cesaris made a rasping, unemotional start at the green light, swift away down Shoreline Drive, but Arnoux out-dragged Lauda and they threaded through Toyota Corner (actually the first of two Toyota Corners, the other on Ocean Boulevard) in that order: de Cesaris, Arnoux, Lauda, Giacomelli, then the pack.

Lauda counselled patience. You put 26 Formula One cars into the confined space which is, by definition, any street circuit, you line that space with concrete blocks, you run the cars on surfaces not normally used for this purpose – so they lack that adhesive film of rubber laid down by previous racing – and you have a menu of many courses.

Borgudd's Tyrrell provided the first by becoming entangled with both ATS cars, Winkelhock's race run already. Salazar in the other ATS got as far as lap 3. Next lap Rosberg overtook Pironi – the only movement in the top eight – but by now Watson was deep into one of his fabled charges. From 11th on the grid he dealt with Alboreto on the opening lap, on the fourth lap dealt with Piquet, on the fifth dealt with Pironi.

Next lap Giacomelli opened the whole thing up by making a 'suicide run'[3] into the Le Gasomet hairpin, out-braking Lauda – who was entirely content to let Giacomelli skitter by – and out-braking himself. Smoke burned from the locked wheels as Giacomelli skittered on, punting Arnoux's Ferrari. In all the

ABOVE *Decisive moment as Lauda takes the lead from de Cesaris.*

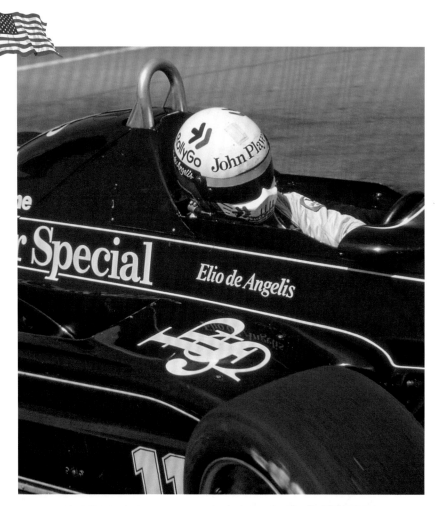

excitement Watson quickly dealt with Rosberg so that the order on lap 7 had become: de Cesaris, Lauda, Villeneuve, Watson, Rosberg, Piquet.

The Rat bared his teeth.

	de Cesaris	Lauda
Lap 8	1:33.3	1:32.3
Lap 9	1:32.3	1:31.7
Lap 10	1:31.4	1:31.5
Lap 11	1:31.2	1:31.1

By then Pironi had hit a wall, Prost had hit a wall, Watson had dealt with Villeneuve, the tow truck was provoking consternation by appearing on the track to hoist wreckage to the knacker's yard (Lauda narrowly missed it) and The Rat stalked de Cesaris moment by moment until, on lap 15, de Cesaris came upon Boesel into the chicane before Shoreline Drive. Boesel did not move aside, holding de Cesaris up, and The Rat watched that, thinking *interesting*. De Cesaris tried the outside and The Rat thought again *interesting*. Then he instructed himself: *take it easy, don't get embroiled and spin.*

Coming out of the chicane de Cesaris was anything but unemotional and began shaking his fist at Boesel as he sailed by – his right fist, the hand you changed gear with. The Rat saw the fist come up and thought: he should be changing gear with

that NOW.[4] The Rat heard the Alfa Romeo's engine howling on the rev limit and, staying wide of him – watch out for anybody who forgets to change gear – went smoothly, logically, to the inside. They ran along Shoreline Drive in tandem but Lauda had the line for the right-hander at the end and de Cesaris had nowhere to go.

The Rat had everywhere to go and went there, shedding de Cesaris immediately:

	Lauda	de Cesaris
Lap 16	1:31.3	1:32.7
Lap 17	1:31.2	1:32.0
Lap 18	1:31.4	1:31.7

The order at lap 18: Lauda 'working the traffic with all the guile in the world,'[5] de Cesaris keeping away from the walls, Watson scenting second place, and Villeneuve and Rosberg in a two-dimensional battle – Villeneuve feeding in turbo power on the straights, Rosberg nippy through the corners. Rosberg noticed how wide Villeneuve's rear wing was – in fact Ferrari were running two rear wings, one in front of the other in staggered formation and as wide as the car.

On lap 21 Rosberg got past Villeneuve and they ran along Shoreline Drive like that to the right-hander, where according to Rosberg the Canadian tried to out-brake him on the outside, which was not possible, and according to Roebuck in *Autosport* Villeneuve appeared not to brake at all! Villeneuve spun into the escape road and came out like a demon, smoke from the tyres, everything, just in front of Piquet.

Rosberg wondered if Lauda could stand the pace. Lauda didn't wonder. He knew perfectly well he could.

Andretti, Daly and Piquet went out in different accidents. 'I think I wound up brushing a wall,' Andretti says. 'I threw it into a corner and I had no grip at all, zero grip.'

On lap 34 de Cesaris had fire and smoke coming from the back of his Alfa Romeo, and crashed hard into Turn 5. 'I had a problem with an oil leak. I was coming into the pits and the oil was coming out from the rear of the engine onto the tyres. All the oil went on the tyres and I had a fire. I had an accident because I couldn't see the fire and because of that – and because of the previous year – people said "Ah, de Cesaris shunted again". That was unfair. You British journalists were so unfair with me. I could not believe

ABOVE *A world in headlines, expressed as only Americans can.*

OPPOSITE TOP
De Angelis keeps the Lotus in perfect balance as he moves towards fifth place.

OPPOSITE BOTTOM
Villeneuve and Michele Alboreto obey and turn before the Do Not Enter sign, while the marshal in white sets a world record. It is impossible to get closer to a Formula 1 car than this and live.

the way news could be manipulated. My team knew I didn't shunt the car because they saw the oil pipe was off. And also de Angelis, who was following me, confirmed to the team that I was coming in to the pits and he had seen the fire on the car.'

That gave a top three of Lauda, Rosberg and Villeneuve and it endured to the end. Rosberg's tyres were worn but he found the drive home 'easy'. Lauda described it as 'uneventful' and into the final stage was satisfied with the standard of his driving. The comeback was no careless thing.

Into the final lap he felt sure the car wouldn't let him down and, even if it had, he'd have carried it to the line. On that lap, allowing his delight to translate itself to shouting and whistling, he suddenly reprimanded himself: don't be silly and drive into a wall.

He beat Rosberg by 14 seconds.

Villeneuve was stripped of third place – it really was that kind of season – when the wing was protested.

Prost 18, Lauda 12, Rosberg and Watson 8, Reutemann and Alboreto 6.

When Rosberg got home he learnt that the Renault and Ferrari protest over Rio had been upheld, so Piquet lost the win and Rosberg lost the six points for second place. With that went the lead in the World Championship.

Yes, it really was that kind of season and it was still only the beginning of April.

Watson eyed it with a guarded optimism because 'Long Beach was the first time I got the car to work as I wanted it to work. I was a lot quicker than the results indicate.'

Rosberg eyed the situation in another mood altogether. He was angry. He pointed out that they'd raced at Kyalami with the cars the way they were and nothing happened, other cars had these water tanks and, worse, Rosberg felt they were in accordance with the rules. Why, he wanted to know, punish only him and Piquet?

He did not get an answer.

Footnote: 1. *To Hell And Back*; 2. *Autosport*; 3. *Grand Prix International*; 4. *To Hell And Back*; 5. *Autosport*.

LEFT *Niki Lauda scales the heights at Long Beach, beating Rosberg by 14 seconds.*

OPPOSITE TOP *Rosberg putting together a strong second place and already he looked a real Championship contender.*

Race Result

WINNING SPEED 131.12kmh/81.47mph

FASTEST LAP 135.86kmh/84.42mph
(Lauda 1m 30.83s on lap 12)

LAP LEADERS de Cesaris 1–14 (14.5);
Lauda 15–75 (61)

	Driver	Team	Engine	Laps	Time
1	N. Lauda	McLaren MP4B	Cosworth V8	75	1h 58m 25.31s
2	K. Rosberg	Williams FW07C	Cosworth V8	75	1h 58m 39.97s
dq	G. Villeneuve	Ferrari 126C2	Ferrari V6t	75	Irregular wing
3	R. Patrese	Brabham BT49C	Cosworth V8	75	1h 59m 44.46s
4	M. Alboreto	Tyrrell 011	Cosworth V8	75	1h 59m 46.26s
5	E. de Angelis	Lotus 91	Cosworth V8	74	
6	J. Watson	McLaren MP4B	Cosworth V8	74	
7	N. Mansell	Lotus 91	Cosworth V8	73	
8	J. Mass	March 821	Cosworth V8	73	
9	R. Boesel	March 821	Cosworth V8	70	
10	S. Borgudd	Tyrrell 011	Cosworth V8	68	
r	E. Cheever	Talbot Ligier JS17B	Matra V12	58	Gearbox
r	A. de Cesaris	Alfa Romeo 182	Alfa Rom V12	33	Accident
r	B. Henton	Arrows A4	Cosworth V8	32	Accident
r	R. Guerrero	Ensign N181	Cosworth V8	27	Accident
r	J. Laffite	Talbot Ligier JS17B	Matra V12	26	Spin
r	J.-P. Jarier	Osella FA1C	Cosworth V8	26	Gearbox
r	N. Piquet	Brabham BT49D	Cosworth V8	25	Accident
r	D. Daly	Theodore TY02	Cosworth V8	23	Accident
r	M. Andretti	Williams FW07C	Cosworth V8	18	Accident
r	A. Prost	Renault RE30B	Renault V6t	10	Brakes/accident
r	D. Pironi	Ferrari 126C2	Ferrari V6t	6	Accident
r	R. Arnoux	Renault RE30B	Renault V6t	5	Accident
r	B. Giacomelli	Alfa Romeo 182	Alfa RomV12	5	Accident
r	E. Salazar	ATS D5	Cosworth V8	3	Accident
r	M. Winkelhock	ATS D5	Cosworth V8	1	Accident
nq	T. Fabi	Toleman TG181C	Hart 4t		
nq	R. Paletti	Osella FA1C	Cosworth V8		
nq	C. Serra	Fittipaldi F8D	Cosworth V8		
nq	M. Baldi	Arrows A4	Cosworth V8		
npq	D. Warwick	Toleman TG181C	Hart 4t		

dq = disqualified; npq = did not pre-qualify; nq = did not qualify; r = retired

CHAMPIONSHIP

	Driver	Points
1	A. Prost	18
2	N. Lauda	12
3	K. Rosberg	8
	J. Watson	8
5	M. Alboreto	6
	C. Reutemann	6
7	R. Arnoux	4
	R. Patrese	4
	N. Mansell	4
10	E. de Angelis	2
	M. Winkelhock	2
12	D. Pironi	1

	Team	Points
1	Renault	22
2	McLaren	20
3	Williams	14
4	Lotus	6
	Tyrrell	6
6	Brabham	4
7	ATS	2
8	Ferrari	1

A MAN BETRAYED

SAN MARINO, IMOLA

To compete in Grand Prix racing you need to be selfish and you need to be strong because Grand Prix racing constantly marginalises the weak. The strength and the selfishness give the whole thing its distinctive character – very sharp, very hard, and in permanent crisis – but whenever common sense is required these qualities can be brutally destructive. Consensus, which makes most of the rest of the world go round, is viewed with great suspicion.

This destruction, in several of its guises, was to be visited on the genteel, ancient town of Imola and the genteel parkland which so gracefully embraces its racing circuit. The days before, during, and after the San Marino Grand Prix remain a powerful example of what can happen when the strengths get out of control.

It really began with the FIA Tribunal's disqualification of Piquet and Rosberg from the Brazilian. The Tribunal ruled that in future cars would be weighed immediately after races so that no coolants could be added to get them to the minimum weight. The Tribunal was, in effect, closing a loophole in the regulations retrospectively and with no consultation. Mr Ecclestone did not care for this. Mr Williams did not care for this. Mr Rosberg did not care for this, made rude noises about the French (Williams told him to shut up), said plaintively that a lot of people had been running The Water Tank Ploy so why punish only Piquet and him? Rosberg added that applying new rules retrospectively was against natural justice.

RIGHT *The way it was supposed to be – Villeneuve leading Pironi - but, all unknown, Pironi is preparing to enrage Villeneuve, provoke Enzo Ferrari and convulse Formula 1.*

San Marino
Imola

RACE DATE April 25th

CIRCUIT LENGTH 5.04km/3.13 miles

NO. OF LAPS 60

RACE DISTANCE
302.40km/187.90 miles

WEATHER Warm, dry

Piratella

Tosa

Variante
Acqua
Minerali

Variante
Alta

Acqua Minerali

Tamburello

Traguardo

Rivazza

Variante
Marlboro

DRIVER'S VIEW

'I liked Imola a lot because it was a difficult circuit, an extraordinary circuit. You braked as you descended into corners and that heightened the sense of driving but for the brakes it was hard. It was also very hard on the drivers, hence why I say it was difficult. It was also very fast which demanded driving, a great deal of driving. You know, in that era, we didn't have ABS and 50 per cent of the driving was how to accelerate into and out of a corner – all that has gone. Overtaking was done under braking. We didn't have power-assisted steering, which made a place like Imola very physical. You didn't have semi-automatic gearboxes so you took the corners steering with only one hand – the other was changing gear – and it became physical: taking a corner one-handed, with all the aerodynamic load, made for a sport unlike anything today. Imola was for athletes! Tamburello was impressionant! Acqua Minerale was a super corner...'

—— Jean-Pierre Jarier

The ruling meant that Watson's fourth place in Rio now became second and, although nobody knew it then, the extra points would have a material bearing on the Championship. Watson's McLaren had been as innocent (or guilty) as Piquet's Brabham and Rosberg's Williams but nobody protested it...

FOCA felt that the Tribunal were in effect bringing in a new rule – which wasn't their role – and doing so in spite of the Concorde Agreement, itself a rare example of consensus and guaranteeing the way new rules would be brought in.

FOCA asked FISA to postpone Imola so that they could ingest the Tribunal's ruling and FISA refused. On the Wednesday before the Grand Prix, FOCA met in London and decided to boycott it. Tyrrell, sympathetic to the FOCA stance, felt obliged to break ranks because he had an Italian sponsor and bills to pay. The rest, whatever their misgivings and internal divisions, held solid.

John Watson sums it up neatly enough: 'There was a real tussle for the control of Formula One.' He sums up with equal neatness what most of the drivers must have thought: 'My concern was do I get paid for not taking part in a race when it wasn't my fault?'

Rosberg, ruminating on his Brazilian disqualification, says: 'You have to remember we got caught in the middle of a political issue and after that we had Imola so it was that kind of a season. I was very sad we didn't go to Imola because we had a quick car and we should have been racing. I watched the

race on TV. Ken Tyrrell was the only English team who went [apart from Toleman]. He gave Ron [Dennis] and the others the impression he was part of the gang but at the end of the day Ken was looking after his own interests. He said "I've Candy as a sponsor," and of course he had Candy as a sponsor, but everyone who didn't show up had problems like that.'

Brian Henton would make his debut for Tyrrell because Slim Borgudd, a rent-a-driver, hadn't paid the rent for the first three races.

The field for Imola was reduced to 14 cars: the grandee teams – two Renaults, two Ferraris – plus two Alfa Romeos, two Tyrrells, two Tolemans, two Osellas and two ATSs.

'We had been aligned with the FISA teams all the way through,' Alex Hawkridge says. 'Right back to the Concorde Agreement we were part of the grand constructors' group or whatever you like to call it. Our role had been to act as a kind of middle-man because we were an English team. We kept in touch with Bernie and Balestre so we were aware of what was going on on both sides. We were trying to do what little we could to get people together.'

Witty provides the background. 'Alex had always said we would go with the manufacturers – the grandees as they were called – because I think he felt he could achieve more by siding with Ferrari and Renault. He felt the manufacturers were where he wanted to be. The majority of the teams were Bernie boys.'

ABOVE *Impromptu drivers' meeting. Didier Pironi is in the centre with Riccardo Paletti (in glasses) behind him. Derek Warwick is to the right of Pironi (striped overall) and Michele Alboreto above Warwick (white t-shirt). Teo Fabi (balding patch!) is below Warwick. Villeneuve is to the left of Pironi.*

1	**1** 1:29.76 R. Arnoux	**2** 1:30.24 A. Prost
2	**3** 1:30.71 G. Villeneuve	**4** 1:32.02 D. Pironi
3	**5** 1:33.20 M. Alboreto	**6** 1:33.23 B. Giacomelli
4	**7** 1:33.39 A. de Cesaris	**8** 1:33.50 D. Warwick
5	**9** 1:34.33 J.-P. Jarier	**10** 1:34.64 T. Fabi
6	**11** 1:35.26 B. Henton	**12** 1:35.79 M. Winkelhock
7	**13** 1:36.22 R. Paletti	**14** 1:36.43 E. Salazar

BELOW *Before the race belonged entirely to Ferrari, Arnoux led Villeneuve and Pironi.*

These included Arrows, who 'did not go to Imola,' as Jackie Oliver says. 'All the Formula One Constructors got together. The only team that broke ranks was Tyrrell. He had Italian sponsors but I did, too, an Italian tile company, and they said "Well, OK, but there will be sanctions against you if you break the union." They dropped them in the end. Ken wiggled his way back in again and said "Very sorry... had to do it, you know."'

Villeneuve would have no difficulty making sure he was on the grid on time because he'd just bought a new Augusta helicopter, a very advanced machine capable of 160 knots and 16,000 feet. He intended to fly it to all the European races.

Team-mate Pironi had married girlfriend Catherine Bleynie two weeks before Imola, Piccinini the best man. Villeneuve wasn't invited. Ferrari politics extended to the altar as well as, sometimes, the grave.

Balestre issued a public statement which began: 'Blackmail, threats and lies from some car manufacturers will not prevent me from having reforms to save drivers' lives.

'The masks have finally fallen. The public at large can now see the true reasons and the instigators of the campaigns conducted for the past three months to destroy and eliminate the President of the International Federation so that he may be replaced by a more accommodating man.'

Consensus lay in a shallow grave and the grave-diggers were quite prepared to dig it much deeper.

The mess, riven by contradictions, ensnared many. Ligier, for example, issued a press release claiming they were not going to the race for 'technical reasons' even though their transporter was seen returning to France the day before practice began.[1] Cheever arrived at the Novotel, Bologna, unaware Ligier had withdrawn, and the team's motorhome people were at the circuit setting everything up for the weekend. They departed at midday on the Thursday.

The drivers might reasonably have complained that the team owners berated them for withdrawing their labour in South Africa ('The one thing we never do is cancel the show!') and now they had withdrawn their own. Lauda did go to Imola to express his opinions. 'The whole thing,' he said, 'is...' – followed by a naughty word. 'Above all, this is supposed to be a sport.'

He quantified the position. 'There have been mistakes on both sides. First of all, FOCA went much too far on this water bottle business. Second, the FIA Tribunal made a bad move in disqualifying Piquet and Rosberg, because disqualification always stirs things up. Third, I think FOCA made a very big mistake in not coming here. And fourth, I fear that the biggest mistakes of all will be made at Casablanca next week' – where FISA were due to meet to decide the future.

The Italians didn't appear to care about the politics provided the Ferraris raced and, as a consequence, the attendance was greater than the year before despite the fact that Arnoux and Prost in the Renaults filled the front row. Arnoux's pole time (1m 29.7s) was stunningly faster than Villeneuve's of the year before (1m 34.5s). Starkly put, Villeneuve's 1m 30.7s now for third fastest was itself almost five seconds faster. The turbos had become power machines poised to swallow circuits.

Warwick survived a 'moment' in second qualifying when the left front suspension broke at high speed.

ABOVE *A picture which is almost unique. Because the grid was so small, the cameraman was able to get almost all of it into his picture. Who's who? Look at the grid on the left...*

A bizarre tyre situation ensnared the ATS team. They were running on Avon tyres and Avon withdrew. On the Friday they used tyres from Long Beach, which were too soft to be effective. The team boss, Gunther Schmid, cast round and on Saturday his two cars emerged with Avons (crossplies) on the front and Pirellis (radials) on the back. Manfred Winkelhock – like Henton, built for Wakefield Trinity rather than Imola – qualified his ATS on the second last row (with Henton), leaving the final row to young Paletti's Osella and Salazar in the other ATS.

Schmid considered flying in wheels to take Pirellis all round but eventually a search at the factory found Avons from Kyalami and Rio. They were flown in by light plane.

A warm Sunday but cloudy. Warwick's Toleman expired on the warm-up lap and Henton's transmission failed before he'd completed a lap: the 14 were 12 already.

Everybody knew Imola was a thirsty track, a guzzler. Forgheri told Villeneuve and Pironi to save whatever fuel they could and both Ferraris were now topped up on the grid.

At the green light Arnoux led from Prost and they maintained that to Acque Minerale, when Villeneuve went by and Pironi soon after. They crossed the line to complete the opening lap in that order, Alboreto fifth, but Arnoux had constructed a significant lead.

The Ferraris ate into that while de Cesaris (fuel pump) and Prost (engine problem) dropped out. That was on lap 7. Giacomelli went on lap 24 (engine) so that only eight cars circulated.

What might have been a procession across an empty afternoon transformed into a duel between Pironi and Villeneuve, and lively, combative fare it was: wheel-to-wheel. They could not match Arnoux's straight-line pace in the Renault, although eventually Villeneuve pulled away and latched on to the rear of the Renault preparing to attack. On lap 27 he dived past and now Pironi prepared to attack, but three laps later, approaching Tosa, Arnoux used the Renault's pace to regain the lead while Pironi attacked Villeneuve. The three cars duelled until Arnoux pulled clear, leaving the Ferraris to fight amongst themselves. They caught Arnoux again because Salazar, a lap down, slowed him.

Villeneuve, third, overtook Pironi and moved on Arnoux. Wisps of smoke came from the Renault and Villeneuve went by. Into the sweeping Tamburello left Arnoux's turbo caught fire. Pironi ducked across the track and went by.

And then there were two...

Ferrari did what they had traditionally done for generations and signalled from the pits SLOW because the race now belonged to them. It was a question of getting both cars safely home, and that would be done in their race order at the moment Arnoux dropped out, another Ferrari tradition. Villeneuve would have the win: 'If it had been the other way round, tough luck for me.'[2]

Villeneuve would cite several examples of this, notably when, with the Championship at stake, he dutifully followed Jody Scheckter in the other Ferrari during the 1979 Italian Grand Prix and Scheckter became Champion.

ABOVE *The world in headlines, and the Italians had plenty to write about.*

OPPOSITE *Grand Prix racing's two tempos, as the Renault team work on Arnoux's car while up the pit lane people wander about.*

Arnoux went out on lap 44. Villeneuve covered that lap in 1m 36.8s, the next in 1m 36.5s, and after the pit board 1m 38.1.

Villeneuve thought: relax, slow, make sure the fuel lasts.

Pironi did not respond to the pit board and did a 1m 36.4s. Villeneuve made a mistake and put two wheels off, dug a dust storm. Pironi led.

Villeneuve thought: no problem, he'll lead for a couple of laps, hand it back to me.

Pironi forced the pace and made Villeneuve respond.

Villeneuve thought: it's worrying he's going so fast, but I have to run at that pace, you can't obey a SLOW sign if your team-mate hasn't.

What was this pace doing to the fuel consumption?

	Villeneuve	Pironi
Lap 47	1:35.5	1:35.8
Lap 48	1:35.3	1:35.4

In his innocence Villeneuve imagined that, with only seven cars circulating – and some in lonely splendour – Pironi had decided to put on a show for the crowd. They'd duel, the crowd would love it but Pironi would pull over and let Villeneuve into the lead, obeying the tradition. It never crossed Villeneuve's thinking that Pironi would do anything else.

On lap 49 Villeneuve retook him – inside – and that seemed to be the moment tradition reasserted itself. Villeneuve thought: OK, slow the pace again, what's

BELOW *The finish which would become infamous, bitter and controversial within moments of this picture being taken. Didier Pironi beats Villeneuve by 0.3 of a second.*

it going to look like if we both run out of fuel on the last lap? He eased back in this sequence:

Lap 50	1:37.3
Lap 51	1:37.3
Lap 52	1:38.1

On lap 53 Pironi went past into Tamburello and immediately forced the pace UP again, spawning among the curious and the cynical a question: can this really be play-acting or is something else going on?

Villeneuve thought: bloody stupid.

Pironi increased the pace in this sequence:

Lap 53	1:35.4
Lap 54	1:35.5
Lap 56	1:35.3
Lap 57	1:35.2
Lap 58	1:35.9

Two laps remained and they almost collided in a left-hander. They crossed the line in tandem and into Tosa. Villeneuve, getting a tow, thought: he's lifted a little. Villeneuve went through on the inside and

slowed the pace again, into the 1m 37s, and thought: OK, Pironi's left it late to obey the pit signal but that doesn't really matter because he's done it.

John Watson, watching on television at home, saw 'a great race, a very amusing race, but how much of it was racing and how much an act we couldn't tell. We simply didn't know whether it was done as a show as opposed to motor racing and it was only towards the end it became obvious that it wasn't.'

They completed the 59th lap, one remaining. By the posture of the Ferrari Number 28, by its positioning, discerning eyes could read another scenario. Pironi was preparing to strike again. Villeneuve still thought: save fuel, save fuel, and changed gear a thousand revs early to do just that. He had no conception that Pironi would strike at him. On the drag to Tamburello, Pironi drew up and out of Tamburello he tracked Villeneuve tightly. Villeneuve suddenly saw this but at no stage did he mount a defence by blocking because, as it seems, even now he could not bring himself to accept that a team-mate he had worked with for a year and a half would do something so dishonourable – and blocking would have been Villeneuve indicating Didier, I don't trust you.

ABOVE San Marino. Everybody looks happy except one. Villeneuve turns away in disgust as Didier Pironi celebrates his stolen victory. They never spoke again and Villeneuve had two weeks to live.

Running hard towards Tosa, Pironi jinked inside and cut past, wheels almost locked.

'He had been lifting his foot on the lap before,' Pironi said, 'and I stayed behind him, but if you lift your foot going fast like that it causes a high back-pressure in the engine and you can damage a piston. I was afraid of that and Gilles was going so slow I thought that might have happened to him so I overtook.'

Villeneuve thought: he let me take him on lap 59 there so he could do the same to me this lap later. It was the last place before the finishing line where you could overtake and Pironi must have calculated that well in advance. Villeneuve, enraged ('he came at me like a bullet ... after that I had no chance to get by') followed Pironi, who won by 0.3 seconds. It might as well have been three minutes or eternity.

Pironi removed his helmet on the slowing down lap and played the crowd by gestures. Villeneuve wouldn't go near the truck for the celebration lap with Pironi and Alboreto, third. He went to the rostrum and while Pironi sprayed champagne on the adoring mass below looked sombre, withdrawn, isolated. Perhaps he was trying to keep control of himself. He strode to the Augusta immediately afterwards and flew home to Monte Carlo.

He never spoke to Didier Pironi again.

All unnoticed, Jarier came fourth a lap down. 'By my last lap nuts and bolts had come loose on the Osella. The car was just like a ... snake.'

Prost 18, Lauda 12, Alboreto and Pironi 10, Watson and Rosberg 8.

Villeneuve was further enraged when Pironi claimed there had been no team orders, and Piccinini said the same. Enzo Ferrari took the highly unusual step of making a public announcement that the pit signals were shown to Pironi for the last 15 laps, Pironi did not interpret them correctly and he felt sympathy for Villeneuve. The internal politics of Ferrari were not for the faint-hearted or the rational. Perhaps a medieval court would be an appropriate comparison.

At Casablanca, news emerged that the FOCA teams would go to the next race, Belgium, although Balestre's proposals for the future of Grand Prix racing – which seemed to override the Concorde Agreement – ought to have been the main item. Since no agreement could be reached on the water-tank ruling a Group was formed to seek solutions. It contained Piccinini, Larrousse, Ecclestone and Mosley among others.

It drifted into deadlock.

Footnote: 1. Chasing The Title; 2. Nigel Roebuck's 'Fifth Column' in Autosport carried an interview with Villeneuve after Imola. In it Villeneuve explained exactly what had happened and, because of his candour, we will always have his side of it.

ABOVE *The immense crowd on the hillside had a minimum of action to savour – except for the Ferraris. Here they watch ATS team-mates Eliseo Salazar and Manfred Winkelhock – Salazar heading towards points, Winkelhock towards disqualification.*

OPPOSITE TOP *The coming man, Michele Alboreto, with the highest finish of his career so far.*

OPPOSITE BELOW *Jean-Pierre Jarier, about to get the whole Osella team's points total for the season.*

Race Result

WINNING SPEED 187.73kmh/116.65mph

FASTEST LAP 190.91kmh/118.63mph
(Pironi 1m 35.03s on lap 44)

LAP LEADERS Arnoux 1–26, 31–43 (39);
Villeneuve 27–30, 44–45, 49–52, 59 (11);
Pironi 46–48, 53–58, 60 (10)

RACE

	Driver	Team	Engine	Laps	Time
1	D. Pironi	Ferrari 126C2	Ferrari V6t	60	1h 36m 38.88s
2	G. Villeneuve	Ferrari 126C2	Ferrari V6t	60	1h 36m 39.25s
3	M. Alboreto	Tyrrell 011	Cosworth V8	60	1h 37m 46.57s
4	J.-P. Jarier	Osella FA1C	Cosworth V8	59	
5	E. Salazar	ATS D5	Cosworth V8	57	
dq	M. Winkelhock	ATS D5	Cosworth V8	54	Car underweight
nc	T. Fabi	Toleman TG181C	Hart 4t	52	
r	R. Arnoux	Renault RE30B	Renault V6t	44	Engine
r	B. Giacomelli	Alfa Romeo 182	Alfa V12	24	Engine
r	R. Paletti	Osella FA1C	Cosworth V8	7	Rear suspension
r	A. Prost	Renault RE30B	Renault V6t	6	Engine
r	A. de Cesaris	Alfa Romeo 182	Alfa V12	4	Fuel pump
r	B. Henton	Tyrrell 011	Cosworth V8	0	Clutch
ns	D. Warwick	Toleman TG181C	Hart 4t		Electrics, parade lap

dq = disqualified; nc = did not complete; ns = did not start; r = retired

CHAMPIONSHIP

	Driver	Points
1	A. Prost	18
2	N. Lauda	12
3	D. Pironi	10
	M. Alboreto	10
5	K. Rosberg	8
	J. Watson	8
7	C. Reutemann	6
	G. Villeneuve	6
9	R. Arnoux	4
	R. Patrese	4
	N. Mansell	4
12	J.-P. Jarier	3
13	E. de Angelis	2
	M. Winkelhock	2
	E. Salazar	2

	Team	Points
1	Renault	22
2	McLaren	20
3	Ferrari	16
4	Williams	14
5	Tyrrell	10
6	Lotus	6
7	Brabham	4
	ATS	4
9	Osella	3

DARKEST HOUR

BELGIUM, ZOLDER

Nobody loved Zolder, lost in gloomy, sandy woodland near the town of Hasselt, and who knew where Hasselt was? The people spoke Flemish and what the hell were they saying? There used to be a bittersweet little joke within Formula One about the only redeeming feature of the circuit: the French fries and mayonnaise in the paddock. Gilles Villeneuve, at least, took pleasure from some of the 90-degree corners which the track offered, but that was about it.

Grand Prix racing only went there because, in the early 1970s, the drivers condemned the full 14km of Spa as too dangerous despite easing some of the corners. Zolder measured 2.6 miles and, purpose-built as a race track, had to be safer than Spa's ordinary country roads on which the drivers were averaging more than 150 miles an hour.

Zolder brooded in much the same way as the Nürburgring did and in 1981 a mechanic was killed in the pit lane, another injured on the grid at the start.

Villeneuve flew himself there.

At 6.40 on the Thursday evening 'a thick layer of grey cloud hung over a wet and cold Zolder paddock. Above the monotonous hum of the motor-home generators there came a louder hum from behind the trees which burst into a roar as the streamlined shape of Gilles Villeneuve's new Augusta helicopter sped over the pits low and fast. At the far end Gilles pulled it up into an almost vertical climb, its speed quickly dropping to almost nothing before he kicked the nose over into a perfect chandelle [candle] announcing his arrival to all below.'[1]

RIGHT *In any other circumstances, this would be one of the most unremarkable Grand Prix photographs ever taken. When you know what was going to happen to Gilles Villeneuve next, it becomes an epitaph.*

Belgium
Zolder

RACE DATE May 9th

CIRCUIT LENGTH 4.26km/2.64 miles

NO. OF LAPS 70

RACE DISTANCE
298.34km/185.38 miles

WEATHER Dry, warm

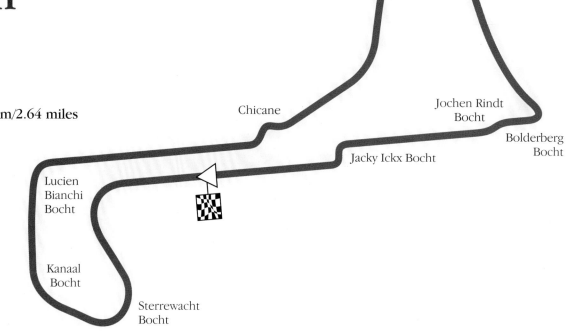

Terlaemen Bocht

Chicane

Jochen Rindt Bocht

Bolderberg Bocht

Jacky Ickx Bocht

Lucien Bianchi Bocht

Kanaal Bocht

Sterrewacht Bocht

DRIVER'S VIEW

'It was a circuit I enjoyed racing on. I suppose it's Belgium's version of Brands Hatch, similar length, good corners on it, a circuit you could get a good feel for. The corners following the pits were good corners. The worst part was the chicane they had had to install some years earlier before the start/finish – the other chicane, Kleine Chicane, was one of the best of any track I raced on. Then you climbed uphill. The car wasn't taking off but it was getting slightly light. Over the top the road dropped away from you and went to the left doing 145, maybe 150 miles an hour. Terlaemen Bocht was quite a quick corner, actually – the two right-handers on that loop were quick, third, maybe fourth gear just depending on your ratio. On the straight you'd reach 160 miles an hour.'

—— John Watson

ABOVE *Derek Daly on his Williams debut, with de Angelis close behind.*

Chris Witty of Toleman 'did see him once do some daredevil stunts with it – I think it was his arrival at Zolder.'

Jarier says Villeneuve 'had bought his Augusta and I went by helicopter too, with a friend. It was a Jet Ranger. When I arrived we talked a great deal about helicopters because he flew the Augusta.'

With Reutemann retired and Andretti committed in the United States, Williams had a vacancy for a driver to partner Rosberg.

'Guy Edwards[2] was my manager at the time,' Derek Daly says. 'First of all he went to Charlie Crichton-Stuart and that started the conversation. It came down to the two Dereks, myself and Warwick. I was not directly involved in the negotiations because Guy handled that but I got a phone call from Frank. I was at home, just up the road from Silverstone. I remember his words: "I think I am going to give you this drive. Can you come down for a seat fitting?" That was it. It came out of the blue.

'Frank wanted to deal with the money himself and Theodore had me under contract. They insisted that Frank bought out the contract and it was £75,000. Of course I didn't care what it took. Frank agreed to pay them and the first £75,000 I'd make at Williams was going to go straight there. I want to say my deal was a hundred grand, so I was going to make £25,000 net – which I didn't care about. The money meant nothing to me at all. If you are being offered a drive

with Williams the only decision is to go for it and forget the money.

'I never got close to Keke although we are very friendly to this day. I never connected with Keke. His lifestyle was different to mine. There was a lot about his lifestyle that I admired but couldn't do. He was out at night, drinkin', smokin' – I didn't do stuff like that. [Actually Rosberg wasn't doing much stuff like that either, as he says in this book, although he may have been giving the impression he was.] There was no doubt he had brilliant raw speed, didn't understand what the car was doing but had that speed. And balls. Oh, yes. One of the bravest guys I'd ever seen. I'd known that from Formula 2.'

On the Friday the tension within the Ferrari pit was so pronounced that bystanders noticed it, a strange, silent waltz with Villeneuve staying away from Pironi and Pironi staying away from Villeneuve. They would not even look at each other. Villeneuve said he didn't intend talking about the situation, he'd do his talking on the track.

Zolder brooded again, the weather dull and overcast. In first qualifying Arnoux went fastest from Prost, Piquet third and Alboreto in the Tyrrell fourth, then Villeneuve – Pironi 15th. Villeneuve said the car was undriveable on Goodyear A compound tyres but better on the softer Bs. He added that at one point – in left-right curves over the hill – the

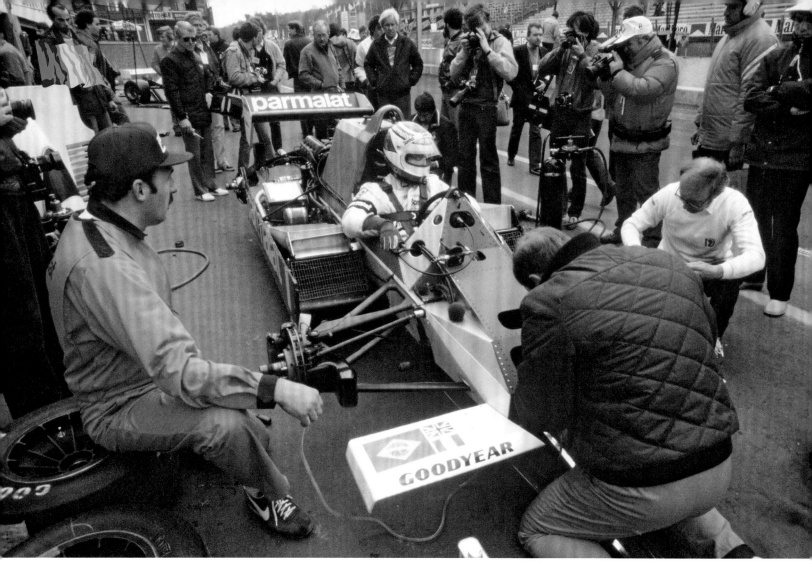

ABOVE *Nelson Piquet and the naked Brabham in the pits. He didn't have a happy qualifying or race.*

steering seemed to lock solid for an instant and he couldn't go through the section flat out.

Towards the end of the afternoon he gave an interview to some Belgian journalists. 'The actual cars,' he said, 'are now absolutely insane. The slightest unevenness in the track surface to the point where it affects the suspension's clearance causes terrible vibrations for the driver – so bad that vision is affected and it causes terrible pain in the head and neck. Because of a track's unevenness the car bounds from left to right without you touching the steering wheel. In these conditions you can't take the kerb coming out of the corner.

'The cars are too fast for the drivers. The ideal formula for me would be cars with very large tyres, like they were a few years ago, and a very powerful engine because, now, the Formula 1 cars are underpowered. Contrary to what a lot of people think, the actual performance has nothing to do with the power of the engine.

'Above all, the chassis must be flat under the driver and the ground effect will be completely removed and the speeds in the corners considerably diminished. I am thinking of the public when I say that. Now the cars turn like they are on rails and if I

was a spectator I wouldn't come to see the Grands Prix. They have nothing truly spectacular.'

He spoke of the Augusta.

'Of course, I often move around piloting myself but what I prefer above all is to pilot with a visibility virtually zero, at 150 metres for example – that's a kind of sport! To be World Formula 1 Champion once doesn't represent anything special to me, I want to be Champion three times or not at all. That said I am quite keen on other branches of motor sport, like rallying, Formula Indy, the stock cars or even Formula Atlantic again to be able to win in my own country. If someone made me an offer I'd drive at Le Mans but in any case I can't do anything without the agreement of the Commendatore [Enzo Ferrari] and I am almost certain he would refuse.'

He discussed Zolder.

'The corners in the woods are very fast. In the second right in the woods, which we take in fifth, if I have a problem and at that instant I have to swerve or I have to lift off it's a guaranteed spin [he made the sign of the cross] – and then mother would come looking for her little lad...

'That said, I do the maximum to take the minimum risks. However, in a season I know I can go off two or three times. That's part of what I do. I like Zolder because it retains corners of 90 degrees when the driver can still do something. In the long curves there is nothing to do, it happens by itself, the car does everything. It's for that reason that I like circuits such as Monaco, Las Vegas or Long Beach, circuits which bring feelings to a driver.'

That evening Villeneuve dined in his hotel near Zolder with a Belgian friend. Preoccupied with the whole Ferrari business, he seemed to be in the wrong mental mood for a Grand Prix weekend.

Zolder brooded on the Saturday, the weather dull and overcast again for the morning untimed session. The newspaper *La Libre Belgique* wrote: 'Spring had been announced, the transformation from winter welcomed, a close Championship promised, a race of passion at the circuit among the pine trees anticipated but – Saturday already – pleasure was really to be found somewhere else, at the seaside.

'Families did come to Zolder, however, wearing hats or T-shirts or anoraks with a thousand and one logos on them. They were a bit like the Formula 1 cars. Little folding chairs under their arms and freezer bags heavily loaded, people melted in the undergrowth beneath the pines and the silver birches or onto the brownish yellow sand covered in flowers. The shriek of the engines has something inhuman and tragic in them, in contrast to the commercial area of stalls from which the smell of French fries and hot sausages constantly floats. People have come a long way to see the racing and what inevitably accompanies it.

'Italian, British, French, German, American and Japanese photographers gather, talking loudly as if they were in a conquered country, sure of themselves as if the national colours on their backs gave them more right to look at their drivers than other people had. Telephoto lenses on their shoulder straps, they shoot carefully at anything that moves down the straight but ignore what is happening in the grandstands in front of them.

'The sound of a whistle rends the air. Arnoux is coming back to his pit. At 12.18 the session ends, like a blanket of silence redescending on the circuit which trembled a moment ago with the announcement that Eddie Cheever had gone off.'

When the second qualifying began, at 1.00, many front-runners made early runs – Pironi out at 1.01, Arnoux and Villeneuve a minute later, Prost at 1.04 and Lauda at 1.06, Villeneuve at 2.37. Rosberg and Alboreto remained in the pits. The front-runners felt their way: Prost four laps and a 1:20.7, Arnoux three circumspect laps and a 1:41.3, Lauda five laps and a 1:16.4, Pironi three laps and a 1:17.1. Only Villeneuve made a concerted attempt at this stage,

essentially alternating fast bursts and slow laps. He was on his first set of new tyres.

1:31.1.
1:32.2.
1:17.7.
1:17.9.
1:46.6.
1:19.2.
1:18.9.
1:48.8.

During this run, Rosberg emerged for five laps and a 1:16.0. Villeneuve returned to the pits at 16 minutes past one and Pironi went out, did a 1:16.8.

With a potential 30 cars or any permutation of 30 cars circulating at any moment – some on installation laps, some on flying laps, some getting their breath back, some touring for the pits – a clear lap became, as Villeneuve said, something you had to create. The pressure within Ferrari, and the pressure within Villeneuve himself, shifted the instant Pironi's time came up.

Lauda did a 1:16.0.

Villeneuve put on his second set of tyres and made a run at 26 minutes past one. It would have to be brief if he wanted to try and conserve these

ABOVE *Think tank: Frank Williams, designer Frank Dernie and Rosberg.*

tyres for a third run before the session ended. Immediately he did a 1:16.6, backed off, and Pironi responded by coming out while Villeneuve headed for the pits. Pironi worked through a 1:22.5 to 1:16.5. That tenth shifted the pressure back onto Villeneuve and it may be the tenth grew into something approaching a taunt and a torment in his mind. As a proud man, as a betrayed man, as a man with a great truth to proclaim, as a man who spent his youth and adulthood living entirely by the currency of speed, he had to be quicker than Pironi. Many powerful currents must have flowed through Villeneuve now, and the rest of the drivers – Arnoux and Prost into the 1:15s, Rosberg joining them there, Alboreto joining Lauda in the 1:16s – were irrelevant.

Pironi returned to the pits.

Villeneuve knew his second set of qualifying tyres might have one lap left in them, which increased the pressure because on it he would be able to afford neither mistake nor lifting off if, or rather when, slower cars got in the way.

Forghieri and Villeneuve spoke. The team were of course fully aware that after a fast lap the tyre degradation was, as Forghieri says, 'about 20 per cent'. If you consider the tiny margins by which everyone in Formula One prospers or fails, 20 per cent represents a chasm. In spite of this, and behaving typically or compelled by the taunt and torment, Villeneuve asked to try the third time. Forghieri said he should do the warm-up lap, the flying lap and then back off and come round to

the pit lane, the modern pit complex sheer as a cliff-face to his right. The Ferrari ran smoothly over the pit lane surface even though, here and there, it looked worn into small patches. He went out and lined up the big attack.

1:29.3.

He launched the attack, did the lap – presumably the fastest lap of which he was capable – and as he approached the line the Ferrari held up their board: IN. He crossed the line and the timing devices froze at 1:17.0.

Without an on-board radio Villeneuve could have guessed he'd not beaten Pironi – drivers feel fractions of a second – but could not know definitively until he was back in the pits and they showed him the timing sheets.

John Watson explains that 'you'd go out, come around and start your first flying lap. Any information on the board at that time isn't relevant other than, say, giving you how many minutes to go to the end of the session. You complete your first flying lap and start the second flying lap, and it is only at the end of that lap you find out what you did on the first one.'

The question of whether Villeneuve was able to gauge the exact time of his lap, and therefore whether he had beaten Pironi or not, is problematical. 'If you'd had a good lap and a clear lap you'd have been elated,' Watson says. 'You'd have sensed that you'd done a good job but you wouldn't have known. In those days you didn't know other than the feeling you get from driving the car – you know you have picked up rpm on the exit of corners, you've been quicker in a corner, you've picked up speed in the straight. On the other hand, if he'd made a mistake or out-braked himself or got caught up with another car he'd have known that that had compromised his lap. Those things the driver would know instantly: you'd lost the chance.'

There is a measure of mystery about what happened next because Villeneuve, tyres done and signalled in, ought to have toured watching his mirrors for anyone on their flying lap. It is what drivers did and what he now did not. Instead he seems to have mounted a final assault on Zolder. Was that propelled by an anger which wouldn't go away, an anger fuelled by the suspicion that he hadn't beaten Pironi? Was it that Villeneuve, perfectly calm, simply drove the Ferrari round at great speed because that is how he drove racing cars, and that is how he felt they were made to be driven, regardless of circumstances?

René Arnoux gives what might be a clue. 'Gilles was a little bit the madman of the steering wheel. That is to say, I believe that he was trying to do a qualifying lap in spite of his worn tyres, in spite of a car which perhaps was not capable of doing the

the pits 'to avoid unnecessary effort'. Not even Villeneuve could wring yet another competitive flying lap out of the tyres. No, Forghieri would signal him in after the single flying lap. Villeneuve agreed.

Nigel Roebuck spent the qualifying session in the Ferrari pit 'as you could do in those days'. He remembers Villeneuve sitting perfectly calmly in the Ferrari waiting. The mechanics poured water over the tyres from a watering can to keep them cool. 'If the situation was getting to him it didn't show. He was usually calm at those moments when he sat. I crouched, as you have to do with someone in the cockpit, and wished him good luck. I remember someone saying "Expletive traffic."'

Villeneuve had sat for 21 minutes. Now he brought the Ferrari out a last time. He flowed down

LEFT John Watson, calmest of men in all circumstances, will win the Belgian Grand Prix and put himself a single point behind Prost in the championship.

time, but that was Gilles – he exploited the car to the maximum in the present. It was always like that. He didn't think of the future.'

Mauro Forghieri says: 'He was coming in but not so slow. For him, slow did not exist.'

Watson says: 'That was Villeneuve. But Imola had poisoned him to the point where his rationale, his judgement, his emotions were dictated by what had happened there.'

Villeneuve thrust the Ferrari into an opposite-lock power slide round the right-handed loop called Sterrewacht Bocht, travelled urgently through the right called Bianchi, ran down the mini-straight behind the pits and flicked the Ferrari through the little chicane – the Kleine Chicane. He was catching the March of Mass who proceeded much more slowly, in fifth gear and trying to keep his tyres cool: simultaneously Mass was watching for a gap in the traffic – so he could move into it and create a fast lap – and looking in his mirrors to see who might be coming up at speed.

The circuit ahead: a left-right kink and a lunge into the braking area for the hard right called Terlaemen Bocht.

Mass saw Villeneuve and thought: he will pass me on the left, on the outside. That would enable Villeneuve to position the Ferrari to take the racing line through Terlaemen Bocht.

Villeneuve must have assumed Mass, a careful and intelligent man, would have seen him. He guessed Mass would go left to get out of his way, leaving him the inside line.

Mass went through the kink placing his March to the right, opening the outside to Villeneuve who was coming through at between 140 and 150 miles an hour.

In an instant of sheer disbelief, Mass realised Villeneuve was on him.

The Ferrari's left front wheel struck Mass's right rear and the March became a launching pad. The Ferrari flew, literally flew, through the air for more than a hundred yards.

Brian Henton arrived and 'the car was flying through the air – the car was in half. It was just on a hill at the back. I was coming up behind it and all of a sudden this Ferrari took off almost like a plane and seemed to have been snapped in half in the air. I can still see this red car going through the air and sort of breaking up.'

If it had landed on tarmac its impetus would have flung it forward, dissipating its frantic energy. It did not. It speared into sand. That tore it apart, giving Villeneuve a deadly hammerblow. In strictest medical terms he was clinically alive, in the real world he was dead.

BELOW *The endless problem of the clear lap. Here, as it seems, Villeneuve has just found a way past Manfred Winkelbock in the ATS.*

ABOVE *The terrible*
ferocity of Villeneuve's
accident is revealed
by what remained of
the Ferrari.

The impact was so savage that it wrenched his helmet off his head, his socks and driving shoes off his feet, and Villeneuve himself – still in his seat – was flung almost 50 yards in the air and then through two layers of catch fencing before his body came to rest. The car made a series of wild convulsions, shedding bits.

It thrashed itself back onto the track, almost wiping away Mass's March. He swerved and missed it.

Arnoux, on an 'in' lap, says that 'unfortunately I was looking far ahead and I saw the car of Gilles land. I saw him come down on the track and break his neck.' Arnoux stopped and was the first to get to Villeneuve. 'I saw immediately that he was no longer with us. Gilles was truly a friend – I liked him a lot. My reaction was to start crying.'

De Cesaris was on an 'in' lap too: 'I saw a big accident. I didn't realise what really happened and although I saw the engine in the middle of the track I didn't realise how bad it was. Of course I thought it must have been big because of the engine. I didn't see Gilles.' He continued to the pits because 'normally you can't stop on the track.'

But this was in no sense normal. Mass stopped and ran back to try and help.

Watson 'was on the circuit – an "in" lap, I think. I came over the top of the hill and there were flags going everywhere. As I came down the hill and the road goes to the left I could see there had been a pretty substantial shunt. I'm not sure where Jochen's car was, I'm not even sure if Jochen drove back to the pits. I realised that one of the cars involved was a Ferrari because you could see bits of Ferrari everywhere. You'd see bits of a car wrapped up in the catch fence and there was a body lying. I stopped my car, got out of it, walked over and there was no helmet on. I recognised it was Villeneuve, looked at his eyes and to me the eyes were dead. That's what I did, looked down, no more than that. There's nothing you can do. Clinically he may have been alive but in my view he was dead. He was brain dead.'

One report says Arnoux was vomiting and turned away.

'Arnoux physically sick? I had no such reactions,' Watson says. 'As a driver you have to have a mechanism, a shield, to protect yourself from allowing something which is very shocking – and obviously very tragic – to affect you so I put the shield up. I got back in the car, got it push-started, went back to the pits and said "Villeneuve's had an accident, he's dead." Then the word came back that technically he wasn't, he was on a respirator – but you can look into somebody's eyes and tell when the lights are out.

'Villeneuve's speed was probably undiminished when he hit Jochen's car. It wasn't the impact, it was the consequence of doing the barrel roll and nose-to-

ABOVE *The familiar,
and deceptive, face of
1982 with the Renaults
straddling the front
row – but not finishing
the race.*

tail rather than side-to-side which killed him.'

Warwick 'stopped the car on the right-hand side,
I ran back to the Ferrari because obviously I thought
he was still in it. I remember pulling a bit of fibreglass
away and there was nothing there. I looked around
and I saw him huddled into the catch fencing. I ran
over there. Wattie had got there just before me and we
pulled him out of the catch fencing. He didn't have his
helmet on – it had come off. It was one of those that
clicked at the front and back. It wasn't broken but it
had pulled off his head. I looked at him and I knew he
was dead. He was blue. I thought: this guy ain't going
to make it.'

Arnoux has no idea 'who else came,' Warwick,
Watson or anybody else. Arnoux 'stayed.'

Roland Bruynseraede, Clerk of the Course, stood
at the exit of the pit lane with a red flag to stop the
session. He signalled to Professor Watkins, sitting in a
Mercedes station wagon with a young Belgian driver,
to go out. As the Mercedes moved it pulled in front of
Pironi, preparing to make a final, late run.

A surgeon on the medical staff was there in 35
seconds. Someone attempted mouth-to-mouth and
heart massage.

Henton 'kept on going to the pits, came in and said

"I think Villeneuve's a goner."'

Watkins was there in about two minutes, the
Mercedes first reaching the wreckage and then what
remained of the Ferrari. Watkins knew immediately
it had to be Villeneuve because, of course, Pironi
had ceded right of way as Watkins emerged in the
Mercedes. Watkins remembered the first thing
Villeneuve had said to him years before: 'I hope I
never need you.'[3]

'The medics arrived, the Prof got there and I saw
the Prof work on him and he beat the hell out of him
trying to revive him. He could see it was a desperate
situation,' Warwick says.

Pironi halted his Ferrari, clambered out and
came to the scene. Watkins looked up and saw him,
watched him turn and walk away.

Warwick says that 'when I walked away I started
to get really upset. I got back into my car, got the car
going, I went back round and into my garage, ran
into the back of the lorry and cried my eyes out. I
sobbed and sobbed and sobbed.'

Witty remembers 'Derek came back, got out,
came into the back of the truck – we didn't have a
motorhome – and was visibly moved. It had really hit
home. It was the first time he had seen something

STARTING GRID

1 1:15.70 **A. Prost**	**2** 1:15.73 **R. Arnoux**
3 1:15.84 **K. Rosberg**	**4** 1:16.04 **N. Lauda**
5 1:16.30 **M. Alboreto**	**6** 1:16.57 **A. de Cesaris**
7 1:16.94 **N. Mansell**	**8** 1:17.12 **N. Piquet**
9 1:17.12 **R. Patrese**	**10** 1:17.14 **J. Watson**
11 1:17.76 **E. de Angelis**	**12** 1:17.87 **M. Winkelhock**
13 1:18.19 **D. Daly**	**14** 1:18.30 **E. Cheever**
15 1:18.37 **B. Giacomelli**	**16** 1:18.40 **J.-P. Jarier**
17 1:18.56 **J. Laffite**	**18** 1:18.96 **E. Salazar**
19 1:18.98 **D. Warwick**	**20** 1:19.15 **B. Henton**
21 1:19.30 **T. Fabi**	**22** 1:19.58 **M. Surer**
23 1:19.59 **C. Serra**	**24** 1:19.62 **R. Boesel**
25 1:19.77 **J. Mass**	**26** 1:19.81 **M. Baldi**

1 2 3 4 5 6 7 8 9 10 11 12 13

like that. I never talked to him about what he did at the scene.'

Daly was 'in the pits waiting to go out. Patrick Head was plugged into my radio and Frank could obviously hear at the same time. I heard Patrick say to Frank "He's out of the car." Patrick didn't know at the time how Villeneuve had got out of the car. I don't know how Patrick heard that – somehow the word came back. We were thinking: that's a good sign.'

Patrese was in the pits while changes were being made to his Brabham so 'I didn't go past the place of the accident.' He is still relieved about that.

Watkins judged Villeneuve's condition very, very bad. The marshals, holding blankets, shielded him from the public gaze as he was lifted onto a stretcher and into an ambulance to be taken to the medical centre for stabilisation. Eleven minutes after the accident a military helicopter on standby at the circuit took him, accompanied by Watkins, to a clinic at Louvain, but there was nothing anybody could do and in essence there hadn't been since 1.52, the moment the Ferrari launched. In the crash his neck fractured fatally.

'It was an ambulance which took me back to the pits,' Arnoux says. 'When I got there I went to the Renault motorhome and I kept on crying.'

'The crash involved one of my drivers, Jochen Mass,' Jackie Oliver says. 'Villeneuve was a high risk taker and I think that's what made him a very appealing driver but sometimes the risks catch you out. As you can imagine Jochen felt responsible – he wasn't – because he is the type of man he is. We didn't know the extent of the accident and when the full impact of it came he felt even worse. We did not discuss it. Nothing could be gained by bringing the subject up. It was something he had to deal with himself.'

Jarier 'was in the pits. I saw Jochen Mass and he told me what had happened. He was very shocked, and it was not his fault because he was in front. The one behind has the responsibility for safety. If the person in front does a zigzag that's different but Jochen stayed on the side of the track.'

Someone rang Jody Scheckter in Monaco. He went immediately to the Villeneuves' home and Joann. She flew to Louvain. At the hospital she was told her husband was on a life support machine and had to make the decision to switch it off. That wasn't necessary. He was pronounced officially dead at 9.12 pm.

After any motor racing fatality three factors come into play and always in the same order: grief, then the physical aspects of the crash, then the overall context. There's a fourth which fits somewhere into this, depending on how fast the other three happen.

The grief began immediately, even as Ferrari hauled

the metal shutter down on their pit and loaded the transporters for Maranello. Gilles Villeneuve was the last of the innocents in that he was a man without guile or malice for whom only driving at the limit represented the life process itself. In that sense an age of innocence died at 1.52 pm on 8 May 1982. Perhaps he retained the wonderful, unsullied enthusiasms of a schoolboy into an age when nobody else could, and everybody left behind felt suddenly old: something of them had died at 1.52, too. Many strong men cried, not only Derek Warwick and René Arnoux, and are not ashamed of that.

Others, reflecting later, were more circumspect because there are degrees in pushing your luck and Villeneuve had constructed a career on habitually pushing it to the absolute limit. It meant that by the law of averages, somewhere, sometime, he risked finding himself in a situation where, at this limit, he had nowhere to go.

Rosberg condensed his feelings into a single word: numb. He had no wish to speak to anybody.

Forgheri said 'I have known many drivers but never anyone like Gilles. He was truly something else. An enormous character, a professional 24 hours out of 24. We often had "collisions" but his obstinacy made me respect him.'

Quite what Enzo Ferrari felt is not at all clear, despite his protestations of paternal love. Brock Yates[4] has suggested that Enzo had 'seen too many eager young men die at the wheel of racing cars to let himself be seduced by their charm.' Yates further suggests that to his intimates Enzo showed a minimum of remorse and expressed concern, instead, about whether Pironi was good enough to win the Championship.

Roebuck, one of those who had been to the scene of the accident and sensed immediately that he was in the presence of death, made his way back to the paddock. 'Inevitably,' he wrote, 'a few zombies munched on their chips and talked glibly of his replacement in the Ferrari team. It may have been genuine callousness or a bluff macho act but whatever the explanation it was abhorrent to most human beings.'[5]

Another journalist, Jeff Hutchinson,[6] wrote: 'No sooner had the news of Gilles Villeneuve's accident spread round the Zolder paddock than the political factions started to make capital of the tragedy. It was a distasteful method of advancing one's arguments, albeit not unexpected given the struggles which continue to rack the sport.'

Lauda dissected the situation, insisting the physical aspects were the consequence of the overall context. The qualifying tyres with their soft rubber made 'the drivers drive at the extreme limit for two or three laps only to get a good time' and,

compounding that, there was a very real difference in speeds between some of the slower cars and the rest.

Pironi, speaking calmly – and as head of the Drivers' Association – said 'we have been protesting since the start of the season. The cars have become too dangerous. The conflicts of interest in Formula 1 are stronger than all the feelings about safety. We proclaim that it is necessary to get rid of the lateral skirts. Gilles's death is a dramatic consequence of ground effects. The cars are at the limit of their adherence and flat to the ground. And they go faster and faster. At the least shock they take off, transformed into an uncontrollable missile.'[7]

'Since the introduction of ground effects and wings, the cars have made incredible progress in the corners. At the place where Gilles had his accident you're doing 250–260kmh [155–160mph]. A few years ago, when skirts didn't exist, we were doing only 180 [110].'

Balestre, who was on the Tour of Corsica, telephoned and promised the FISA executive committee would meet.

OPPOSITE Prost, Lauda and Andrea de Cesaris waltzing through the Little Chicane in the opening laps of the race.

BELOW A world in headlines, and one terrible phrase: the wages of death.

ABOVE *Rosberg stalking Arnoux across the first four laps of the race before the Renault's unreliability crippled it.*

The fourth factor is in some ways the most difficult of all: the world, altered to a greater or lesser extent, goes on. In the whole history of Grand Prix racing there is no instance of a race being cancelled in the wake of a fatality.[8]

As Alex Hawkridge says, 'the only point at issue there is do we go on or don't we? Obviously if you are in racing you have sponsors so the business has to go on. You don't have too much latitude, really. Derek was a pretty resilient guy. That day really brought things close to home: we are not immortal and he had just seen that. He was affected by that but it didn't affect him driving the car. In a sense my job was to let him work it out for himself. You can't put pressure on him.'

Warwick 'got back to the hotel with Rhonda [his wife] and we didn't go out that night, we ate in the room because I was so upset. Later on it was announced that he'd died.' Warwick remembers 'the one thing that really shocked Rhonda was the next morning I got up, had a shower, got ready for the track, and Rhonda said to me "What are you doing?" I said "I'm going to the track." She said "You're not racing?" I said "Of course I'm racing." She could not understand how somebody who'd seen what I'd seen, tried to help and then had that reaction afterwards could go racing as just another day. You have to have that because otherwise you can't do it.'

All the drivers had to cope with it, of course. A question to Rosberg: How do you get back in a car after something like Gilles's accident had happened?

'I have probably faced that I don't know how many times. When you go racing or you do sport, I always said that if your grandmother passes away Sunday morning you have to be able to race in the afternoon as if nothing had happened. That's the way it is. It's a lot closer when it's a colleague or a race accident or something like that, of course.'

While Zolder continued to brood that Sunday morning something significant was happening at McLaren. 'Pierre Dupasquier [Michelin racing director] gave me a tyre to try, a hard tyre on the left-hand side,' Watson says. 'It was a tyre that had last been seen in Las Vegas the year before. As far as I was concerned, that was concrete and clay. I said "Forget it, I'm not going to run that stupid tyre." "No, no, you've got to do it." So I put it on the left and my normal tyre on the right. I went out, bloody awful – no, not that awful. Then it got better and better and in the end, after a five-lap run, I had done a time which was within a tenth of a second of what I'd done on the matched set of softer tyres. I came in and said "If the day remains as warm as it is now" – it was a warm morning – "leave it alone." Niki had done his runs and in the debriefing there was a fairly free, open exchange of information.' Here is the dialogue...

FAN'S EYE VIEW

'After growing up mainly on a diet of racing at Brands Hatch from the mid-1960s, I was living and working for a car parts sales company in Holland in 1982, where I even did some racing myself in the Benelux FF1600 Championship – which included numerous races at Zandvoort and Zolder.

'Thankfully I grew up in a time when access to the paddock was possible and affordable, cars were not locked away in garages and Formula One drivers roamed free. From the racing point of view, the big difference with now is that the results were far less predictable, and the risks, of course, far greater. In that sense, 1982 had the lot.

'Another big difference is that without huge gravel traps a paying spectator was closer to the action and could still find good spots to take some decent photos.

'I remember most of all the – literally – deathly silence that suddenly fell over Zolder in final qualifying and hearing the commentator talk of a massive crash for one of the Ferraris.

'Minutes later when Pironi drove slowly past, helmet off and very emotional, this and the commentator's lack of further information confirmed my worst fears. Difficult to imagine these days, but the next day it was business as usual: a good race and a great win from behind for Wattie, who looked after his tyres better than Rosberg.'

GARETH REES
TOKYO, JAPAN

FROM TOP *Piquet, looking hard into the corner; Mansell qualified the Lotus on the fourth row; Jochen Mass, a strong man who needed all his strength at Zolder; and the winner is ... John Watson.*

Lauda: 'What did you do?'

Watson: 'I did this, this and this, and I ran this set of tyres.'

Lauda: 'Why?'

Watson: 'I tell you now, Niki. I have always been honest with you, never lied to you. I'm going to run those on the left side and if I was you I'd do the same thing – because if you don't, you're going to end up after five laps, ten laps with understeer on the entry to corners.'

Lauda (thinking for a moment): 'No, no.'

Watson: 'Tell me why you won't do it.'

But Watson didn't really need an answer to that. He knew. 'It boiled down,' he says, 'to the fact that Niki hadn't had a chance to try them himself so therefore his mantra, his own ideas about how you go motor racing, would have been compromised. And so he wouldn't run the tyre. That was a great opportunity for me to see into Niki in a way which I had not seen before. You take chances and do things from time to time but part of his discipline was that he did things by the book. His whole philosophy of racing was testing, preparation, testing, preparation and you establish what you are going to run. It's a very logical, very Teutonic way of doing it. You don't suddenly throw all that up in the air and say "Ah, let's do something different."'

Twenty-six cars lined up on the grid. Arnoux had one thought: win the race to be able to dedicate it to Villeneuve. There had been a bond between the two men since the French Grand Prix at Dijon in 1979 when, in the closing laps, they fought an audacious, breathtaking and seemingly dangerous duel, banging wheels and overtaking constantly. Both men trusted the other and both pushed their luck to the absolute limit but both constantly gave the other just enough room.

Now Arnoux waited for the green light at Zolder.

In the stampede to the first corner Rosberg got his Williams past Prost and tucked in behind Arnoux. All unnoticed, Watson gained a place from the grid and ran ninth. With those hard tyres the race would come to him. Arnoux held the lead for four laps before he slowed with a mechanical problem and Rosberg led a Grand Prix for the first time in his career, Lauda now behind him – Watson eighth and making a charge. On lap 6 he took Piquet, on lap 8 Alboreto and on lap 9 Prost drifted back – Watson fifth.

The order settled, solidified: Rosberg, Lauda, de Cesaris, Patrese and Watson.

'I got stuck behind Patrese for about 20 laps and it broke my heart because I was all over him everywhere on the race track,' Watson says.

Warwick's Toleman went to lap 29 when the driveshaft failed. 'In my mind during the race I never ever saw Gilles lying there until my last lap

and again I started to feel the emotion of losing a colleague. I didn't back off, never, up until that point and I just eased off.'

On lap 30 de Cesaris took Lauda and set off after Rosberg.

On lap 31 Watson 'finally managed to get past Patrese coming into the chicane. I got right under his wing – a Watsonesque move. Once I'd got past, Patrese disappeared in the mirrors. There's no doubt BMW weren't able to run in the race at the pace they'd showed in qualifying and they were on Pirellis, which may not have been as good.'

De Cesaris, enduring the frustrations of unreliability in a competitive car, insists 'Zolder was another race I could have won. That was the race where I was the quickest. I was catching Rosberg like one second a lap and then the clutch broke and I stopped as usual. I was much quicker.' It happened on lap 34.

By lap 45 of the 70 Watson was catching Lauda so decisively that when he drew up two laps later Lauda let him through. 'I passed him in front of the pits,' Watson says, 'and I did a metaphorical fingers up to him, not just to Niki but to all the Marlboro people [who were paying Lauda a lot more money than Watson]. And I disappeared.'

That left only Rosberg ahead and his tyres, which had been wearing since the middle of the race, were now all but finished. He kept his eye on his pit board and noted that Watson gained a second a lap. Rosberg did the only thing he could and pressed on, although he seemed in constant trouble with back-markers and, given the state of his tyres, couldn't out-brake them. By lap 55 he led by 15 seconds and that produced a superb symmetry: 15 laps to go and Watson gaining that second every lap...

On lap 61 Watson almost lost the race in the strangest way. At the first corner Daly went off into the catch fencing and walked back to the pits. Watson had been getting pit signals telling him how fast he was catching Rosberg and into lap 62, as he passed the abandoned Williams, he assumed it must be Rosberg's. That, mused Watson, gives me the race. He backed off. He'd been rapping out 1m 20s and now slowed to a 1:22.9, but the pit board said P2 – you're in second place. Next lap he did a 1:21.5 and got the P2 again. He accelerated and the statistics reveal Rosberg's plight.

	Rosberg	Watson
Lap 64	1:22.8	1:20.9
Lap 65	1:23.5	1:20.8
Lap 66	1:22.5	1:21.8
Lap 67	1:21.0	1:20.2 – Watson's fastest of the race
Lap 68	1:22.0	1:20.7

LEFT *Mauro Baldi didn't manage to qualify the Arrows but got onto the final row of the grid because of Ferrari's withdrawal. This spin in the race cost him a long pit stop to have the sand cleaned from the throttle and he was running at the end, 19 laps down.*

Into the second-last lap they reached the hairpin. Marc Surer (Fittipaldi), three laps down, was going through and Rosberg thought: I have to get him and have him between Watson and me up to the chicane. That would buy Rosberg a precious moment or two and if he could hold the lead into the final lap he'd back himself to keep Watson at bay. Rosberg tried to late-break Surer but he locked the rear wheels: the tyres were too far gone to respond. The Williams slid wide and Watson thrust the McLaren through, the race decided.

'Keke had pretty much worn his rear tyre down virtually to nothing, he had no grip and I sailed past him,' Watson says. 'Gangbusters! The thing about Keke was, he was very, very honest and fair as a racing driver, no dirty tricks, no nasty moving or anything like that. I always found Keke very correct in a car – good racer, but he also had this sense of knowing when something was about to happen or when he was about to be beaten. I was pulling him in at two, three seconds a lap at that stage.'

Initially Rosberg vented his frustration on Surer but, reflecting later, realised that Surer had in fact done nothing wrong. He just happened to be there. The frustration was easy to understand, of course. Since 1978 Rosberg had driven 40 Grands Prix for five teams and not won one. At Zolder he'd been within some four miles of it.

Frank Williams was not pleased with Rosberg, a sentiment shared by others. They felt he'd made a mistake and he knew perfectly well that he had – overdriving the car – but could find consolation in a great truth: to win the race he could have done nothing else. Watson beat him by 7.2 seconds.

At post-race scrutineering Lauda's McLaren, which finished third, was found to be 3lb underweight and disqualification followed. It didn't seem much then, but it would.

Jarier flew home on the Sunday night in the Jet Ranger. 'I saw Gilles's helicopter because mine was next to his. When I left it was still there where he had left it.'

Prost 18, Watson 17, Rosberg 14, Lauda 12, Alboreto and Pironi 10.

So Watson was now within the one point of Prost but 'you don't think of Championships at that stage, you're trying to accumulate points,' Watson says. 'When you get a lot of different teams and drivers winning races it dissipates the points so much. In the last ten years we have become accustomed to having a driver win the Championship with 100-plus points. That wasn't the case in 1982, and due to the unreliability of the turbos there were two teams – McLaren and Williams – who could compete, and latterly the Tyrrell. Dissipation? Don't forget the BMW was a bloody quick engine, plus you had Alfa Romeo, plus the two Tolemans – ten turbo-engined cars.'

Like Jarier, many people remember leaving the circuit and seeing Villeneuve's helicopter where he'd left it. Rosberg hadn't been on the track when Villeneuve crashed. 'My recollection of that is entirely overshadowed by Monday morning when I left the hotel in my car and passed the track, where rubbish was flying around. It was a dead place and Gilles's helicopter was still there.'

A young Brazilian had been taking part in a Formula 2000 race, supporting the Grand Prix, and he and his team manager, Dennis Rushen, passed the helicopter. The young man's name was Ayrton Senna, and when, years later, people said he took risks because he had no personal experience of a fatality at a race meeting they were quite wrong.

Here it was.

OPPOSITE Lap 30 and Alboreto's engine – and race – go up in smoke.

BELOW Watson was entitled to feel happy, Lauda entitled to feel sombre – he'd be disqualified from third place.

Footnote: 1. Grand Prix International, May 1982; 2. Guy Edwards, former racing driver, later known as an expert on motor racing sponsorship; 3. Life At The Limit, Professor Sid Watkins, Macmillan, London, 1996; 4. Enzo Ferrari: The Man and the Machine, Brock Yates, Bantam, London, 1992; 5. Autosport, 13 May 1982; 6. Grand Prix International, 13 May 1982; 7. Pironi actually used the word obus, meaning a military shell; 8. Specifically, Riccardo Paletti would die at Montreal a month after Villeneuve. The Canadian Grand Prix was restarted. Elio de Angelis died in testing at the Paul Ricard circuit in 1986 but the Belgian Grand Prix went ahead quite normally a few days later, although many drivers were still visibly upset. The death of Roland Ratzenberger during qualifying for the San Marino Grand Prix in 1994 did not affect the race, and the race itself was restarted after the death of Ayrton Senna.

Race Result

WINNING SPEED 187.04kmh/116.22mph

FASTEST LAP 191.27kmh/118.85mph
(Watson 1m 20.21s on lap 67)

LAP LEADERS Arnoux 1–4 (4);
Rosberg 5–68 (64); Watson 69–70 (2)

RACE

	Driver	Team	Engine	Laps	Time
1	J. Watson	McLaren MP4B	Cosworth V8	70	1h 35m 41.99s
2	K. Rosberg	Williams FW08	Cosworth V8	70	1h 35m 49.26s
dq	N. Lauda*	McLaren MP4B	Cosworth V8	70	Car underweight
3	E. Cheever	Talbot Ligier JS17B	Matra V12	69	
4	E. de Angelis	Lotus 91	Cosworth V8	68	
5	N. Piquet	Brabham BT50	BMW 4t	67	
6	C. Serra	Fittipaldi F8D	Cosworth V8	67	
7	M. Surer	Arrows A4	Cosworth V8	66	
8	R. Boesel	March 821	Cosworth V8	66	
9	J. Laffite	Talbot Ligier JS17B	Matra V12	66	
r	D. Daly	Williams FW08	Cosworth V8	60	Accident
r	J. Mass	March 821	Cosworth V8	60	Engine
r	A. Prost	Renault RE30B	Renault V6t	59	Spin
r	R. Patrese	Brabham BT50	BMW 4t	52	Accident
r	M. Baldi	Arrows A4	Cosworth V8	51	Throttle/spin
r	J.-P. Jarier	Osella FA1C	Cosworth V8	37	Rear aerofoil
r	A. de Cesaris	Alfa Romeo 182	Alfa V12	34	Gear linkage
r	B. Henton	Tyrrell 011	Cosworth V8	33	Engine
r	M. Alboreto	Tyrrell 011	Cosworth V8	29	Engine
r	D. Warwick	Toleman TG181C	Hart 4t	29	Driveshaft
r	T. Fabi	Toleman TG181C	Hart 4t	13	Brakes
r	N. Mansell	Lotus 91	Cosworth V8	9	Clutch
r	R. Arnoux	Renault RE30B	Renault V6t	7	Turbo compressor
r	M. Winkelhock	ATS D5	Cosworth V8	0	Clutch
r	E. Salazar	ATS D5	Cosworth V8	0	Accident
r	B. Giacomelli	Alfa Romeo 182	Alfa V12	0	Accident
ns	D. Pironi	Ferrari 126C2	Ferrari V6t		Withdrawn
ns	G. Villeneuve	Ferrari 126C2	Ferrari V6t		Fatal accident
nq	R. Guerrero	Ensign N181	Cosworth V8		
nq	J. Lammers	Theodore TY02	Cosworth V8		
npq	R. Paletti	Osella FA1C	Cosworth V8		
npq	E. de Villota	March 821	Cosworth V8		

dq = disqualified; npq = did not pre-qualify; nq = did not qualify; ns = did not start; r = retired * Lauda's time: 1h 36m 50.132s.

CHAMPIONSHIP

	Driver	Points
1	A. Prost	18
2	J. Watson	17
3	K. Rosberg	14
4	N. Lauda	12
5	D. Pironi	10
	M. Alboreto	10
7	C. Reutemann	6
	G. Villeneuve	6
9	E. de Angelis	5
10	R. Arnoux	4
	R. Patrese	4
	N. Mansell	4
	E. Cheever	4
14	J.-P. Jarier	3
15	M. Winkelhock	2
	E. Salazar	2
	N. Piquet	2
20	F. Serra	1

	Team	Points
1	McLaren	29
2	Renault	22
3	Williams	20
4	Ferrari	16
5	Tyrrell	10
6	Lotus	9
7	Brabham	6
8	ATS	4
	Talbot Ligier	4
10	Osella	3
11	Fittipaldi	1

REMEMBERING GILLES

—————— A RISK TOO FAR ——————

'Zolder,' John Watson will say, 'was a deadly mixture of bitterness and frustration.'

'The accident? Gilles liked to play with death,' Jean-Pierre Jarier will say. 'He wanted a game with death. Me, I adored driving in Formula One but I wanted to remain alive.'

Chris Witty captures the essence of Villeneuve in a handful of simple words: 'I was in South Africa in 1977 when he did the Formula Atlantic series and he never lifted off the gas. Ever. He didn't give 100 per cent, he always gave 110 per cent.'

Villeneuve's father Séville spoke on French television the day after the crash. 'He was doing what he loved with all his heart, all the strength he could summon and with complete sincerity. He was a lad who, when he wanted something, worked towards it and, believe me, he got it. And that's the biggest memory that I will keep of Gilles: going out and searching for what he wanted.'

Séville recounted what Villeneuve had frequently said: 'When you are master of the racing car it obeys your commands.'

He added: 'We were constantly in contact with the clinic. It was not easy to get through to it – and, since I accepted that Gilles had become an idol of the people, I also decided to live with the consequences, however hard they may be.'

Séville understood that at any moment during his career Villeneuve might have had a serious accident 'but not serious to that extent. You say you're ready to understand when destiny strikes so brutally, but in reality it's still a real shock.

'I have no doubt Gilles died happy. He always did what he loved the most. He gave himself entirely to motor racing and motor racing itself made him renowned. If Jacques [Villeneuve's brother] decided to follow the career of a driver and attempted to have a chance in Formula One again I would encourage him.'

John Watson analyses what happened at Zolder.

'To me the key was that he was so screwed up about Imola and now Pironi going quickest. It was this poison that completely infected his judgement to such a degree that he lost all sense of rationale. I wouldn't say it was bitterness per se, I would say it was out and out frustration. Villeneuve was never in my understanding of the word a rational driver. He was a racer, which was fine, I've no problem with that.

'Secondly he wasn't as bright as some of his contemporaries – compared to the likes of Alain Prost, Niki as well, and even Pironi for that matter. Pironi was much more intelligent than Gilles, but Gilles had other qualities apart from his driving – a certain amount of peasant guile, if you want to call it that. It went to the quick of Villeneuve's personality and character that he always felt he had the beating of Pironi – but Pironi was a political creature, not necessarily a particularly nice creature, but a political one.

'There was like a virus in Ferrari which encouraged Villeneuve to hyper-activate. This is why we saw so many occasions like Zandvoort[1] and the burst tyre, that the Italian Press particularly loved all this. He had a hooligan element in him. It wasn't a malicious one, it was innocent, it was naïve – which is why they all fell for it. He didn't rationalise motor racing the way Jackie Stewart did or Niki or Prost, and so on. There are drivers who use intelligence behind the wheel, there are others out there who are, you know ... hooligans. Then you have your hugely gifted person, which Villeneuve was, combined with the devil-may-care attitude, and it was being fostered by the virus in Ferrari. They wanted him to be doing what he was doing.

'Once Pironi got half a decent car his ability – and he had a lot of that – combined with an utter, ruthless, single-mindedness was always going to create a problem with Villeneuve, who was really a kid with a big toy box.'

Watson remains unsentimental. 'Villeneuve wasn't my sort of guy. I didn't have the star-struck thing. I was critical of what he and Arnoux did at Dijon in 1979 when they went round the back of the circuit side by side banging wheels. That, in Gilles's mind, made me seem a bit of a conservative. He was a naturally – you could use the word phenomenally – gifted racing driver, but I thought that level of driving at Dijon had no place in Formula One.'

Ah, Dijon in 1979.

'The duel with Gilles? We appreciated each other, we liked each other and it's for that reason that we had the duel,' Arnoux says. 'We shared a lot of things and that's why his death struck me so hard. What I think, firstly, is that we had a certain respect for each other and it's important that people know this. The second thing is that there were some moments in some races where you can do anything. You are a bit like extraterrestrials, eh? You do anything and get away with it. There are others where you don't – like the stupid accident Gilles had at Zolder. It was a matter of misunderstanding between Gilles and Mass. But at Dijon you had two drivers with the same understanding as well as respect. Neither let go. Gilles was hard but fair.'

'Arnoux versus Villeneuve, Dijon, 1979? Typical Gilles,' Rosberg says. 'He would do that – but it was unhealthy at that speed, it was crazy, it was more luck than judgement that it didn't end in tears. In those days you didn't have carbon suspensions which snap as soon as they touch, the suspensions were steel...'

Watson remembers taking a pole position one time and Villeneuve expressing incredulity. 'I don't

think he meant to be rude particularly, I think he was trying to be amusing.' It did not amuse John Watson.

Rosberg 'knew Gilles quite well because I came through the ranks with him in Canada and America. We raced against each other for two years and we weren't on talking terms at the end because we were always banging wheels. It was either him or me won the races. I don't think we'd be considered the greatest of friends in Formula Atlantic. His kids loved me and Gilles would be mad because they'd play with me and talk to me.

'What did I make of Gilles? Crazy? Yes. Crazy in everything he did – in a car, helicopters, flying without oxygen at high altitude. It's not a nice thing to say afterwards when a thing like that has happened but he really had no fear, that boy. Fear is actually a very good self-defence. I don't know what percentage that is, because sometimes it's more and sometimes it's less, but I think Gilles had none.

'As a racer he was fair, absolutely fair. He was a hard driver like hell but always fair. With him you could go into a corner no problem but you would also know that he wasn't going to be the one who gives. Either you have him or you're going to bang wheels with him. We had some hard fights in Canada. The best one was in Mosport. There was this huge hump coming back from the bottom and the car used to go airborne. We hit each other in the air – that was the best I had with him.

'When I came back to Formula One he was a big Ferrari star already. I was little Rosberg and he was big Villeneuve.'

'I always lived with a great deal of respect for Gilles,' Arnoux says. 'I think it would have been

BELOW *The last moments of his life: final qualifying, 8 May 1982 (Gareth Rees).*

difficult for him to become World Champion. He won races, he did beautiful races, but it is true that he exploited the car so much lap by lap and that took him, from time to time, into delicate situations with the tyres, the brakes, the engine and so on.

'Was he a man without fear? In a car during the races I would say yes. He wasn't conscious of danger. You remember the Grand Prix at Imola in 1980? He crashed and broke the car. I was concerned because I was ahead in the Renault and after the Grand Prix I saw him in the pits. His car was completely destroyed: the chassis had been on one side of the road, the engine and gearbox on the other. Gilles was with his son Jacques. I said immediately "How are you?" He was standing there looking at the car. He said "I'm in super shape." I said "You haven't done anything to yourself?" "No, no."

'Gilles spoke a phrase which stays all the time in my head. He said "You know, I am content." I said "Content about what?" He said: "Because I hit the wall at 280kmh [170mph] and the car took it – resisted it. That means the car is solid and I can drive it like that again." Only Gilles could have said it. In one way his phrase shocked me, but, coming from him, in another way it didn't. He said it spontaneously and sincerely. He was just like that. For me, the only one like that.'

Jarier says Villeneuve 'lived near Monaco like me and, like me, he had a house in the mountains. I knew him in Canada because I'd driven against him there. The first Grand Prix he won, in Canada, I had a 40-second lead over him five laps before the end and then I had a problem losing oil. I drove against him in Formula Atlantic. I was in front of him and I had half a lap lead. On the last lap there was someone who came out of the pits and I swerved, damaged the car and I finished second. Each time against Villeneuve I lost because of a connerie [something crappy]! Truly incredible!

'I found him overconfident judged by what I saw him do in racing cars. For example, in qualifying at Monza he went off in the Ferrari in a corner and lost a couple of seconds but he continued as if he could still do a good time. It was bizarre. At Zandvoort he had that puncture but continued to run on three wheels like a madman towards the pits. He left bits of aluminium on the track, which was not proper. He saw the damage to the driveshaft, the suspension, too, everything broken, but he got back to the pits. He sat there with his helmet on imagining the mechanics could simply change the wheel and he'd set off again. Those things I do not understand.'

Footnote: 1. During the 1979 Dutch Grand Prix Villeneuve had a puncture and drove the Ferrari almost fully round the circuit to regain the pits and change the wheel. As he went round the tyre became an octopus and the car so damaged it wouldn't be able to continue. That Villeneuve did keep going to the pits distilled opinion about him: the never-say-die racer or the child of his own immaturity.

ABOVE *How Quebec read about the fatal lap at Zolder. The funeral, Gilles' widow Joanne Villeneuve supported by the Canadian Premier, Pierre Trudeau.*

23 MAY

LEADING QUESTION

—— MONACO, MONTE CARLO

The received wisdom, endlessly recycled, is that pole position at Monaco represents the equivalent of winning big at the Casino. From pole you use the grid's stagger to hustle through eye-of-the-needle Ste Devote in first place, protect your back, keep away from the Armco, and a couple of hours later you'll be standing on the little podium with members of the House of Grimaldi.

This is precisely how Keke Rosberg, among others, approached it. He had his reasons for caution because he'd tried three times before to qualify for the race – with Theodore in 1978 and Fittipaldi in 1980 and 1981 – and now at last he'd find himself on the grid. 'You can,' he'd insist, 'win it from the back and the trick is to avoid risks at the start.'

The recycling ought to have stopped forever in the late afternoon this 23 May, destroyed by a sequence of events so beautifully bizarre that even the Casino had seen nothing like it. The fact that the recycling has continued in spite of this seems to confirm that followers of Formula One do not want Monaco to be a real place at all, and perhaps it isn't. It resembles a Hollywood set, complete with castle, princes and princesses, and right from the start in 1929 rational people expressed incredulity that even irrational people could dream of a Grand Prix here. No good would come of it.

The cussed nature of the circuit – tight, narrow, claustrophobic – had the opposite, almost perverse, effect. Far from follow-my-leader on an annual basis

RIGHT *The two principal players in the Principality: Riccardo Patrese in front of Alain Prost. Patrese did win, Prost ought to have won – and almost anybody else might have done. Grand Prix racing had produced its most improbable and chaotic finish.*

Monaco
Monte Carlo

RACE DATE May 23rd

CIRCUIT LENGTH 3.31km/2.05 miles

NO. OF LAPS 76

RACE DISTANCE
251.71km/156.40 miles

WEATHER Warm, dry, rain later

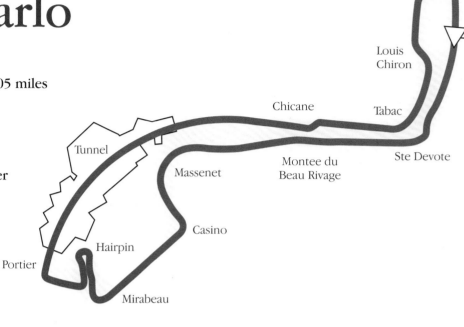

DRIVER'S VIEW

*'It was one of my favourite circuits.
I'm not sure why but maybe it was
because I came from karting and
technically that is similar to street
circuits. Of course there was always a
great atmosphere at the Grand Prix,
born of tradition, and the night after
I won was fantastic. A really big party
with the Prince and Princess – not
all the Grands Prix have this kind
of atmosphere! Normally it's just the
airport and home. You can call it a
kart track with houses but it had some
real corners, not only stop-and-go,
stop-and-go. You had Casino corner,
Tabac corner, the corner into the
tunnel – like a proper circuit.'*

–Riccardo Patrese

the Grand Prix packed powerful surprises, and often enough they came fast and from nowhere.

If you disagree with any of the above, please read on.

Because of the perception of pole position – vital in the true sense of that word, namely essential to success – qualifying was always taut, edgy, and sometimes charged with recrimination as drivers searched out a clear lap.

The structure of the Grand Prix weekend reflected Monaco's quirks with first qualifying on the Thursday, the Friday kept free for promotional activities washed down with the produce of Rheims vineyards, and Saturday centred on the inevitable dramas of second qualifying.

You can postulate that everything about the Monaco Grand Prix was (and is) quirky, starting with actually running Grand Prix cars and their awesome performance round streets normally limited to 50kph (31mph). Pole in 1982 would be set at an average of 143kph (89mph). Ponder that. Grids comprised 26 cars except here (20) because the track wasn't big enough. The Press Room was in a musty theatre, complete with scenery, until its later move to a floor of a multi-storey car park. Some of the marshals had been taught in the Third Reich. Even the waiters in the Hôtel de Paris looked rich and in physical terms they were, because the Grand Prix cars went past just there, smack in front of them. Residents paid a fortune for that.

In fact everybody looked rich except you and the Formula One photographers, always dressed as if they had just come back from Vietnam.

Because 31 drivers entered and only 26 were allowed into the qualifying sessions – again the track not being big enough for more – a pre-qualifying session was held from 8.00 on Thursday morning. The 23 drivers whose teams scored points in 1981 were exempt, leaving the remaining eight to contest three places. Livening this up further, the organisers sent out the municipal watering-truck to cleanse the track, which it did by making it the equivalent of wet for half the session. (Some drivers used wet tyres until it dried.) This was taut and edgy, and it built and built to the final few moments, when Jarier's Osella went fastest from Mass in the spare March (the race car had an engine problem) and Warwick in the Toleman. He went 55/100ths of one second quicker than team-mate Fabi, who now became a spectator along with Paletti (Osella), Boesel (March), Serra (Fittipaldi) and de Villota (March).

Recriminations? The Toleman team, torn between delight for Warwick and regret for Fabi, claimed that the March which was weighed after the session was not the one which Mass had used to set his time...

In first qualifying Arnoux went out after 13 minutes and worked down, 1:51 then 1:40 then two laps in the 1:25s. He backed off, gathered himself – 1:37 – and launched the Renault at the circuit. It had a turbo tailored to this track, more flexible and with

STARTING GRID

1		**1** 1:23.28 **R. Arnoux**
	2 1:23.79 **R. Patrese**	
2		**3** 1:23.93 **B. Giacomelli**
	4 1:24.43 **A. Prost**	
3		**5** 1:24.58 **D. Pironi**
	6 1:24.64 **K. Rosberg**	
4		**7** 1:24.92 **A. de Cesaris**
	8 1:25.39 **D. Daly**	
5		**9** 1:25.44 **M. Alboreto**
	10 1:25.58 **J. Watson**	
6		**11** 1:25.64 **N. Mansell**
	12 1:25.83 **N. Lauda**	
7		**13** 1:26.07 **N. Piquet**
	14 1:26.26 **M. Winkelhock**	
8		**15** 1:26.45 **E. de Angelis**
	16 1:26.46 **E. Cheever**	
9		**17** 1:26.69 **B. Henton**
	18 1:27.00 **J. Laffite**	
10		**19** 1:27.01 **M. Surer**
	20 1:27.02 **E. Salazar**	

OPPOSITE From the start Arnoux leads with the familiar crocodile stretched behind him as they come up the hill.

reduced lag. Physically it demanded strength as well as judgement and, as Arnoux punched it round, it kept punching him – especially blows to the head. He used whatever width the track offered, the Renault at all manner of angles and sometimes virtually sideways.

1:24.543.

Only two other drivers – de Cesaris and Patrese – reached the 1:24s by the end of the session, Rosberg fourth, Prost sixth, and Watson 12th. (Like Mass, in the spare because of an engine problem.)

Arnoux said that, given a clear lap, he thought he could go a second faster on the Saturday.

Patrese spiced that Saturday by doing a 1:23 in the morning untimed session, Mansell next and Alboreto after that. Patrese had a Cosworth engine, team-mate Piquet the BMW turbo. Mansell's Lotus had a Cosworth, Alboreto's Tyrrell had a Cosworth. What might that portend?

Patrese struck early. Out after only three minutes he worked down to a 1:25, backed off, did a high 1:23 and next lap hammered in 1:23.791, provisional pole. Giacomelli was bubbling, too. Out after nine minutes he worked down to a 1:35 and pitted, emerged four minutes later and in three laps did 1:23.939. They'd put up a roadblock in front of Arnoux, who played a long, waiting game. With ten minutes of the session left he took it on. Someone has described his lap as violent but, of more importance, the track was clear and Arnoux feasted on that.

1:23.281.

Prost came fourth, Pironi fifth, Rosberg – blocked by slower cars who, he'd swear, weren't looking in their mirrors – sixth. It was a familiar complaint, eternally made down the years but no less frustrating for that.

In one of the practice sessions Daly 'arrived in the pits with the engine blown up and I was fastest on the timesheets. Instead of allowing me to get into the spare car that was available and ready to go it was kept for only Keke. They had to go back and get a fourth car which they rolled up, and I was never comfortable in that car. I could not go as fast on qualifying tyres as I could on race tyres and it was a bit of a struggle. Even so I qualified eighth – not bad.

Watson struggled to tenth.

The weather on Sunday shifted from azure to cloudy and Rosberg captured all the physical aspects when he remembered that, in the untimed session, his head bounced 'around like a ball' on the bumpy section by the swimming pool – and the race would be over 76 laps, a total of 156 miles.

You can have tactics at Monaco and these invariably involve patience: the received wisdom on this May day revolved around an assumption that if Arnoux led the others would form a traditional crocodile behind him and circle until the Renault broke down, by which time Prost's Renault would probably have broken down too and the rest of them could get on with it.

Roebuck noticed a banner 'Gilles sei sempre con toi' ('Gilles we are always with you') and when Pironi saw it he crossed himself.

In the drivers' briefing the etiquette for the finish was explained. Whichever driver won would do his

ABOVE *Watson joined by Derek Daly, who might have won the race. Watson retired with an oil leak after 36 laps.*

slowing down lap in the usual way but, instead of turning into the pits, would continue to the start-finish straight and halt at the podium, opposite the pits. The driver was 'presenting' the car to the Prince and Princess Rainer, who would already be there. The driver then got out and stood on the podium. The other cars would turn into the pits at the end of their slowing down laps.

Arnoux did lead Giacomelli through Ste Devote, Patrese third, but Daly already had problems. 'Mansell got ahead of me on the run to the first corner and I'd have to follow him for most of the rest of the race. He was blocking me, I couldn't get by. I could see his eyeballs in his mirror looking at me. That allowed the rest to pull away.'

Across the opening lap Arnoux squeezed and forced a substantial lead:

Arnoux	1:34.230
Giacomelli	1:36.752
Patrese	1:39.009

On lap 2 Prost went past Patrese and next lap Giacomelli's gearbox began to fail, giving: Arnoux,

Prost, Patrese ... Rosberg eighth, Watson eleventh. The leaderboard remained static until lap 15, when Arnoux spun at the swimming pool. The Renault slewed, smoke churning from the wheels, and came to rest facing the right way but stalled. Arnoux could not restart the engine and, anyway, a skirt on the Renault had been damaged, disturbing the handling. It opened the race to Prost, with Patrese and Pironi held prisoner behind him. That endured from lap 15.

Further back Rosberg hunted down Alboreto and went by, Alboreto on his best behaviour. Rosberg hunted down de Cesaris and brandished the Williams at him a time or two but de Cesaris wasn't having any of that. Watson circled further back and would get no higher than ninth.

Lap 20: Prost, Patrese, Pironi, de Cesaris, Alboreto, Rosberg, Mansell, Daly, Watson, Lauda.

On lap 23 Salazar retired when his fire extinguisher went off and on lap 29 Cheever's engine failed. Sixteen cars left.

Lap 30: Prost, Patrese, Pironi, de Cesaris, Rosberg, Alboreto, Mansell, Watson, Daly, Lauda.

On lap 31 Laffite retired with a handling problem,

on lap 32 Winkelhock's differential failed, and on lap 37 Watson's ignition failed. Thirteen cars left.

Lap 40: Prost, Patrese, Pironi, de Cesaris, Rosberg, Alboreto, Mansell, Daly, Lauda – the other four runners a lap down.

Prost began to increase the pressure, pulling further and further away from Patrese while Pironi, who lost his nosecone lapping de Angelis, battled on in third.

At the end of lap 46 Mansell pitted for new tyres. That freed Daly 'and then I started a charge, absolutely started a charge.' Daly had been doing 1m 28s, 1m 29s behind Mansell, but now he went down to the 1m 27s.

Lap 50: Prost, Patrese, Pironi, de Cesaris, Rosberg, Alboreto, Daly. Everybody else ran a lap down.

On lap 51 Piquet's gearbox failed and on lap 58 Lauda's engine failed, leaving 11 cars.

On lap 59 Daly set his fastest time of the race, 1m 27s, although Prost was in the 1m 26s.

Around lap 60, the order unchanged, drizzle fell and moistened the surface.

On lap 65 Rosberg, frustrated by the robust de Cesaris reluctance to let anybody past, hit a kerb and broke the Williams's suspension. As he'd reflect, he misjudged it by an inch and a half and that destroyed his whole effort. His hands were raw from grappling the Williams round. De Cesaris says cryptically 'Rosberg couldn't pass me and eventually he went off.'

'I was catching cars almost every lap,' Daly says. 'I caught Keke right before the chicane on the seafront and saw him hit the kerb on the right side going through it. I still remember it in slow motion. I saw him break the pullrod on the front suspension and I just drove by him. I was actually driving over the limit, the car dancing everywhere. I was flying, I really felt I was flying.'

Lap 70: Prost, Patrese. Pironi, de Cesaris, Daly. Alboreto had gone with a front suspension failure. Nine cars left.

Lap 71: Prost, Patrese, Pironi, de Cesaris, Daly. The other four cars were a lap down.

Next lap Daly, his visor coated in oil, lost control of the Williams at Tabac and it struck the Armco. Daly thought instantly: it is destroyed. 'I am coming into the Tabac corner, the car is oversteering and gets away from me. I have a lazy spin, the rear wing hits the Armco. I straightened the car and away I go again. Never stopped. However, the Armco barrier broke off the rear wing with the gearbox oil cooler on it so I drive around but I now have no rear wing. Charlie Crichton-Stuart is telling me "GO! GO! GO!" from the pit lane wall – four laps left. I drive around a full lap with my gearbox dumping the gearbox oil out on the racetrack.'

Prost overtook him up the hill to Casino so Daly ran a lap down, Prost pulling decisively away. Prost completed lap 72 in 1m 30, Daly 1m 44.

Lap 73: Prost, Patrese, Pironi.

Pironi covered the lap in 1m 35, a figure which

BELOW Cheever's engine lets go on lap 29 and de Angelis is already moving wide and preparing to move through.

ABOVE *Winkelbock*
would only cover
31 laps before the
differential failed.

would become very important and very suggestive
very soon.

One lap down, Daly, de Angelis, Mansell.

Four laps down, Henton.

Six laps down, Surer.

Lap 74: Prost, some seven seconds ahead of
Patrese, came up to lap Surer again, but exiting
the chicane on the seafront the Renault suddenly
snapped out of control. Daly's oil? It rammed the
barrier, was pitched across into the other barrier,
pitched back again and lay motionless. A wheel,
torn off, bounded away and debris lay everywhere.
Any accident at 130mph is shockingly sudden
but more so when there is nowhere – absolutely
nowhere – to go. As Prost clambered out, shaken, a
cluster of marshals churned yellow flags. Danger.

That enabled Patrese to pick a way through and
complete the lap in the lead. 'I thought: now maybe
it is my turn to win. I saw my mechanics cheering
me from the pits when I went past them after the
Prost accident. I was leading Pironi comfortably. I
had no need to push hard ... I was not ready to take
any risks on the wet surface.'

The order: Patrese, Pironi, de Cesaris.

Pironi covered the lap in 1m 43, markedly slower
than the previous lap. He was suffering, he thought,
a misfire and assumed the wet weather had seeped
into the electrics.

Daly ran on, ever slower.

'I wasn't worried about Daly because I was fully
aware that he was a lap down,' de Cesaris says.

Lap 75: Patrese lapped Surer down from Casino
Square and the Italians in the crowd saluted
him with raised fists as he moved safely towards
victory. On the descent to the Station Hairpin, he
lurched under braking – the track like ice – slewed

sideways, turned round and ran over the inner kerb
backwards, stopping there. 'I braked normally, maybe
even a bit early. The back end of the car suddenly
went away and I was going backwards.

'It wasn't as if I came from nowhere. I'd qualified
on the front row and spent most of the race a couple
of seconds behind Prost. Then I spun on the oil – oil
which I only found out about a couple of years ago
when I read an interview with Derek Daly! Twenty
years later I understood what had happened! I never
thought it was a mistake but I always wondered why
I spun off when I was going so slowly. The car just
went away from me like it was suddenly on ice.'

'That's why Patrese spun and stalled,' Daly says.
'He spun on my oil. So he spins and goes backwards
and gets stuck. I pass him.' Interesting...

Because the Brabham had come to rest in a
potentially dangerous position marshals prepared to
give it a push but waited for a gap in the traffic.

Pironi went past and into the lead, de Cesaris chasing him hard.

De Cesaris went past and into second place. Seeing Patrese beached, de Cesaris thought: he'll have to have a push. 'I didn't think that was allowed. I thought he would be disqualified.' De Cesaris didn't realise you could legally be pushed if your car was in a dangerous position.

Patrese, immobile and impotent, watched them both go. 'That almost finished me. Chance gone.' He'd never won a race although he had led Kyalami in 1978 before the engine failed and Long Beach in 1981 before an oil filter failed. Now this. The marshals pushed and he set off down the Station Hairpin back into the race – the slope allowed him to bump-start the engine – but with no remote idea of the running order. 'Anyway, I got going.' He'd continue to the finish and have time afterwards to examine his sadness.

Pironi completed the lap in 1m 58 and was clearly in trouble. He might have been exercising prudence in the wet but his time was much slower than that.

De Cesaris did 1m 42 – a gain of fully 16 seconds.

As Pironi crossed the line to begin the last lap – 76 – he gesticulated to have the race stopped, even as the Ferrari pit held out a signal ONE MORE LAP. Pironi was running out of fuel: that is what had been slowing him.

A Lotus unlapped itself.

With Pironi limping, Monaco suddenly spread itself in front of de Cesaris. Pit signals told him that Pironi had a problem so in effect 'I was leading the race. I said to myself: maybe this time you're going to make it. [Like Patrese, he'd never won.] I was very good through the race and I was really quick. Then – and the car was unreliable – it went to 11 cylinders.' De Cesaris thought: I'll have to settle for

BELOW *Role reversal for the principal players: Prost leads Patrese – here at Rascasse – against a backdrop of mountains and money (well, mountains of money).*

LE FIGARO

★ X X VENDREDI 21 MAI 1982 (N° 11 730) – Édition de 5 heures – PRIX 3,50 F

SP

Patrese gagne le Grand Prix de Monaco

AUTOMOBILE

Les J.S. 19 non conformes à Mon

Ligier en mini jupe

Le ciel sur la tête de Prost

SPORTS

AUTOMOBILE   Le pari du turbo Renault à Monaco

Les essais à transformer

23

---

third. That assumed Pironi would manage to finish, Patrese's push was legal, and Patrese could get back past him.

'Monaco,' de Cesaris says, 'had become a lottery.'

'Monaco,' Patrese says, 'was very strange.'

De Cesaris 'got to the top of the hill and at Casino Square the engine died. I swore. I knew I couldn't win.' The circuit is downhill from Casino to the tunnel and de Cesaris let the Alfa freewheel.

Pironi nursed the Ferrari to the tunnel where it slowed and came to a complete halt, the last of its fuel drunk.

De Cesaris 'came to a stop just at the beginning of the tunnel – in fact, just before Pironi's car.' He got out and sat on a wall nearby. One report said he was in tears but he denies that. 'I didn't cry.'

Daly pressed on. 'Then I pass Pironi, who'd stopped in the tunnel,' Daly says – and de Cesaris stopped in the tunnel, too. Very interesting...

Patrese passed Pironi but in the tunnel's darkness didn't recognise the Ferrari. He was beginning to think, however, 'there are a lot of cars stopped round this circuit.' His lap 75, a nightmarish 3:04.2 while he waited for the push, receded into memory.

Daly did not, of course, know that Patrese had restarted. 'I'm coming down to the Rascasse hairpin to start my last lap leading the race and I hear the differential grind and grind and grind and grind and eventually break.' Daly clambered out and walked away. He still feels 'the decision not to let me use the third car potentially cost me the race win, I think.'

Patrese, driving prudently, completed the race and took the chequered flag, thought nothing of that. All finishers get the chequered flag. He estimated that perhaps he'd come as high as second but who knew? 'Of course in those days there was no radio so nobody could tell me anything.' He'd remember 'on the slowing down lap a lot of people were cheering and waving flags but that was normal for anyone finishing in Monaco.' He thought nothing of that, either. In the tunnel he drew up next to the Ferrari and gave Pironi a lift back. Pironi had been jerking his thumb 'like a student hitch-hiker waiting on the autostrada.'

Patrese reached the entrance to the pits but marshals gesticulated no, no, keep on to the podium. He couldn't understand why, because at

ABOVE *A world in headlines, and yes, the sky fell on Prost's head.*

OPPOSITE *Patrese coming up to Casino Square in lonely splendour and no idea what position he was in the race.*

the drivers' briefing, as he remembered so well, they'd been told only the winner would be required to do that. Well, Patrese concluded, they must have changed the rules to include cars in the first three positions.

He parked the Brabham beside the podium and got out looking bemused. 'I asked somebody "What happened?" and they said "You won!" I had so many doubts. After I spun I saw so many cars going past...'

As de Cesaris says, 'I didn't know who'd won, even on the podium nobody knew who'd won.'

Eventually Riccardo Patrese really believed because, in a great moment, he brandished the trophy and grinned like his head had just exploded. Pironi, classified second, quickly turned his back

– sensing, no doubt, the champagne shower coming his way. De Cesaris, classified third, stood to one side looking withdrawn, uncomprehending, resigned to the final reality. Amid the delicious uncertainty de Angelis made his way to the podium, no doubt because, running at the end, he deduced he must have been in the top three. He was actually fifth.

Prost 18, Watson 17, Pironi 16, Rosberg 14, Patrese 13, Lauda 12.

Patrese would never win Monaco again, de Cesaris would drive 208 races and never win one, Pironi and Daly never drove Monaco again.

Apart from that it was all very processional, predictable and uninteresting – you know, the way Monaco always is.

OPPOSITE *Patrese still doesn't look completely convinced he's won.*

BELOW *Pincer movement: Pironi puts the squeeze on de Cesaris and dares him to resist.*

Race Result

WINNING SPEED 132.26kmh/82.18 mph

FASTEST LAP 138.07kmh/85.79mph
(Patrese 1m 26.35s on lap 69)

LAP LEADERS Arnoux 1–14 (14);
Prost 15–73 (59); Patrese 74, 76 (2);
Pironi 75 (1)

RACE

	Driver	Team	Engine	Laps	Time
1	R. Patrese	Brabham BT49D	Cosworth V8	76	1h 54m 11.25s
2r	D. Pironi	Ferrari 126C2	FerrariV6t	75	Electrics
3r	A. de Cesaris	Alfa Romeo 182	Alfa Rom V12	75	Out of fuel
4	N. Mansell	Lotus 91	Cosworth V8	75	
5	E. de Angelis	Lotus 91	Cosworth V8	75	
6r	D. Daly	Williams FW08	Cosworth V8	74	Accident/gearbox
7r	A. Prost	Renault RE30B	Renault V6t	73	Accident
8	B. Henton	Tyrrell 011	Cosworth V8	72	
9	M. Surer	Arrows A4	Cosworth V8	70	
10r	M. Alboreto	Tyrrell 011	Cosworth V8	69	Front suspension
r	K. Rosberg	Williams FW08	Cosworth V8	65	Front suspension
r	N. Lauda	McLaren MP4B	Cosworth V8	57	Engine
r	N. Piquet	Brabham BT50	BMW 4t	50	Gearbox
r	J. Watson	McLaren MP4B	Cosworth V8	36	Oil leak/battery
r	M. Winkelhock	ATS D5	Cosworth V8	31	Differential
r	J. Laffite	Talbot Ligier JS19	Matra V12	30	Handling
r	E. Cheever	Talbot Ligier S19	Matra V12	28	Engine
r	E. Salazar	ATS D5	Cosworth V8	22	Fire extinguisher
r	R. Arnoux	Renault RE30B	Renault V6t	14	Spin
r	B. Giacomelli	Alfa Romeo 182	Alfa Rom V12	5	Transmission
nq	M. Baldi	Arrows A4	Cosworth V8		
nq	J. Lammers	Theodore TY02	Cosworth V8		
nq	J. Mass	March 821	Cosworth V8		
nq	D. Warwick	Toleman TG181C	Hart 4t		
nq	J.-P. Jarier	Osella FA1C	Cosworth V8		
nq	R. Guerrero	Ensign N181	Cosworth V8		
npq	T. Fabi	Toleman TG181C	Hart 4t		
npq	R. Paletti	Osella FA1C	Cosworth V8		
npq	R. Boesel	March 821	Cosworth V8		
npq	C. Serra	Fittipaldi F8D	Cosworth V8		
npq	E. de Villota	March 821	Cosworth V8		

npq = did not pre-qualify; nq = did not qualify; ns = did not start; r = retired

CHAMPIONSHIP

	Driver	Points
1	A. Prost	18
2	J. Watson	17
3	D. Pironi	16
4	K. Rosberg	14
5	R. Patrese	13
6	N. Lauda	12
7	M. Alboreto	10
8	E. de Angelis	7
	N. Mansell	7
10	C. Reutemann	6
	G. Villeneuve	6
12	R. Arnoux	4
	E. Cheever	4
	A. de Cesaris	4
15	J.-P. Jarier	3
16	N. Piquet	2
	M.Winkelhock	2
	E. Salazar	2
19	D. Daly	1
	F. Serra	1

	Team	Points
1	McLaren	29
2	Renault	22
	Ferrari	22
4	Williams	21
5	Brabham	15
6	Lotus	14
7	Tyrrell	10
8	ATS	4
	Talbot Ligier	4
	Alfa Romeo	4
11	Osella	3
12	Fittipaldi	1

6 JUNE

STREET FIGHTING

—————————————— USA, DETROIT

I've recorded my initial reaction – curiosity and bemusement – to Grand Prix racing in the Introduction. I had covered Le Mans since 1976 but that wasn't the same thing. No national newspaper journalist dreamed of going for the practice sessions or the weigh-in there. Grid positions were utterly meaningless in a 24-hour race. Like annual migrants we made our way from England to the town on the Friday (in time for dinner), went to the circuit on the Saturday for a leisurely lunch, watched the race until about midnight (the last moment you could get a story into the final editions of the Sunday papers: memories of the crash in the 1955 race lingered). Then we went off to get a good night's sleep.

On the Sunday we returned and frequently the leading cars were running in the same order as when we'd left. It was all very gentlemanly and slightly surreal. We wrote our race reports as soon as possible after the race and headed for home. Jacky Ickx and Derek Bell seemed to win every year in the Rothmans Porsche and that added a soothing quality to the whole weekend: it would have been entirely possible to write the race report before setting off from England on the Friday, merely adding details like how much they beat the second Rothmans Porsche by.

The delights of rural France are well known, which is why so many Britons buy homes there. Even if you have never been to Detroit you'll know enough about the place to understand the shocking contrast. Detroit was dangerous if you turned the corner into the wrong neighbourhood. There were

RIGHT *The Renaissance Center made anything at Monaco almost diminutive. In its shadow, Bruno Giacomelli, Winkelbock and Mansell jostle for positions in midfield.*

USA
Detroit

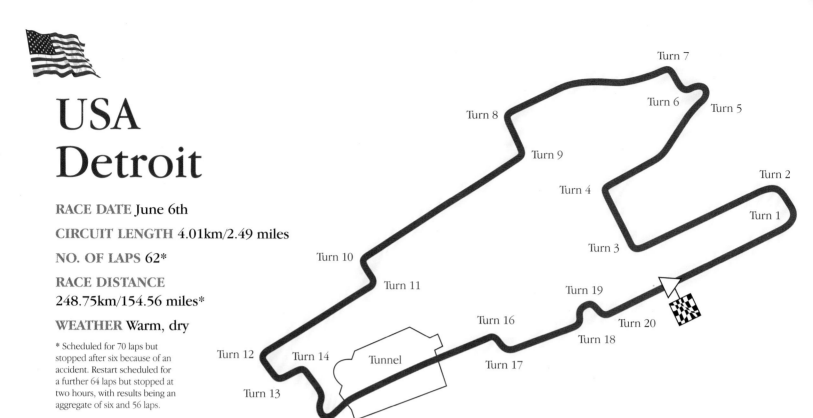

RACE DATE June 6th

CIRCUIT LENGTH 4.01km/2.49 miles

NO. OF LAPS 62*

RACE DISTANCE
248.75km/154.56 miles*

WEATHER Warm, dry

* Scheduled for 70 laps but
stopped after six because of an
accident. Restart scheduled for
a further 64 laps but stopped at
two hours, with results being an
aggregate of six and 56 laps.

Turn 7
Turn 6
Turn 5
Turn 8
Turn 9
Turn 4
Turn 2
Turn 1
Turn 3
Turn 10
Turn 11
Turn 19
Turn 20
Turn 16
Turn 18
Tunnel
Turn 17
Turn 12
Turn 14
Turn 13
Turn 15

DRIVER'S VIEW

*'Fundamentally it was an urban street
track in North America on the grid system
– the typical layout of a city there – so
you were just going from intersection
to intersection. The quality of the roads
was pretty poor in a number of places,
not so bad in others. It was the nature
of the tarmac itself to be very low grip,
so fundamentally we had low grip too.
On street circuits, because you get all the
usual rubbish going down on it – every
contaminant you can think of – for
decades, when you put a race car on it it
just slides over the surface. Eventually it
wears it down and lays its own rubber. That
didn't really occur. The thing that was most
unusual about Detroit was that it was in
the downtown area, and in North America
they are predominantly poor. You might
call them ghettos. It was not the sort of place
you'd go out to at night-time on your own,
wandering around the streets.'*

—————— *John Watson*

neighbourhoods where taxi drivers refused to take you. These were two good reasons, among many, why Britons were not buying homes there and still aren't.

On the airport bus in, the cluster of skyscrapers looming and enlarging, a roadside electric sign carried the total of cars made in Detroit so far in the year. It was continually updated so that the final two numerals rotated slowly as they recorded the latest cars off the production lines. I mentioned to an American journalist how impressive this was and he replied 'No, no, no! That damned sign shows how bad things are. The last two numbers should be turning so fast you can't read them…'

Detroit was different, all right. You wouldn't be sitting at a pavement café in the Place de la Republique sipping a glass of Loire wine (a succulent Sancerre, perhaps) and watching the girls go by; you'd be in the plastic and formica Hungry Tiger – where fast food meant fast – sipping Coke (or was it Pepsi?) and watching the police cars go by, sirens screaming into the fetid evening air.

Downtown Detroit, built on the usual American grid pattern, was a series of cliff-face buildings rising, as it seemed when you stood beneath them, all the way to the sky, but many were from the 1920s and

1930s and curiously art deco. There was a feeling of decay, or something approaching genuine poverty. At night the white middle class fled to the leafy suburbs spread out into Michigan, leaving the middle and inner suburbs exclusively to African-Americans, who had a way of flashing mean, mournful, distrusting eyes at you. They had their reasons, good reasons, but all in all it was a hell of a place to hold a Grand Prix.

John Watson remembers 'everybody turned up at Detroit and thought it was a dump, partly because of the location and partly because of the circuit – you had this wonderful Renaissance Center but inner city decay around it. The local media, typically American, expected the influx of Grand Prix drivers would be more polite in the way they would give an opinion of Detroit, or whatever, and by and large most of the opinion was pretty blunt and pretty rude. People don't like to be told their city is a dump.

'I was one of a number of drivers they spoke to and I said something which was very positive and it worked for me. I said "I've dreamed of coming to Detroit for God knows how long because of Tamla Motown, the Supremes," and so on. At that time

BELOW *Actually, some drivers do like each other as Cheever, Piquet and Lauda prove as they sit on the waterfront.*

Motown was big, big music. "Just to come here is absolutely magical." I didn't talk about the race track, I gave them the chance to say "Well, here's a guy who's got something good to say.'"

The drivers found problems immediately. Because it was a new circuit there ought to have been an introductory session on the Thursday so they could make its acquaintance. That was cancelled, the track unready. Work went on and the drivers walked round seeking out and analysing the points of maximum danger.

An office worker, Debra Krzesowisk, was quoted as saying: 'I wish they'd fix up some of the other streets ... there are holes and I mean holes! I'd like to see these Grand Prixers race in those craters. If the whole thing brings in money to fix our streets, then it's worth it. I'll just race around in my own Grand Prix until then.'

A clergyman, due to hold a wedding Mass, foresaw a problem with traffic getting in and out for the church. 'We need some flag-waving down there.'

The untimed session on Friday ought to have started at 10.00 but the track still wasn't ready and no car went out until 3.55 in the afternoon, the first qualifying session abandoned. When the drivers came back after their initial runs they complained about the manhole covers, the bumps, the walls, the narrowness of the track, the escape roads and the absence of sufficient protective tyre walls. Apart from that they adored it...

The great American public, nurtured on 200mph ovals, knew nothing about Formula One and many showed no sign of wanting to know anything about it (but see the comments of local residents the Thompsons on page 127). One man asked what speed these Formula One cars were doing round the track and, when he was told they averaged about 80mph, said 'My car goes faster'n thaat.' It caught the mood: irritation that the middle of their city had been fenced off mingled with incomprehension as to why.

Nor was that all. In a hotel four blocks away, something called the Poetry Resource Center was sponsoring the Sixth Annual Michigan Poetry Festival. They described it as 'the Grand Prix of poetry' and insisted the noise of the cars wasn't putting off any of the 300 attending. Elsewhere a convention of librarians, 3,000 strong, began. Weren't they the total opposite of Grand Prix racing? One of the 3,000, Emily Mobley, responded by insisting the race added to the excitement and added: 'We just hate to see a stereotyped image of librarians. We're very outspoken and aggressive.'

The cars were just down the road, ma'am, if you fancied giving that aggression an outlet.

OPPOSITE *Baldi hits Henton as the midfield bunches in the shadow of the skyscrapers.*

STARTING GRID

1 1:48.53 A. Prost	**2** 1:48.87 A. de Cesaris
3 1:49.26 K. Rosberg	**4** 1:49.90 D. Pironi
5 1:50.06 M. Winkelhock	**6** 1:50.25 B. Giacomelli
7 1:50.29 N. Mansell	**8** 1:50.44 E. de Angelis
9 1:50.52 E. Cheever	**10** 1:51.02 N. Lauda
11 1:51.03 R. Guerrero	**12** 1:51.22 D. Daly
13 1:51.27 J. Laffite	**14** 1:51.50 R. Patrese
15 1:51.51 R. Arnoux	**16** 1:51.61 M. Alboreto
17 1:51.86 J. Watson	**18** 1:52.27 J. Mass
19 1:52.31 M. Surer	**20** 1:52.86 B. Henton
21 1:52.87 R. Boesel	**22** 1:52.98 J.-P. Jarier
23 1:54.08 R. Paletti	**24** 1:54.33 M. Baldi
25 1:55.63 E. Salazar	**26** 1:55.84 M. Serra

ABOVE *Detroit distilled into an image, concrete walls, Armco barriers, geometrical turns. Here Mansell leads de Angelis but neither finished.*

The Grand Prix clearly formed part of a rejuvenation plan for Detroit, just as the immense Renaissance Center – several tower blocks side-by-side – did. The name told you everything. The central tower contained a hotel and the drivers stayed there. Since the pits were just below it they took the elevator down there, and never saw Detroit except as some monstrous backdrop from their bedroom windows. At one point Rosberg actually 'felt a prisoner of it all.'

I stayed in a very basic self-catering apartment far from this and was astonished to get back alive every evening. I don't think they'd ever seen a white man walking the streets at night and it was the shock factor which protected me as I made my way towards the delights of the Hungry Tiger again.

In the Press Room the Formula One journalists spoke a patois entirely of their own. You'd hear talk of compounds, hear expressions like 'rock ape' – which I took as an allusion to the hilarious Peter Ustinov spoof Grand Prix of Gibraltar[1] – 'quallies' and 'welly' and 'wets'. Perhaps they indulged in rain dancing. There were 'marbles,' although I couldn't imagine these millionaire jet-setters playing anything as humble as that, even to pass the time in the Renaissance Center. Some drivers did 'banzai laps', whatever they were. Some took corners 'balls

to the wall' and I didn't plan to investigate that. All of them tried 'to keep it on the island'. One car had evidently come 'straight from the box'.

The nuances of the qualifying, beyond the complaints of the drivers, were lost on me, never having seen it before, and, with both sessions now on the Saturday after Friday's cancellation, nobody else had seen it in that form either. As a matter of tradition, whoever covered motor racing for the *Daily Express* also filed to its sister the *Sunday Express* (which of course went to Press on the Saturday evening: hence staying up late at Le Mans). They habitually showed as much interest as the American public and were content with a single paragraph recording who had pole and where the Brits came. Even this was not always used. It meant that that Saturday at Detroit I had no incentive to discover the nuances and, once Canada was out of the way a week later, wouldn't ever need to discover them. I didn't even know if there were any.

Alain Prost was a good enough driver to ignore his instinctive dislike of the track – 'all you can see is bumps, corners and walls' – and take pole from de Cesaris, Rosberg and Pironi on the second row, but the McLarens were all over the place, Lauda on the fifth row and Watson on the ninth.

Prost bided his time in first qualifying, not

venturing out until the session was just over five minutes old, and did one slow lap, looking around him. He pitted and re-emerged ten minutes later for a five-lap run, reaching 1:49.187. He pitted again and re-emerged 14 minutes later for a single lap, a 1:49.8. He made his final run 24 minutes after that, a 1:57 followed by 1:48.537 – provisional pole at an average speed of 82.6 miles an hour. De Cesaris in the Alfa Romeo was the only other driver into the 1:48s.

Rain fell, making the second session wet. That meant average speeds in the 60mph range and guaranteed Prost pole, although his right foot remained painful after the whack against the Armco at Monaco. Without the rain, Prost judged he could have found another second. Gazing ahead to the race he felt overtaking would be more problematical than Monaco and out-braking a car ahead was all but impossible in the ten right-hand corners.

The 25 cars came to the grid on the shoreline straight in the shadow of the Renaissance Center, accompanied by – inevitably – Motown music. They faced a left-handed horseshoe at the end of the straight and then the staccato sequence of mini-straights and geometrical corners which worked their way back past the other side of the Renaissance Center. They joined the straight at

the other end, the shoreline again to one side, although reaching towards the start-finish line they'd have to negotiate a tight little right-left and a sort of chicane.

The race began on time at 2.20 on the Sunday afternoon, Prost strongly away and Rosberg trying to squeeze by. That didn't work and Rosberg slotted in behind de Cesaris. Watson picked up a couple of places from the start and inherited another when Winkelhock crashed, making him 14th. De Cesaris pitted on lap 3 with a broken driveshaft, but Watson didn't inherit another place because Mass got past him.

The leaderboard at lap 6, just over ten minutes into the race: Prost, Rosberg, Pironi, Mansell, Giacomelli, Cheever.

Into lap 7 de Angelis and Guerrero crashed and Patrese became entangled too, his Brabham briefly on fire. The race was stopped and not resumed for an hour, which drew a mischievous barb from Lauda: 'If they stop it for all the crashes round here I'll be able to have a drink every ten minutes.' Rosberg observed trenchantly 'A Grand Prix driver can only stand so many starts in a one-day period.'

The positions at the end of lap 6 determined the restart grid, and after the full 62 laps the result would be decided on aggregate times. Prost had been leading Rosberg by three seconds, which

BELOW *Roberto Guerrero (Ensign) and de Angelis both crashed at Detroit, and Patrese joined them by rearranging the tyre wall. It was enough to halt the race.*

seemed useful to carry forward. Watson was now on the seventh row.

The main part of the race would be enacted in two distinct dimensions: the fight for the lead and Watson fighting to get to the leaders. Lap by lap the two dimensions would come closer and closer.

'We struggled all the way through practice and qualifying to find grip,' Watson says. 'In the intermission when the race was stopped Pierre Dupasquier of Michelin, who was one of the smartest men I've ever met within motor racing – a very, very smart engineer – came to me and said "John, you're on the 06 (or whatever it was), the softest tyre. Please go and put on a set of 05s, one compound harder." Actually it wasn't so straightforward because in those days there were extremely subtle differences between grades, compounds and construction of tyres and Michelin operated with great secrecy anyway. I'm not sure Pierre didn't even say "You will win the race." I went to my mechanics and said "Look, have you guys got some of my 05s?" They dragged some out, strapped them on, the race recommenced, and bit by bit I found myself able to pick up pace. Michelin would never have gone to Niki and said the same thing to him because he always ran the 06s whenever he could, so it would have been pointless...'

Prost led again from Rosberg and Pironi.

Watson ran a distant 13th to lap 16 when he surged past the Lotuses – de Angelis had a gearbox problem, Mansell a handling problem. A lap later he took Mass, two laps after that he took Arnoux, who had a misfire. Watson ran ninth.

He describes the problems of finding a rhythm. 'From the exit of Turn 20 you'd probably get about 140 miles an hour. It was a difficult corner, 180 degrees. You could never get the car to enter the corner, never get bite, and at McLaren we were chasing our tails to get the car to do that. Because it was a lighter car, it was very gentle on its tyres compared to Renault. Turns 3 and 4 were geometrical, a horrible little tight squiggle, 6, 7, 8 geometrical. Along the back straight you hit the maximum speed into Turn 1 and that was 140, 150mph in an aspirated car, maybe 10mph more in a turbo.'

Prost's fuel metering unit slowed him and Rosberg hustled the Williams through into the lead on lap 23.

Next lap Watson dealt with Laffite, the lap after that Daly, so that on lap 25 he ran seventh. Prost, travelling ever more slowly, came back to him on lap 29, Watson moving past him and into the points. He dealt with Giacomelli, who slid wide in a corner – but Giacomelli retaliated and ran over Watson's rear wheel. Giacomelli retired, Watson continued, now fifth. Ahead, in the order he would reach them: Lauda, Cheever, Pironi, Rosberg.

Watson produced an extraordinary lap. Around a track on which, as you remember, Prost judged overtaking more difficult than Monaco, he was poised to strike.

OPPOSITE *Giacomelli put together a feisty race, at one point running as high as fourth, until he tangled with Watson.*

BELOW *Reverse order: Pironi leads Cheever but Cheever would finish second, Pironi third.*

'I caught up to a run of three cars, Niki, Cheever and Pironi. In the space of one lap I passed Niki into Turn 1. He said "I saw you coming and I made way for you to go through" but the point is that Niki, again, was acting archetypically. He had convinced himself it couldn't be done so he wasn't doing it. I took Cheever into Turn 8 and Pironi into Turn 10. Positive thought is actually as important as anything in any part of motor racing. Look at overtaking. You can send out a message to a car you're wanting to overtake, and the message is clear: I am coming through. I am not going to be put off by you, I AM coming through.

'Niki never was someone who would fight you wheel to wheel right into the last millimetre of track, Cheever I didn't know so much about and he was probably less predictable, Pironi was certainly somebody who would possibly be unpredictable as well. Anyway, I was coming through with such positiveness: bosh, bosh, bosh, job done. The power of positive thought is an exceptionally powerful tool in all of life but it's knowing how and when to apply it.

'It was my little tsunami, if you like. I had a

FANS' EYE VIEW

'The excitement was palpable and everyone was so thrilled that Detroit was hosting a Grand Prix race for the very first time. The city was buzzing with anticipation because we didn't know what to expect from the sophisticated European drivers, their glamorous women, and of course the world press. Would they like our old "rust-belt" working class city?

'All weekend we were out on the downtown streets soaking up the carnival-like atmosphere, drinking beer and eating food from the many street vendors. Seeing the cars at the practice runs blew us away. How did the drivers manage to navigate such a crazy route?

'The city had promised that there would be spots where you could view the Sunday action for free so we didn't buy passes. We scrambled around fences and barriers and wound up holding onto some tree branches down by the Detroit River, amazed by the roar and speed of the beautiful Formula One cars racing around "our" town.'

BARBARA AND CHUCK THOMPSON
DETROIT, USA

GRAND PRIX: Detroit Doesn't Race American

12. Part III/Saturday, June 5, 1982

Carnival flavor surrounds Prix

By NANCY CAIN
Macomb Daily Staff Writer

DETROIT —Rosemary and Rick Frohock drove in from Mount Clemens at 9 a.m. Friday to make sure they got good seats in the bleachers.

The couple brought their sons, Brian, 10, and Craig, 8.

"It's not every day that a Grand Prix comes to Detroit," Frohock, an engineer at Fisher Body, noted. "We felt they could miss a day at South River Elementary School for this."

The boys nodded enthusiastically as Frohock added, "I've always loved fast cars. This is exciting."

The Mount Clemens family was among countless thousands of Grand Prix-watchers who flocked to the downtown Detroit area, filling bleachers and lining up shoulder-to-shoulder along the race course for a glimpse of Detroit Grand Prix 1982.

Sports cars, drivers and celebrities were the order of the day.

Detroit Doesn't Race American

Residents Unhappy About Chaos and Presence of Foreign Cars

By SHAV GLICK, *Times Staff Writer*

DETROIT—What could be more ludicrous than having a bunch of French, English and Italian cars—driven by Europeans and South Americans—racing through downtown Detroit, the depressed and decaying center of what's left of the American motor-car industry?

Grand Prix no prize for 3 churches

By HARRY COOK
Free Press Religion Writer

The Detroit Grand Prix race scheduled for Sunday, June 6, may cause at least one downtown church to cancel services. It promises also to create problems for two other churches inside the race course.

And Detroit Renaissance, which is promoting the race, hasn't got many answers for concerned pastors and parishioners.

The Rev. Richard W. Ingalls, rector of Mariners' Church — one of three churches within the race course — said Monday he was irked that Detroit Renaissance hadn't called together the clergy of the affected parishes "long ago."

"I've tried to find out what the plans were and kept getting stonewalled," the priest said.

RICHARD FERRIS, vice-president of Detroit Renaissance, said officials are determined to limit access to the race area. He said they are concerned that a large number of people might, under the guise of going to church, try to save the $15 admission to the race area.

ABOVE *A world in headlines, and they had no idea what to make of the stranger.*

OPPOSITE *Yes, there were trees in Detroit but Watson didn't let them distract him.*

'Then,' Watson says, 'I started to reel in Keke and I was picking up two to three seconds on average a lap.'

	Rosberg	Watson
Lap 33	1:54.5	1:52.2
Lap 34	1:55.2	1:51.3
Lap 35	1:53.8	1:51.4
Lap 36	1:55.9	1:51.2

That was Watson's fastest lap of the race and on the next lap 'I passed him into Turn 1. You got the momentum off Turn 20 and you'd take a slingshot down the inside. Keke said afterwards "You know, you were catching me by so many seconds a lap – I'd just done my best lap and you'd taken four seconds out of it. There's no answer to that." So I took the lead in the race on the road but I wasn't actually leading on time because it was the aggregate. I had to pull out 15 seconds or something, which I was able to do fairly comfortably.

'While all this was going on, behind me my good old team-mate and friend Niki suddenly went: oh, oh, you can pass – reprogramme the computer chip in the brain. He got past Cheever and Pironi and he had a better chance of winning the race than me. He was fewer seconds behind Keke than I was and he could have finished second on the road but won on aggregate. He tried to pass Keke, got it wrong and shunted, which Keke found very amusing. Whereas I was quiet, clean, positive, Niki was will I won't I? Keke shut the door, and that was it.'

On lap 37 Cheever, who had been following Pironi since lap 26, made his move: 'I had followed him for so long that at one point I said: I have to get by him now or forget about it. I did it when I came out of the hairpin. I took the wrong line but I kept my foot on it and closed my eyes.'

It worked.

Watson pressed on, alone and untroubled. Rosberg limped in fourth, wracked with doubts about the Championship. As Napoleon said, when you're choosing a general you ask 'Is he lucky?' This mid-season Rosberg wasn't lucky at all and mild-mannered John Watson was showing himself hard enough to take whatever anybody threw at him.

Eddie Cheever, in his fourth season, finished 15 seconds behind and had never been as high as second before. 'John was unbeatable today,' he said. 'He would have been the winner under any circumstances. I had to take risks to get by drivers but I did it without any mistakes. I didn't take any crap from anybody and I didn't give anybody any crap.'

---

rhythm, I had a car which, suddenly, was reborn with the tyres. Ironically if you were looking for rhythm you couldn't come to a better city than Detroit, home of Tamla Motown.'

As Rosberg went past the pits a Williams board told him Watson now ran second and was only 12.9 seconds behind. Rosberg had a concise thought: damn! Then he asked himself a question: is this going to be Belgium all over again? Rosberg confessed that Watson's tyres seemed 'magical', and he – Rosberg – had a gearbox problem. He couldn't get third and fourth.

Watson 26, Pironi 20, Prost 18, Rosberg 17, Patrese 13, Lauda 12.

A tremendous race by any standards and, despite the five-hour time gap to London and the endlessly delayed restart, it was straightforward to cover. Well, Charlie Vincent of the *Detroit Free Press* didn't find it like that. He wrote: 'No one seems quite sure how fast he went, or how far, or how many people watched him do it, and some even question whether he did, indeed, win the first Detroit Grand Prix Sunday afternoon. But John Watson, a 36-year-old Irishman driving for Team McLaren, took the checkered flag and easily beat American-born Eddie Cheever to the finish on the last lap of the time-shortened race.'

Clearly Mr Vincent hadn't seen it before, either.

He quoted Watson as saying: 'The car was bloody awful in practice. I wasn't particularly hopeful, based on that. I found I could pass people in a few places, and once I found that, it seemed to happen relatively easy. I didn't expect to be able to overtake people. I didn't see places to do that in practice, but today I did. I really had to start racing all over again once I passed Rosberg. It was a bit of a disappointment but I overcame it.'

Another *Free Press* writer, Curt Sylvester, wrote that after Cheever's exertions all Cheever 'had in mind at 6:15 p.m. Sunday were three things – a beer, a shower and a nap. The beer was no problem. It was waiting for him at the interview table, right next to race winner John Watson. But the shower and the nap were being delayed by the throng of journalists who closed in on him before the formal Watson

BELOW Rosberg, hungry for points, prepares to make a power play on Chico Serra's Fittipaldi by lapping it.

interview was completed.' Sylvester pointed out that Cheever was the only American in the race and 'so what if he has lived the last 24 years in Italy?'

Whenever a Briton wins, and you're working for a British newspaper, it is invariably easy to report it. I still knew nothing about how Grand Prix racing functioned and really did have no sense of its habits and habitats. The following day the *Express* wanted a full-scale interview with Watson. I imagined that the teams would naturally spend Monday relaxing in the Renaissance Center and make their leisurely way up to Canada on the Tuesday, perhaps driving through the tunnel under the Detroit River into charming Windsor on the far side and then, travelling north, take in the countryside.

One of the organisers said the barriers and fences which lined the course would take about ten days to remove (although, amazingly, they hadn't decided where to store them, or the bleachers – outdoor uncovered bench seats arranged in tiers – for the race the following year). Because Detroit was very much a working town, getting it back to work was an

imperative, and dismantling the barriers had begun shortly after the race ended.

As I walked to the Renaissance Center and saw the crews working on dismantling the barriers I was confident Watson would be there, and everybody else too.

They had all long gone, of course, fled faster than the white middle classes' daily exodus to Detroit's suburbs. Where they had gone I had no idea and nobody could tell me. The girls on the hotel reception were as helpful as they could be given that the whole Grand Prix entourage had simply checked out and decamped.

'Forwarding address for any of them?'

'No, sir!'

Here was an important insight. The Grand Prix entourage, singly and collectively, were almost pathologically restless, which is why Rosberg regarded a day and a half waiting in the Renaissance Center – an opulent place replete with floors of shops and restaurants – as the physical and mental equivalent of a prison sentence. I would come to

know the controlled stampede from any circuit once the race was over, something so intense that, only two or three hours after the chequered flag, the paddock which had been teeming with transporters and equipment and lavish hospitality units would be completely empty, just tarmac and litter blowing in the breeze.

The future was always somewhere else, and these people felt an irresistible compulsion to head off towards it now. The idea of reminiscing about the race, savouring the fresh-minted memories, having wild parties – all that had been discarded a generation ago, lost in the rush to the future.

I'd covered sport for a long time and never confronted anything like this. Who on earth were these people and what drove them – yes, drove them – to behave in the way they did? I'd reported a Grand Prix weekend and not spoken a single word to any driver. Wherever you happened to be at the circuit they were somewhere else. It was all very mysterious, like something very private being enacted in public.

ABOVE *Team-mates Rosberg and Daly come charging up to lap Alboreto.*

Outside the work went on, and by the evening rush hour the main thoroughfares – Jefferson, Larned, Congress, Woodward and the Chrysler Freeway – had normal traffic flowing down them.

The *Daily Express* never did get their interview with John Watson and I never did find out where he went.[2] I do remember one thing, though. I had a very leisurely journey up to Canada, taking in the scenery, and if the Grand Prix people didn't care to be nostalgic about the race, I didn't care to be about the nightly visits to the Hungry Tiger either.

Perhaps, to the Grand Prix people – even the ones who were 'rock apes' – the whole world had come to resemble Hungry Tigers.

There was actual proof, if any more were needed,

of the degree of mysteriousness. Watson's winning speed, 78.2mph, was 'open to question' according to the *Detroit Free Press* because 'varying officials' couldn't decide how long the track was. One party said 2.493 miles, the other 2.59. Nor did anybody seem to know the attendance, although many of the 65,000 seats were unoccupied. Some people thought 45,000, the organisers and police claimed 100,000.

Yes, all very mysterious.

Perhaps I'd find out more in Canada.

Footnote: 1. Riverside Records produced records of interviews with racing drivers and a spoof of Monaco by Peter Ustinov, called The Grand Prix Of Gibraltar. He made the engine noises (he had a cold) and dealt mercilessly with the (pseudonymed) drivers; 2. I did find out where he'd gone, but only when I started researching this book. He went to New York.

OPPOSITE *Harmony at McLaren between Lauda, designer John Barnard and Watson.*

RIGHT *Most happy fella. Victory at the USA Grand Prix. Watson crafts a superb burn from the stern to beat Eddie Cheever's Ligier by 15 seconds.*

Race Result

WINNING SPEED 125.75kmh/78.14mph.

FASTEST LAP 130.78kmh/81.26mph
(Prost 1m 50.43s on lap 45).

LAP LEADERS Prost 1–22 (22);
Rosberg 23–36 (14); Watson 37–62 (26)

* Scheduled for 70 laps but stopped after six because of an accident. Restart scheduled for a further 64 laps but stopped at two hours, with results being an aggregate of six and 56 laps. Lap leaders are given 'on the road'.

RACE

	Driver	Team	Engine	Laps	Time
1	J. Watson	McLaren MP4B	Cosworth V8	62	1h 58m 41.04s
2	E. Cheever	Talbot Ligier JS17B	Matra V12	62	1h 58m 56.76s
3	D. Pironi	Ferrari 126C2	Ferrari V6t	62	1h 59m 09.12s
4	K. Rosberg	Williams FW08	Cosworth V8	62	1h 59m 53.01s
5	D. Daly	Williams FW08	Cosworth V8	62	2h 00m 04.80s
6	J. Laffite	Talbot Ligier JS17B	Matra V12	61	
7	J. Mass	March 821	Cosworth V8	61	
8	M. Surer	Arrows A4	Cosworth V8	61	
9	B. Henton	Tyrrell 011	Cosworth V8	60	
10	R. Arnoux	Renault RE30B	Renault V6t	59	
11	C. Serra	Fittipaldi F8D	Cosworth V8	59	
nc	A. Prost	Renault RE30B	Renault V6t	54	
r	N. Mansell	Lotus 91	Cosworth V8	44	Engine
r	N. Lauda	McLaren MP4B	Cosworth V8	40	Accident
r	M. Alboreto	Tyrrell 011	Cosworth V8	40	Accident
r	B. Giacomelli	Alfa Romeo 182	Alfa V12	30	Accident
r	E. de Angelis	Lotus 91	Cosworth V8	17	Gearbox
r	E. Salazar	ATS D5	Cosworth V8	13	Accident
r	R. Guerrero	Ensign N181	Cosworth V8	6	Accident
r	R. Patrese	Brabham BT49D	Cosworth V8	6	Accident/fire
r	A. de Cesaris	Alfa Romeo 182	Alfa V12	2	Transmission
r	J.-P. Jarier	Osella FA1C	Cosworth V8	2	Ignition
r	M. Winkelhock	ATS D5	Cosworth V8	1	Accident
r	R. Boesel	March 821	Cosworth V8	1	Accident
r	M. Baldi	Arrows A4	Cosworth V8	0	Accident
ns	R. Paletti	Osella FA1C	Cosworth V8		Accident
nq	E. de Villota	March 821	Cosworth V8		
nq	N. Piquet	Brabham BT50	BMW 4t		
nq	J. Lammers	Theodore TY02	Cosworth V8		Accident/injury

nc = did not complete=; nq = did not qualify; ns = did not start; r = retired

CHAMPIONSHIP

	Driver	Points
1	J. Watson	26
2	D. Pironi	20
3	A. Prost	18
4	K. Rosberg	17
5	R. Patrese	13
6	N. Lauda	12
7	M. Alboreto	10
	E. Cheever	10
9	E. de Angelis	7
	N. Mansell	7
11	C. Reutemann	6
	G. Villeneuve	6
13	R. Arnoux	4
	A. de Cesaris	4
15	D. Daly	3
	J.-P. Jarier	3
17	N. Piquet	2
	M. Winkelhock	2
	E. Salazar	2
20	J. Laffite	1
	F. Serra	1

	Team	Points
1	McLaren	38
2	Ferrari	26
	Williams	26
4	Renault	22
5	Brabham	15
6	Lotus	14
7	Talbot Ligier	11
8	Tyrrell	10
9	ATS	4
	Alfa Romeo	4
11	Osella	3
12	Fittipaldi	1

13 JUNE

DEATH ON THE GRID

CANADA, MONTREAL

The Île Notre-Dame could hardly have been drawn in greater contrast to the Motown streets, any more than Detroit could be a greater contrast to Montreal. The Île was verdant, and scenic in places. Ah, so that's what 'keeping it on the island' must have meant, although how that could be applied to Detroit, firmly anchored into continental USA and no island whatsoever, was another mystery.

The Île was decorated by amazing pavilions from EXPO 1976,[1] which loomed from the trees and provided the photographers with unusual backgrounds for racing pictures. The artificial Olympic rowing basin lay directly behind the pits and small boats ferried team personnel to and from the distant paddock. The breeze brushed the surface of the basin, sculpting the water into gentle, restful wave fronts.

Nobody could truly gauge what Gilles Villeneuve meant in Canada, and specifically to the Canadian Grand Prix, because for the last four years he had been there in the Ferrari. His victory in 1978 provoked a compound of hysteria and euphoria, and thereafter the event centred on his presence. The gauge would now be his absence. The fact that the Circuit Île Notre-Dame had been renamed the Circuit Gilles Villeneuve kept his name constantly in play and there had to be edges of sadness to that. A great deal had happened since Zolder on 8 May – Monaco and Detroit – but as the drivers played a 'friendly' football match against the journalists[2] on the Wednesday at Montreal, Villeneuve's death

RIGHT *Horror film. Pironi (left, 28) has stalled, most cars have threaded and dived safely past but young Riccardo Paletti – almost certainly unsighted – is about to strike the Ferrari a blow of terrible savagery.*

Canada
Montreal

RACE DATE June 13th

CIRCUIT LENGTH
4.41km/2.74 miles

NO. OF LAPS 70

RACE DISTANCE
308.70km/191.81 miles

WEATHER Cold, dry

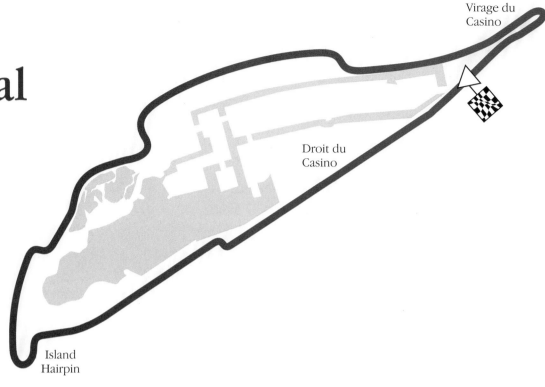

Virage du Casino

Droit du Casino

Island Hairpin

DRIVER'S VIEW

'I liked it. It was fast but as a consequence a circuit where you couldn't use too much downforce because of the speed, especially the top speed. The configuration was different from today: we had two quick esses. One, after the pits, was taken flat, the other in maybe fourth gear. Montreal was also very critical for brakes. You had the very slow hairpin before the pits and that was a bit like Monaco, stop-and-go, stop-and-go and extremely hard on the brakes. You needed special brakes to avoid problems. You can't say this particular circuit was more physical than that circuit because in those days all the races were physical. We didn't have automatic gearboxes and there was no power steering. The circuits were more challenging, for sure. Now with all the chicanes and all the places where they can go off it's a different story.'

—*Riccardo Patrese*

was only just over four weeks past. The local papers ran endless eulogies to him to the point where, as someone remarked, the Grand Prix seemed 'of little actual consequence.'[3] The television channels carried endless tributes.

Pironi had to deal with this because it directly involved him whether he liked it or not, and initially he adopted the tactic of keeping his head down and his mouth shut. Eventually he did give his side of it in sober interviews with local radio stations.

The Grand Prix organisers were concerned enough about the impact of the absence to make entry free on the Friday. There, before the morning untimed session began, sat John Watson by himself on a wall beside the McLaren pit.

I introduced myself and said how well his Detroit victory had been received at home.

'That's nice to know,' he murmured in that softened Ulster accent.

I didn't say more and he didn't say more. No matter. I'd finally spoken to a Formula One driver. True, I hadn't unlocked any of the mysteries of their compulsions for movement, and I hadn't enquired where he'd been since Detroit because that didn't matter any more, but at least I'd looked him in the

eye and found he appeared not just entirely normal but rather polite in an Olde Worlde sort of way. Perhaps they were all like that if only you could find them.

There was, however, a way to find them: set up a proper interview through a team's Press Officer. Mansell was an obvious subject – British newspapers really did want Brits – and the John Player Special Lotus man went by the name of Tony Jardine, young, affable and accommodating, a gifted mimic with a great crease of a smile which stretched full across his face. Since, by chance, I was in the same hotel as Jardine and Mansell he was sure it wouldn't be a problem.

'After Saturday qualifying at the hotel?' he suggested.

'Fine.'

There was a Close Encounter of the Second Kind (a crash being the First, any team's Press Release being the Third) between the Brazilians Serra and Boesel during the morning untimed session. On the track they both laid claim to the same piece. Off the track they had rather less than a meeting of minds. Serra went to Boesel and explained the facts of life, which involved Serra trying to ram his fist

BELOW Rosberg pow-wow in the pits. Charlie-Crichton-Stuart talks, Frank Dernie watches and former driver Innes Ireland (second left), now a journalist, prepares to take notes.

through the visor of Boesel's helmet. Serra turned to leave and Boesel aimed a juicy kick at his posterior, whereupon Serra turned again, fists raised, and weighed in. Six mechanics were needed to drag them apart.

Ah, so they weren't all gentle by nature and polite in an Olde Worlde sort of way...

It rained during the afternoon qualifying session and the weather wasn't warm, itself a cruelty because traditionally the race was at season's end – cold in Canada then – but finally the organisers got a June date when it ought to have been very warm indeed. De Cesaris went quickest followed by Rosberg, who'd felt this was a turbo circuit and slim pickings, if any, for him.

In the dry on Saturday the turbos swallowed the circuit – Pironi, the Renaults, Piquet – leaving no-surrender Watson to pant along sixth and no-surrender Rosberg seventh.

Grandiose terms like International Media Centre were not yet giving ordinary reporters delusions of splendour, and the Press Room was a homely place – as they used to be in most sports – with plain chairs in the interview room and a plain table for the drivers. Pironi appeared, very handsome in a well-bred, well-groomed Parisian way. He sat and said

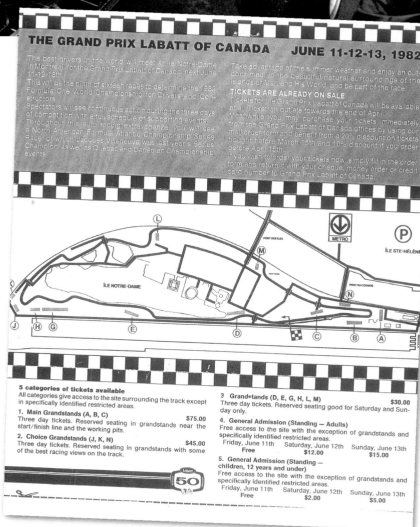

THE GRAND PRIX LABATT OF CANADA   JUNE 11-12-13, 1982

The best drivers in the world will meet at Ile Notre-Dame in Montreal for the Grand Prix Labatt of Canada, next June 11-12-13th.

This will be the ninth of sixteen races to determine the 1982 Formula One World Championship for Drivers and Constructors.

Spectators will see continuous action during the three days of competition with a full schedule of supporting events. Throughout this auto racing extravaganza, you will see a North American Formula Atlantic Championship Series Race, of which Jacques Villeneuve was last year's Series Champion, as well as Quebec and Canadian Championship events.

Take advantage of the summer weather and enjoy an outdoor meal in the beautiful natural surroundings of the Islands of Man and His World, and be part of the race!

TICKETS ARE ALREADY ON SALE

Tickets for the Grand Prix Labatt of Canada will be available at all Ticketron outlets towards the end of April.

Meanwile, you may purchase your tickets immediately from the Grand Prix Labatt of Canada offices by using our mail order form and benefit from a 20% discount on tickets bought before March 15th and 10% discount if you order before April 15th.

If you wish to order your tickets now, simply fill in the order form and return it with your cheque, money order or credit card number to Grand Prix Labatt of Canada.

5 categories of tickets available

All categories give access to the site surrounding the track except in specifically identified restricted areas.

1. Main Grandstands (A, B, C) $75.00
Three day tickets. Reserved seating in grandstands near the start/finish line and the working pits.

2. Choice Grandstands (J, K, N) $45.00
Three day tickets. Reserved seating in grandstands with some of the best racing views on the track.

3. Grandstands (D, E, G, H, L, M) $30.00
Three day tickets. Reserved seating good for Saturday and Sunday only.

4. General Admission (Standing — Adults)
Free access to the site with the exception of grandstands and specifically identified restricted areas.
Friday, June 11th   Saturday, June 12th   Sunday, June 13th
Free $12.00 $15.00

5. General Admission (Standing — children, 12 years and under)
Free access to the site with the exception of grandstands and specifically identified restricted areas.
Friday, June 11th   Saturday, June 12th   Sunday, June 13th
Free $2.00 $5.00

quietly, almost to himself, 'We all know who would have been on pole if he had been here.' It came from a deep place within. Pironi looked down, away from everybody, and tears welled in his eyes.

Cynics are fully entitled to suggest this was theatre, designed so Pironi could prove he was neither cheat nor bastard but a caring, feeling human being. If I'm any judge it was not. This man was very, very close to breaking down completely, as if he'd erected all sorts of barriers since Imola and Zolder, and now a combination of geography and circumstances had destroyed the barriers, leaving him sitting there not so much vulnerable as naked. Frankly, he could barely speak.

The Press Room was very quiet, no chair leg scraping the wooden floor.

And then we all went away, quietly, to wherever we were going.

All unnoticed, young Riccardo Paletti managed to get the Osella onto the second last row of the grid. Enzo Osella, satisfaction pouring from all his pores, said 'He has been brave – a bomb.' You know what Enzo meant.

Montreal was the sort of city which, by its ambience, invited you to relax. It was Paris erected in the New World and several cultures removed from Detroit. The women, slender and dressed in the casual chic way French women do, knew all the arts of swishing their bottoms as they walked, the

restaurants knew all about seducing you with their food, and you didn't hear, as the in-crowd disported themselves in the evenings, the constant wail of police sirens.

That translated into the mood for the Mansell interview and, anyway, it was high time to listen to a Grand Prix driver speaking more than one sentence. We met in a corner of the hotel lobby, comfy chairs, all very relaxed. If the first impression of Pironi had been handsome boy the first impression of Mansell, which never needed subsequent revision, was strong man. I soon learnt about the paradoxes he carried round with him. After the interview I wrote: 'He sits, trim and bouncy, and speaks about coming to terms with dying – and, almost in the next breath, of the two geese he has back home in Warwickshire and the seven eggs they are hatching at this moment. He is very proud of things like that.'

His wife Rosanne was resting upstairs, their first child due in August.

He discussed the toll exacted by each race, how it left a driver bruised and half a stone lighter. He discussed how the G forces from the ground effects were so extreme that, to accommodate them, his neck muscles had had to develop so that the neck was 'a size bigger than it should be. It's muscle-bound now.' He touched his collar and said he didn't wear ties any more because, the neck so large, he couldn't do the collar up. He smiled at that. He

139

STARTING GRID

1		**1** 1:27.50 **D. Pironi**
	2 1:27.89 **R. Arnoux**	
2		**3** 1:28.56 **A. Prost**
	4 1:28.66 **N. Piquet**	
3		**5** 1:28.74 **B. Giacomelli**
	6 1:28.82 **J. Watson**	
4		**7** 1:28.87 **K. Rosberg**
	8 1:28.99 **R. Patrese**	
5		**9** 1:29.18 **A. de Cesaris**
	10 1:29.22 **E. de Angelis**	
6		**11** 1:29.54 **N. Lauda**
	12 1:29.59 **E. Cheever**	
7		**13** 1:29.88 **D. Daly**
	14 1:30.04 **N. Mansell**	
8		**15** 1:30.14 **M. Alboreto**
	16 1:30.51 **M. Surer**	
9		**17** 1:30.59 **M. Baldi**
	18 1:30.71 **J.-P. Jarier**	
10		**19** 1:30.94 **J. Laffite**
	20 1:31.23 **R. Guerrero**	
11		**21** 1:31.75 **R. Boesel**
	22 1:31.86 **J. Mass**	
12		**23** 1:31.90 **R. Paletti**
	24 1:32.20 **E. Salazar**	
13		**25** 1:32.20 **G. Lees**
	26 1:32.32 **B. Henton**	

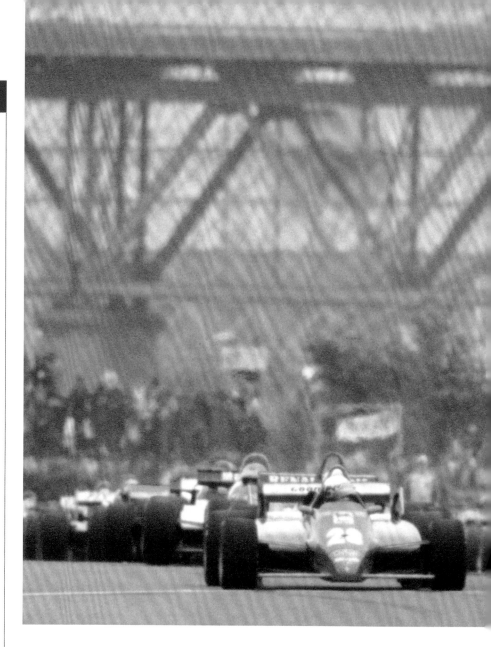

ABOVE *The deadly time as the clock moves to 4.15 and in an instant the cars will be unleashed.*

had a dry sense of humour, more Yorkshire than Warwickshire you'd have thought.

He discussed driving a racing car in the wet. 'You can't see anything. That's eerie, that's really eerie.' He stressed that turbo engines were what you had to have, full stop. He concluded: 'I know I can win the World Championship. The big question is when. I'm a practical man. Listen. I know I'm good enough to win it.' One day he'd back that statement by doing it, but that one day would have seemed impossibly far away as we sat with the hum of the Montreal traffic filtering in from the road outside. In August, Rosanne would give birth to a daughter, Chloe, and she'd be ten when he did do it.

Mansell was easy to talk to, quite open in a disarming way, and spoke well. I thought: if they're all like this I won't have any problems.

I would have, and they'd be with him, but that's another story.

A former *Express* man, Malcolm Folley, introduced me to one Eoin Young in the bar just round the

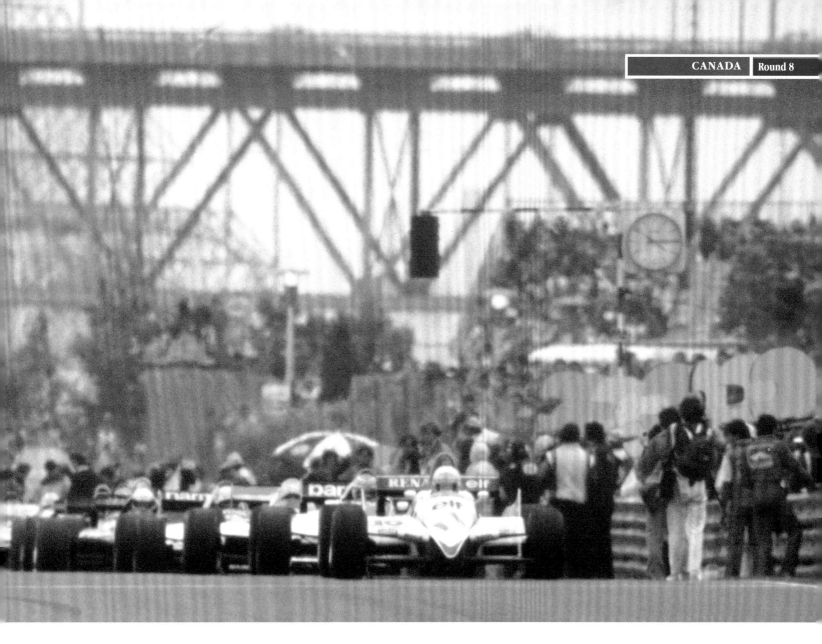

corner from where the interview had taken place, and somehow we took an instant dislike to each other. Young can be brusque, has a quiver-full of put-down lines and had spent his whole adult life in motor racing, at this time as a columnist among much else. Word filtered back to me that he thought I was an upstart which, of course, in motor racing terms I was – although I had been a professional journalist since 1962. It couldn't have mattered less because, after Montreal, we'd never meet again anyway.

That evening Riccardo Paletti and his mother Gianna had dinner. She'd write in a tribute to Riccardo[4] that 'you did not know and I could not have foreseen that they were the last minutes where you could have smiled to me, spoken to me, cried, touched me.' She'd remember having a long wait for the meal but 'we were happy'.

He told her: 'I know that you are more relaxed when I do not qualify but I know that you want my happiness.'

She replied: 'Yes dear, I really wanted your happiness,' and she'd add she wanted it so much that it overruled everything else. He sensed how worried she was and tried to calm her.

Sunday dawned cloudy and overcast. In the morning session Piquet and Patrese went quickest and everybody settled to wait. Accommodating television schedules, the race was not due to start until 4.15. Rain hung in the air but never came – and neither did the trains to the Île's metro station, which ordinarily served as a wonderful people-mover to and from the Grand Prix. A strike crippled it.

At some unrecorded moment as the clocks ticked towards the race, Paletti's mother made her way towards the tower where the hospitality suites were. It overlooked the grid. Paletti ran towards her and she'd remember 'You are smiling, beautiful, happy. Your face is shining because, inside, you have the joy of being on the starting-grid – of having qualified a wheel-barrow.' He gripped her arm strongly and said he'd pulled a joke on someone. It would make them both smile when they got back to Milan. Their eyes met and she sensed he was telling her, as he always told her, don't be afraid. 'Bye, mamma.'

From the hospitality suite she watched him emerge from the drivers' briefing and he still seemed happy. She saw him walking towards the Osella chatting with Boesel.

There was a long wait for the red light to blink on, the longest, Mansell would say, that he had known in racing.

Paletti's mother remembered it as the slowness.

Professor Watkins waited behind the right-hand column in one chase car with his usual driver at the Canadian Grand Prix, Mario Valli. Another chase car waited behind the other column. Both had garish neon lights on their roofs and these pulsed on and off, on and off – bright yellow on the Watkins car, blood red on the other. They'd follow the grid and get to an accident faster.

The Formula One car – a nervy, highly-strung creature, each component taut, each integral part loaded with torque – is designed to be stationary for only very brief periods or alarming processes start within it. Pironi's Ferrari began to creep. He pushed the foot brake and stopped it. Still he waited. The Ferrari crept again, he braked again and that cut the revs. The engine died and, in the traditional gesture to warn all those behind, he raised his arm: I've stalled, miss me.

Paletti's mother remembered seeing that.

It was an instant of very great peril and everything afterwards happened at ferocious, ever rising speed.

Paletti's mother remembered shouting 'Riccardo.'

The cars were getting from 0 to 100mph in four seconds. Each row of the grid was separated by eight metres, giving 104 metres (113 yards) from Pironi at the front to Lees at the back. Under that ferocity of acceleration, 104 metres is nothing at all.

The red light blinked to green and all the cars accelerated as hard as they could. The sheer power unleashed in that instant can make concrete tremble. Arnoux accelerated away and 'I didn't see Pironi stall, I didn't see anything.'

Prost, directly behind Pironi, couldn't help seeing and twisted the Renault left to go round the Ferrari. That alerted cars behind and they went left too in a great, almost frantic, ripple of motion.

Watson, from the third row of the grid, was 'long gone' before anything happened.

Rosberg 'only just managed to get past.'[5]

Derek Daly had Mansell 'on the same row as me but on the left-hand side and I was in front of him in the stagger. Before I saw Pironi I could see cars were moving in an unusual way – couldn't work out what it was. Suddenly I see Pironi had stopped and I'm probably doing 100 miles an hour at this

stage, maybe more. Mansell was beside me. I saw what was going to happen, and in an instinctive moment I thought: the only thing I can do here is yank hard to the left to miss Pironi – I hope Mansell sees me. I believe Mansell saw what I was confronted with and understood my thought pattern because the very instant I turned left he turned left with me. I avoided Pironi, Mansell avoided me in perfect, synchronised steering movements – because I was sure my crash was going to happen with Mansell. It was pure, instinctive reaction by two people seeing a similar thing, realising the danger level and understanding how to save themselves.'

Neither man was able to lift off the accelerator so it was done flat out. Mansell would describe this as subliminal: you have no time to think, only act, and it is governed entirely by self-preservation.[6]

Boesel couldn't avoid the Ferrari and his March struck its left rear wheel. The March was pitched away and Lees struck it helplessly. Behind Boesel, Paletti was coming: bespectacled Paletti, inexperienced Paletti, ambitious Paletti determined to seize his moment, prove his great truth as a Grand Prix driver. He had the Osella up to 120 miles an hour and at 10,200 revs. He must have been unsighted by Boesel's March because Boesel hadn't been able to swerve and reveal to him, even for a millisecond, that the Ferrari was there.

'Paletti? That could have been me,' Henton says. 'We both qualified quite low on the grid and I was on the left, Paletti was next to me but one row ahead. They dropped the flag and I remember to this day that because I am left-handed it saved my life. Pironi had stalled at the front and all of a sudden there were cars going everywhere – we'd all dropped our clutches and were flat out. I just whipped to the left. Paletti hit the back of Pironi, straight in, trapped his feet. I saw him hit out of the corner of my eye as I was going past. He would have been going quite quick. Construction wasn't the same as today. It was that sandwich aluminium that they used and it just collapsed very easily on impact.'

The Osella struck the Ferrari so hard that it pitched it into the air and flung it 40 yards across the track in a moment of savage, shocking violence. The Watkins chase car drove between the Osella and the Ferrari – Watkins saw Pironi was not only moving but undoing his seat belts to get out.

The other chase car stopped behind the Osella. It had taken nine seconds to get there.

The Watkins car stopped in front of the Osella. It had taken 16 seconds to get there and by then Pironi, with the movements of a man demented, had sprinted to the Osella and began tearing at the wreckage of the car to get to Paletti and help him.

Paletti sat trapped, the steering wheel rammed against his chest, his legs broken. He was, mercifully,

OPPOSITE *The horror film in three frames. Paletti hammers Pironi's Ferrari across the track. Then both cars are stationary as the rescue vehicles accelerate towards them.*

FAN'S EYE VIEW

'My father worked for the local VW-Audi dealer in my home town of Danbury, Connecticut. You could say I was in or around the car business from about the age of two. Being in a VW family, and having seen the film Le Mans at the age of eight, I naturally became interested in both Porsche and Ferrari. My Italian heritage favors the Ferrari side.

'In my teens I discovered Formula One, and around 1980 really started following it actively, which was difficult because TV coverage in the US was sporadic, at best. No surprise that Gilles Villeneuve became my hero.

'The racing was really great (passing for the lead on track, wow!) I talked my father into taking my brother and I on the trip to Montreal. I was set to graduate from High School so it was a kind of graduation present.

'Tragically, we lost our Gilles the month before. I'll never forget that moment when the report came on during ABC's Wide World of Sports on the Saturday of Gilles' accident. It was a devastating blow. At that time, driver fatalities were still all too common but Gilles was seemingly invincible.

'Still, we had already bought our tickets and I was determined to see Formula One cars for the first time so off we went to Montreal. It was a lot of fun. The shriek of the Cosworth V8, Matra V12, Ferrari and Renault Turbo V6s, etc, was worth the price of admission. We were seated in the grandstand at what used to be the Turn 1 and 2 esses just beyond the old starting grid. The grey and cold weather seemed appropriate given the loss of Villeneuve.

'We weren't sure what happened in the Paletti accident and didn't find out about the outcome until the next day. The restart took a long time to organise. I understand now that it took a very long time to get poor Riccardo out.'

JAY GILLOTTI
MERCER ISLAND, WASHINGTON

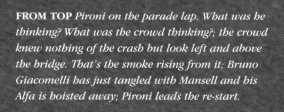

FROM TOP *Pironi on the parade lap. What was he thinking? What was the crowd thinking?; the crowd knew nothing of the crash but look left and above the bridge. That's the smoke rising from it; Bruno Giacomelli has just tangled with Mansell and his Alfa is hoisted away; Pironi leads the re-start.*

unconscious. Watkins ran, stooped and opened Paletti's visor. He got an airway into his mouth and lifted his eyelids but the pupils were dilated. Watkins sensed liquid running.[7] Suddenly the 40 gallons of fuel in the Osella burst into flames. That was 38 seconds after impact. The fire – hellish molten yellow and red – became a funeral pyre, Paletti lost forever within it.

Pironi saw a firefighter pointing his extinguisher in the wrong place and, realising he had no time to grapple it off him, seized the fire fighter and pointed him. The first extinguisher – this one? – was doing its work in 1.8 seconds. The fire seemed to be out but then, in a further moment of horror, it started again, licking like the flames of hell from under the Osella. The petrol must have seeped everywhere.

Time is a very strange thing. The fire was completely out in between 50 and 70 seconds, but it felt like forever. Lauda said: 'What disturbed me the most was that it took so long for the fire to be put out. The fire extinguishers they were using did nothing.'

That was a harsh judgement and what Lauda surely meant was that they did nothing instantly.

Paletti's mother remembered it was daylight but she had only darkness. She thought of how many millions of people must have died in this second, how many millions of mothers embraced their babies and all she had was nothing.

Watson, like almost all the other drivers 'didn't know about it at all until we came round at the end of the first lap.'

Watkins and team owner John McDonald wrenched the steering column and steering wheel from Paletti's chest. His crash helmet was taken off. The medical team took 28 minutes to get him from the wreck, and that felt like a lot longer than forever. It was so long that Murray Walker, watching from the BBC studio in London, would never forget it when, across the coming years, other details of the tragedy had softened from memory.

Paletti was put on a helicopter. It took 98 seconds to reach hospital, but he was beyond medical help and had been since the Osella struck the Ferrari. He died at 5.45 on the operating table.

The Île Notre-Dame in late afternoon: the sky was grey like a shroud and darkening, a bitter wind had come up and even as the workforce cleared the wreckage away, so that the race could eventually be restarted, the circuit seemed spiritually emptied.

ABOVE *And it seemed the horror film would never end. Firefighters confront a molten mass of flames from underneath Paletti's Osella.*

Any journalist working for a daily newspaper
has to respond instantly to an event like this and
the days of mobile phones and laptop computers
were a whole technological age away, unimaginable
as well as unanticipated. To speak to the *Daily
Express* Sportsdesk you had to place a collect call
with a Canadian operator who then rang the paper's
number in London and waited for the switchboard
to answer. When they did, the Canadian operator
gave your name, where you were calling from and
would the newspaper accept the charge? The man
on the switchboard said 'Yes' and you were through,
asking him to connect you to the Sportsdesk so
that you could say: a driver's just been killed in an
horrific crash.

There was no live television coverage on the BBC
(you got edited highlights late at night), and who
knew which Press agencies were present to send a
newsflash round the world?

The Sportsdesk at the *Express* may well have
been blissfully unaware of any of the events on
the Île Notre-Dame. My job was firstly to tell them,
secondly to write about it. The Canadian operators
had a rule (same in America) that they would
only allow a number to ring for a short time and
then they'd say 'Sorry, no answer' and disconnect.
Newspaper switchboards were notably tardy,

especially if a lot of calls came in at the same time,
and I kept getting disconnected before anyone in
London would answer. At one point I placed three
calls simultaneously on different phones in the Press
Room in the hope one would make it.

They never did and eventually I got through to
the Manchester office.

Of course, you don't care about the
communications problems of 1982, but in retrospect
they assumed an importance to me, which is why
I've mentioned them. Contemplating the full horror,
discussing it endlessly as everyone does, wringing
meanings out of it, gathering drivers' reactions – I
didn't do any of that under the imperative of getting
the call through.

I was thinking more about telling people Paletti
had died than thinking of Paletti's death.

I am ashamed to write these words for many
reasons, not least because they are true. In
mitigation I was there to do my job and nothing else,
and that was what I was doing. Professionally I was in
no position to recoil any more than, say, the rescue
workers had been, however much more important
their work was than mine.

If I had been drawn into the aftermath instead,
I am sure I would have decided that I never
wanted to see this literally infernal thing ever again.

BELOW *Young men in a hurry: Daly leads Alboreto but neither finished.*

Sportswriters do not become sportswriters to describe young men being burnt to death. On the contrary, sport is – or ought to be – a celebration of being alive. In nearly 20 years of it I'd been at only one event where somebody died – the 24-hour race Le Mans in 1976 when a restaurant owner from Strasbourg crashed fatally; but that happened in the middle of the night and on the far side of the circuit. Before the era of TV cameras monitoring the whole circuit, it might as well have happened in another universe, and in a sense had. After all, I'd been back at my hotel and sound asleep anyway.

Paletti was utterly different. Paletti was a sequence of images which wouldn't be going away and I see them still, particularly Pironi's sprint to try and help, particularly that awful fire reigniting under the car and, strangely, the burnished rubber marks in a criss-cross over the track left by many tyres.

In all the claustrophobic circumstances closing in on Pironi, from Imola to Zolder to here, it is impossible to imagine his anguish when facing the restart. Professor Watkins sought him out because drivers have to be fit, physically and mentally, to race, and if Watkins judged they weren't they didn't. He found Pironi very uptight and still shocked, and advised him to take it easy.[8]

Evidently Pironi hesitated before making the decision and then reacted like a racer when he had

made it. He brought the cars round to the grid again in gathering gloom – it was now 6.15 – and this time they moved cleanly away, Pironi holding the lead from Arnoux, Prost running third.

On the second lap Giacomelli, who had an engine problem, intended to pit. Daly and Mansell were behind as they reached the hairpin before the pits. Daly got by and Mansell didn't see Giacomelli raise an arm signifying I am pitting for the most logical of reasons: Giacomelli did not, as it seems, raise his arm. They crashed. Giacomelli kicked his car as he walked away from it but Mansell remained in the cockpit for some time, his left arm painful. When he got out a marshal gripped him by that arm and

Le Grand Prix a-t-il encore sa raison d'être?

par Richard Milo

Riccardo Paletti est mort sous les yeux de sa mère, Gina. Et Séville-Villeneuve, le père de Gilles, a remis le trophée Gilles-Villeneuve au vainqueur de l'épreuve, le Brésilien Nelson Piquet.

Comme quoi la mort a mauvais goût. Il était déjà déplacé que le père de Gilles remette au stade l'honneur de son fils sur la tribune d'honneur. Mais après la mort de Paletti, après le spectacle d'horreur auquel a eu droit le monde entier, fallait-il que Séville-Villeneuve fasse obligatoirement la présentation, cinq semaines après la mort de son fils?

Riccardo Paletti

Riccardo Paletti meurt à son premier départ

Il aurait eu 24 ans, mardi...

Nelson Piquet remporte le Grand Prix du Canada, sur Brabham turbo

LEFT *A world in headlines, and a question from Quebec: has Grand Prix racing lost its right to live?*

it hurt so much Mansell aimed a swipe at him with the other.

Pironi, in the spare car of course, fell back and once Piquet had dealt with Arnoux on lap 9 he was not to be caught. Patrese worked up to second place by half distance and stayed there while Watson lurked like a predator in fifth: on lap 67 of the 70 Cheever ran out of fuel (and kicked his car), Watson fourth. On lap 69 de Cesaris ran out of fuel (and cried, even though he'd be classified sixth). When Piquet and Patrese came onto the podium Watson joined them. He'd been hoping for a point or two and expressed amazement that he was there. What did Napoleon say about generals and luck?

Watson remembers Canada as a 'hard race.' It was that, all right.

De Cesaris remembers Canada as bringing at least one advance in safety. 'After Paletti they changed the starting procedure so that if a car stalls on the grid they couldn't give the start.'

Watson 30, Pironi 20, Patrese 19, Prost 18, Rosberg 17, Lauda 12.

Because of the five-hour time gap and the delays, I filed my story the following day and it appeared under the headline: DEATH IN THE AFTERNOON AND A WREATH AT DUSK. It seemed to represent perfectly all the reasons for getting back to writing about the living and forget all about the bizarre rituals which constituted a Grand Prix weekend, the deadly sting lurking within them, and the people who spoke their incestuous patois like an impenetrable code.

The Falklands war was ending and British troops moved towards the capital, Port Stanley. On the British Airways flight back, as the plane slogged out over the Atlantic, the intercom crackled. 'Captain here. Spot of good news. White flag over Stanley.' The plane erupted, people standing and cheering. An American next to me asked plaintively 'What did that guy say?'

'Never mind. Family business.'

The Canadian Grand Prix seemed such a small thing compared to that, and was: one dead, not many, many dead.

At the baggage carousels at Heathrow Eoin Young, who'd been on a different flight, waited for his suitcase. He had his back to me and I thought: well at least I'll never see you again. This upstart is upping and starting back in his real career as of this moment.

I didn't see him again for – oh, a couple of weeks.

Arietto Paletti and a colleague flew from Milan to Montreal and were met there by a senior Osella executive and one of the team's technicians, an old friend. The friend would remember it was 'just them, from all the racing world'. They confirmed Riccardo was dead.

They all went straight to the hospital, and seeing his son had such an impact on Arietto that he had difficulty standing up.

Riccardo looked serene.

Footnote: 1. The 1967 International and Universal Exposition (EXPO) was a world fair held at Montreal as part of the country's centennial celebrations; 2. The drivers won 3–2 despite facing 'the Latin elite of the journalists, led by a strong pack of Italians and South Americans' (Grand Prix International). Slender, wan young Italian Riccardo Paletti played for the drivers but wasn't mentioned in the report. Patrese, however, starred; 3. Grand Prix International; 4. Riccardo Paletti, a family tribute privately printed; 5. Keke: An Autobiography, Keke Rosberg and Keith Botsford, Stanley Paul, London, 1985; 6. My Autobiography, Nigel Mansell, CollinsWillow, London, 1995; 7. Life At The Limit; 8. Ibid.

OPPOSITE *Piquet won and here Patrese is on his way to giving Brabham a double by finishing second.*

BELOW *Didier Pironi, the man carrying many burdens into and through the Canadian Grand Prix. He'd finish ninth.*

Race Result

WINNING SPEED 173.65kmh/107.90mph

FASTEST LAP 179.74kmh/111.69mph
(Pironi 1m 28.32s on lap 66)

LAP LEADERS Pironi 1 (1);
Arnoux 2–8 (7); Piquet 9–70 (62)

RACE

	Driver	Team	Engine	Laps	Time
1	N. Piquet	Brabham BT50	BMW 4t	70	1h 46m 39.57s
2	R. Patrese	Brabham BT49D	Cosworth V8	70	1h 46m 53.37s
3	J. Watson	McLaren MP4B	Cosworth V8	70	1h 47m 41.41s
4	E. de Angelis	Lotus 91	Cosworth V8	69	
5	M. Surer	Arrows A4	Cosworth V8	69	
6r	A. de Cesaris	Alfa Romeo 182	Alfa Rom V12	68	Out of fuel
7r	D. Daly	Williams FW08	Cosworth V8	68	Out of fuel
8	M. Baldi	Arrows A4	Cosworth V8	68	
9	D. Pironi	Ferrari 126C2	Ferrari V6t	67	
10r	E. Cheever	Talbot Ligier JS17B	Matra V12	66	Out of fuel
11	J. Mass	March 821	Cosworth V8	66	
nc	B. Henton	Tyrrell 011	Cosworth V8	59	
r	K. Rosberg	Williams FW08	Cosworth V8	52	Gearbox
r	R. Boesel	March 821	Cosworth V8	47	Engine
r	M. Alboreto	Tyrrell 011	Cosworth V8	41	Gearbox/fuel pressure
r	A. Prost	Renault RE30B	Renault V6t	30	Engine
r	R. Arnoux	Renault RE30B	Renault V6t	28	Spin
r	E. Salazar	ATS D5	Cosworth V8	20	Transmission
r	N. Lauda	McLaren MP4B	Cosworth V8	17	Clutch
r	J. Laffite	Talbot Ligier JS17B	Matra V12	8	Handling
r	R. Guerrero	Ensign N181	Cosworth V8	2	Clutch
r	B. Giacomelli	Alfa Romeo 182	Alfa Rom V12	1	Accident
r	N. Mansell	Lotus 91	Cosworth V8	1	Accident/injury
r	G. Lees	Theodore TY02	Cosworth V8	0	Accident*
r	J.-P. Jarier	Osella FA1C	Cosworth V8	0	Withdrawn*
r	R. Paletti	Osella FA1C	Cosworth V8	0	Fatal accident
nq	M. Winkelhock	ATS D5	Cosworth V8		
nq	E. de Villota	March 821	Cosworth V8		
nq	C. Serra	Fittipaldi F8D	Cosworth V8		

nc = running, not classified; nq = did not qualify; r = retired *Retired after first start

CHAMPIONSHIP

	Driver	Points
1	J. Watson	30
2	D. Pironi	20
3	R. Patrese	19
4	A. Prost	18
5	K. Rosberg	17
6	N. Lauda	12
7	N. Piquet	11
8	M. Alboreto	10
	E. Cheever	10
	E. de Angelis	10
11	N. Mansell	7
12	C. Reutemann	6
	G. Villeneuve	6
14	A. de Cesaris	5
15	R. Arnoux	4
16	J.-P. Jarier	3
	D. Daly	3
18	M. Winkelhock	2
	E. Salazar	2
	M. Surer	2
21	J. Laffite	1
	F. Serra	1

	Team	Points
1	McLaren	42
2	Brabham	30
3	Ferrari	26
	Williams	26
5	Renault	22
6	Lotus	17
7	Talbot Ligier	11
8	Tyrrell	10
9	Alfa Romeo	5
10	ATS	4
11	Osella	3
12	Arrows	2
13	Fittipaldi	1

REMEMBERING RICCARDO

———— A GRID TOO DEADLY ————

'He had just come to Formula One and we didn't know him much,' Patrese says. 'I think I only exchanged a few words with him. Of course he seemed a nice guy and he was trying to make his way in Formula One – then this tragedy, this bad luck, but in those days the cars were not really very safe, especially in the front. If an accident like that happened today maybe it would not be so big.'

It's no consolation. It never is.

The man they did not know much about was born in Milan on 15 June 1958 so his 24th birthday would have been on the Tuesday after Montreal.

One of his schoolteachers, Padre Cristina, remembers him as 'always smiling and in love with the mountains, in love with skiing. He had plenty of trophies for that. He had enthusiasm, courage, loyalty and generosity. He was a competitor – he also loved karate.'[1]

A fitness trainer, Franco Franchi, confirms that. Paletti, he says, was 'very shy. He never wanted to create problems, he watched everything closely during the karate lessons and then repeated all the movements.'

The motor racing career began at Monza in 1976 in obscure circumstances. Father Arietto and Riccardo were there and, as a joke, one of them challenged the other to a driving test. Riccardo, who hadn't a licence yet, won...

Arietto had a building company so Riccardo was born into money but he set out to learn the business. A partner in the company, Claudio Lossa, says Riccardo was 'professional and very serious on the job'. He was learning, examining buildings and taking pictures of them. 'He knew how to judge a building. He said "If the Formula 1 world doesn't give me what I aspire to, I will put all my energies into my father's company."'

In 1978 he competed in the Italian Super Ford championship driving an Osella, and a journalist, Guido Schittone, became a companion.

They travelled together in a camper – Schittone remembers passing through the province of Liguria one starlit night to a race, the world so full of promise. Paletti, driving the camper, seemed a young 19, slim but wearing big glasses. He looked just like any Italian's image of an Oxford University student. He was very rich.

They'd take evening meals together, talk. Once Paletti said to him 'I haven't a lot of friends and I find establishing a rapport with people of my own age particularly difficult. Doing sport is a way to be with other people, get closer to them. I've competed on the ski slopes, I've taken part in measured kilometre events on skis and then I came to car racing. It is a strange world but when I am inside the cockpit everything seems beautiful to me. And I feel happy.'

Schittone remembers Paletto's father Arietto staying in his green Porsche during their races reading a book and murmuring 'I am suffering ... I am suffering.'

Paletti did nine Super Ford races (two second places) and finished third overall. He did one round of the Italian Formula 3 in a Ralt Toyota and moved fully into that championship in 1979 using a March car with the Toyota engine. It was a story of retirements and lowly finishes (highest two fifth places). He was 12th overall.

He stayed in Italian Formula 3 in 1980 but that only brought more retirements and lowly finishes.

'In 1980,' Mike Earle of the Onyx team says, 'we were running Johnny Cecotto in the Formula 2 car and we were on M and H tyres. He wanted to get into Pirelli so he moved on, so we had an empty seat. Robin Herd [of March] rang and said he had a young Italian kid called Riccardo Paletti who wanted to drive. He'd been doing Formula 3. I had never heard of him. I said "Yes, sure, send him down."

'A very frail looking, pale young man walked in, bespectacled, with a mop of black curly hair. To my horror he spoke zero English, which was slightly

ABOVE *Paletti managed
to get the Osella onto
the Canadian grid and
prepared to confront
the consequences of the
destiny he had chosen:
to be a Grand Prix
racing driver.*

more than my Italian. We managed to nail a few bits
and pieces together and ran him in some rounds
at the end of 1980. His reputation then was that he
managed to do two races a year when he didn't crash.

'Anyway, he did a couple of rounds and he crashed
and then we took him to Monza, by which time his
English was improving at an amazing rate, mostly the
wrong words. We used to engineer him by having a
sheet of paper and on it was written the Italian and
next to it the English. He'd point to what he wanted
and we'd point out what he was doing! So we went to
Monza and he qualified pretty well up, fourth, and he
ran second for a long time.'

Paletti had a long battle with an experienced Italian
driver, Alberto Colombo in a Toleman, and 'just got
done in the last lap'. Warwick won, Colombo second,
Paletti third.

'He was sponsored by Pioneer, the hi-fi people,
and we had a long discussion with them. By
November of that year they had decided they were
going to put a full budget up for him to do Formula 2
the following year. We did a deal with March for a car
for him, got it early, did a lot of testing with him,
hell of a lot of testing, and he got better and better
and better.

'We went to Thruxton with the car and he ran well,
we went to Hockenheim and he led that until three
laps from the end when his battery said enough. He
went right through the year like that and at one stage
he was well up the championship, second or third.
He was obviously much, much better than people
thought he was.

'We got to know him well. He was a lovely, lovely
man, really seriously nice, a super guy. Sensitive,
educated. He could play the piano. We got to know
his family quite well, too. When he was over he
used to stay at my house and he became a very
good friend.

'At the end of that year he wanted to go Formula
One and we weren't ready to do that. We didn't have
a car. I was against it and I said to his father "Better
to do another year of Formula 2, win it and then go
Formula One." He was young, only 22 even by then.'

Pioneer wanted to finance the Formula One
season. Paletti discussed the choice with his family: he
could stay in Formula 2 without any financial worries
and be in a kind of comfort zone or risk Formula
One without money – the sponsorship presumably
paid only for the drive. He reasoned that he'd made
a sacrifice by spending a long time in England, so far
away from Italy's warmth, to further his career. He'd
dreamed of Formula One and getting there would
reward his sacrifices. Moreover you might only get
one chance at Formula One. With the full support of
the family he decided to take it.

'Anyway,' Earle says, 'he did a deal with Osella and

off he went. It was a disaster: the car wasn't very good and he was struggling at the back of the grid.

'In the meantime John McDonald had come to see us and he'd done a deal with [Spaniard] Emilio de Villota to run him in a March Formula One car and a few weeks after he'd done that deal Rothmans came along wanting him to run their outfit. He asked if we'd run di Villota as a sort of satellite team. We said "Fine, OK, no problem at all." We went to the races and he never qualified, never looked like qualifying...'

...specifically, Belgium, Monaco, Detroit, Canada.

Nor was Paletti faring much better with Osella: dnq South Africa, dnpq Brazil, dnq Long Beach; did get in at Imola where only 14 started, covered seven laps and the rear suspension failed; dnpq Belgium, dnpq Monaco, did qualify for Detroit but had an accident at the start.

'He had decided that he was going to pack it up, and roughly at that point – the weekend of Montreal – we'd had a conversation with him. We had also spoken to his father. They were going to leave the Osella thing, come back to us and work with the March. Riccardo said "What's happening?" I explained the Emilio situation and he said "Well, why don't I come and drive for you? I know you all, we get on well and we've worked well together." I said "Yes, great, great." We just about had everything arranged.

'We [March and Villota] hadn't qualified at Montreal so I went back to the hotel, I didn't even go to the circuit on race day. I'd watch it on TV. I saw the accident. He was at the back of the grid and it's a bit like driving down a motorway in fog – all the tyre smoke's hanging about – and the trouble was for someone coming from a hundred yards back he'd generated quite a lot of speed. Right at the last minute there's cars going right and left out of this cloud of smoke and then there's a car in front of you. I dashed down to the circuit, by which time he was away. I went to the hospital to look after his mum. She was distraught.'

John Watson felt a particular sadness. 'One of the things that made it slightly more personal to me was that Paletti had driven for Mike Earle, who was a great friend, at Obyx in Formula 2. I knew Riccardo because of that.

'The Paletti family became very friendly with Mike. Riccardo was a young guy from a wealthy family who was indulging his aspiration to be a racing driver. He was out of his depth at this point in his career, no question. He wouldn't have been as savvy as others maybe even of the same age. He was just a very nice, sweet guy. He put his helmet on and when you do that you still have to keep your peripheral vision open. By peripheral vision I mean nous and sense and reading that things are happening. I don't

think that he had that. He went flat out, straight in, and probably he'd didn't see Pironi's car until the millisecond before he hit the back of it.'

Earle agrees. 'I do believe Wattie's theory has some relevance. Whilst Riccardo'd been around a lot in Formula 2 it was only his second Formula One start and he was right from the back. It wasn't even a glancing hit, it was full in. Unfortunately the deformation round the front of the car meant he was trapped and in the end they pulled him out with a strop – kind of yanked him out – because his injuries were such that if they'd left him there he was going to die anyway.'

There was a consensus among the people who met, knew and worked with Riccardo Paletti: he was a gentleman and not through his education or affluent situation. It was his character. In adversity he never blamed others, only himself.

In the tribute book which the family produced after Montreal, Arietto wrote these beautiful words: 'Your mother and I knew that motor racing was your way in life and we could not stop you from following it. Goodbye Riccardo, our beloved and beautiful child, no one can forget you for what you have suffered.'

And we haven't.

Footnote: 1. The background here is from Arietto Paletti's tribute book to his son, and used with his kind permission.

BELOW *Happy families – as seen in the privately printed tribute book* Riccardo Paletti *and used by kind permission of Arietto Paletti.*

THE TIGHTENING

HOLLAND, ZANDVOORT

A Saturday race to avoid clashing on television with the Wimbledon final on the Sunday, and that tells you where the tennis correspondent of the *Daily Express* would have to be: London SW19, watching Jimmy Connors beat John McEnroe 3-6, 6-3, 6-7 7-6, 6-4, and definitely not among the sand dunes facing the North Sea a pleasant train ride from Amsterdam. Oh well, one more race wouldn't hurt.

Mansell hadn't recovered from his Montreal crash and Lotus selected Roberto Moreno, who'd arrived in England from Brazil only three years before, knowing no English at all and having driven nothing more than a kart.

Now in 1982 he'd done a little testing with Lotus but four problems confronted him: a race weekend is a compound of many pressures which are absent from empty circuits and repetitive test days; Zandvoort was widely considered a place for turbos, which of course he did not have; the grid was restricted to 26 drivers but 30 entered, so he had to qualify; and he had hardly driven the current Lotus, the 91, before.

Ferrari reached for Patrick Tambay to partner Pironi and here was another introduction to Grand Prix racing's habits and habitats. Far from entering a lengthy period of mourning for Villeneuve, speculation had linked a whole variety of drivers to the drive – eight alone in one magazine, excluding Tambay.

He'd driven Formula One since 1977, but since the Kyalami drivers' strike had been in the

RIGHT *Derek Warwick leads Bruno Giacomelli (Alfa Romeo) on lap 8. Two laps later he pitted and three laps after that set fastest lap.*

Holland
Zandvoort

RACE DATE July 3rd

CIRCUIT LENGTH 4.25km/2.64 miles

NO. OF LAPS 72

RACE DISTANCE 306.14km/190.22 miles

WEATHER Warm, dry

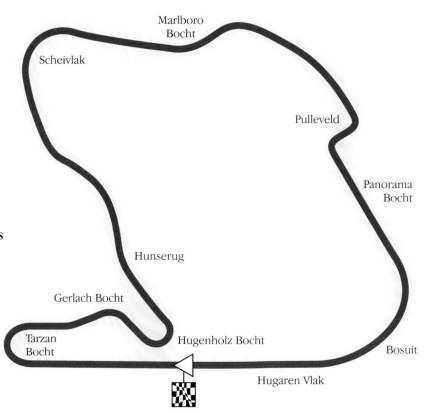

Marlboro
Bocht

Scheivlak

Pulleveld

Panorama
Bocht

Hunserug

Gerlach Bocht

Tarzan
Bocht

Hugenholz Bocht

Bosuit

Hugaren Vlak

DRIVER'S VIEW

'I loved the venue. I thought having a Dutch Grand Prix was magnificent because the area was great, they really loved their motor racing and you have people from a lot of European countries come to watch the race. You were on the beach front and the circuit was (a) demanding and (b) very, very fast. That long straight going in to Tarzan was pretty phenomenal.

'The car was quite good and quite dangerous, wasn't very strong – it flexed a lot. That wasn't necessarily significant at Tarzan but it became so in the quick corners out the back. You just knew if you got it wrong you were going to hurt yourself. I've looked back and thought of the amount of times I climbed into that Toleman, especially in '81 and '82, and thought: if I have an accident in this car I'm going to hurt myself. But you never ever eased off'.

—— *Derek Warwick*

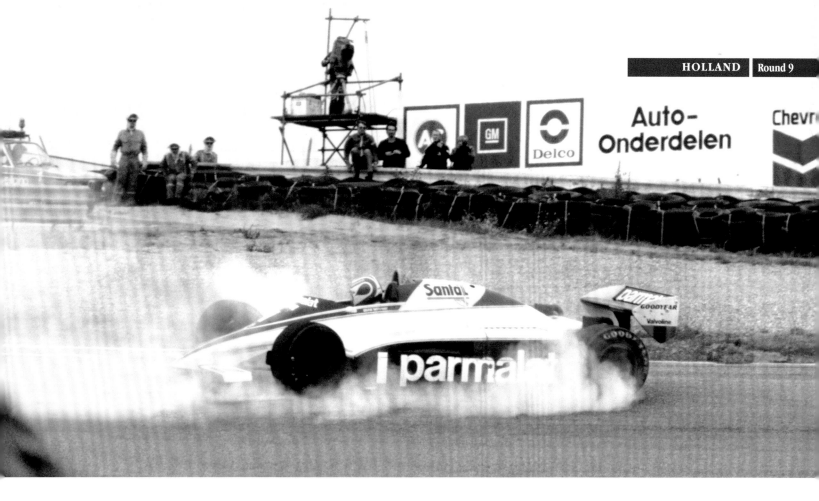

United States. He spoke near-fluent English in a refined Gallic purr. Pironi was handsome in a boyish, cherubic, choirboy sort of way – although in character certainly not angelic; Tambay was handsome as Hollywood defined it. He was softly spoken, gentlemanly, and something about him suggested he understood there was life outside a motor racing circuit as well as inside.

'Enzo decided then he told somebody go get him,' Tambay says. 'That's the way the company worked. Piccinini was his go-for and Piccinini first asked Pironi to call me. I was in Hawaii. Pironi called me and said "Are you interested?" I said "OK, why not?" Piccinini called me then.

'Why did I say yes? I had turned down Ferrari at the end of '77. I was supposed to have a Ferrari contract that year after the Austrian Grand Prix – I was supposed to have a meeting with the Old Man after Zeltweg where I had run between the Ferraris of Niki Lauda and Carlos Reutemann. I got a telex saying that the meeting was cancelled – well, put back. I went to London to meet with John Hogan [senior Marlboro executive] and in the meeting Teddy Mayer turns up. This was the Tuesday before the next CanAm race in the States. In that meeting they produced a contract for '78 and '79 with McLaren.

'We had a discussion. I said "Well, I have a Ferrari possibility" and they said "We'd like you to be alongside James Hunt, it's going to be a lot more fun

with him as a team-mate than Carlos Reutemann" – and James Hunt had been World Champion the year before that. "You're going to have the Goodyear tyres and Ferrari will have the Michelin tyres. They are coming in and for the first year it's going to be a shambles. Here's the contract. If you sign it now you have a sure Formula 1 drive for '78 and '79 and an option for '80."

'I didn't have any agent, I didn't have any managers, I was doing the negotiations by myself. So there I was with a possible contract with Ferrari, and the Old Man has cancelled that meeting, and a McLaren contract on the table in front of me – Teddy Mayer there for McLaren, John Hogan there for Marlboro. I signed.

'I went to the States – the CanAm race in, I think, Trois Rivieres. I said to Gilles "I just signed the contract with McLaren that you were going to have" – because he started in '77 at the British Grand Prix in the McLaren M23 and I drove the Ensign. They had an option on him for '78 and Teddy didn't take it up, he signed me instead. I said "But, Gilles, I have an offer also from Ferrari. They want a young guy for next year with Carlos. Maybe you should ring them up and come to Monza and see if there is a possibility that it's for you." That's the way it happened. He came to Monza and met them.

'Before Monza, I went with Mauro Forgheiri to meet Mr Ferrari – first meeting – and I excused myself for not waiting to sign the contract with

ABOVE *Piquet gets the Tarzan horseshoe wrong in practice and is lucky not to hit anything.*

Ferrari. I said I was not sure that the offer would be genuine but I had one that was confirmed and on the table. The Old Man said "You made a mistake. You would have won races with us and you would have won a lot more money with us than you will at Marlboro McLaren." I said "The money is not the purpose."

'In '82 when Gilles passed away the Old Man – and I don't know for what reason – must have thought: well, I'll give this guy a chance again. And he did.

'Who was Enzo Ferrari? He was Enzo Ferrari! He was everything you can imagine and more, very impressive, very, very powerful in the sense that he decided if you were going to work for Scuderia Ferrari either as a mechanic, an engineer or a driver. That is power. It was totally different from any other operation, totally, totally different. He was very smart, very – I wouldn't say wicked, but very shrewd and also a manipulator in order to be able to get the best out of people. To produce the team's best performance you have to get the best out of everyone in the team. Sometimes it was controversial and difficult for some people but in the end that's what he tried to do.

'He didn't go to the races but he had his "Moscow eyes" – spies – there. He had Italian press guys or some trusted people that he talked to. They were calling him and giving him a report on the way the team was behaving, the way drivers were behaving, who was doing what.'

Motor sport, including Grands Prix, was quite

STARTING GRID

1		**1** 1:14.23 R. Arnoux
	2 1:14.66 A. Prost	
2		**3** 1:42.72 N. Piquet
	4 1:15.82 D. Pironi	
3		**5** 1:15.83 N. Lauda
	6 1:16.15 P. Tambay	
4		**7** 1:16.26 K. Rosberg
	8 1:16.51 B. Giacomelli	
5		**9** 1:16.57 A. de Cesaris
	10 1:16.63 R. Patrese	
6		**11** 1:16.70 J. Watson
	12 1:16.83 D. Daly	
7		**13** 1:17.09 D. Warwick
	14 1:17.23 M. Alboreto	
8		**15** 1:17.62 E. de Angelis
	16 1:18.02 M. Baldi	
9		**17** 1:18.29 M. Surer
	18 1:18.35 M. Winkelhock	
10		**19** 1:18.43 C. Serra
	20 1:18.47 B. Henton	
11		**21** 1:18.47 J. Laffite
	22 1:18.65 R. Boesel	
12		**23** 1:18.95 J.-P. Jarier
	24 1:19.08 J. Mass	
13		**25** 1:19.12 E. Salazar
	26 1:19.27 J. Lammers	

different to most other sports in that the circuits and tracks reflected what French wine-growers call terroir, meaning the importance of the exact place where the growing is done. A football pitch is a football pitch anywhere. Tennis surfaces for the Grand Slam vary but the courts are always the same size and flat. Athletic stadiums are athletic stadiums and the race distances always precisely the same, rugby pitches are ... rugby pitches, swimming pools the same. Even horse-racing circuits have a striking uniformity, albeit with certain variations, but nothing approaching the difference between Detroit, Montreal and now Zandvoort, different again. When the wind blew they had to sweep the sand off it. Only golfers, competing across many terroirs, face as much variety, and anyway they have an advantage: if they make a mistake with, say, a long putt they won't need Prof Watkins in a fast car coming towards them or a military helicopter to take them to the nearest hospital.

That knowledge changes everything.

Zandvoort, evidently made from concrete German coastal defences, had been a Grand Prix circuit since 1952 and looked tired. Circuits did not, then, routinely spend huge sums on improvements obeying the mantra we must be world class.

The races came once a year and the same crowd came once a year to the circuits which were as they had been the year before. Each season had more or less the same rhythm.

I did not realise Zandvoort, like Montreal, was unusual in that you could get close to it on public transport and walk the rest of the way – an astonishing contrast to the rural circuits where five-mile traffic jams were normal, getting out into the traffic jam from the car parks might take a couple of hours, and people unable to afford helicopter rides plotted devilish strategies to find ways round it all.

Arnoux went fastest in first qualifying on the Thursday from Prost, then Piquet and Pironi, confirming that the turbos did rule. Someone described their speed as 'frightening' and their cornering no less so. Frank Williams went out to the Hunserug, the right-and-left some distance behind the pits, to inspect the handling of his two cars and that of everybody else, and what he saw was raw

BELOW Unhappy debut. Roberto Moreno, deputising for the injured Mansell, is about to discover that a Grand Prix weekend can be a very tough experience.

speed. Around Zandvoort's loops and bends Arnoux averaged 128 miles an hour, which is 58 more than the legal limit on Britain's motorways, for example.

Lauda was fifth, Tambay a whisker behind, Rosberg a whisker behind that and Watson 11th. Poor Moreno came last and the only driver in the 1:21s, despite de Angelis showing him the way round. All very predictable.

On behalf of Lotus, Tony Jardine hosted a dinner for journalists in Amsterdam that evening and, the wine flowing, they all gossiped away like women are supposed to do, catty, cruel, salacious, irreverent, scurrilous – and wonderful. Here was something else. A small, enclosed world like Grand Prix racing seeps and heaves with rumours all the time and, because it is small and enclosed, the rumours become important entities for an hour or two, until the next one comes along. You find yourself getting drawn in to this and, before you know it, you're behaving like an insider looking out. Eoin Young, when he no longer went to the races, wrote plaintively that what he missed most was exactly this gossip.

Next day the weather turned hot, cutting the cars' speeds so that the grid remained essentially undisturbed. Moreno hadn't qualified and a lot of people wondered what Colin Chapman made of that.

Thus far the Renault cars had been, overall, unreliable and the question of the moment became

what happens when one of them holds together? Prost lay only 12 points behind Championship leader Watson and, although Arnoux had only four, half the season remained.

That evening I'd arranged to dine in Amsterdam with Murray Walker, still one of the few people – courtesy of the interview at his home – that I actually knew. The whole evening passed in a moment. How else could it have been when you have, across the table from you, a gifted raconteur with a snorting sense of humour, an ease about everything he did and a rich store of stories harvested from all those years of being on the inside? Not to mention taking the tank into Nazi Germany, or the Indian villages and the aspirins...

Back at my hotel some time shortly after one in the morning the phone rang. An excited voice from the *Daily Express* Foreign Desk announced that Murray Walker had been killed and what did I know about it? I only knew I must have been one of the last people to see him alive. I had no idea where he was staying – this is Amsterdam – and who the hell do you ring at one in the morning to find out? David Benson, who had covered Grand Prix racing for the paper years before, was on a trip to Singapore and the voice said it would ring him there to see if he knew. Quite how someone in Singapore would know Murray Walker's hotel in Holland was not my problem. Getting back to sleep was.

BELOW *Tambay contemplating ... how to get past the Renaults from the third row of the grid?*

Race day dawned overcast and dry. At the circuit another version of the night's events emerged. Someone had rung the BBC after midnight claiming to be Walker and telephoning from Holland. This someone said John Watson had been killed in a road crash and a friend critically injured after emerging from a nightclub – the name of a real nightclub was given. BBC Radio 2 carried it as an item on their 1.00 am news bulletin – hence my phone ringing a few minutes later. Quite how Walker's name became juxtaposed with Watson's is mysterious and it may be that, plucked from deep slumber, I garbled the message from the voice from the Foreign Desk myself.

Murray Walker had one of the most distinctive voices in Britain and quite how anyone working at the BBC did not instantly recognise an impersonator remains even more mysterious.

It all served to reinforce my impression that everything about this Grand Prix racing really was ... strange.

Watson, as an Ulsterman always sensitive to what can be loosely called matters of security, expressed concern that his parents were on holiday and hoped they wouldn't hear. Beyond that, and understandably, he didn't want to discuss the matter and in fact there wasn't much to discuss. Nobody knew anything.

To watch the race you could, with the right pass, wander from the paddock to the horseshoe corner called Tarzan at the end of the start-finish straight and stand on the semi-circle of grass which comprised the infield. Apart from the raw excitement of 26 cars being pitched into it from the flag, Tarzan was a favoured overtaking place and spectacular anyway, with a ground effect car going round it at full belt. The Sports Editor was curious to know what Grand Prix drivers earned and so, at Tarzan, I was standing next to one Nick Brittan, then – among many other things – John Watson's manager, trying to prise out of him what Watson earned.

'Never going to tell you that!'

'But ... just a general figure ... a guideline...'

'Never going to tell you that, either!'

This was yet another strange aspect. Grand Prix racing had a most ambivalent relationship to money and the public domain, and you wouldn't have anticipated that because it offered itself as an exclusive activity fashioned precisely by money, lots of it. Hence the exclusivity and, by extension, how special it was.

All the insiders seemed agreed that Grand Prix racing was a big deal, and many insisted it was the only deal in the whole wide world. Beyond that,

ABOVE *The start and already the Renaults are in front. Prost leads Arnoux into the Tarzan horseshoe.*

almost everything to do with it was laboured secrecy. Sponsors paraded their involvement but baulked at any suggestion of how much, leaving the amount to implication.

The prize money was completely unknown beyond a tight inner circle who distributed and received it. If Arnoux won the Dutch Grand Prix, due to start in a moment, we had no idea how much he got, or the first three, or if the prize money went lower down the finishing order than that. Was pole position worth money? Was the fastest lap? Was there, in effect, start money for showing up?

Every year Wimbledon held a Press Conference to announce that year's prize money, which is how everybody knew what Connors and McEnroe would be getting as winner and loser. The tennis authorities issued lists of prize money during a season, constantly updated. Football transfers were announced routinely. The value of every horse race appeared in the morning papers every day. The prize money in major golf tournaments was freely available and aroused no controversy.

But this...? Mystery again.[1]

Arnoux and Prost catapulted from the grid, Pironi with them, and into Tarzan Prost cut across and took the lead. Rosberg could hardly see the starter's signal and cars surged by – from the fourth row he'd be running 11th.

At the chicane on lap 2 Pironi took Arnoux. The

order after that: Piquet, Tambay, Lauda, Giacomelli, Watson, de Cesaris, Rosberg. Pironi out-braked Prost into lap 5 at Tarzan.

Young Derek Warwick found the Toleman could be wrestled round Zandvoort, and although it ran between one and two seconds slower than Pironi's Ferrari he matched Tambay. The lap times are interesting:

	Tambay	Warwick
Lap 2	1:24.1	1:23.0
Lap 3	1:24.3	1:22.4
Lap 4	1:22.9	1:23.7
Lap 5	1:22.8	1:22.5

That took Warwick from fifteenth to tenth. Rosberg was moving on Giacomelli and Lauda. He took Giacomelli, himself in combative mood and ceding nothing, on lap 8 after a protracted and at times alarming struggle. Next lap he out-braked Lauda into Tarzan. That gave, at ten laps: Pironi, Prost, Arnoux, Piquet, Tambay, Rosberg, Lauda, Giacomelli, Daly, Watson – but Warwick in the pits because the rear wing had blown off on the straight. He wasn't aware of that until he reached Tarzan but he was certainly aware of it when he did reach Tarzan.

Rosberg hustled past Tambay after slipstreaming him tightly along the straight and ducking by into Tarzan – again on lap 12. He pushed the Williams as hard as he could even though he could see a tyre was losing pressure. By now Warwick has emerged from the pits with a new rear wing and hurled the Toleman, covering lap 12 in 1:23.1 and next lap doing 1:19.7, the fastest of the race so far and, as it would prove, unassailable. Only one other driver got below 1:20, Piquet on lap 68 with 1:19.8.

Therein lies a tale or two.

'The reason I got fastest lap, of course, was because at the time we were struggling for sponsors so we came in and put a new set of tyres on just to do a fast lap,' Warwick says with his accustomed candour. 'That's bloody quick round there in a flying pig: 20 miles an hour was quick in that car! The idea was to get some publicity and show that we were quicker than we really were, and it did help us to keep the sponsor for the following year. The car didn't have a lot of downforce but did have quite good power, but the problem was its inconsistency because the engine didn't have enough money put into it.'

Witty, with his accustomed candour, sets out the background. 'Holland was quite simple in a way. We were struggling. We were all staying not that far away from the track and in the evening Alex, myself, Roger Silman [team manager] and Rory Byrne met. We were

trying to get sponsors, we really needed them. Rothmans were sponsoring the March team and I'd made some overtures into Rothmans because the first thing you do in Formula One is try and nick each other's sponsors.

'We thought: we've got the British Grand Prix coming up, why don't we consider running the car light and sacrifice any chance of a result for track performance? We did. Rory and Roger agreed to it – Derek was OK, Fabi was OK but he didn't qualify. Derek was on the seventh row, not a bad effort in qualifying. It was probably our best qualifying and that was legal. Derek made a pit stop quite early for a problem and took on fresh tyres. That's what helped as well.'

Hawkridge, with his accustomed candour, says 'I don't think we were ever in the running to get Rothmans as a sponsor. Chris was off on his own quite often chasing rainbows [which is what sponsor chasers have to do]. He may well have had some contact with them but I wasn't aware of it.'

No, the point was to get the Toleman round Zandvoort at serious speed to create publicity to attract sponsors, whether Rothmans or not. It would also create publicity for the team in the run-up to the British Grand Prix, only two weeks away. In

BELOW One went off (de Angelis) and one stayed on (Cheever) in qualifying. Cheever didn't get into the race.

terms of a showcase, that is The Big One to every British team, but especially to a small team looking for money.

The publicity worked, which is why I am writing about it these 25 years later and you are reading it.

From lap 15 the race settled into an orderly rhythm, Pironi commanding it from the front from Prost and Piquet, Arnoux and the slogging Rosberg. Watson, 11th, could make no kind of progress and there'd be nothing for him today, not even lowly points to maintain his Championship momentum.

The orderly rhythm was shaken up into lap 22 and inevitably, perhaps, at Tarzan. For a lap or two Arnoux had felt some sort of vibration from the steering and made the reasonable assumption that tyre wear was causing it or a wheel was out of balance. He approached Tarzan quite normally at 190mph, moved into the late braking area – again quite normally – and suddenly the left front wheel keeled over and broke away completely. The steering arm had broken under braking and the Renault could not be controlled. In an instant Arnoux knew I have no steering, no brakes, I am helpless. He braced himself for the impact which would have to come.

The Renault screamed straight ahead and as it left the track the kerbing flipped it briefly into the air. Then it was screaming onto the sand and scrub run-off area like a missile being pitched through its own dust-storm. It rammed its snout into the tyre wall – a proper, solid thing about five tyres high and three rows of tyres deep, all bound together – and the impact made a deep, reverberating, shocking shriek.

I thought he was dead.

The Renault rode upwards, the snout boring with such ferocity that it scattered tyres like a bomb burst, flinging a dozen of them into the air towards the people cowering behind the barrier and the ranks of people in the grandstand behind that. It bored all the way to the metal guardrail and came to rest there, battered and at a grotesque angle.

Paletti and Montreal remained horrifically vivid in the memory and now this. What was I doing here? What was anybody doing here?

Arnoux's helmet moved, and in such circumstances it is a movement of mercy because it means life.[2] He was lifted from the cockpit and didn't need the ambulance. He'd escaped with no more than a bruised right ankle.

Rosberg now ran fourth, trying to reel in Piquet, and that became much more relevant to the Championship when Prost's engine lost power and then failed. Piquet now faced the prospect of reeling in Pironi, but this day Pironi

had a fast, reliable car and drove a masterful race, controlled and unhurried. Prost was gone after 33 laps (of the 72) and Rosberg could see all sorts of enticing, intriguing possibilities up ahead and no threat behind, Lauda too far away.

	Pironi	Piquet	Rosberg
Lap 34	1:21.5	1:22.9	1:22.5
Lap 35	1:21.1	1:22.4	1:22.7
Lap 36	1:21.2	1:22.1	1:22.4

It was the story of the race. Pironi could keep the Ferrari in the 1:21s at will whereas Piquet and Rosberg didn't get there for another five laps and when they did Pironi went into the low 1:20s. Rosberg drove the final ten laps as fast as he could make the Williams go, disregarding the health of tyres, engine and everything else. He actually caught Piquet on the final lap but in his own phrase 'the

OPPOSITE *After Villeneuve and Paletti, Grand Prix racing was a nervy place – and the sound of Arnoux thumping the tyre barrier at Tarzan corner echoed a long, long way. He was shaken, stirred and unhurt.*

BELOW *A world in headlines, and the Dutch papers highlighted their own Jan Lammers.*

De Fransman Arnoux wordt bevrijd uit de stapel sloopbanden waarin hij per ongeluk verzeild raakte

car had nothing more to give,'[3] and anyway Piquet always seemed to have a bit in hand if he needed it.

Rosberg's bad run was ending, Watson finished ninth and Pironi was talking about the Ferrari's power and reliability. He was also talking about the Championship and it looked his for the taking. Brands Hatch might not suit the turbos but Paul Ricard would, and Hockenheim, and the Österreichring, and Monza. That left twisty Dijon and contorting Las Vegas, and even in those places Pironi could anticipate scoring points.

Watson 30, Pironi 29, Rosberg 21, Patrese 19, Prost 18, Piquet 17.

In the immediate aftermath of the race two men faced quite different situations.

Derek Daly had found himself in a 'dust-up with Prost in Tarzan. We were exchanging positions. I was fast down the straight and Prost would get me on the inside, then I'd pass him again. He couldn't quite make it stick and he eventually had two or three tries. Then the same thing happened with Alboreto. He'd pass me, I'd pass him. Well, going in to Tarzan he was trying to pass me and we touched. We'd got too close and he believed it was a deliberate act. He spun, I continued.

'End of the race I'm standing talking to three or four people. I suddenly see this punch come over the top of their shoulders. Didn't quite connect. Alboreto had a big red face on him and he said "Next time I keeeell you." That was all. A scuffle erupted, somebody pulled him back and off he went.'

Alan Jenkins, newcomer to the McLaren team, got into a dust-up with Tyler Alexander, forthright American, a team-member from way back and consummate exploiter of one-liners. To appreciate this, you need to cast your mind back to my plight at Detroit where I assumed everyone would linger and savour, and instead everyone headed away in something approaching a stampede.

'I got on famously well with Tyler except at Zandvoort,' says Jenkins. 'Everybody was rushing to the plane, as everybody did just about before the cars had actually slowed down on the last lap! At Zandvoort the people who knew went out in their hire cars and used half the track to get to an exit and beat the traffic. I hadn't got a clue. I said to Tyler "What happens now, how do I get to the airport?" – I seemed to have been in a different hire car with different people every day. As he

FAN'S EYE VIEW

'As I was living in Holland I was lucky there was a Dutch Grand Prix in 1982 – the race was added to the calendar at quite short notice. Even better, I was able to get away from work to attend testing a couple of weeks before. That's when I actually shot most of my photos, taking advantage of an ideally placed platform on the outside of the Hugenboltz Bocht, as the hairpin behind the pits was known.

'For the race I chose to watch from a temporary grandstand erected on the outside of Bos Uit, the fast undulating and crucial curve which led onto the long main straight. I had a special reason for picking this spot. Just a few months before I had started doing some Formula Ford racing myself and this was my "home" track.

'Zandvoort was a pretty fast circuit anyway, but Bos Uit was the daunting challenge that really set the men apart from the boys – and I was very much one of the boys, still mustering the courage to take it flat on every lap in my FF1600, so I wanted to see the Formula One stars at work.

'Needless to say, the blinding speed of these last-generation ground-effect cars in the swooping Bos Uit was sensational – and all the more spectacular because, despite having no suspension to speak of, the non-turbo Cosworths had to give it their all just to stand a chance of keeping in the slipstream of a turbo on the long straight that followed.

'Rosberg, of course, was the big hero who even passed a couple of turbos under braking for Tarzan on his way to third place, and was visibly on the limit in Bos Uit. I recall Lauda in the McLaren was also right up there too. From my seat I could see them burst over the brow from the Panorama Bocht and drop flat out into the long sweeper and then watch all the way down the long straight until they turned into Tarzan. It was the first time I had ever experienced the odd phenomenon of my eyes seeing the cars turning into Tarzan well before the sound of them lifting off the gas in the braking zone reached my ears. Weird.

'It turned out to be Pironi's last win, but at the time he seemed to be heading irresistibly towards the title. Though I wasn't a fan of his, I can remember wondering at his psychological make-up. He'd survived a couple of massive crashes at Ricard in pre-season testing, followed by his selfish actions at Imola and the supposed aftermath at Zolder. Then, in the previous race in Canada, this man had inadvertently been the cause and then close witness of Ricardo Paletti's fiery end.'

GARETH REES
TOKYO, JAPAN

FROM TOP *A hard season for Cheever, who failed to qualify the Ligier; Lauda kept his Championship alive with fourth place; Rosberg picked up very useful points for third place – and at season's end they'd be more than useful.*

disappeared between two motorhomes, Tyler said "Well, you're free, white and 21 – you sort it out." I got a lift with another team in the end, saw Tyler at the airport and said "Thanks." He was a bit gruff but later on we hung out a bit together, went and had a meal or a beer together, so we got on fine.'

Alexander once distilled Formula One like this: 'It's dangerous. It says so on the back of the ticket.' He also distilled injustice in Formula One as 'Well, hell, that's life in the big city.'

At Zandvoort that's what he was telling Alan Jenkins and it was, as it remains, a good lesson to learn early.

John Watson still led the Championship but 'I had a bad run after Canada – some of it was my fault, some of it wasn't.' The internal balance within a team is always a delicate thing because it has twin, rival centres of gravity, the two drivers. If one of those drivers happened to be Niki Lauda you risked having just one centre of gravity. That was having a direct bearing on Watson, and as he discusses it he insists 'this is not sour grapes, this is a fact of life: Niki's achievements were probably greater than the expectations of him in 1982. Marlboro principally brought Niki in and it was going to be a great story for them if Niki could be World Champion,

front page news. That's part of the reason he was brought in, and as a bonus he did a very good job in 1982.

'Not that Ron Dennis would necessarily have gone along with all that unless there was something advantageous to the team' – Dennis wouldn't pander to Lauda or Marlboro for the sake of it, especially if Watson was doing better – 'but the bigger problem did occur at some point, and it did have a big effect on me: the overall engineering control of the McLaren was in the hands of John Barnard and he was also engineering Niki's car. I had Teddy Mayer running mine and there was an element of friction, partly because Teddy had basically just given up the company [to Dennis] that he'd been a very big part of for many years.

'Also, I don't think John and Teddy were natural soul-mates. Teddy would have enjoyed winding up John, which wasn't particularly difficult, and Ron once said to me "You're lining yourself up against John." I said "Well, I've got to work with what I've got. I'm not working against John, I'm working for my position." It was a bit of a difficult situation to deal with.

'Niki had fame, skill, political contacts, presence, and they were paying him a hell of a lot of money

BELOW *Pironi, winning the last race of his five-year career.*

so I had a number of issues. I was doing as best I could. Maybe it wasn't always perfect but it was the best I could – and that was another element. At times I might have got upset because I felt I wasn't getting what I should have been getting.

'Equally, and slightly amusingly, John would send out a job sheet for the car set-up for the race. Teddy had worked out that there's no point in taking a horse to water and kicking it to death if it isn't going to drink. You have to find a way to get the bloody thing to drink' – presenting Watson with a car set up the way he didn't want. 'So by having the job sheet presented on a Saturday night they ticked everything, but in fact what they were doing was making changes. I don't know if John Barnard was aware but ostensibly he wasn't. It enabled me to drive the car the way I wanted and I was quite effective in the car.

'There wasn't sufficient flexibility coming from John in respect of what I needed. The trouble with engineers, particularly where theory is concerned – and wind tunnel technology wasn't particularly sophisticated at that time – is that if you can't drive the car, if the front end of the car was too pointy and it didn't suit me, then what's the point?

'Teddy had a very simple philosophy, and I have used it to explain things to other people: a racing driver doesn't actually need to think too much, his job is to drive the racing car – not to

ABOVE *The floral touch so this must be Holland. Zandvoort was also known for its sweeping corners. This is Patrese – he'd have an unhappy race.*

171

OPPOSITE *Pironi's podium, Piquet seeming unimpressed by it all and Rosberg (left) obscured.*

BELOW *Salazar kept the ATS going and finished two laps behind the winner, Pironi.*

engineer the racing car, not to do a hundred other things, but get in and drive it. If you can give the driver the opportunity to open the throttle and turn the steering wheel with total confidence then it's down to his ability and his skills. It's a very simple philosophy, and that's what I was given. It's what it's about, absolutely. Fundamentally, Teddy had a lot of good, useful experience.'

This background is centred on Zandvoort because, as Watson says, that's where his bad run began. It would endure for another five races and only in the sixth, Monza in September, did he score points again. In that sense his misfortune opened the whole season up to Pironi, Rosberg, Prost and The Rat himself.

Footnote: 1. The only real figures I ever heard were: (a) when, after the crowd invaded the track at Monza on the last lap of the Italian Grand Prix, and Mansell – running in a lowly place – backed off, another driver overtook him and a member of the Lotus team said 'that cost us $8,000'; and (b) one time at the Williams factory, when someone asked how much it cost to run the team and Frank began with the usual never-talk-about-that answer and then suddenly said 'We're a business, what's the big secret?' and told us. Amazingly the world didn't stop but continued to rotate precisely as it had before. Equally amazingly, it still does; 2. It is not always the case. When Ayrton Senna hit the wall at Imola in 1994 the crash looked instantly very, very serious. His head moved, offering a second or two of hope, but it was caused by a muscular spasm. He was no more than clinically alive and, despite the best medical treatment at the scene, in a helicopter, and in hospital in Bologna, he was beyond saving; 3. Keke.

Race Result

WINNING SPEED 187.33kmh/116.40mph

FASTEST LAP 191.86kmh/119.22mph
(Warwick 1m 19.78s on lap 13)

LAP LEADERS Prost 1–4 (4);
Pironi 5–72 (68)

RACE

	Driver	Team	Engine	Laps	Time
1	D. Pironi	Ferrari 126C2	Ferrari V6t	72	1h 38m 03.25s
2	N. Piquet	Brabham BT50	BMW 4t	72	1h 38m 24.90s
3	K. Rosberg	Williams FW08	Cosworth V8	72	1h 38m 25.61s
4	N. Lauda	McLaren MP4B	Cosworth V8	72	1h 39m 26.97s
5	D. Daly	Williams FW08	Cosworth V8	71	
6	M. Baldi	Arrows A4	Cosworth V8	71	
7	M. Alboreto	Tyrrell 011	Cosworth V8	71	
8	P. Tambay	Ferrari 126C2	Ferrari V6t	71	
9	J. Watson	McLaren MP4B	Cosworth V8	71	
10	M. Surer	Arrows A4	Cosworth V8	71	
11	B. Giacomelli	Alfa Romeo 182	Alfa V12	70	
12	M. Winkelhock	ATS D5	Cosworth V8	70	
13	E. Salazar	ATS D5	Cosworth V8	70	
14	J.-P. Jarier	Osella FA1C	Cosworth V8	69	
15	R. Patrese	Brabham BT50	BMW 4t	69	
r	J. Mass	March 821	Cosworth V8	60	Engine
r	J. Lammers	Theodore TY02	Cosworth V8	41	Engine
r	E. de Angelis	Lotus 91	Cosworth V8	40	Handling
r	A. de Cesaris	Alfa Romeo 182	Alfa V12	35	Electrics
r	A. Prost	Renault RE30B	Renault V6t	33	Engine
r	R. Arnoux	Renault RE30B	Renault V6t	21	Suspension/crash
r	B. Henton	Tyrrell 011	Cosworth V8	21	Throttle linkage
r	R. Boesel	March 821	Cosworth V8	21	Engine
r	C. Serra	Fittipaldi F8D	Cosworth V8	18	Fuel pump
r	D. Warwick	Toleman TG181C	Hart 4t	15	Oil leak
r	J. Laffite	Talbot Ligier JS19	Matra V12	4	Handling
nq	R. Guerrero	Ensign N181	Cosworth V8		
nq	T. Fabi	Toleman TG181C	Hart 4t		
nq	E. Cheever	Talbot Ligier JS19	Matra V12		
nq	R. Moreno	Lotus 91	Cosworth V8		
npq	E. de Villota	March 821	Cosworth V8		

npq = did not pre-qualify; nq = did not qualify; r = retired

CHAMPIONSHIP

	Driver	Points
1	J. Watson	30
2	D. Pironi	29
3	K. Rosberg	21
4	R. Patrese	19
5	A. Prost	18
6	N. Piquet	17
7	N. Lauda	15
8	M. Alboreto	10
	E. Cheever	10
	E. de Angelis	10
11	N. Mansell	7
12	C. Reutemann	6
	G. Villeneuve	6
14	A. de Cesaris	5
	D. Daly	5
16	R. Arnoux	4
17	J.-P. Jarier	3
18	M. Winkelhock	2
	E. Salazar	2
	M. Surer	2
21	J. Laffite	1
	M. Baldi	1
	F. Serra	1

	Team	Points
1	McLaren	45
2	Brabham	36
3	Ferrari	35
4	Williams	32
5	Renault	22
6	Lotus	17
7	Talbot Ligier	11
8	Tyrrell	10
9	Alfa Romeo	5
10	ATS	4
11	Osella	3
	Arrows	3
13	Fittipaldi	1

LAIR OF KING RAT

— GREAT BRITAIN, BRANDS HATCH

The attraction of Donington, so far from prying eyes, was the same for Gordon Murray and Brabham as it had been for Ron Dennis, McLaren and Niki Lauda. As Murray says, 'We went there and booked the whole circuit privately. We had security round the perimeter.' Murray, designer of the Brabham and original thinker, was about to produce another coup.

Alain Prost, if you remember, had been forced to pit in South Africa with a puncture, took on four new tyres, and they enabled him to go so fast that he cut through the field and won. The possibilities of such a tactic, he felt, were not lost on Murray or Ecclestone at Brabham. This has entered the folklore of the sport but, as Murray points out, it wasn't like that: 'It was totally independent of the Prost thing. That went unnoticed, certainly for me and I'm sure for Bernie as well. It really was one of those brainstorm things where you could work out how much 1lb of fuel cost you in lap times, which of course they do every race now. In those days it was roughly 1lb equals one-hundredth of a second.

'I'd always thought about that because obviously I was trying to get the car as light as possible. I thought: you also get a degradation in the tyres, and I started doing some maps. It was all on paper, all mathematical, it was nothing to do with physical evidence. I did some calculations on how long you could be in the pits, including the slowing down and the warming up afterwards, and still win the race with the combined advantage of three things: less

RIGHT *Rosberg ought to have been leading the pack from the start but he was at the back and the Brabhams helped themselves. The rat is in the middle of the pack.*

Great Britain
Brands Hatch

RACE DATE July 18th

CIRCUIT LENGTH
4.20km/2.61 miles

NO. OF LAPS 76

RACE DISTANCE
319.71km/198.66 miles

WEATHER Hot, dry

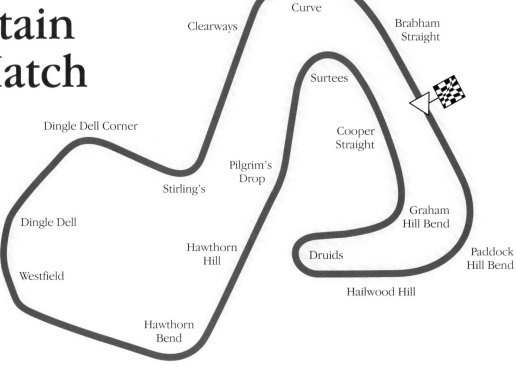

Clark Curve

Clearways

Brabham Straight

Surtees

Dingle Dell Corner

Cooper Straight

Pilgrim's Drop

Stirling's

Graham Hill Bend

Dingle Dell

Druids

Paddock Hill Bend

Hawthorn Hill

Westfield

Hailwood Hill

Hawthorn Bend

DRIVER'S VIEW

'Brands was the best circuit in England, no doubt about that. I'm a BRDC member and I love Silverstone but as far as Grands Prix go it was a driver's circuit: undulating, you came past the pits and you went into Paddock and it was all off camber. In those days if you made a mistake you went off big time. When you go out into the country you were going bloody fast and you've only got to look at the accidents. Johnny Herbert crashed there [in Formula 3000 in 1988] and was lucky to get out alive. You were getting G forces and you were thrown about because it was a bumpy old circuit as well. When you came from the country under the bridge and had the grandstands and pits before you, you only thought: I've got Paddock coming at me. Paddock was a challenge, it was an overtaking place – round the outside or even down the inside – but the trouble was one clip there and you were straight into the barrier. And, more embarrassing, there's 100,000 people watching you do it. You certainly had nowhere to go then. The Tyrrell went very well there – it was a very solid car – but Ken wasn't as innovative as some of the others and the car was a brick outhouse, really.'

—— *Brian Henton*

weight – obviously, with a lower fuel load – new tyres when you went out and, also, an average lower centre of gravity for the car because the fuel tank was never full. The fuel tank made a huge difference because of where the tanks were behind the driver. A full tank raised the centre of gravity of the car enormously.

'So with those three things – and it's quite easy to do the mathematics – I worked out, if I remember correctly, that we needed to lose not more than something like 26 or 27 seconds in total making the pit stop and then we'd be sure to win the race.

'The first time anything physical happened was when we went out on cold tyres [as new tyres were when you pitted for them] and you lost so much on the first one or two laps while the tyres warmed up. I thought: well that's blown that, but I stopped and thought about it again. I spoke to the tyre company and I asked them "Well, what would happen if you put the tyres on already at their operating temperature?" They said "As long as you don't over-heat them and burn the compound off you will be quick immediately."

'When I think back now to the first equipment it was ridiculous! I designed a thing that looked like a Tardis or a blue telephone box. We put a gas burner in the bottom and a funnel at the top so the air was circulating right through this box and stacked four tyres up in it. We had a little window and through it we could prod them – we had no thermostat or anything, we opened the window and

prodded the tyres to make sure they were at the right temperature. We kept that burning in the pits, well just out the back of the garage, then slowly but surely we developed different fuel systems.'

This was because of a pressure problem which, ordinarily, didn't exist because cars were only being fuelled before a race, and it wasn't being done against the clock. You took as long as you needed to fill the tank and then you were ready to go the full distance. The problem? 'As the fuel went down, the remaining air in the barrel expanded and there wasn't enough pressure to squeeze the last bit out.'

Murray thought that through and 'eventually I had two barrels, one next to the other. One was just compressed air and the other one had the fuel in. One bled into the other one.'

Using this, getting 33 or 35 gallons in took three and a half seconds.

'Basically we had to invent the fuel rig and we had to invent tyre-warmers.'

A week before the British Grand Prix they went to Donington.

'We did our first test. In the meantime, of course, I had done a lot of video work and practising with the crew on wheel changing to see how you could change wheels very quickly – because in three and a half seconds you could get the fuel in. We got special wheel nuts and wheel pins, did all sorts of special things for the wheel changing. We trained the people like crazy.

ABOVE *The speedy and the static: compared with Roberto Guerrero's Ensign, the parked Mini looks positively substantial.*

'We went to Donington and lo and behold we
were under the 26 second mark. I said to Bernie
"That's it. Next year we'll build a half-tank car." In
fact the tank would be big enough to do Detroit
and Monaco without stopping, so it was like a 60-
per-cent-tank car, if you want to put it like that. Of
course, it gave you much more freedom on the
mechanical layout of the car as well.'

The first example of The Pit Stop Ploy was to be
the British Grand Prix.

Brands Hatch spread itself like a feast for the
eye. That phrase has not been chosen carelessly. A
spectator could actually see a great deal, building
into a fund of precious memories to be carefully
hoarded for future delight. In a grandstand,
permanent or temporary, the track uncoiled like
a mighty gesture: you saw the cars flee under the
bridge at Clearways, come full bore round the great
curve to the undulating start-finish straight, saw
them dive into Paddock Hill Bend and down the dip
beyond before they rose to the Druids horseshoe.
They were lost in the trees there but emerged a
moment later on the downhill to the left, along
the back straight and fast uphill left-left-left out
into the country.

Only Austria (and maybe Kyalami) was like this
and it must have been something to do with the
contours of the land. You needed elevation. The
flatland circuits might have been missile ranges

– whoosh, there goes another one. At Brands you
could see who was gaining on whom, who losing,
and, as a race developed, you might have a dozen or
more cars simultaneously in your sight spread round
the mighty gesture. At moments there was simply
too much to watch, your eye drawn helplessly this
way and that.

Paddock Hill Bend, adverse camber, was a
favourite overtaking place which demanded, in the
vernacular, big balls. You got to see all that, too,
especially the ones who had them and the ones
who hadn't.

Rosberg (who certainly did) came brimming
with confidence. He lived in England so this was
his home race, involving a minimum of travel and
inconvenience. He liked Brands Hatch, he knew
the Williams would be fast there and he knew, too,
that in terms of the Championship he needed to do
well. Where better than here? The circuits to come
favoured the turbos.

He didn't fear the Renaults or Brabhams or
Ferraris in the British Grand Prix, he feared Watson
and Lauda.

Rosberg was fast on the opening day despite
tangling with Arnoux at Druids – Rosberg went to
the inside and evidently Arnoux wasn't looking – and
did a 1m 09.5s lap, provisional pole which became
pole the following day.

The Brabhams had built-in air jacks and big fuel

STARTING GRID

1	**1**	**2** 1:09.54 **K. Rosberg**
	2 1:09.62 **R. Patrese**	
2	**4** 1:10.06 **D. Pironi**	**3** 1:10.06 **N. Piquet**
3	**6** 1:10.64 **R. Arnoux**	**5** 1:10.63 **N. Lauda**
4	**8** 1:10.72 **A. Prost**	**7** 1:10.65 **E. de Angelis**
5	**10** 1:10.98 **D. Daly**	**9** 1:10.89 **M. Alboreto**
6	**12** 1:11.41 **J. Watson**	**11** 1:11.34 **A. de Cesaris**
7	**14** 1:11.50 **B. Giacomelli**	**13** 1:11.43 **P. Tambay**
8	**16** 1:11.76 **D. Warwick**	**15** 1:11.72 **T. Fabi**
9	**18** 1:12.43 **J.-P. Jarier**	**17** 1:12.08 **B. Henton**
10	**20** 1:12.69 **J. Laffite**	**19** 1:12.66 **R. Guerrero**
11	**22** 1:13.18 **M. Surer**	**21** 1:13.09 **C. Serra**
12	**24** 1:13.30 **E. Cheever**	**23** 1:13.21 **N. Mansell**
13	**26** 1:13.72 **M. Baldi**	**25** 1:13.62 **J. Mass**

fillers behind the roll bars, the meaning clear. Herbie Blash of Brabham confirmed The Pit Stop Ploy and insisted it had not been adopted because the cars couldn't go the distance: no, it's the quickest way to make them go the distance. Naturally some suspicious minds in the paddock thought it no more than a feint to sow doubt and confusion, and Rosberg called it 'a hoax'. Others wondered, if The Ploy happened and if it worked, what impact it would have on Grand Prix racing. They had to conclude it could only be fundamental.

Tambay pointed out that it was 'done all the time in Cam-Am racing. I'm sure it would be terrific for television and for the crowds but it would mean redesigning all the pit lanes to separate refuelling from other activities or else there could be a lot of dead journalists and some charred pretty girls. The tanks would be made lighter, everyone would get into the act and we'd have a whole new set of tricks and wheezes. Aren't exit and entry from the pits already dangerous enough?'[1]

Jean Sage said Renault had thought of it a long time before but 'it didn't seem practical. We will be very interested to see if Brabham can make it work.'

Of more immediate concern to Brabham was that Goodyear's compounds did not enable the team

BELOW *'Right, I'll have that one.' Frank Williams is on top of every detail.*

FAN'S EYE VIEW

'My love affair with motor sport started in 1952 with a ride in an MG TD – top and windscreen down – to a stock car race at a nearby dirt track. Another jump to road racing occurred when I acquired George Monkhouse's two books, Motoraces and Motor Racing with Mercedes Benz. I still have the books. From there to being an avid fan and competitor was a short jump. I stopped competing in 1971 and went into insurance brokerage.

'In 1976 we went to Monaco for our first Grand Prix. A British couple sitting at the next table helped us with the French menu. We have been fast friends since. We went to the UK annually and they visited us at our home in New York on occasion.

'We had been to Brands in a previous visit to the UK for some club racing so a Grand Prix visit was in order. Our friends obtained excellent tickets and made the necessary arrangements. It was quite an experience: incredible crowd, fantastic air show and great racing.

'Lauda and Pironi seemed to have their spots well in hand, but Tambay, de Angelis, Daly and Prost were within a breath of each other.'

CHARLES J. BOUGH
UTAH, USA

FROM TOP *A traditional Brands feature, the air display: Red Arrows, the Harrier jump jet which usually blew the marquees down, and Concorde; the early running order, Piquet, Lauda, Pironi and de Angelis; the great Rosberg charge – he's just about to overtake Tambay on lap 11.*

to run softer – and therefore faster – tyres, getting through one set up to the pit stops and another set afterwards. Instead Brabham ran standard A compounds like the other Goodyear runners.

In great secrecy another team, Toleman, were preparing to use an amazing variant of The Ploy. 'After Zandvoort and the fastest lap, no, we didn't get Rothmans, but we then went to the British Grand Prix and we had to make a decision: what are we here for?' Witty says. 'We'd looked at it and thought: well, our reliability record is so poor that you can go round and round and hope you might get a tenth but nobody is going to notice you – and that was if you finished. So we took a gamble.

'When you are trying to create a profile and you've got budgets, you're trying to pay for Brian Hart, you're trying to do this, do that, you're trying to better yourself, you look at all kinds of things. It was Alex or myself who said "Why don't we run half tanks?" That was the one that really fooled everyone. The decision was taken on race morning and both drivers agreed. We felt that a performance was needed in order to raise our profile. It's probably against the spirit but it's a dog eat dog world in Formula One.'

'In terms of the relativities of it,' Hawkridge says, 'we were racing on exactly the same tyres we had had a year earlier but they were particularly good at Brands Hatch. I don't think we could use them anywhere else, but at Brands they really were very, very quick both as a qualifying and a race tyre. So we had this tyre advantage and we were virtually on the pace of the McLarens with it. We said to ourselves: how do we get the best out of this weekend? What do we most want?'

There were sponsor pressures to be on the television.

Right, Hawkridge & Co decided, you want to be on television, we will put you on television.

They took a further decision: if either Warwick or Fabi lasted long enough to roll to a halt because they have no more fuel, we'll call it driveshaft failure.

An immense crowd came on race day, a Sunday bathed in sunshine. They saw that if Brabham were preparing to perpetuate a hoax it was both elaborate and convincing. At their pit they laid day-glo strips like signs so that Piquet and Patrese would know exactly where to stop. They had fuel churns, in the livery of sponsor Parmalat, ready. They had mechanics in fireproof clothing bearing Parmalat logos.

BELOW *Rosberg, entirely heroic round Brands, and in the end it was all for nothing. He was not pleased.*

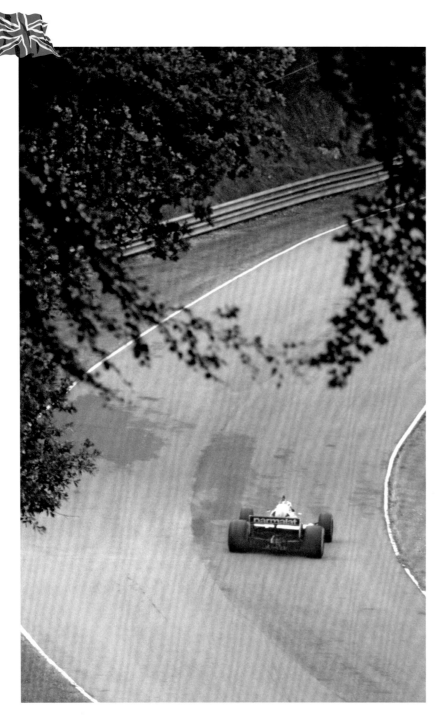

ABOVE *Bountiful, beautiful Brands – and Nelson Piquet proceeds on his way to the pit stop that never was.*

OPPOSITE *The panorama of Brands, because – like Austria – it wasn't flat. Prost leads Tambay down from Druids while in the far background a couple of cars prepare to ascend to that fabled horseshoe.*

On the warm-up lap Rosberg's Williams suffered a problem with fuel pressure and the car wouldn't start. 'I knew the problems of starting at Brands. I had to place my car pointing slightly downhill into the wall to avoid a slide. I had it all figured out.'[2] Mechanics pushed him as the other cars flowed round, and it wouldn't fire. Eventually it did and he attacked the warm-up lap to re-catch the rest of the field and take his position on pole. He reached them when they had formed up and so he had to start from the back. Well, he thought, it will look even better when I win it from here.

Reflecting now, Rosberg says: 'I was on pole and the car didn't start, so I lose the pole and had to start

from the back. It wasn't a question of understeer or anything like that. We had a super car. So we lost the pole and that's one of the bad memories because that race would have been mine, I'd have walked it. It's not that that would have been a step towards the Championship so much as, being a racing driver, you want to win races and to win at Brands, which is a man's track, that's where you want to win. It's not about 100,000 spectators, it's about me and the rest of the drivers.'

Patrese stalled, his arm raised high instantaneously. Pironi corkscrewed past, Arnoux slewed and clouted the rear of the Brabham, Prost turned sharp left on to the grass, Daly dipped just past but still on the track, Watson went on to the grass but Patrese and Arnoux, cars seemingly locked, ebbed across forcing Watson wider and wider. Arnoux was out, Patrese was out and so was Fabi, so he'd never find out what he could have done fuelled light.

The Ploy rested on Piquet now and he led from Lauda. Rosberg came from afar like an avenger against fate: on the opening lap he surged past Mass, Baldi, Mansell, Laffite, Surer, Henton and Watson.

If Lauda could stay with Piquet as the race unfolded, The Ploy would be in disarray...

	Piquet	Lauda
Lap 2	1: 16.1	1: 16.5
Lap 3	1: 14.8	1: 16.4
Lap 4	1: 15.4	1: 17.1

So it was working.

By now Rosberg had dispatched Guerrero, Serra was out after an accident with Jarier, and Watson spun avoiding that. The McLaren wouldn't restart. Rosberg was 12th and coming strong but Goodyear had produced a new tyre and on full tanks he had serious understeer.

By lap 5 he was 11th and now he proceeded to dispatch Giacomelli. He was only some 30 seconds behind Piquet, and of course Piquet was going to be pitting. He never did. On lap 10 he had a fuel injection problem and toured, arm raised. It opened the race to Lauda and gave this running order behind him: Pironi, Daly, de Angelis, Warwick, de Cesaris.

Warwick moved up to de Angelis and moved straight past into Westfield, a power play, especially on half tanks. Still Rosberg came – sixth by lap 14. Pironi and Daly circled together.

	Pironi	Daly	Warwick
Lap 15	1: 16.4	1: 16.3	1: 15.4
Lap 16	1: 15.8	1: 16.1	1: 15.1
Lap 17	1: 15.9	1: 15.9	1: 15.4

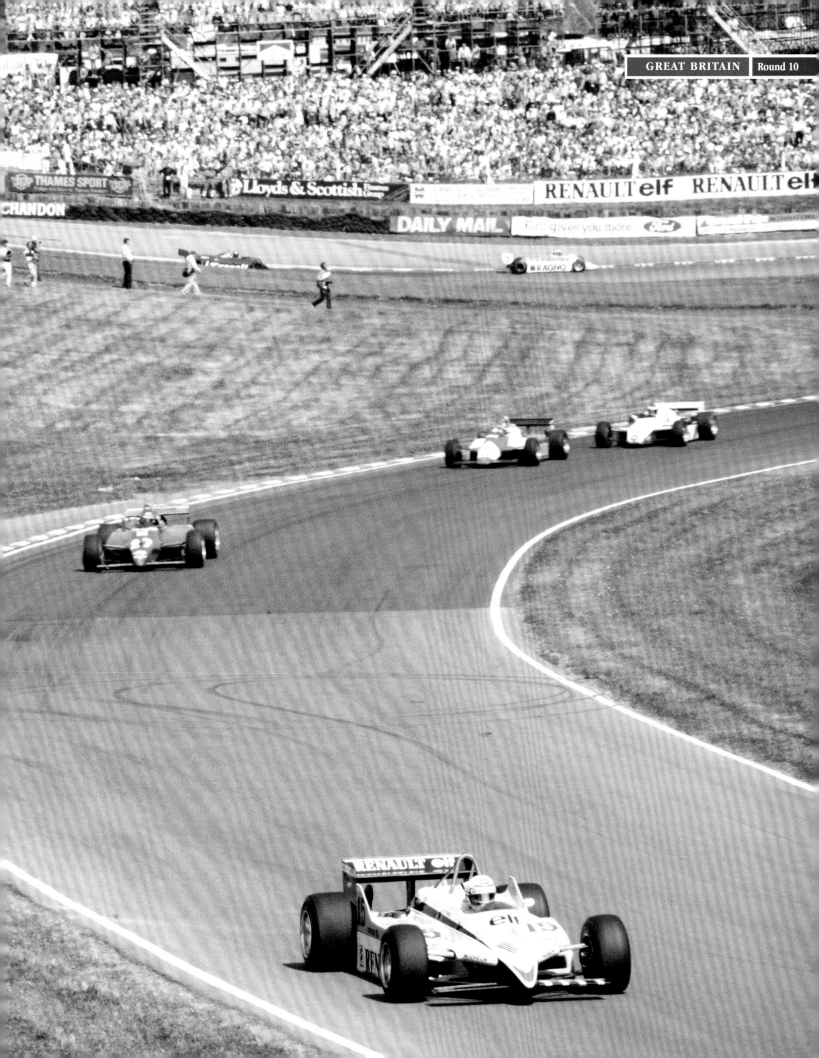

Warwick was catching them, although on that lap 17 Rosberg pitted for tyres. He'd explain that understeer puts too much heat into the tyres and you progressively destroy them. As he reached his pit he saw the team 'in despair' and as they tried to get him back out as fast as possible they panicked. He saw Patrick Head, designer Frank Dernie and Frank Williams himself looking downcast. Rosberg felt his world collapsing because, on top of all this, he knew perfectly well that the understeer would destroy the tyres the team was struggling to put in. He resumed at the rear of the field – again.

Warwick reached Daly and Pironi and was about to put himself, Toleman and Hart all over the world's television screens as per request.

Round the Clearways sweep into lap 18 the Toleman – imperious in its pace – drew full up to the Williams and, as Paddock Hill Bend loomed, Warwick simply placed it to the inside and sailed by. James Hunt, commentating on the BBC, found a phrase: Warwick 'ate Daly alive.'

He saw Pironi directly ahead and for six laps stayed with him.

Witty was 'watching it from behind the pits and I thought we'd do well to get to lap 25,' either running out of fuel or unreliability ending it. 'That came, and lap 26...'

On lap 26 Warwick hugged in behind Pironi round Clearways, hugged tight as they reached the flickering bays of the grid. Pironi made a move to go to mid-track but Warwick was already inside. Pironi

left him room on the inside through Paddock and Warwick had done it. At the instant he went by he cheered in the cockpit and then he saw the flags and banners waving to him.

'It was one of the great moments,' Warwick says. 'I'd had a bad start, the car was really difficult, and if those moments come along you have to grab them with both hands. Because the car wasn't particularly quick we qualified mid-field, the Pirellis were working fantastically and I remember, when I passed Pironi on the outside, I saw the crowd for the first time in my whole life. There was so much banner

ABOVE *In the end it was a straightforward run home for Lauda, who beat Pironi by 25 seconds.*

OPPOSITE *Warwick about to make Brands Hatch explode, and the truth of it all only emerged much later.*

LEFT *A world in headlines, and let's have a little British restraint from* The Times, *please.*

THE TIMES MONDA

Lauda's victory without a lapse

By John Blunsden

Nicki Lauda drove an immaculate race at Brands Hatch yesterday to give the Marlboro McLaren team their second consecutive victory in the RAC British Grand Prix. Lauda, who moved into the lead on the tenth of the 76 laps, went on to dominate the race and win a decisive victory on behalf of the users of the three-litre Cosworth Ford engine over the increasingly powerful opposition provided by the turbo-charged teams.

Nevertheless, turbo power proved useful on the final laps when Patrick Tambay mounted a successful attack on the JPS Lotus of Elio de Angelis to snatch third place in his Ferrari behind his teammate, the new world championship leader, Didier Pironi. Derek Daly recovered from a pit stop for replacement tyres to finish a close fifth, a few yards ahead of the surviving Renault of Alain Prost.

It was a race full of drama and again it began on the starting grid. The first upset was when Keke Rosberg's Saudia Williams, sitting in pole position, failed to start for the warm-up lap because of fuel pressure problems. Eventually he got away, very late, and although he caught up the remainder of the field he had to start the race from the back of the grid.

Meanwhile, up front, the second fastest car in practice, the Braham-BMW of Riccardo Patrese, slipped out of gear just before the starting light turned to green, and although Pironi weaved his way past the stranded car, Rene Arnoux caught it a glancing blow with his Renault, which lost a wheel and slewed back into the Brabham. Teo

second lap Jean-Pierre Jarier's Osella lost a wheel and was hit by Chico Serra's Fittipaldi, which rolled and caught fire, but both drivers emerged unharmed. Keke Rosberg, had to take violent avoiding action and damaged a

Back among the trophies: Lauda celebrates

been in 16th place on the grid with his heavyweight car, and he picked up a place a lap for the first five laps, then displaced De Cesaris's Alfa Romeo on lap seven to run sixth.

Piquet's retirement made

meeting when he outmanoeuvred the Ferrari at the same point for a while he went through to begin the chase of Lauda.

RESULTS: 1 N Lauda (Marlboro Me Ford) 76 laps, 1 hr 35 min 33.812 sec

Rosberg: team leader who leads from the front

Crashing the 70 barrier

By John Blunsden

Keke Rosberg, leader of the TAG Williams team, became the first and only driver to lap the 2.61-mile Grand Prix circuit in under 70 seconds at Brands Hatch yesterday. During the hour-long first qualification period for tomorrow's Marlboro-sponsored RAC British Grand Prix his Cosworth Ford-powered Saudia Williams was timed at 1min 9.54sec, an average speed of 135.302mph, to put the 33-year-old Finnish driver in pole position at this stage. The second hour of qualification runs will begin at 1.0 today.

The undulating nature of this circuit, which puts a bigger premium on ultimate road-holding than on top-end power, has been a leveller between turbo and non-turbo teams. For much of yesterday's practice Rosberg, his league Derek Daly and...

ABOVE *A picture
you normally never
see because the
photographers are
invariably elsewhere:
the cars form an orderly
queue to come in to the
pits when it's all over.*

waving, scarves, and you could hear them over the
noise of the engine, earplugs and everything. Quite
amazing. That moment did my career a huge amount
of good. Brands was quite a local track for me and I
knew it very well, I knew the right place to overtake
him. It ran out of fuel, which must mean it wasn't
carrying very much...'

Pironi, all unknowing, said 'Nothing I could do,'
and there would have been nothing he could have
done even if he had known.

Witty, watching intently, says 'Lap 27, the car's
still running and I began to have doubts, began
to wonder if they had changed their minds about
fuelling the car light.'

Easy to miss, in the communal fervour, was
that Lauda was actually going faster than the
Toleman, this Lauda who had perfected economy of
movement, who dealt in precision and efficiency and
logic, this Lauda who led by some 25 seconds.

Warwick slowed on lap 41.

Witty knew what had happened when, 'obviously,
he didn't appear.'

Warwick, interviewed on TV, said 'The car was
fantastic, the engine was superb, the Pirelli tyres

were just as good as when the race started. What
can I say? It's a bitter disappointment for Toleman
because the team above all else needs the break and
we just didn't get it.'

Witty remembers that. 'When Derek got back
Barrie Gill was doing the TV interviews and Derek
gave an Oscar-winning performance, which surprised
me somewhat.'

Hawkridge remains unrepentant. 'Even if you
take the light fuel, we ran 41 laps so we were light
but we weren't empty. People could draw their own
conclusions but what you couldn't take away from
it was that the car was a competitive package at
Brands Hatch. Derek got the Renault drive [in 1984]
and it didn't do Toleman any harm. It was a strategic
decision to try and make the best of that weekend
– and we knew that, if we'd been on the tyres Pirelli
wanted us on, we wouldn't have been competitive
at all...'

On lap 44, Lauda led Pironi by 42 seconds.

The race drifted into stalemate, or rather
remained in Lauda's control. He did not relinquish it
and was never going to relinquish it.

'Everything worked very well right from the

FAN'S EYE VIEW

*'Having finished school for the summer holidays
I spent five glorious days at Brands Hatch – that
fantastic amphitheatre of motor sport – sneaking past
security guards and volunteer marshals to gain access
to the pits at every available opportunity.*

*'On the Saturday I hid under a team transporter,
only emerging when the general public had long gone.*

*'I was able to photograph the drivers and teams
during lunch and official qualifying.*

'During the race I stood at Graham Hill bend.'

JULIAN EYRES
HIGH WYCOMBE, UK

FROM TOP CLOCKWISE
*Beautiful bodies, all in a
row; Teo Fabi, contemplating
outqualifying Warwick? The
court of soon-to-be-king
Rosberg, plus obligatory
cigarette; Eddie Cheever
contemplating not finishing?
Henton, contemplating
setting fastest lap? Ken
Tyrrell (left) might be
contemplating it too.*

beginning,' he said. 'I was surprised to be in the lead so early.' He was given a genuinely emotional reception by the crowd. 'I think the British people like me and I saw that at the finish. I wasn't perhaps the man they wanted to see win but they gave me real tribute.' He paused and surveyed his Championship chances, because he was now third. 'I think Brands is one of the last tracks where we can beat the turbos. At the others it's going to be very difficult.'

Rosberg had dropped out after 50 laps with low fuel pressure and let the team know his feelings. Echoing Lauda, he realised that if you didn't have a turbo you had to win here and he'd got nothing.

On lap 63 Brian Henton set fastest lap in the Tyrrell with yet another variation of The Ploy, this one entirely unplanned. 'You know why I did the lap? Because I had Alboreto's spare car. My race car had blown up in practice so I was in Alboreto's spare and that was much quicker. We did come in – I think the nosecone was loose – and they did put new tyres on. That's what you do. I went out and I was pulling people in and I finished eighth. That fastest

lap is about the only thing I managed to achieve in Formula One!'

Pironi 35, Watson 30, Lauda 24, Rosberg 21, Prost and Patrese 19.

After the race Denis Jenkinson of *Motor Sport* approached Witty and 'said he thought he heard Warwick's engine cough. He was pretty astute and the only guy who suspected something. I said "Oh!" We always said we would keep stum. Obviously the team knew about it and I wondered how long they would keep quiet but it stayed silent for the event. It got Derek the Renault drive and it launched Toleman. I had Michael Turner do a painting of it, Derek going past Pironi. Anyway, after Brands we went back to normal service.'

That would be the French Grand Prix, only a week away, which is to say that the truckies, the mechanics and everybody else needed to be down by the Riviera on the Wednesday, and they weren't even out of Brands Hatch into the traffic jam yet.

Well hell, yes, that's life in the big city.

Footnote: 1. Grand Prix International; 2. Keke.

OPPOSITE *Not a bad result for Marlboro.*

BELOW *Faces of the race: Lauda keeping his emotions under control, Pironi, too, but Tambay (right) finds a smile.*

Marlboro

Race Result

WINNING SPEED 200.73kmh/124.73mph

FASTEST LAP 207.38kmh/128.86mph
(Henton 1m 13.02s on lap 63)

LAP LEADERS Piquet 1–9 (9);
Lauda 10–76 (67)

RACE

	Driver	Team	Engine	Laps	Time
1	N. Lauda	McLaren MP4B	Cosworth V8	76	1h 35m 33.81s
2	D. Pironi	Ferrari 126C2	Ferrari V6t	76	1h 35m 59.53s
3	P. Tambay	Ferrari 126C2	Ferrari V6t	76	1h 36m 12.24s
4	E. de Angelis	Lotus 91	Cosworth V8	76	1h 36m 15.05s
5	D. Daly	Williams FW08	Cosworth V8	76	1h 36m 15.24s
6	A. Prost	Renault RE30B	Renault V6t	76	1h 36m 15.44s
7	B. Giacomelli	Alfa Romeo 182	Alfa V12	75	
8	B. Henton	Tyrrell 011	Cosworth V8	75	
9	M. Baldi	Arrows A4	Cosworth V8	74	
10	J. Mass	March 821	Cosworth V8	73	
r	A. de Cesaris	Alfa Romeo 182	Alfa V12	66	Electrics
r	E. Cheever	Talbot Ligier JS19	Matra V12	60	Engine
r	M. Surer	Arrows A4	Cosworth V8	59	Engine
r	K. Rosberg	Williams FW08	Cosworth V8	50	Fuel pressure
nc	M. Alboreto	Tyrrell 011	Cosworth V8	44	
r	J. Laffite	Talbot Ligier JS19	Matra V12	41	Gearbox
r	D. Warwick	Toleman TG181C	Hart 4t	40	Out of fuel
r	N. Mansell	Lotus 91	Cosworth V8	29	Broken skirt/driver discomfort
r	N. Piquet	Brabham BT50	BMW 4t	9	Fuel injection
r	R. Guerrero	Ensign N181	Cosworth V8	3	Accident/oil line/engine
r	J.-P. Jarier	Osella FA1C	Cosworth V8	2	Accident
r	C. Serra	Fittipaldi F8D	Cosworth V8	2	Accident/fire
r	J. Watson	McLaren MP4B	Cosworth V8	2	Spin
r	T. Fabi	Toleman TG181C	Hart 4t	0	Accident
r	R. Arnoux	Renault RE30B	Renault V6t	0	Accident
r	R. Patrese	Brabham BT50	BMW 4t	0	Stalled on grid/accident
nq	M. Winkelhock	ATS D5	Cosworth V8		
nq	J. Lammers	Theodore TY02	Cosworth V8		
nq	E. Salazar	ATS D5	Cosworth V8		
nq	R. Boesel	March 821	Cosworth V8		

nc = did not complete=; nq = did not qualify; r = retired

CHAMPIONSHIP

	Driver	Points
1	D. Pironi	35
2	J. Watson	30
3	N. Lauda	24
4	K. Rosberg	21
5	A. Prost	19
	R. Patrese	19
7	N. Piquet	17
8	E. de Angelis	13
9	M. Alboreto	10
	E. Cheever	10
11	D. Daly	7
	N. Mansell	7
13	C. Reutemann	6
	G. Villeneuve	6
15	A. de Cesaris	5
16	R. Arnoux	4
	P. Tambay	4
18	J.-P. Jarier	3
19	M. Winkelhock	2
	E. Salazar	2
	M. Surer	2
22	J. Laffite	1
	M. Baldi	1
	F. Serra	1

	Team	Points
1	McLaren	54
2	Ferrari	45
3	Brabham	36
4	Williams	34
5	Renault	23
6	Lotus	20
7	Talbot Ligier	11
8	Tyrrell	10
9	Alfa Romeo	5
10	ATS	4
11	Osella	3
	Arrows	3
13	Fittipaldi	1

ORDERS & DISORDERS

FRANCE, PAUL RICARD

Paul Ricard was a very strange place and very strange things were to happen there. That was entirely appropriate because the circuit and its location reflected with unerring accuracy the separation between the seductive imagery of Grand Prix racing and the reality of it.

The circuit lay some distance from the Mediterranean coast, the topless beaches and the beautiful people, although this was sometimes claimed for it to sustain the imagery. In truth it lay dry like a dead snake somewhere in the tree-clad hills of Provence along narrow, contorting roads which clogged solid at Grand Prix time with many thousands trying to get in and, later, the same many thousands trying to get out. In purely logistical terms, or rather an absence of logistics, access was at least as bad as any British Grand Prix at Silverstone (which alternated with Brands) – itself an utter nightmare. Whole families (French or British according to the venue) grew visibly older as they waited in enormous, static columns of cars in the countryside.

Paul Ricard had its own airstrip so that the rich people, not always beautiful, could gaze down from their executive jets on the poor bloody columns as they rose, free, and turned towards the delights of Paris.

The roads up (and back down) were – because of the hills – like rides on a big dipper when the traffic did move. You could hear the crickets – the authentic background music of Provence – making

RIGHT *The mighty Mistral straight, stretching into infinity. This is Prost, who'd have such an unhappy race.*

France
Paul Ricard

RACE DATE July 25th

CIRCUIT LENGTH 5.81km/3.61 miles

NO. OF LAPS 54

RACE DISTANCE
313.74km/194.94 miles

WEATHER Hot, dry

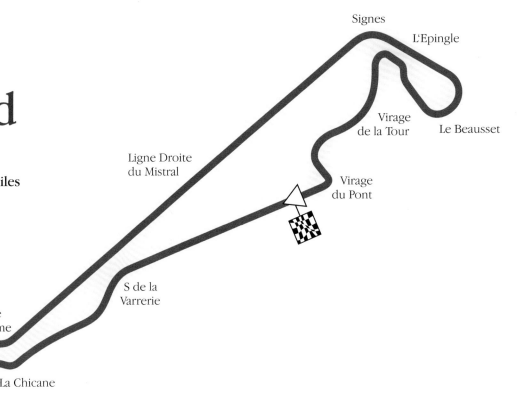

Signes

L'Epingle

Virage
de la Tour

Le Beausset

Ligne Droite
du Mistral

Virage
du Pont

S de la
Varrerie

Ste
Baume

L'Ecole

La Chicane

DRIVER'S VIEW

'It was a long circuit and you had the Mistral straight. Once you got to the end of that it was more technical but also driven at high speed. You remember the "S" of de la Varrérie after the pits? You took that at more than 170mph. That was where Elio [de Angelis] was killed [in 1986] and afterwards it was made into a right turn. When you had a car which was well balanced, as I had for the Grand Prix, it was OK in fifth gear. That means flat out. And taken with your eyes wide open, not shut! On the Mistral we were doing 330kmh [205mph] but it wasn't exciting. You were going straight ahead, you didn't have much to do so you could rest. It was when you got to the end and went into Signes: you'd be doing 280, 300kmh [170, 185mph] and that became a difficult corner. I liked Ricard a lot. You couldn't really compare it with any other circuit because you had this long, long straight and then the technical part – and you had plenty of problems with the tyres because the track was very abrasive.'

—— René Arnoux

their incessant knitting noises with their knees, strident as a sharp sziss sound. You could also see, in clearings, ladies sitting on battered chairs wearing very little and promising a good time either in the bushes or on the back seats of cars they'd parked nearby. They were completely shameless in – forgive me – their body language, just in case anybody misunderstood what was on offer, and they were, physically as well as geographically, about as far away from the creatures on the topless beaches as you could get. They gave the term Service Station a whole new meaning.

The circuit itself, the artificial creation of the Ricard family and their fortune from the drink which bore their name, was in 1982 a very modern facility although 12 years old: a mere fresh-faced child in the context of most other circuits which (again in 1982, before The Ecclestone Imperative) resembled widows fallen on hard times.

Ricard, however, was fearsome fast, its Mistral Straight (named for the wind which rakes the Rhône-Saône valley) the longest on the calendar and permitting the absolute maximum speed of which a Grand Prix was capable. Tambay would do 339kmh (210mph) whilst at Signes, the right-hander at the end of it, Rosberg was doing 278kmh (172mph). Even in a world living through the medium of speed these were stunning. Marseilles, the sprawling port where many people stayed for the Grand Prix, was 484 miles from Paris. Tambay would have covered

that in two and a half hours at his Mistral speed. The fabled TGV high-speed trains, traversing France in competition with air travel, couldn't have stayed with him. They did a mere 200mph.

The whole area around the circuit was bleached by sunlight and little rainfall, boulders were strewn here and there, and the ensemble resembled a lunar base. It was also wonderfully quixotic in a particularly French way in that they issued passes to get out as well as in (Derick Allsop of the *Daily Mail* wondered 'If you haven't got one, do you have to stay forever?'); and when there was no racing, to keep the coarse, sparse grass under control they shepherded hundreds of sheep in and let them graze. If you chanced to be there then, the Mistral, the shimmering pits complex and the enormous, shifting tide of sheep suggested you'd wandered into an avant-garde film rather than a lunar base.

To the French it was a precious place, part of what they call their patrimoine, a strong word meaning their heritage, just as everything else in France was, but – and the but is significant – even more important to them as a place where they (in this case Renault, Prost and Arnoux) could challenge and defeat the best the rest of the world could put against them. There were many, many delights in France but they did not include the ladies on the chairs and they did not include French chauvinism, which was about to be played out in full measure. I cannot tell you whether the French have raised sex

ABOVE *The other home match: Frenchman Jarier qualified the Osella but the driveshaft broke and he didn't complete a lap.*

ABOVE *The home
match: two Frenchmen
(Arnoux nearest
camera) put two
French cars on the
front row for the
French Grand Prix*

to an art form (as they claim) but they have achieved
a comparable level with the chauvinism.

It brought a truly great weight onto the Renault
team and was passed on through the team to the
two drivers. That refracted, splintering the team into
acrimony, mistrust and recrimination; and what the
team and drivers did divided France to the point
where Prost, afterwards, was abused at a real service
station because the attendant thought he was Arnoux
and thus felt liberated to say what he thought about
that Prost, imagining he was saying it to Arnoux.

Yes, Paul Ricard was a very strange place and very
strange things were about to happen there.

The Renaults dominated qualifying, Pironi splitting
them on the first day (Prost fastest, Arnoux third)
but Arnoux taking pole from Prost on the second.
Arnoux's pole lap was driven at an average speed
of 137.6mph which, leaving Paris at 9.00 on any

morning, would have got him to Marseilles nicely in
time for lunch.

Only Arnoux and Prost did laps in the 1m 34s.
This really was turbo territory although they were
now delivering so much power that, as Pironi
confessed, Signes could no longer be taken in one
without lifting off the accelerator.

Lauda was the leading non-turbo driver on the
fifth row, having done 1m 37.77s, Rosberg – talking
in terms of needing miracles – next on 1m 37.78.
They'd had a moment in second qualifying when
Rosberg asserted that Lauda had deliberately blocked
him after making a rude gesture. Rosberg was visibly
angry after the session and went forth to clarify
matters. You could do that with Lauda, as Rosberg
knew, and he did.

Watson qualified two places behind Rosberg and
needed miracles just as much.

STARTING GRID

1	
1:34.40	**2**
R. Arnoux	1:34.68
	A. Prost

3	**4**
1:35.79	1:35.81
D. Pironi	**R. Patrese**

5	**6**
1:35.90	1:36.35
P. Tambay	**N. Piquet**

7	**8**
1:37.57	1:37.70
A. de Cesaris	**B. Giacomelli**

9	**10**
1:37.77	1:37.78
N. Lauda	**K. Rosberg**

11	**12**
1:38.76	1:38.94
D. Daly	**J. Watson**

13	**14**
1:39.11	1:39.30
E. de Angelis	**D. Warwick**

15	**16**
1:39.33	1:39.60
M. Alboreto	**J. Laffite**

17	**18**
1:39.90	1:39.91
J.-P. Jarier	**M. Winkelhock**

19	**20**
1:40.18	1:40.33
E. Cheever	**M. Surer**

21	**22**
1:40.42	1:40.67
T. Fabi	**E. Salazar**

23	**24**
1:40.85	1:40.97
B. Henton	**G. Lees**

25	**26**
1:40.99	1:41.57
M. Baldi	**J. Mass**

Brabham, meanwhile, prepared to try and implement The Pit Stop Ploy.

Based on qualifying, and making the necessary assumption that both their cars would function for the full 54 laps, Renault could divide the race up as they wished. Here an imperative came into play: the Championship. The full extent of the French government's financial involvement in the company was never absolutely clear but French taxpayers' money was going in and what the French government wanted was the Championship: a Frenchman in a French car beats the world. Under the logic of this, Renault would maximise their chances whenever and however they could, and you did not have to be a mathematician to see the implications of the points table. Prost had 19, Arnoux 4 and with only six races left (including this one) the chances of Arnoux catching Pironi, Watson, Lauda and Rosberg looked slight. It would be hard for Prost, too, but possible. A win here and he would be among the Championship leaders.

Team manager Jean Sage said: 'Before the race we all decided that, if we were running first and second then Alain should win. René agreed to that, and there was no discussion about "if the lead is so many seconds". Whatever the gap between them, Prost was to win – unless the cars were being threatened by another, in which case the order was to stay the same.'

Prost would write[1] 'Gérard Larrousse told René to let me through if the two of us were among the points coming up to finish [...] I must stress that I didn't make any such request to René or Gérard Larrousse, simply because if I had been in Réne's shoes, I would have refused point blank. Réne didn't protest against Larrousse's instructions.'

Arnoux, as it seems, kept his own counsel and for the most obvious of reasons: a motor race is a

BELOW Patrese before his Brabham caught fire, setting fastest lap.

tumultuous journey into the unknown and any one of a hundred factors can alter it at any instant. The team orders might never be implemented because the circumstances simply hadn't arisen (which is what invariably did happen).

Looking back now, Arnoux explains: 'We were half way through the season and I had a contract with equal status to Prost and it was a season where drivers didn't have too many points.'

The atmosphere at a French Grand Prix, especially Ricard, was the opposite to the British. At Ricard, people came to be seen. In Britain – Silverstone or Brands – people came to see the people they hadn't seen since this time last year. It gave the British Grand Prix the feel of a giant club meeting, or a reunion, and Ricard an affinity with the Cannes Film Festival where, no doubt, you'd meet a lot of the same crowd.

The grid that hot afternoon teemed with so many people you could no longer see the cars. Who were these people? A small number were the drivers, team members and mechanics. The rest? They strutted with an air of importance, stooping to examine the cockpits and then, all at once as the countdown began, they were gone to the shade where, perhaps, loose-limbed lovelies in skimpy uniforms soothed them with aperitifs.

Arnoux led from Prost, Pironi tight up to them and the Brabhams predatory. They travelled through the long sweep called Sainte-Baume and onto the Mistral. Patrese went past Pironi but Rosberg went off, dropping him to 12th and needing even more of a miracle.

Down the start-finish straight Piquet dealt with Pironi. On the Mistral he dealt with Prost.

By lap 5 Patrese led from Piquet, as they would have to do if they were running light to make their fuel stop. Arnoux was content to let them go. 'I spared my tyres at the start when I had full tanks. I didn't want to overheat them while I stayed in touch with the Brabhams, out on half tanks. I wasn't going to fall for that game. For the first ten laps I drove with my head, not my hands. I tried to stay as cool and lucid as possible. It would have been dumb to fall apart so early.'

On lap 9 Patrese suddenly slowed, flames from the rear of the car, and Piquet went through. The engine had blown. Patrese got it back and parked it in front of the pit lane wall, the flames a proper fire now. He looked in his mirror and thought blimey. He scrambled to get himself out and a fire marshal yanked him, dragging him clear.

Piquet pulled away from Arnoux at the rate of a second a lap.

On lap 11 at Signes, the corner where the cars carried such terrible speed in, Baldi and Mass touched. They went off into the small run-off area, tearing down catch fencing as they went. Baldi came to rest on the trackside of the guardrail protected by a tyre barrier but, 20 yards further on, Mass struck the tyres and guardrail a tremendous blow. His March vaulted across the little access road behind it and came to rest upside down and burning on the densely-populated spectator slope beyond. Several people suffered burns but by sheer good fortune no one was killed.[2] While the firefighters arrived Baldi sprinted over and tried to haul Mass out. Mass emerged with light burns.

It could have been an horrific thing.

On lap 12 Piquet led by nine seconds and that represented the focal point because, lap after lap, the order remained Piquet, Arnoux, Prost, Pironi. On lap 14 Watson retired with an electrical problem.

On lap 22 the Brabham pit crew came out and made ready for the stop, Piquet leading by 17

GRAND PRIX DE FRANCE - FORMULE 1

Tant qu'il y aura des turbos

Alain Prost et Renault sont en tête à l'issue des premiers essais au Castellet

Envoyé spécial : PATRICE FARDEAU

Hier au Castellet, Didier Pironi, leader du championnat du monde, entouré, des deux conducteurs de « Renault » : Alain Prost et René Arnoux.

FORMULE 1 AU CASTELLET

Ce fut un championnat de France !

Renault renoue avec le succès, René Arnoux l'emportant sur son « coéquipier » Alain Prost et les Ferrari de Pironi et Tambay

Envoyé spécial : PATRICE FARDEAU

Champagne évidemment français pour un podium qui / Alain Prost, à gauche de René Arnoux qui lui tourne le / apprécier. Il a peut-être quelques rancœurs...

FORMULE 1

La victoire en grinçant...

René Arnoux a-t-il eu raison ?

Avec son doublé au Grand Prix de France, l'écurie « Renault sport » a tout pour être heureuse. Et pourtant ce n'est pas vraiment aujourd'hui la joie chez les « jeunes », où l'heure est plutôt à quelques grincements de dents.

Il est permis de rester quelque peu sceptique quand René Arnoux, pour justifier son refus de laisser la victoire à son coéquipier de l'écurie Renault, Alain Prost, à l'arrivée de la course du Castellet dimanche, dit : « Je n'ai pas perdu espoir d'être champion du monde. Les circuits à venir, très rapides, me plaisent. »

Arnoux est tout de même à 26 points du leader actuel du Championnat du monde, son compatriote Didier Pironi, et en est encore séparé par six pilotes (dont Prost...), et si mathématiquement, en cinq courses restant à disputer, tout est possible, il faudrait tout de même qu'il bénéficie d'un étonnant concours de circonstances, lui qui, depuis le 1er mars 1980 à Kyalami (Afrique du Sud), date de sa deuxième et dernière victoire, avait connu la malchance plus souvent qu'à son tour.

Et c'est sans doute, en raison de ce qui précède, qu'il faut respecter ce qui avait été sa réaction première, à chaud, quand il avait lâché : « Moi aussi, j'ai droit à la victoire ».

Gérard Larrousse, le directeur de « Renault-sport », était plus partagé. S'il versa dans un premier temps une larme d'émotion à voir ses deux voitures arriver les premières, après avoir si longtemps souffert des comparaisons avec « Ferrari » et « Brabham », il analysait plus tard la situation, à froid : « Il était de mon devoir de directeur d'écurie de passer le panneau privilégiant Prost, puisque tous nos efforts sont tendus vers le titre mondial. Cela dit, il faut se mettre à la place d'Arnoux. J'ai également été pilote et humainement je ne peux complètement le blâmer. »

Mais les trois points dont Arnoux n'a pas voulu faire cadeau à Prost peuvent coûter cher, au moment des comptes, fin septembre à Las Vegas, car maintenant, si les « Renault » ont renoué avec la fiabilité sur les circuits ou les « turbos » doivent dominer, la lutte sera serrée entre les « Renault » de Prost et Arnoux et les « Ferrari » de leurs compatriotes Pironi et Tambay.

À Las Vegas, on saura déjà comment les équipes seront composées pour 1983, on saura ce que Prost voulait dire quand il lâchait : « L'an prochain, nous ne serons plus dans la même écurie ». À ce sujet, Arnoux est resté très vague : « Bien sûr, j'ai des contacts avec d'autres écuries, comme tout le monde ». Et Gérard Larrousse, plus encore : « Rien n'est fait...

LEFT *A world in headlines, and the 'victory which grates.'*

OPPOSITE *On lap 9, Patrese had an engine fire but, unaware, made his way to the pits. By then everybody else on the circuit was fully aware.*

seconds. On lap 23 Piquet did not pit but surely would next time round. On the Mistral smoke belched from the Brabham and through Signes he pulled off. The Ploy remained untested in the only place which matters, the heat of battle.

Then there were two, Arnoux and Prost, and the Renault plan could be implemented. On lap 25 Arnoux led Prost by ten seconds, Pironi running a steady third 16 seconds behind Prost. Pironi was rapping out laps of 1m 44s regular as a drumbeat, but so was Arnoux and so was Prost. Sometime after this Prost lost a skirt, making the Renault a handful and making the catching of Arnoux problematical.

Arnoux showed no signs of being caught. That created a dilemma within Renault, because with 20 laps to go the order had solidified – Arnoux, Prost, Pironi, Tambay, Rosberg, Alboreto – and if it finished like that, but Arnoux contrived to give Prost the win,

the Championship would look very, very different: Pironi 39, Watson 30, Prost 28, Lauda 24, Rosberg 23.

They ran towards the end and what the French call a denouement, meaning the conclusion but carrying theatrical implications of surprises. There would be those, all right, not least because Arnoux now led by 23 seconds. The Renault team held out a pit board and nothing could be lost in translation to the drivers:

T 10   1 ALAIN   2 RENE

– ten laps to go [T = tours, laps], Prost to win, Arnoux second. Arnoux's response came in statistics and decimal points, and they could not be lost in translation back to the pit lane wall, the team and their board – even though Renault would hold the board out again four more times.

BELOW *Arnoux leads Prost through the chicane and when the race finished like that the Renault team detonated.*

'I found it completely abnormal to give my leading place up,' Arnoux says, 'and at one moment my lead was 35 seconds.'

	Arnoux	Prost
Lap 45	1:44.0	1:44.0
T 9	1 ALAIN	2 RENE
	Arnoux	Prost
Lap 46	1:44.4	1:43.7
Lap 47	1:44.8	1:44.2
Lap 48	1:44.7	1:44.1
Lap 49	1:44.9	1:44.2

'Of course I saw the pit boards!' Arnoux says. 'What did I think? I didn't think – I simply continued with my race.'

T5	1 ALAIN	2 RENE
	Arnoux	Prost
Lap 50	1:44.4	1:44.1
Lap 51	1:44.6	1:44.8
T 3	1 ALAIN	2 RENE
Lap 52	1:45.3	1:44.3
T 2	1 ALAIN	2 RENE
Lap 53	1:45.2	1:44.9
Lap 54	1:46.6	1:44.8

ABOVE *Sacré bleu! Pironi gives France a hat-trick podium by finishing third, behind Arnoux and Prost – oh, and Tambay was fourth.*

Arnoux won it by 17 seconds, Pironi 42 seconds away, and the crowd bathed in that: Renault 1–2 in France, both drivers French, Arnoux a chirpy, cheeky chappie who'd had shocking luck so far and, perhaps, reflected the irreverence of the ordinary Frenchman. Arnoux was extremely popular and more so after the one hour 33 minutes and 33 seconds of the French Grand Prix.

Pironi 39, Watson 30, Prost 25, Lauda 24, Rosberg 23, Patrese 19.

Arnoux walked into a storm. He said: 'Halfway through the race, unfortunately, I ran into serious vibration problems. I was shaken like a bag of beans and on the long straight I suffered from very painful hands just trying to keep the steering wheel steady. I couldn't slow down because I could foresee a pit stop to change tyres.'

That might have sounded like a justification for not slowing down, particularly since he expanded on it. 'When you have 23 seconds lead over the man behind you, you might as well stop to let him by. I did not want to take any risks in case I had to

ABOVE *Paul Ricard's straights were no place for a normally-aspirated engine and even Rosberg could not get the Williams any higher than fifth.*

OPPOSITE *If there was dissent in the Renault camp the drivers didn't show it. Prost (left) looks just as delighted as Arnoux – and Pironi looks happy, too.*

stop' – for tyres – 'during the last laps.' It was not a justification, because Arnoux added: 'What I really mean to say is this: if I hadn't had those vibrations I would have been even further ahead.'[3]

Prost countered with 'I don't care whether his lead was one second or 30. His orders were to let me by. Our situation is too critical and it is too important for us to win the title for our chances to be treated with such high-handedness.'

Sage said that 'from a human point of view one can understand René's decision to keep ahead, but from the team's point of view it is rather different. Obviously, we want to win the World Championship and Alain has a lot more points.'

Reflecting, Arnoux says: 'Was there a great drama within the team after the race? Yes and no, because first Renault were very happy: we had come first and second in the French Grand Prix, we were two French drivers and in French cars. And the man who finished third was Didier Pironi, the man who finished fourth was Patrick Tambay – four French drivers. But to get back to the main point: when you sign a contract with a team as No 2 driver, with precise clauses saying you are No 2 and you have to respect what the team demands of you, the moment you sign you are saying you are in agreement. I signed a contract without clauses about being No 2, or No 1 for that matter. With Alain, our contracts were equal. I wasn't a No 2 driver in my career!

'If we had been, say, two Grands Prix from the end of the season and I had had virtually no points and Prost had the possibility of winning the World Championship, why shouldn't I have played the team game? But in the middle of a low-scoring season... it was ridiculous.'

Reflecting,[4] Prost would say that Larrousse was 'crazy even to propose such an arrangement' because it fundamentally misjudged how racing drivers thought but, even so, he felt embittered that Arnoux had 'welshed'.

Hence Prost's decision to speak publicly.

It brought him to the service station, the attendant, the mistaken identity and the tirade against that Prost on his way home. Monsieur Prost could hardly pay with his credit card – letting the attendant see who he was – so he paid cash and drove out of there at racing speed.

Footnote: 1. Life In The Fast Lane; 2. This crash gave rise to a celebrated story within Formula One media circles. Barrie Gill, entrepreneur and much else, was covering the race for The Sun newspaper in London. He rushed to a phone and rang them. 'Something terrible's happened down here,' he said breathlessly, 'dozens dead.' Another journalist, overhearing, started to make hand-signals and Gill lowered the receiver. The journalist explained that there weren't fatalities. 'No one?' Gill said, loudly and incredulously in his Leeds accent. 'No one?'; 3. Quoted in Grand Prix International; 4. Life In The Fast Lane.

Race Result

WINNING SPEED 201.21kmh/125.02mph

FASTEST LAP 209.00kmh/129.86mph
(Patrese 1m 40.07s on lap 4)

LAP LEADERS Arnoux 1–2, 24–54 (33);
Patrese 3–7 (5); Piquet 8–23 (16)

RACE

	Driver	Team	Engine	Laps	Time
1	R. Arnoux	Renault RE30B	Renault V6t	54	1h 33m 33.21s
2	A. Prost	Renault RE30B	Renault V6t	54	1h 33m 50.52s
3	D. Pironi	Ferrari 126C2	Ferrari V6t	54	1h 34m 15.34s
4	P. Tambay	Ferrari 126C2	Ferrari V6t	54	1h 34m 49.45s
5	K. Rosberg	Williams FW08	Cosworth V8	54	1h 35m 04.21s
6	M. Alboreto	Tyrrell 011	Cosworth V8	54	1h 35m 05.55s
7	D. Daly	Williams FW08	Cosworth V8	53	
8	N. Lauda	McLaren MP4B	Cosworth V8	53	
9	B. Giacomelli	Alfa Romeo 182	Alfa V12	53	
10	B. Henton	Tyrrell 011	Cosworth V8	53	
11	M. Winkelhock	ATS D5	Cosworth V8	52	
12	G. Lees	Lotus 91	Cosworth V8	52	
13	M. Surer	Arrows A4	Cosworth V8	52	
14	J. Laffite	Talbot Ligier JS19	Matra V12	51	
15	D. Warwick	Toleman TG181C	Hart 4t	50	
16	E. Cheever	Talbot Ligier JS19	Matra V12	49	
r	A. de Cesaris	Alfa Romeo 182	Alfa V12	25	Front tyre/accident
r	N. Piquet	Brabham BT50	BMW 4t	23	Engine
r	E. de Angelis	Lotus 91	Cosworth V8	17	Fuel pressure
r	J. Watson	McLaren MP4B	Cosworth V8	13	Battery lead
r	J. Mass	March 821	Cosworth V8	10	Accident
r	M. Baldi	Arrows A4	Cosworth V8	10	Accident
r	R. Patrese	Brabham BT50	BMW 4t	8	Engine/fire
r	E. Salazar	ATS D5	Cosworth V8	2	Accident
r	T. Fabi	Toleman TG181C	Hart 4t	0	Oil pump drive
r	J.-P. Jarier	Osella FA1C	Cosworth V8	0	Driveshaft
nq	J. Lammers	Theodore TY02	Cosworth V8		
nq	R. Guerrero	Ensign N181	Cosworth V8		
nq	C. Serra	Fittipaldi F9	Cosworth V8		
nq	R. Boesel	March 821	Cosworth V8		

nq = did not qualify; r = retired

CHAMPIONSHIP

	Driver	Points
1	D. Pironi	39
2	J. Watson	30
3	A. Prost	25
4	N. Lauda	24
5	K. Rosberg	23
6	R. Patrese	19
7	N. Piquet	17
8	R. Arnoux	13
	E. de Angelis	13
10	M. Alboreto	11
11	E. Cheever	10
12	P. Tambay	7
	D. Daly	7
	N. Mansell	7
15	C. Reutemann	6
	G. Villeneuve	6
17	A. de Cesaris	5
18	J.-P. Jarier	3
19	M. Winkelhock	2
	E. Salazar	2
	M. Surer	2
22	J. Laffite	1
	M. Baldi	1
	F. Serra	1

	Team	Points
1	McLaren	54
2	Ferrari	52
3	Renault	38
4	Williams	36
	Brabham	36
6	Lotus	20
7	Tyrrell	11
	Talbot Ligier	11
9	Alfa Romeo	5
10	ATS	4
11	Osella	3
	Arrows	3
13	Fittipaldi	1

8 AUGUST

IMAGE FROM HELL

—— GERMANY, HOCKENHEIM

Somebody had to cover the German Grand Prix and the Austrian the week after. Since I'd been at four of the last five races, refusing was scarcely an option and, slowly but surely, I was being drawn in. Motor racing is very much about insiders and outsiders, with physical barriers (the metal fencing round the pits and paddock) standing eternally in between. Insiders get a profound sense of being at the centre of something very powerful because that's where they are. It can be intoxicating and so can the racing: Nigel Roebuck used the word 'narcotic' about Formula One recently.

There were many aspects to addiction but the most potent was that young men were prepared to risk, and were risking, their lives to fulfil their desires. You watched Connors and McEnroe and neither they, the officials nor the crowd were in any remote danger: fluffy ball, grass. Then you thought of Villeneuve and Paletti.

This season of 1982 held something else, too. Nobody, nobody, had the remotest idea what was going to happen next, and if you were getting close to it you had to be curious. I'd met Allsop at Brands Hatch and we agreed to travel together. Journalists invariably did (Roebuck and Alan Henry, Eoin Young and Maurice Hamilton, Pat Mennem of the *Mirror* and Colin Dryden of the *Daily Telegraph*, and so on). It was company and made life easier.

The week before Hockenheim, and for a reason I have completely forgotten, the *Daily Express* were offered an interview with a young Irishman called

RIGHT *The aftermath of the crash which almost killed Pironi in practice. His brutalised Ferrari is back in the pits, the damage a mute testament to the ferocity of what had happened to the car – and to him.*

Germany
Hockenheim

RACE DATE August 8th

CIRCUIT LENGTH
6.79km/4.22 miles

NO. OF LAPS 45

RACE DISTANCE
305.86km/190.05 miles

WEATHER Hot, dry

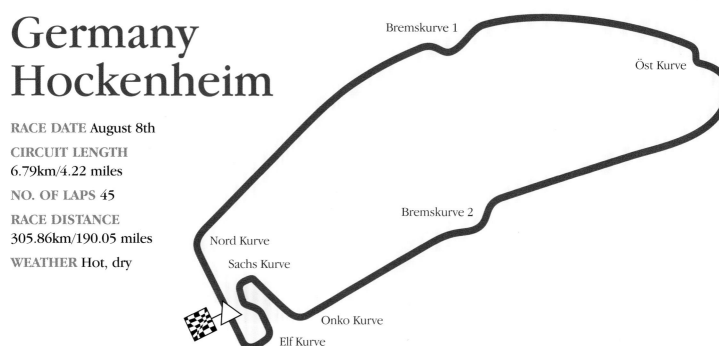

Bremskurve 1

Öst Kurve

Bremskurve 2

Nord Kurve

Sachs Kurve

Onko Kurve

Elf Kurve

Opel Kurve

DRIVER'S VIEW

'I liked Hockenheim, yes – the old Hockenheim – but I don't like the new one. In Formula 2 it was big fun and a very exciting place to drive around and in Formula One a very, very good track for the Ferrari. Once, twice, three times, four times you reached maximum speed and every time you had plenty of opportunity – and time – to get yourself ready for the high or low speed corners, for the heavy braking. Very exciting! Every time you reached maximum revs you didn't know whether you were going to be getting the engine blown in your face or not. We used to slipstream and you had time to look in your mirror to see if you had gained a few centimetres, a few inches or even a few metres on the guy following you or the guy in front of you. The chicanes were regarded as overtaking places.

'The Stadium Complex was very tricky to set the car up for because it also had to be set up for the long straights and you had to have stability under braking for those chicanes – very low downforce, and obviously low downforce when you went into the Stadium. It meant that the car was sliding away so you had to find a proper balance: it was a compromise between stability under braking, the high speeds that you had to reach, and the handling of the slow speed stuff in the Stadium.

'That made it interesting technically.'

Patrick Tambay

Tommy Byrne who was due to make his Grand Prix debut in a Theodore. I met him in a house in north London – again I have completely forgotten why. The interview, which appeared the following morning, began:

'Tommy Byrne was born on the back seat of a car on its way from Blackrock to the hospital in Drogheda thirty miles away. It was a good sign.'

He told a wonderful tale, of how he, brothers, sisters (five in all), parents and the occasional rat lived in a two-bedroomed house until it burnt down. He worked as a petrol pump attendant, borrowed money to race and was good enough to win the Formula Ford Festival at Brands Hatch in 1981 in Ayrton Senna's car: Senna didn't return from Brazil for the Festival and at that time had no intention of returning at all.

Byrne said: 'You jump into the car and it's just life, isn't it?'[1]

Imagining Byrne in Grand Prix racing was not at all difficult because who knew the backgrounds of any of them? And who cared?

The Hockenheim circuit is named after the town next to it. You come from one of two autobahns which slice past and there's a very German feel: the town's architecture is slightly portly, woods mask most of the circuit, and the immense stretch of stone grandstands – one of the autobahns is so close it allows glimpses of them – are uncompromisingly solid in a Germanic way. First built in the 1930s for motorbike racing and used as a test track for Mercedes-Benz in 1939, the extensive rebuild after the War (to accommodate the close autobahn) did not remove the atmosphere of the 1930s.

Motor racing people generally don't care about any of this any more than drivers' backgrounds and it is true the configuration of the track and the likely weather are infinitely more important than a circuit's surrounding geography. A pity. Each circuit, as I was discovering, brings a different terroir to the calendar and so does each country. That's why it's called the World Championship. The Hockenheim terroir, before it was gelded in 2002 and made to look like everywhere else, contained immensely fast straights in the forest and three chicanes (overtaking places, incidentally, under braking) to stop the speeds from going insane.

The fact that each track offered great danger is self-evident but the dangers were subtly different

BELOW From last place on the grid Marc Surer has a storming drive to take Arrows to sixth place, his second points finish of the season.

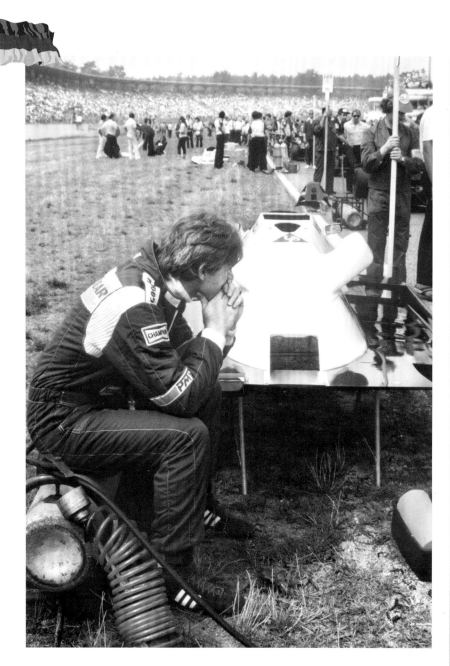

ABOVE *Derek Daly contemplates starting from the tenth row of the grid.*

depending on the configuration. Hockenheim was about to demonstrate that, and give me – apart from the Mansell interview – a sudden and profound insight into how drivers actually think.

On the Friday Lauda was hustling the McLaren round but even he could not force it to the pace of the turbos. Lauda bided his time, making his first run 20 minutes into the session and, on his only hot lap, did 1:52.6. It would be his best time but still more than four seconds slower than Pironi on provisional pole. Lauda bided his time again and, moving towards the end of the session, emerged. On his first hot lap he had to take to the grass to avoid Rupert Keegan's March and it may be his tyres picked up some dirt.

He fled along the start-finish straight but into the right-hander at the end spun off at high speed and the McLaren tore down some safety fencing

1	**1** - Vacant	**2** 1:48.89 A. Prost
2	**3** 1:49.25 R. Arnoux	**4** 1:49.41 N. Piquet
3	**5** 1:49.57 P. Tambay	**6** 1:49.76 R. Patrese
4	**7** 1:52.62 M. Alboreto	**8** 1:52.78 A. de Cesaris
5	**9** 1:52.89 K. Rosberg	**10** 1:53.07 J. Watson
6	**11** 1:53.88 B. Giacomelli	**12** 1:54.21 E. Cheever
7	**13** 1:54.47 E. de Angelis	**14** 1:54.59 D. Warwick
8	**15** 1:54.98 J. Laffite	**16** 1:55.22 M. Winkelhock
9	**17** 1:55.47 B. Henton	**18** 1:55.86 N. Mansell
10	**19** 1:55.87 D. Daly	**20** 1:56.25 J.-P. Jarier
11	**21** 1:56.48 R. Guerrero	**22** 1:56.53 E. Salazar
12	**23** 1:56.68 M. Baldi	**24** 1:57.24 R. Boesel
13	**25** 1:57.33 C. Serra	**26** 1:57.40 M. Surer

with great, rotating violence before it hit the barrier beyond. Yes, you do look for movement, and Lauda was moving all right, out of the car and on the move. I remember thinking: it's an entirely normal human reaction to get away from a place where something dangerous has just happened. At that moment Niki Lauda of the seared face appeared just like you and I. But appearances, as the old saw has it, really can be deceptive. He'd crashed at perhaps 150 miles an hour – faster than any shunt you or I are ever likely to have – and his arms had suffered whiplash. His thought processes were: there is just enough time to get into the spare car before the end of the session.

That's why he was running...

Rain drowned the Saturday morning untimed session but seven cars ventured out and were soon leaving roosters of water behind them. Pironi did

three laps and was easily quickest, 2:10.9 against Tambay's 2:14.2.

Pironi came fast from the chicane feeding onto the straight towards the Stadium Complex. Up ahead Prost travelled slowly (125mph!) on the left intending to pit and reached Derek Daly, who pulled the Williams over to the right. 'I know Prost is trying to pass me so I move over to the right side.' The fact that both intended to pit, and neither of course knew the other was pitting, is relevant only in that they were both travelling comparatively slowly.

Pironi, peering ahead into the water, noted Daly's movement and assumed it was to give him – Pironi – overtaking space. Pironi could not see Prost and, at about 150mph, his left front hit Prost's right rear, launching the Ferrari.

'I didn't know at the time that Pironi was beside Prost – Pironi was, I think, running two seconds

ABOVE *Turn one and Arnoux leads from Prost, Alboreto (3) right up there.*

ABOVE *By its nature, Hockenheim favoured the turbos but Rosberg rode the kerbs and attacked the chicanes to get the Williams to third.*

faster than everybody else. Absolutely flying,' Daly says. 'Pironi only sees a ball of spray, well, a ball of mist. When I pulled over to let Prost go by, just before the Stadium, Pironi saw the ball of mist pull over to the right side. He's thinking: there's only one car creating it. So he ploughs straight through the mist that is still there thinking: the other car will be gone when I reach that point. He doesn't realise Prost is in the middle of it – or he realises too late, hits him doing full chat and does the end over end. I never saw him.'

Prost watched Pironi 'actually overtake me in the air' and Pironi himself remembered seeing the tops of the trees. The Ferrari landed on its rear and somersaulted for 300 yards down the track. Prost had no brakes – the Renault badly damaged – and struggled to miss Pironi as the Ferrari came to rest the right way up after hammering the Armco. Some drivers stopped and Piquet removed Pironi's helmet. One report[2] said he 'nearly fainted' when he saw Pironi's injuries 'and had to walk away, ill, as the rescue crews started work.'

Professor Watkins was in a fast-response Porsche in the Stadium Complex and consequently had to go all the way round to reach Pironi. By then medical cars positioned nearer were already at work.

As it happened, Allsop and I reached the circuit just after the accident, anticipating the shrieking and droning of cars going round – what someone called That Certain Sound. We heard silence. It is no ordinary silence and there are reasons, not least that a racing circuit exists to generate sound because highly-stressed engines are loud and, if you're close to them, abominably, almost unbearably loud. Marlboro used to give away earplugs as a normal part of their publicity machine.

Silence is ominous because it can only mean something has happened, and invariably it takes an accident to stop the cars.

Hockenheim sounded like a tomb.

Pironi was conscious when Watkins reached him and he 'implored' Watkins to save his legs. Watkins gave his word that he would. Watkins, surveying the

personality. I always thought there was a hidden side to Pironi. You never quite saw the full picture. Believe it or not, the ruthless side of him I did not see. I partnered him in Austria, in Canada and at Watkins Glen – remember Ken Tyrrell ran a third car there because he was looking at me to replace Pironi, which is what I did the following year. So I got to know him a little better than I did Keke – no, I connected with him better. It hit me more personally when he got hurt than, say, Paletti because I didn't know Paletti at all.'

Tambay was also in the pits. 'Didier went out because he wanted to test a new set of wets. Whether he should have tested those wets or I should have tested them I can't remember exactly, or even why he went out. Franco Lini[4] came up to me and said "You're on your own, kid. Now you've got to do it for yourself and not for somebody else" – because I was always somebody else's team-mate.'

Humanitarian concerns aside, Pironi's career as a Grand Prix driver seemed over and consequently the Championship opened up. His 39 points were unlikely to withstand the efforts of the pursuing pack across a further four Grands Prix.

The rain lingered into second qualifying where Piquet went fastest with 2:03.4, a statistic which illustrates the perils of a wet track because, the day before, every driver had been under 2:00.

Someone took a photograph of Pironi in the midst of the wreckage. The Ferrari looked as if it had been crushed around him and, bareheaded, eyes closed, contorted face bloody, his head was

BELOW *Frank Williams, on top of every detail – again.*

state of both Pironi and the Ferrari, was 'amazed' he was still alive. Then the anaesthetic worked and Pironi drifted out of consciousness. His legs were so badly mangled that amputation was considered and the car had to be cut open to get him free. He was taken by helicopter to Heidelberg University Hospital where a surgeon said amputation might be necessary. Watkins again assured Pironi that that would not happen, certainly at this stage.[3]

Daly drove 'to the pit lane because I was going there anyway. I go to the pits and I'm sitting there. Suddenly a photographer arrives and then there's two or three more, and then there's more and more and more. I'm thinking: something unusual's going on here. Then I heard Pironi's crashed, then the session stopped. It was only when I backtracked that I put the pieces of the puzzle together.

'I was more connected to Pironi than I ever was to Keke because I drove with Pironi in three races [for Tyrrell in 1979] when Jarier got hepatitis. We drove from the airport together and I got to know him. He was a very unusual, quirky kind of

Sport

Frankfurter Allgemeine Zeitung

Hockenheim ohne Jochen Mass / Eine gefährliche Idee im Geschwindigkeitsrausch der Formel 1:

Mit halb gefülltem Tank in jeder Runde eine Sekunde schneller?

HOCKENHEIM. Was macht schnelle Autos noch schneller? Das ist alles, was in der Formel 1 wirklich interessiert. Für ein paar Zehntelsekunden wird also gewagt. Die Tüftler und Bastler in den Konstruktionsbüros der Rennställe haben praktisch Narrenfreiheit. Mit tausend Tricks wird da gearbeitet, jede noch so winzige Lücke in den technischen Auflagen für Formel-1-Fahrzeuge bedingungslos genutzt. Nach außen demonstrieren die konkurrierenden Konstrukteure zwar immer wieder Ei-

Als zwischen den Turbomannschaften und den anderen Rennställen sogar so etwas wie ein Burgfrieden geschlossen wurde und die Formel 1 Mitte der Saison beim Großen Preis von Belgien in Zolder endlich in geordnete Bahnen zu kommen schien, zerrte der tödliche Unfall des kanadischen Ferrari-Fahrers Gilles Villeneuve die Branche doch wieder ins Zwielicht.

Zu Ehren des Toten wurde die Rennstrecke in Montreal in „Gilles-Villeneuve-Kurs" umbenannt. Das erste Rennen

Jochen Mass freilich wird auf einen Start beim Großen Preis von Deutschland auf dem Hockenheimring verzichten. Er hat sich von den Folgen seines Unfalls noch nicht erholt. Beim freien Training sagte Mass am Freitag, seine gestauchte Wirbelsäule und zwei „angeknackste Rippen" machten das Fahren zur Tortur. „Man spürt erst im Auto, wie höllisch weh das tut", sagte der Bad Dürkheimer. Wie es aussehe, könne er auch beim Großen Preis von Österreich in Zeltweg und beim Grand

Zeitgewinn je Runde: eine weitere Sekunde. Abgesehen davon sorgt weniger Benzinballast an Bord für eine gewisse Schonung von Bremsen und Getriebe, die durch die urwüchsigen Kräfte des bayerischen Turbomotors schon mehrfach überfordert wurden.

So weit, so gut, auch wenn die weitere Erhöhung der wahnwitzigen Kurvengeschwindigkeiten in den flachen, kaum gefederten Ungetümen an sich schon ein Wahnsinn ist. Denn die Zentrifugalkräfte, die den Kopf des Fahrers mit mehrfacher Erdbeschleunigung nach außen drücken, erreichen bereits Grenzwerte, die kaum noch zu verantworten sind. Aber die gefährlichste Konsequenz des Brabham-Tricks liegt in der Notwendigkeit, in der Mitte des Rennens nachzutanken und zugleich die weichen Reifen zu wechseln. Um den Zeitgewinn, der bei einem Rennen wie dem Großen Preis von Deutschland am Sonntag in Hockenheim nach der Hälfte der Distanz (insgesamt 45 Runden = 305 Kilometer) etwa vierzig Sekunden betragen mag, durch den Stopp nicht völlig zu verspielen, müssen die Fahrer natürlich mit höchstmöglichem Tempo durch die enge Boxengasse jagen, womit eine weitere beträchtliche Gefahrenquelle durch die Findigkeit der Formel-1-Teams geschaffen wäre. Denn vor den Boxen halten sich bei jedem

Mary Meagher

Großer Preis von Deutschland / Tambay Sieger am Hockenheimring

Kollisionen und handgreifliche Auseinandersetzungen beim Großen Preis von Deutschland / Tambay Sieger am Hockenheimring

Pironi schwer verunglückt, Piquet und Salazar prügeln sich nach Unfall

heg. HOCKENHEIM. Die Formel 1 und ihre Hauptdarsteller haben beim Großen Preis von Deutschland am Hockenheim-Ring wieder einmal bewiesen, wie lebensgefährlich und hemmungslos es in dieser Gesellschaft immer mal wieder zugeht. Die Bilder vom letzten Training am Samstag und vom Rennen

Metern weit verstreut liegenbleiben. Doch diesmal ist der Fahrer nicht aus dem Wrack herausgeschleudert worden. Dies hat Pironi vermutlich das Leben gerettet. Zwanzig Minuten dauerte es, bis die Helfer den in die Trümmer eingeklemmten Franzosen herausgeschnitten haben. Selbst hartgesottene

Graf Berghe von Trips, Giles Villeneuve) schreiben, dies können auch viele fürs Leben gezeichnete Piloten wie Lauda und nun Pironi sagen. Ferrari, immer wieder Ferrari. Die roten Rennwagen aus Maranello zählten und zählen zwar stets zu den Schnellsten, was diese Formel auf die Räder bringt, aber offensichtlich auch zum Gefährlichsten.

ken. Auch über die technischen Besonderheiten der Formel-1-Rennwagen, die durch alle möglichen aerodynamischen Tricks auf die Piste gepreßt werden. Doch wehe, wenn dieses ausgetüftelte künstliche Gefüge mit Flügeln, Schürzen und Spoilern versagt. Dann sind die Wagen auch von reaktionsschnellen

ABOVE A world in headlines, and the quality German newspapers are restrained over the Grand Prix weekend while (right) the British magazine Grand Prix International *showed the full horror. The picture (bottom) of Pironi trapped in the carcass of the Ferrari was the one which, like a haunting, went round the world.*

210

locked into a posture of agony. This photograph, or variations of it, went round the world and lingered for days so that you might be wandering a street anywhere and suddenly be confronted by it assaulting you from a newspaper hoarding, might sit next to someone in a bar reading the evening newspaper and find your eye helplessly drawn to it, might switch on the television news in the hotel and couldn't escape it.

The full weight of Ferrari expectation now fell on Tambay.

And that broth of a boy Byrne? nq – did not qualify. The full weight of his own expectations would take him to Austria a week later to have another go.

The Press Room was high up in the grandstand opposite the pits and Allsop and I made a high-powered decision. Rather than stay in there watching the race on television, as most journalists habitually did, we'd go to the seating just outside the Press Room entrance – every journalist had a reserved seat – and actually watch the cars. From so high up in the grandstand you could see them coming into the Stadium Complex, going round it, along the start-finish straight and then out into the country again. If anything happened, and in 1982 there was always that, we could get to the Press Room in seconds. So we sat and watched, just like normal spectators, as Prost took his position on the front row. (Because of the Pironi accident this became effectively pole, just as Arnoux, behind Pironi's vacant position, became effectively the front row.) Lauda, wrist sprained in his Friday crash, withdrew.

Brabham were due to try The Pit Stop Ploy and informed opinion suggested Piquet would pit after 25 laps of the 45.

In the morning warm-up Rosberg hadn't been happy with his engine and decided to take the spare car into the race. That was a scramble and the only lap he did was the parade lap to the grid, the car's set-up all but unknown to him. He faced a gruelling afternoon and estimated that seventh was as much as he could hope for.

Arnoux seized the lead, Prost behind, but Piquet slotted inside Prost braking for the first chicane. Piquet hustled Arnoux as he would be bound to do

ABOVE *The Renaults with the race at their mercy – Arnoux (16) would at least finish but Prost had a fuel injection problem after 14 laps.*

ABOVE *A study of Hockenheim's darkened forest backdrop – and Tambay passing safely by.*

with the Brabham so much lighter and took him on the second lap. Piquet's advantage was startling.

	Piquet	Arnoux
Lap 2	1:54.1	1:57.0
Lap 3	1:54.5	1:55.8
Lap 4	1:55.0	1:56.4
Lap 5	1:54.8	1:56.0

So the advantage was translating to around a second and a half a lap, amounting to 35 seconds by lap 25, enough time for a successful pit stop and a tactical revolution in Formula One.

Tambay went past Prost and moved up to Arnoux, moved past on lap 10. Prost had a fuel injection problem so that the position became: Piquet, Tambay, Arnoux, Patrese, Watson, Rosberg.

Patrese's engine expired in wisps of smoke at the Brabham pit and now, clearly, Watson and Rosberg could anticipate gaining points. The turbo advantage here reduced them to the art of the possible. The race seemed becalmed, or rather moving at an established rhythm, as races often can when the initial skirmishing is complete and the cars have settled into their running speeds. Sitting in the grandstand watching was proving to be an entirely agreeable experience on a pleasantly warm afternoon.

On lap 19 Piquet came up to lap the Chilean Eliseo Salazar in an ATS at the Ostkurve chicane, far out of our sight. Piquet went ahead into the mouth of the chicane but Salazar steamed into the side of him, punting him off. The ATS came to rest on the track and by then Piquet had sprung from the Brabham consumed by a truly terrible rage. As he landed on the ground he brandished both hands towards Salazar, who was still clambering out. Salazar made his way onto the run-off area and Piquet came for him, his body language very pronounced indeed. As he came he raised his hands again. What the hell were you doing? He gesticulated then pushed at Salazar's helmeted face, gave him a left hook and a right cross combination, and as Salazar backed away tried to kick him in what appeared to be a delicate place.

He missed.

He stalked urgently away raising both hands above his head in a gesture meaning: what can you do with idiots like this?

Salazar, head bowed, walked some distance away behind Piquet who, when he reached some grass, turned, ripped a glove off and flung it to the ground in a great theatrical gesture, did the same with the other glove. Salazar turned round and walked back where they had come from, helmet held slack in his hand. He looked distracted as Piquet climbed over the Armco and vanished into the trees, perhaps looking for a pack of wolves to kill with his now bare hands.

And just eight weeks before, when I'd spoken to Watson and interviewed Mansell, I'd been thinking how touching it was that these Formula One drivers had guarded Olde Worlde courtesies.

When we didn't see Piquet come round, Allsop and I concluded he'd had a mechanical problem and we'd find out the details afterwards.

It gave the race to Tambay, Arnoux tracking him distantly into second but Watson, running third, had a front suspension failure with nine laps to go so that Rosberg came third.

Enzo Ferrari was not remote as such a moment. 'You got telexes from Enzo Ferrari and a phone call straight away into the Ferrari motorhome,' Tambay says.

Pironi 39, Watson 30, Rosberg 27, Prost 25, Lauda 24, Patrese 19.

Tambay says that when Piquet crashed he told himself to be careful with the back markers, but he had a feeling this was his day even when he missed a gearchange and thought he might have damaged the engine. As he came from the Ferrari some of the mechanics, who'd been through Zolder, Montreal and the Saturday here, were in tears.

Reflecting now, Tambay says: 'If you look at the race, I won because I was second to Piquet and he got involved with Salazar. This is why I won the race. Like Murray Walker would say, "You win the race by covering the distance before the others."

'After the accident of Gilles, I don't know what happened to the team, to the car or to the construction of the car or the engines, but the car started to be very reliable and performed very well. I don't know if they strengthened it or made progress with the engine or whatever, but straight away with Didier we started having a lot of results.'

When any race is over a journalist checks with his office to have a tactical talk, not least to find out how much space he has been allocated. I did that and Allsop did that in adjoining telephone booths and we were both asked the same question: what about the fight? We both tried to stall: oh, the fight? Because it had happened out of sight we had no way of knowing it had happened and in those days there were no endless replays on Press Room television screens. The coverage finished when the coverage finished. That meant we had no opportunity of watching a recording to see what Salazar had done to Piquet and what a few instants later Piquet had done to Salazar.

By now Piquet would be in Rio de Janeiro, still wearing his overalls, having flown back without the

BELOW A majestic study of Watson negotiating a Hockenheim chicane, although a broken front suspension would halt him.

OPPOSITE *Not only victory for Tambay but a decisive one – 16 seconds in front of Arnoux.*

BELOW *It's still the most effective – and theatrical – way to finish a motor race, and Tambay will have reached the line in a milli-second.*

need of an aeroplane. Salazar, however, sat on the ground in the ATS pit, leaning against the wall.

'For me it is not a problem when he starts to punch me,' he said. 'I 'ave my 'elmet on. He can punch me all day and I don't care. But when 'e try to kick me zere...' He looked up, face bleak, and didn't smile at all.

Anyway, we reconstructed the crash and the fight, and photographs lifted from television proved irresistible to any red-blooded daily newspaper. We didn't dare watch a race from anywhere except the Press Room and its comprehensive television coverage ever again.

I never did see the fight until I got home and watched the video.

Rosberg had quite other concerns when he got home. He'd been burgled.

He'd always said 'I don't need a bloody alarm system here, you know. My front door had been kicked in – really kicked in. It had boot marks like this. It was lying on the floor when I came home. My gold coins and souvenirs and things like that had gone. I got alarm systems but I never felt comfortable in the house after that.'

Footnote: 1. Byrne had a brief Formula One career: five meetings, of which he qualified for two and retired both times; 2. Grand Prix International; 3. Life At The Limit, Watkins; 4. Franco Lini was an Italian journalist who in the 1960s became Ferrari team manager, evidently because Enzo wanted him to talk to people. He could do that, all right.

Race Result

WINNING SPEED 209.92kmh/130.44mph

FASTEST LAP 214.57kmh/133.33mph
(Piquet 1m 54.03s on lap 7)

LAP LEADERS Arnoux 1 (1);
Piquet 2–18 (17); Tambay 19–45 (27)

Note: Pironi qualified for pole position, but did not start because
of an accident in qualifying. Pole position was left vacant.

RACE

	Driver	Team	Engine	Laps	Time
1	P. Tambay	Ferrari 126C2	Ferrari V6t	45	1h 27m 25.17s
2	R. Arnoux	Renault RE30B	Renault V6t	45	1h 27m 41.55s
3	K. Rosberg	Williams FW08	Cosworth V8	44	
4	M. Alboreto	Tyrrell 011	Cosworth V8	44	
5	B. Giacomelli	Alfa Romeo 182	Alfa V12	44	
6	M. Surer	Arrows A4	Cosworth V8	44	
7	B. Henton	Tyrrell 011	Cosworth V8	44	
8	R. Guerrero	Ensign N181	Cosworth V8	44	
9	N. Mansell	Lotus 91	Cosworth V8	43	
10	D. Warwick	Toleman TG181C	Hart 4t	43	
11	C. Serra	Fittipaldi F9	Cosworth V8	43	
r	J. Watson	McLaren MP4B	Cosworth V8	36	Front suspension
r	J. Laffite	Talbot Ligier JS19	Matra V12	36	Handling
r	D. Daly	Williams FW08	Cosworth V8	25	Engine
r	R. Boesel	March 821	Cosworth V8	22	Tyre/accident
r	E. de Angelis	Lotus 91	Cosworth V8	21	Transmission
r	N. Piquet	Brabham BT50	BMW 4t	18	Accident
r	E. Salazar	ATS D5	Cosworth V8	17	Accident
r	A. Prost	Renault RE30B	Renault V6t	14	Fuel injection
r	R. Patrese	Brabham BT50	BMW 4t	13	Piston
r	A. de Cesaris	Alfa Romeo 182	Alfa V12	9	Accident
r	E. Cheever	Talbot Ligier JS19	Matra V12	8	Handling
r	M. Baldi	Arrows A4	Cosworth V8	6	Misfire
r	J.-P. Jarier	Osella FA1D	Cosworth V8	3	Steering
r	M. Winkelhock	ATS D5	Cosworth V8	3	Clutch/gearbox
ns	D. Pironi	Ferrari 126C2	Ferrari V6t		Accident/injury
ns	N. Lauda	McLaren MP4B	Cosworth V8		Accident/injury
nq	T. Byrne	Theodore TY02	Cosworth V8		
nq	R. Keegan	March 821	Cosworth V8		
nq	T. Fabi	Toleman TG181C	Hart 4t		

nq = did not qualify; ns = did not start; r = retired

CHAMPIONSHIP

	Driver	Points
1	D. Pironi	39
2	J. Watson	30
3	K. Rosberg	27
4	A. Prost	25
5	N. Lauda	24
6	R. Patrese	19
	R. Arnoux	19
8	N. Piquet	17
9	P. Tambay	16
10	M. Alboreto	14
11	E. de Angelis	13
12	E. Cheever	10
13	D. Daly	7
	N. Mansell	7
15	C. Reutemann	6
	G. Villeneuve	6
17	A. de Cesaris	5
18	J.-P. Jarier	3
	M. Surer	3
20	M. Winkelhock	2
	E. Salazar	2
	B. Giacomelli	2
23	J. Laffite	1
	M. Baldi	1
	F. Serra	1

	Team	Points
1	Ferrari	61
2	McLaren	54
3	Renault	44
4	Williams	40
5	Brabham	36
6	Lotus	20
7	Tyrrell	14
8	Talbot Ligier	11
9	Alfa Romeo	7
10	Arrows	4
	ATS	4
12	Osella	3
13	Fittipaldi	1

15 AUGUST

CHAPMAN'S LAST FLING

AUSTRIA, ÖSTERREICHRING

A different terroir again, this one looking at first glance more suited to *The Sound of Music* than racing cars. Imagine a hillside contoured by great, grassy undulations rising to the rim of a tree-lined horizon. Imagine dense, tall copses of firs here and there like nature's decoration. Imagine more than three and a half miles of track threaded like a ribbon into this, travelling through immense loops and sweeps up the hillside and even more immense loops and sweeps down again. Now imagine Nelson Piquet's pole lap at an average within an eye-blink of 152 miles an hour.

We were in the theatre of giants, no place for persons of a nervous disposition.

The Österreichring felt Austrian. You saw people wearing lederhosen and hats with feathers not for effect but because that's just what they wore. You saw comely wenches serving big beers to the lederhoseners from rustic wooden bars. You smelt sausages – wurst – drifting on the breeze.

We'd come from Hockenheim through Munich by car because, however much Grand Prix teams and drivers felt the need to go to airports at the first possible opportunity after a race – which had thrown me completely in Detroit – and come back through airports at the last possible moment for the next race, other members of what someone called the Grand Prix Family had no need of that. You took a couple of days off and meandered instead.

Strolling in Munich, that picture of Pironi seemed everywhere, as if it haunted a whole Continent. You

RIGHT *The cap has been hurled in celebration and now the Lotus team celebrate around Colin Chapman after the thrilling de Angelis victory.*

Austria
Österreichring

RACE DATE August 15th

CIRCUIT LENGTH
5.94km/3.69 miles

NO. OF LAPS 53

RACE DISTANCE
314.92km/195.68 miles

WEATHER Hot, dry

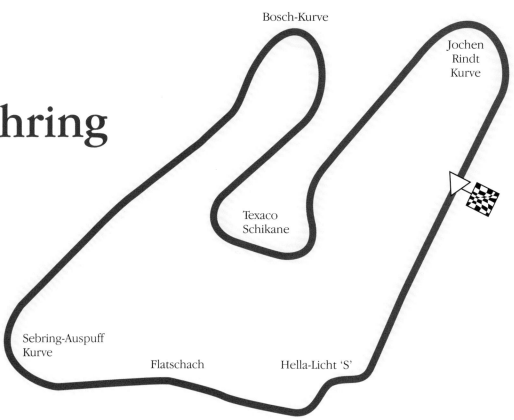

Bosch-Kurve

Jochen
Rindt
Kurve

Texaco
Schikane

Sebring-Auspuff
Kurve

Flatschach

Hella-Licht 'S'

DRIVER'S VIEW

'It was a frightening place to drive. It's funny, the place was all a bit over the top but my main memory is of Bosch-Kurve. I don't know why. Every track you have a little something you remember better than others. The Bosch-Kurve was very furious. You came down from the altitude and in the wet ... well. Into the Bosch-Kurve in a non-turbo – that would hardly get you up the hill! – in my first year, 1978, you could slide the cars without getting wet pants, you know. Modern cars, however, would be going flat round Austria. We just couldn't do it, we couldn't use the power. [Authentic Rosberg insight – Hilton: 'From the grid there was a hill you couldn't see over.' Rosberg: 'But there was nothing there to see.' Hilton: 'But when you went from the grid there might be all hell on the other side.' Rosberg: 'Nooo. You wouldn't qualify that far back. Come on!']

'Unfortunately after that a chicane was built. That was an awful chicane – every chicane is an awful chicane. Whoever invented them should be banned from motor racing. OK, after Mark Donaghue was killed [in practice, 1975] something needed to be done but the corner there wasn't the worst on the track, was it? It had no run-off area – like all the others. There was quite a big difference in altitude from the pits to the top of the hill. The last corner was a fairly steep hill. It was the altitude that made it an interesting track, and you only had that at Spa and Brands Hatch.'

Keke Rosberg

wondered what ordinary people made of it and how difficult it was to justify as the consequence of a sporting event. Pironi wanted to be in the car and nobody ordered him to go suicidally fast in the wet, of course, but no doubt most of the kamikaze pilots in the Second World War were volunteers too. Since 1945 we'd been at peace for five decades and that's why the hoardings carrying Pironi's bloodied agony seemed to reflect another time and another mentality, not a Saturday session of no particular importance up the autobahn past Stuttgart a couple of days before.

You wondered if being a volunteer was itself really a justification, an excuse-all, for what had happened at Zolder, Montreal and Hockenheim, wondered if a great responsibility did not fall on the people who accommodated the volunteers by giving them cars which were lethal – and justified doing that by murmuring well, they want them. Presumably the pilots wanted the planes too.

These were the questions an outsider would ask. As far as anyone could tell, the insiders never asked them at all. They had grown up within it, it had always been like that, they had dedicated virtually every moment of their waking, working lives to it and beneath the well-rehearsed world-weary cynicism a profound affair of the heart was going on. Drivers, team principals, designers, mechanics, tyre manufacturers, uniformed girls who handed you drinks and biros and notebooks and badges, sponsors of all shapes and sizes, married couples who ran motorhome hospitality units, Press Officers, journalists, photographers, all manner of officials, truckies, the Longines timing team, the medical staff, the guys who flew the helicopters, the woman who toured the circuits in a red caravan developing the photographers' films and, on top of all these, shifty people you couldn't quite place – they were all in love with it.

Sometimes Allsop and I felt lonely because we were not. We came from that other world, the one beyond the paddock, he a football man in those distant days when that sport did not sprawl monstrously across every minute, hour, day, week and month of the whole year making no differentiation between winter and summer. It enabled the *Daily Mail* to deploy him to the Grands Prix with a surprisingly short overlap at either end of the Grand Prix season, something utterly unimaginable 25 years later.

BELOW *De Angelis getting ready for an extraordinary race, which produced the second closest finish to that date.*

Allsop had begun covering it the season before – 1981 – and, in Belgium, confronted a mechanic being run over and killed in the pit lane, another run over and almost killed on the grid.

We hadn't grown up with motor sport, we hadn't subconsciously absorbed and accepted from childhood the ethos well, it happens and continued.

It took a long time for that to begin to happen to me and after 1 May 1994 I knew it never really would. I can't speak for Allsop but I'd be surprised if he didn't feel the same.

Now imagine, against this background, that you are surveying the vast, undulating hillside for the first time and about to witness Piquet's lap which would make the Österreichring the fastest Grand Prix circuit then in use. The circuit was frightening and – in the context of 1982, Zolder, Montreal, and that picture – very frightening indeed. A glance up the hillside was enough.

The Österreichring nestled into its beautiful setting but the pits and paddock were in no sense beautiful. The equivalent of today's immaculate Media Centre, humming with technology and relaying everything instantly round the world, for example, was a large, egg-shaped, permanent marquee on the opposite side of the track to the pits. It was so old its original white had discoloured to a soft, sour yellow. By definition, being a marquee, it had no windows and consequently the heat within it – Austria can be very hot in summer, and was – gathered in much the same way that, we are assured, has made the planet Venus an inferno.

BELOW *All Austria is watching the return of Lauda the Austrian but he can get no higher than fifth.*

STARTING GRID		
1	**1** 1:27.61 **N. Piquet**	**2** 1:27.97 **R. Patrese**
2	**3** 1:28.86 **A. Prost**	**4** 1:29.52 **P. Tambay**
3	**5** 1:30.26 **R. Arnoux**	**6** 1:30.30 **K. Rosberg**
4	**7** 1:31.62 **E. de Angelis**	**8** 1:31.81 **M. Alboreto**
5	**9** 1:32.06 **D. Daly**	**10** 1:32.13 **N. Lauda**
6	**11** 1:32.30 **A. de Cesaris**	**12** 1:32.88 **N. Mansell**
7	**13** 1:32.95 **B. Giacomelli**	**14** 1:32.95 **J. Laffite**
8	**15** 1:33.20 **D. Warwick**	**16** 1:33.55 **R. Guerrero**
9	**17** 1:33.97 **T. Fabi**	**18** 1:34.16 **J. Watson**
10	**19** 1:34.18 **B. Henton**	**20** 1:34.18 **C. Serra**
11	**21** 1:34.42 **M. Surer**	**22** 1:34.62 **E. Cheever**
12	**23** 1:34.71 **M. Baldi**	**24** 1:34.77 **R. Keegan**
13	**25** 1:34.98 **M. Winkelhock**	**26** 1:34.98 **T. Byrne**

It's called the greenhouse effect: the air has nowhere else to go. Inside the marquee lay strewn, for some inexplicable reason, theatrical props and artefacts.

The telephone room was cleverly situated in a small room built into the marquee's top, reached by a wooden stairway. Yes, heat rises. Yes, the heat rose as it gathered. Yes, it had nowhere else to go. At one point the temperature in the telephone room reached 140° and dictating a story became extremely difficult because you were peering at your notes through a constant cascade of your own sweat. It was exactly like taking a shower without the shower. I saw one man take his shirt off and use that to dab-dab-dab his eyes. I saw Jardine, hair matted, wandering heat-struck looking as if he'd been doused.

From that room, despite everything, the stories went out that in first qualifying Piquet had done the 151mph, Patrese slightly slower but in the 151s as well, Tambay next on 148, then Prost with Rosberg fifth fastest on 145, a genuine feat for a car without a turbo engine. One report claims other teams were 'staggered' by the Piquet lap.

The turbos were fearsome here and Piquet's lap, on his third run near the end of the session, became an overall marker of progress. The year before, Arnoux in the Renault turbo took pole with 1:32.0, an average speed of 144mph. Piquet's 1:27.6 annihilated that. Didier Braillon wrote in *Grand Prix International*: 'However spectacular the Brabham performance, it obviously was also frightening, and certain drivers did not hesitate to say what they were thinking – that the current cars are missiles and that a lap record nowadays is more concerned with ballistics than auto racing...'

Arnoux's 1:32 would have put him fifth on the 1982 grid, behind not only Rosberg but the non-turbo Tyrrell of Alboreto too.

It was a curious session in that many drivers spent a long time in the pits watching the light, pastry-puff clouds and hoping they would move across the sun, cooling the track even a little.

That night a tremendous storm brought merciful fresh air in its wake but Saturday was hot again, the times fractionally slower. Patrese went quickest from

ABOVE *Mid-grid chaos as the race starts. The two Alfa Romeos (front and right) have collided and Daly (against the pit wall) is involved – and out – too.*

ABOVE *De Cesaris walks*
briskly back after a
crash at the very start.
He hasn't far to go.

Piquet, then Prost, Tambay and Arnoux – who'd had
a wretched Friday when his race car and the spare
car kept breaking down. Rosberg, sixth again, led
the non-turbos from de Angelis but Watson was lost
in 17th place with debilitating understeer on this
Saturday. The day before, he'd been 18th. Tommy
Byrne somehow goaded and coaxed and forced the
Theodore onto the last row.

Because the calendar was (reasonably) stable
from season to season people fell into rituals: the last
thing you did when you checked out of your hotel
was make the reservation for the following year.
Hotels were passed down through the generations
like precious legacies because otherwise you might
end up travelling huge distances to find a room
when the Family came to town in their hundreds,
their rooms safely locked up (as it were) from the
year before.

People had rituals, and among a certain group
on the Saturday of the Austrian Grand Prix it never
varied. The old *Daily Mirror* hand Pat Mennem, a
florid-faced man of great humour and – truly – an
Olde Worlde charm, led the hire-car motorcade up

a winding mountain road to a restaurant perched
at the top where the food and wine were excellent
but, more importantly, the owner had fought in
North Africa for Rommel's Afrika Korps. Mennem
had just missed the War but had a military bearing
and could hold a drink like no other man I have
ever encountered.

The owner and Mennem exchanged warm
greetings, and the feasting began. At a certain
point, when the wine began to talk, either Mennem
made a signal or the owner made a signal. Ready.
The owner had somehow managed to keep
recordings of the songs the Afrika Corps played
to maintain their morale and he put them on. He
and Mennem marched up and down the restaurant
while the rest of the clientele dissolved into great
hilarity and applause.

Those five decades after the madness ended
you could do the marching now. The fact that an
Englishman was doing it to Third Reich military
music guaranteed bonhomie as well as hilarity, and
somehow it made that picture harder and harder
to take.

Never mind. A great, wonderfully eccentric night up a mountain and on the morrow you have an Access All Areas Press Pass for the race, something unimaginably precious to any follower who'd waited all year, slept in a tent and bought a ticket to sit on the hillside as the nearest to it they could get.

The narcotic leads to addiction.

The heat wave reached into race day and a vast crowd came, Austrians celebrating Lauda's return and Italians wanting to celebrate another Tambay victory in the Ferrari. At the green light the hills were alive with the sound of Formula One music as the 26 cars set off.

The crowd saw Piquet cleanly away and Rosberg hustling past Tambay, but the Alfa Romeos played dodgem cars and that of de Cesaris banged into Daly. Even as Piquet led the surge up the hill and out into the country the 26 had become 23 and, after a lap, 22 when Keegan stopped. His steering had been damaged in the Alfas' crash.

A turbo race, of course: Piquet leading from Patrese, Prost, Tambay and Arnoux, de Angelis and Rosberg panting along behind them. The Brabhams, committed yet again to The Ploy, would pull away. Patrese moved into the lead, Tambay had a puncture and motored as quickly as he could to the pits and the Renaults were being shed by the Brabhams.

Lap 5: Patrese, Piquet, Prost, Arnoux, de Angelis, Warwick, Teo Fabi, Mansell, Rosberg.

On lap 8 the Tolemans failed, Mansell fell back and pitted, Arnoux's turbo broke, and on lap 17 Piquet pitted. His tyres had blistered, forcing him

BELOW Rupert Keegan (March) demonstrating just how steep the climb from the grid was.

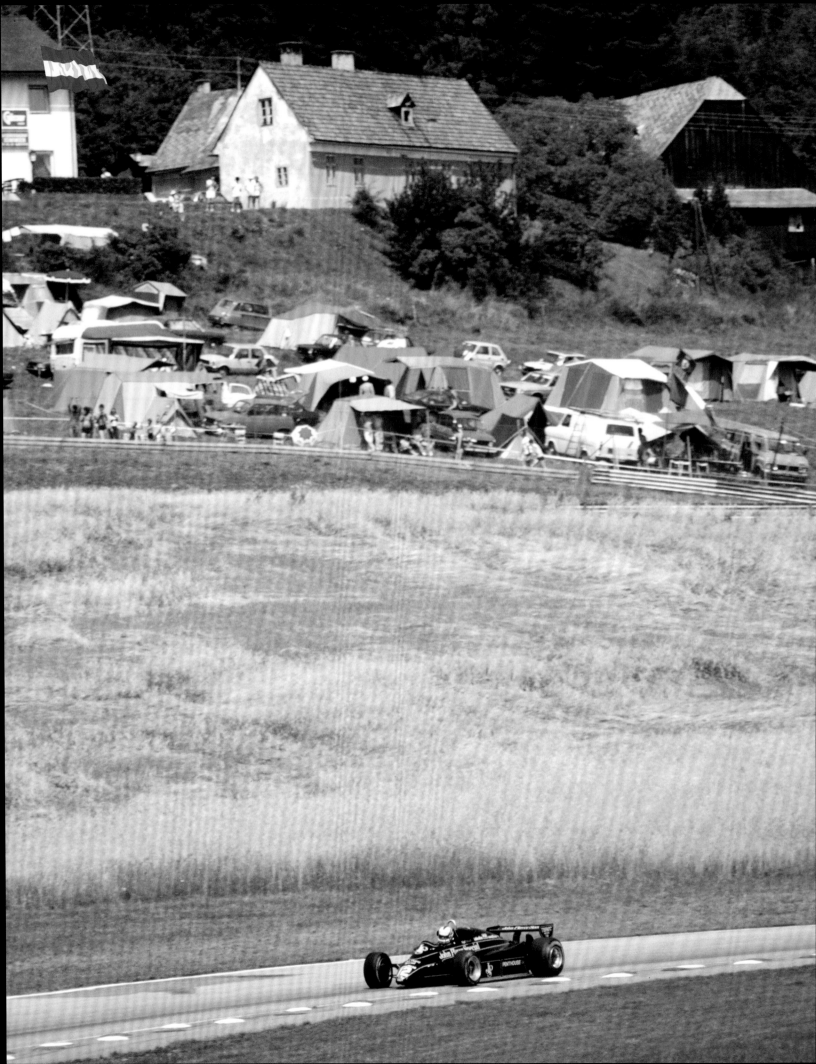

Newspaper clippings

Seite 6 / DIE PRESSE **SPORT**

MIT DEM FORMEL-1-TRAINING BEGINNT NICHT NUR LAUDAS KAMPF – AUCH ATEMBERAUBENDE TEMPOJAGD

Prokop zieht Vergleiche zu den Astronauten
„Kreislaufbelastung wie bei einem Looping!"

Eigenbericht der »Presse« von JOSEF METZGER

Seite 6 / DIE PRESSE **SPORT**

Erster GP-Sieg von de Ángelis im Zeltweg-Drama
Zweiter Rosberg ein Zehntel zurück – Nur ein Turbo kam durch: Tambay als Vierter – Lauda Fünfter

Eigenbericht der »Presse« von JOSEF METZGER

DAS PACKENDE FINISH: DE ANGELIS ...

Viele Ausfälle im Grossen Preis von Oesterreich

De Angelis um Radbreite vor Rosberg im Ziel

Samstag/Sonntag, 14./15. August 1982   **SPORT**   DIE PRESSE / Seite 7

NIKI LAUDA ALS ACHTSCHNELLSTER: MEHR PROBLEME MIT DEM AUTO ALS MIT DER HAND

Piquet brach Schallmauer der Formel 1
„Monte Carlo ist mir schneller vorgekommen!"

Eigenbericht der »Presse« von JOSEF METZGER

RING-SPLITTER

»WELTREKORDLER« NELSON PIQUET AUF BRA...HAM-BMW-TURBO: SCHNITT 244 km/h

---

in early. The pit crew, caught unawares, were unprepared for The Ploy yet and took almost half a minute to do their work. He rejoined fourth.

Lap 22: Patrese, Prost, de Angelis, Piquet, Rosberg, Laffite.

Two laps later Patrese pitted and Murray Walker, commentating on BBC, described it as 'sensational' because the fuel went in and the four tyres went on in 14 seconds.

As Gordon Murray says, 'the cars didn't go far enough for us to do it until Austria. You know, if I look at those photographs now it's bloody stupid. I had all my guys dressed in Nomex and I'm standing in front of the car in a short-sleeved shirt, nothing on my head. If the car had gone up I'd have been a Roman candle...'

Patrese describes refuelling as a 'fantastic idea. It's still a fantastic idea today! After Austria everybody had to start doing it. In Austria Nelson broke down but I did the pit stop. Everybody was watching what we were doing and it worked very well. Of course in those days there was not a limit on how many litres you could have in the car – it was quick, around 120 litres in four, five seconds. With the turbos we needed 240 litres to complete a Grand Prix, so half that made a much easier way for the driving.

'I went out, I was in the lead and we could have won the first race where we did the pit stop – but unfortunately my engine blew up.'

Patrese had got out just in front of Prost but when the engine blew the Brabham rotated off, travelling at speed across a meadow before riding up a bank backwards. Spectators behind a mesh fence watched it come at them and some turned to flee. The bank arrested it.

We did get a race, however. Prost led but of course Renaults didn't finish races, de Angelis ran second, Piquet third but Rosberg was catching him. Piquet's engine was about to expire. At lap 40: Prost, de Angelis, Rosberg and Laffite on the same lap, and only five other runners going round.

The hills remained alive to the sound of Formula One music, but only sporadically now as the nine survivors rose and fell among the circuit's 3.6 miles of undulation. The race remained alive because Rosberg was catching de Angelis, suddenly had him in vision. Watson's engine failed after 44 laps and four laps later Prost was gone with a fuel injection problem, yellow flames belching from the rear of the Renault. Prost clambered out, head bowed, distraught, his body seemingly bowed by rage. He wandered away, trance-like, onto grass, his back to the car which had come to rest half on and half off the circuit.

LEFT *A world in headlines, and they weren't all about the local boy Lauda.*

OPPOSITE *The hills were alive with the sound of engines. Mansell put the Lotus on the sixth row but an engine failure on lap 17 stopped him in the race.*

225

ABOVE *The historic pit stop which enabled Patrese to rejoin in the lead and convinced Gordon Murray everybody would be doing it.*

And still Rosberg was catching de Angelis...

Rosberg's foot hurt and he'd lost time behind Laffite who blocked him when he tried to get by but, typically, he attacked the Österreichring. What followed represented an act of willpower as well as driving.

'I came through to fourth or fifth in a fairly short time. I was catching Elio three, four seconds a lap.'

At lap 50, three to go, he had the gap down to 3.1 seconds and a lap later 2.6. As de Angelis reached the crest of the hill from the start-finish straight Rosberg was half way up it. Out into the country de Angelis stretched away but Rosberg came back at him. Crossing the line into the last lap Rosberg had the gap down to 1.6 seconds and when de Angelis reached the crest of the hill Rosberg was visibly nearer than he had been the lap before.

He thrust the Williams through the little sequence of lefts and rights on the far side of the hill, forced it through the sweepers after that so hard that, emerging, he'd cut the gap to four car's lengths.

He had momentum, something you sensed as well as saw.

As they began the downhill journey through the carving curves towards the finishing line, way down there, he lurked within striking distance and stayed at that distance. It was like a perfect waltz through the lefts and rights, a majesty of movement against such a majestic backdrop. Rosberg jinked left but de Angelis covered that, Rosberg got a tow and jinked left a second time. De Angelis covered that again.

It brought them to the long, sloping right-hander which went on and on into the start-finish straight.

Rosberg weighed his options very calmly, balancing them against the risks and what that would mean for the Championship. He might go inside de Angelis, over the kerb: no 'obstruction' there and grass the other side. The corner was ferociously fast and if he'd been a younger man he might have tried it. Instead he hesitated, for a millisecond maybe.

'I only had one chance and that was the last corner. I knew that the inside was very easy to block. I could have done it on the outside but I thought for sure I'd crash because if you get on marbles at the end of the race on that corner and went off you would hurt yourself. So I decided not to take that risk, which was untypical of me because I knew if I go outside I can win. And I could trust Elio, he was my best friend in Formula One, that wasn't the question. But of course he would block inside, which he then did – and then he gave me a chance. They had this half-round [kerbing] on the inside – strange looking – and I considered running right over that. I decided the car would probably jump too much and jump into Elio's car. I decided not to do it but drive behind him and I knew I'd lost already. If I came out from behind there was not enough distance to the line.'

De Angelis drifted wide as they approached the exit, leaving Rosberg the empty inside.

From there it was a straight power play to the line.

De Angelis got there 0.050 of a second before Rosberg, and Colin Chapman flung his cap high, high into the air, a gesture he'd been making for years whenever one of his cars won. He would never do it again. Chapman's last was de Angelis's first.

'Neither of us had yet won a race and I was very happy for him, I wasn't sad and I gave it all I could,' Rosberg says. 'I was lapping Laffite, that's where I lost the race. Jacques wouldn't let me by and I lost five seconds or six seconds.'

Pironi 39, Rosberg 33, Watson 30, Lauda 26, Prost 25, de Angelis 22.

Between Austria and the next race, the Swiss at Dijon, the teams went testing at Monza. Alan Jenkins remembers that because it gave him an extraordinary insight into how Lauda thought.

'Niki felt in his own mind he could extrapolate things like tyre temperature for example, which we

didn't know a huge amount about. We certainly didn't play with tyre pressures like they do now. This was the early transition from crossplys to radials and it was much more of a black art than it is now but he would tell you he could tell what the car was doing as he left the pit lane. He would often just come back in, wouldn't do a lap. He'd say "No, no, that's not going to work." I think [designer] Steve Nichols was taking over running him from Tyler when I got Wattie. For some reason someone said "You do the Monza test." I don't think I'd done a test prior to that.

'Niki came in and said "That high speed bit there, I want a softer front spring."'

ABOVE *The pit stop didn't solve anything – Patrese retired after 27 laps.*

BELOW *An evocative panorama of the lamented Elio de Angelis, who'd beat Rosberg by an eyeblink. Evocative? No Armco, no run-off area, no sandtrap, no tyre wall, just a field.*

OPPOSITE *The last Lotus win of Colin Chapman's life, and Rosberg is pleased for de Angelis.*

BELOW *If you're curious, No. 11 beat No. 6 by 0.050 of a second.*

Dialogue...

Jenkins: 'No, you don't. You want a harder one and we are going to put more wing in.'

Lauda: 'Nope.'

Jenkins: 'What do you mean, no?'

Lauda: 'I mean that won't work.'

Jenkins: 'Well, I think it will.'

Jenkins 'started to get the wing numbers out and he didn't want to look at it. He sat in the car and I said – this was mid-afternoon – "Can you just try it for me?" He said "OK." I can't remember his exact words but the meaning was I'll try it just this time.

'Then he waved to his buddy in the back of the garage, the bag carrier, to get his stuff and I thought: he's going to leave! But he stayed in the car, went out, did a few laps, came in and said "Hmmm. Very interesting. Now I go." And he left. I got this huge bollocking from Ron [Dennis] as to why I had upset Niki so he'd left before the end of the test. Ron wasn't there but rang to see how we were doing. Ron said "What time did he do?" and I said he'd done a really good time then left.

'It was something like he had to make a point. I had made him do something he didn't want to do, compounded by the fact that I was right. It wasn't a falling out, it was showing who was boss.'

Yes, Herr Andreas Nikolaus Lauda of Vienna had furtive eyes which didn't miss much and a suspicious mind. He was also, in most situations in his life, the boss.

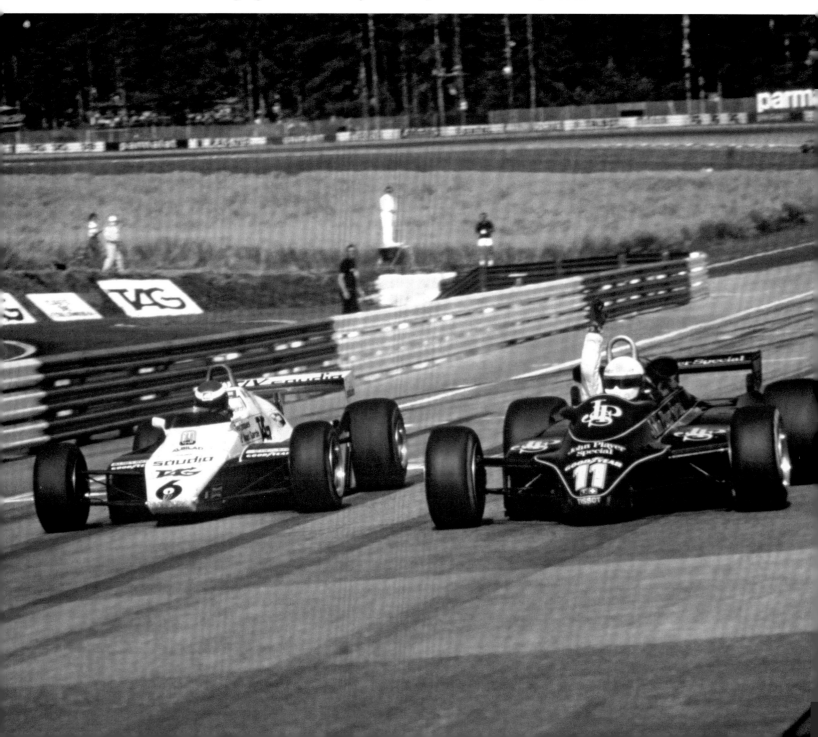

Race Result

WINNING SPEED 222.20kmh/138.07mph

FASTEST LAP 228.29kmh/141.85mph
(Piquet 1m 33.69s on lap 5)

LAP LEADERS Piquet 1 (1);
Patrese 2–27 (26); Prost 28–48 (21);
de Angelis 49–53 (5)

RACE

	Driver	Team	Engine	Laps	Time
1	E. de Angelis	Lotus 91	Cosworth V8	53	1h 25m 02.21s
2	K. Rosberg	Williams FW08	Cosworth V8	53	1h 25m 02.26s
3	J. Laffite	Talbot Ligier JS19	Matra V12	52	
4	P. Tambay	Ferrari 126C2	Ferrari V6t	52	
5	N. Lauda	McLaren MP4B	Cosworth V8	52	
6	M. Baldi	Arrows A4	Cosworth V8	52	
7	C. Serra	Fittipaldi F9	Cosworth V8	51	
8	A. Prost	Renault RE30B	Renault V6t	48	Fuel injection
r	J. Watson	McLaren MP4B	Cosworth V8	44	Water pipe
r	B. Henton	Tyrrell 011	Cosworth V8	32	Valve spring
r	N. Piquet	Brabham BT50	BMW 4t	31	Camshaft drive
r	T. Byrne	Theodore TY02	Cosworth V8	28	Spin
r	M. Surer	Arrows A4	Cosworth V8	28	Fuel system
r	R. Patrese	Brabham BT50	BMW 4t	27	Spin
r	E. Cheever	Talbot Ligier JS19	Matra V12	22	Valve
r	N. Mansell	Lotus 91	Cosworth V8	17	Engine
r	R. Arnoux	Renault RE30B	Renault V6t	16	Turbo
r	M. Winkelhock	ATS D5	Cosworth V8	15	Spin
r	D. Warwick	Toleman TG181C	Hart 4t	7	Rear suspension
r	T. Fabi	Toleman TG181C	Hart 4t	7	Driveshaft
r	R. Guerrero	Ensign N181	Cosworth V8	6	Driveshaft
r	M. Alboreto	Tyrrell 011	Cosworth V8	1	Accident
r	R. Keegan	March 821	Cosworth V8	1	Accident
r	A. de Cesaris	Alfa Romeo 182	Alfa Rom V12	0	Accident
r	D. Daly	Williams FW08	Cosworth V8	0	Accident
r	B. Giacomelli	Alfa Romeo 182	Alfa Rom V12	0	Accident
nq	R. Boesel	March 821	Cosworth V8		
nq	J.-P. Jarier	Osella FA1D	Cosworth V8		
nq	E. Salazar	ATS D5	Cosworth V8		

nq = did not qualify; r = retired

CHAMPIONSHIP

	Driver	Points
1	D. Pironi	39
2	K. Rosberg	33
3	J. Watson	30
4	N. Lauda	26
5	A. Prost	25
6	E. de Angelis	22
7	R. Arnoux	19
	P. Tambay	19
	R. Patrese	19
10	N. Piquet	17
11	M. Alboreto	14
12	E. Cheever	10
13	D. Daly	7
	N. Mansell	7
15	C. Reutemann	6
	G. Villeneuve	6
17	A. de Cesaris	5
	J. Laffite	5
19	J.-P. Jarier	3
	M. Surer	3
21	M. Winkelhock	2
	E. Salazar	2
	B. Giacomelli	2
	M. Baldi	2
25	F. Serra	1

	Team	Points
1	Ferrari	64
2	McLaren	56
3	Williams	46
4	Renault	44
5	Brabham	36
6	Lotus	29
7	Talbot Ligier	15
8	Tyrrell	14
9	Alfa Romeo	7
10	Arrows	5
11	ATS	4
12	Osella	3
13	Fittipaldi	1

ONE & ONLY ROSBERG

SWITZERLAND, DIJON

Ah, Dijon where the real terroir begins because this is Burgundy and Nuits St Georges, Gevrey Chambertin, Volnay, Pommard and the rest are just over there – hallowed names, evocative names, poetic names, and standing in the most direct contrast to the circuit of Dijon-Prenois which was neither hallowed nor poetic but, rather, another place unlikely to survive The Ecclestone Imperative. Dijon-Prenois was your basic unreconstructed circuit with your basic French absence of hygiene to accompany that. Capturing the mood nicely, Nigel Roebuck wrote in *Autosport* that the track 'has one of the most unpleasant and officious administrations to be found anywhere.'

You could, however, make some claim to it being evocative because, as we have seen, here in 1979 during the French Grand Prix Villeneuve and Arnoux explored the outer limits of what Formula One cars can be made to do, and did this side-by-side for three full laps. That the race was now the Swiss Grand Prix concerned nobody in Formula One unduly, if at all. After the brutal crash at the Le Mans sports car race in 1955, where at least 80 people were killed, Switzerland banned all motor racing. Dijon was, literally and figuratively, the nearest they could get even 27 years later. There was a sort of precedent in that the San Marino Grand Prix was regularly run in Italy although San Marino is a Principality in its own right.

Any sport which had taken a drivers' strike, the political strangulation of a race – San Marino, as it happened – two deaths and a maiming in its stride in

RIGHT *Suddenly the horizon looked limitless to Rosberg who now led the Championship.*

Switzerland
Dijon

RACE DATE August 29th

CIRCUIT LENGTH
3.80km/2.36 miles

NO. OF LAPS 80

RACE DISTANCE
304.00km/188.89 miles

WEATHER Hot, dry

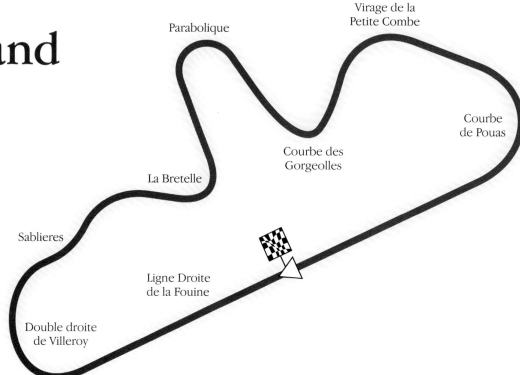

Parabolique

Virage de la
Petite Combe

Courbe
de Pouas

Courbe des
Gorgeolles

La Bretelle

Sablieres

Ligne Droite
de la Fouine

Double droite
de Villeroy

DRIVER'S VIEW ——————

'I thought it was very dangerous – lovely track but very dangerous. It had fast corners, great big corners, it was shortish but – great. You had the sweeping corners where Villeneuve and Arnoux were banging wheels, you had the hill, you had two mega-corners coming back onto the start-finish straight. The track surface was always dirty, sandy and not a very grippy place. It didn't deserve to be part of the Grand Prix calendar every year, no. The facilities were non-existent. There were no hotels, one military airport and all that. You'd run a medium set-up and that was always the compromise there: how fast you got onto the straight. The corners at the back had no run-off areas: I mean none. It was lethal, that place.'

—————— *Keke Rosberg*

eight months was hardly likely to raise an eyebrow about having a Grand Prix in a country other than the one it ought to have been in.

The surrounding terroir was bleached dry, making it resemble a lunarscape not dissimilar to Paul Ricard. Somehow it felt like one, too. Can Burgundy of so many rich pleasures really have been just over there?

Rosberg approached the weekend knowing that the circuit favoured those who could drive rather than just depress accelerator pedals, and qualifying demonstrated that because although the turbo Renaults dominated the first session Lauda got the non-turbo McLaren up to third place; and in the second session the turbo Brabhams dominated but Daly took third now and Rosberg fourth in the non-turbo Williamses.

There's a naughty tale about that involving the escape road, which itself proved to be a naughty place. Behind the paddock you could sit and watch the cars go through the hard left-hand corner called La Bretelle (the Link Road). From there the track described a long, tight loop as it returned towards the rear of the paddock. If you missed La Bretelle you had the escape road directly ahead. It wriggled gently until it rejoined the track where the loop returned and wasn't just a short cut, it was a very short cut indeed.

Tambay had a pinched nerve in his shoulder which proved so painful that after first qualifying he withdrew, and Arnoux had joined Ferrari for 1983.

How would that affect the balance in the Renault team and particularly Prost's championship chances? He could scarcely count on Arnoux helping him...

The Renaults were so quick on the Friday that they chose not to contest the Saturday session but contented themselves with running on full tanks and unmarked tyres.

Rosberg wrestled with understeer – the familiar problem, haunting him like a ghost from race to race. He, Frank Williams and his engineer Frank Dernie struggled with this but what Rosberg described as a 'last minute change to the tyres' solved it. He had three different compounds on the car for the race, a decision taken shortly before the start. 'I tried it on the warm-up lap and it felt really good. I just said "This is the way to go." No argument.'[1]

Watson also suffered understeer, qualifying 11th.

A strange incident enlivened Saturday qualifying because Mansell went off up the escape road into catch fencing, blamed Henton, and they squared up. (Many years later Henton found reminiscing about this amusing and said 'Fist fight? It was handbags at dawn!')

The view from behind the paddock was, in Formula One terms, panoramic. After Austria I'd taken my family on holiday to Italy and motored up to Dijon to cover the race before continuing home. I got my mother a pass for the Saturday and she sat watching La Bretelle as qualifying began. Nothing had prepared her for the late braking, deceleration, road holding

ABOVE *Unseen bravery. Tambay had an injured arm and although he took part in the first qualifying he withdrew.*

and acceleration of the Formula One car, and, as the first few came hard in, she murmured 'Dead!' – they'd have to crash and die. Instead they followed the racing line, got onto the power baaarp-baaarp and proceeded quite normally.

If you are a follower of Grands Prix through the medium of television and have never been to a race weekend or test session your first taste of the reality of it will be a strong experience, as if the basic laws of geometry, physics and gravity are being rearranged before your very eyes.

The other day a magazine called *Evo*, which specialises in road testing hot production cars, did a detailed comparison of such as a big BMW, a Corvette, a Lamborghini, an Ascari, a Mitsubishi and, among others, a Caterham CSR. That was the most potent, doing 0–100mph–0 in 13.7 seconds, but, as the magazine pointed out, the current McLaren F1 car was doing 0–100–0 in 6.6 seconds, more than twice as fast. The McLaren also braked from

185mph–0 in 3.5 seconds, which candidly is very hard to imagine from the driver's point of view. (Circa 1982, Rosberg would recount, the G-forces were so stark under braking that they tried to make your eyeballs rotate.)

Of course, television flattens and slows everything. If you go to Wimbledon the courts seem smaller than the ones you've been watching at home and the ball is travelling a lot faster. You need some time to adjust. Same at Lord's where, sitting side-on to the wicket, a fast delivery is difficult to glimpse and you wonder how any batsman has the time to play it. Now think of a downhill ski race where, at points, the racer may be jumping the length of a football pitch in the air. And so it goes. None of this (in my own experience) equals the sense of complete disorientation when you are confronted with 0–100–0 in 6.6s machines for the first time: the shrieking, echoing bomb-burst of noise, the braking points which cannot be possible, the absolute

STARTING GRID

1		**1** 1:01.38 **A. Prost**
	2 1:01.74 **R. Arnoux**	
2		**3** 1:02.71 **R. Patrese**
	4 1:02.98 **N. Lauda**	
3		**5** 1:03.02 **A. de Cesaris**
	6 1:03.18 **N. Piquet**	
4		**7** 1:03.29 **D. Daly**
	8 1:03.58 **K. Rosberg**	
5		**9** 1:03.77 **B. Giacomelli**
	10 1:03.89 **P. Tambay**	
6		**11** 1:03.99 **J. Watson**
	12 1:04.06 **M. Alboreto**	
7		**13** 1:04.08 **J. Laffite**
	14 1:04.92 **M. Surer**	
8		**15** 1:04.96 **E. de Angelis**
	16 1:05.00 **E. Cheever**	
9		**17** 1:05.17 **J.-P. Jarier**
	18 1:05.39 **B. Henton**	
10		**19** 1:05.39 **R. Guerrero**
	20 1:05.45 **M. Winkelhock**	
11		**21** 1:05.87 **D. Warwick**
	22 1:06.01 **R. Keegan**	
12		**23** 1:06.01 **T. Fabi**
	24 1:06.13 **R. Boesel**	
13		**25** 1:06.16 **E. Salazar**
	26 1:06.21 **N. Mansell**	

precision in cornering – like watching a Japanese bullet train – and the unleashing of so much power out of a corner that the car is already in the distance.

Then, afterwards, you listen to the drivers and they invariably sing the same song. The set-up wasn't quite right ... could have found a tenth of a second here, another tenth there ... understeer in turn two ...tyres started to go off ... I'll be faster next time no question ...

As Frank Williams once observed, however much power a racing car can deliver the driver always demands one and the same thing: more.

Mother never wanted to go again after Dijon but the narcotic was getting to me.

Whether she saw Derek Daly go by on his hot lap I have no idea but plenty of people, including the timing officials, clearly did not.

Daly says that in his relationship with Rosberg 'the only thing that irritated him' – Rosberg – 'was that I started ahead of him on the grid at Dijon and part of the reason he won there was as a result of something I did.'

First, the hot lap. 'Actually that was a bogus time. I didn't do it. Here's what happened: it appeared that the Williamses were faster without the front wings so we were both running in qualifying and practice without them. In the last session I tried with front wings on the car again and immediately I thought: this is a faster set-up. I'm chasing John Watson, who is maybe four seconds ahead of me. You know Dijon? You go down the front straight, you turn right, you do down the hill through these esses. I braked too late at the top of the hill and missed the left turn. I go through this escape road, stop at the top of it and see Wattie coming, let him go by and drive out

BELOW *Singer Leo Sayer, here with Rupert Keegan, loved Grand Prix racing and popped up regularly.*

behind him. Of course when I drove up behind him I am now two seconds closer than I was. I flashed by the timing at a 1m 32. I drive in. Charlie Crichton-Stuart is first up to me.'

Crichton-Stuart: 'Man, the car must be good.'

Daly: 'Charlie, I didn't do the time.'

Crichton-Stuart (looking left, looking right, shouting into Daly's helmet): 'Don't tell anybody – especially Keke. Don't expletive tell him.'

Daly prudently said nothing to anybody except 'the car is faster with front wings on.'

(Momentary diversion. A quarter of a century later I had this verbal exchange with Rosberg:

I've spoken to Derek Daly and he outqualified you.

Rosberg (combative): 'Where?'

Dijon.

Rosberg: 'Yeah, using the short cut!'

So when did you find out?

Rosberg: 'I knew it instantly.'

How?

Rosberg: 'Because he CAN'T be quicker than me, not in Dijon. If you wait long enough, he might have got lucky and had a time which was similar, but Dijon? Nooo. He cut the loop off.'

End of verbal exchange.)

Daly's short cut did, however, lead the Williams team to put front wings on Rosberg's car too, and as Daly says 'It turned out to be the best for the race, which put him in a position to be able to take advantage of everybody else's misfortune.'

Prost had pole from Arnoux, Patrese and Lauda.

A Grand Prix meeting was a more intimate affair then, the paddock large by the standards of the 1960s but ridiculously small by today's. In mood and conduct it was nearer 1967 than 2007. Drivers didn't habitually conceal themselves in air-conditioned motorhomes and if you wanted a word with Rosberg he would invariably be sitting outside chatting, probably provocatively, to people going past. He wore sunglasses, he smoked and he ate real food with a knife and fork, not organic shredded carrot juice and pasta and the like. From time to time a

BELOW *Disaster at Dijon for John Watson. By lap 10 he'd cut a path from mid-grid and ran seventh, between Patrese and Daly. Then everything went wrong – Rosberg won the race and led the Championship.*

sturdy, dedicated little tribe of Finns complete with flags – they followed him from race to race – would suddenly burst into view shouting at great volume Keke! Keke! and things we couldn't understand. He smiled and they smiled and the people going past smiled, and wasn't this the way life was meant to be?

A hot, dry Sunday afternoon. Arnoux took the lead from Prost and they pulled clear and Prost overtook him. Now Prost pulled away and Arnoux held a big gap to Patrese while Piquet, running light for his fuel stop, had to make a move. He needed to be in a substantial lead but only got past Patrese on lap 4. Order at lap 5: Prost, Arnoux, Piquet, Patrese, Rosberg, Lauda ...Watson 11th.

The race assumed its shape, a familiar shape. Piquet caught Arnoux but by then Prost was literally out of sight and at La Bretelle Piquet slithered off onto the dust, came back. Patrese drew up and Rosberg drew up on Patrese.

Piquet took Arnoux on the outside down the start-finish straight on lap 11.

Watson made a concerted thrust so that on this lap 11 he reached eighth and on lap 17 took Patrese. He lost a skirt, however, and pitted three laps later. It took so long for repairs that when he emerged he ran at the back of the field.

Piquet was travelling fast, prising tenths of a second from Prost wherever he could, and cut the gap from 7 seconds to 4.5 He made his pit stop on lap 40 but that could only be a crippling disadvantage because he had not overtaken Prost. The race turned, as others had done before it, on whether the Renault would hold together. The order after Piquet's stop: Prost, Arnoux, Rosberg, Lauda, Piquet, Patrese.

By lap 44 the first five faced a crocodile of cars – Patrese (now lapped), Alboreto, de Cesaris and Daly. The Renaults selected their moments and passed by, but when Rosberg, catching the Renaults at 1.5 seconds a lap, reached de Cesaris he also reached a problem. De Cesaris did not accept the racing etiquette that all is fair in fights for position but a driver being lapped moves courteously aside as soon as he decently can. De Cesaris blocked and, because the Alfa Romeo had the turbo power, Rosberg could not match it on the straights. So Rosberg tried everything he knew in the corners, driving like a 'lunatic' and worried about destroying his tyres. He watched, impotent, as the Renaults sailed away and he was not happy.

ABOVE *A world in headlines, and the Swiss papers treated it all with circumspection.*

'De Cesaris nearly cost me the race. I was very quick but I just couldn't get by this bloody Alfa. I could slipstream it, get alongside it and that was the end of it. I just could not take him because when I was alongside by the end of the straight he was ahead again and there was no chance, I couldn't out-brake him, nothing. In those days blue-flagging wasn't what it is today and this happened lap after lap, lap after lap. The bloke was being lapped! It wasn't for position – he was a lap down.

'Did I speak to him afterwards? No. I knew Andrea quite well but after that, what's the point? You expected bad behaviour from Andrea. I had a very clear idea always about who I was in front of and who I was behind. Can I let him by or can I fight with this guy? Every person you would approach differently because you had a mental picture of every one. You knew his weaknesses, you knew his strengths. You knew his history, what he'd done before, so you just had the feel for everyone. And you treated them all differently. Andrea was unfair. I was so angry I was tempted to bang wheels. That was the only time I nearly lost control of myself in a

racing car. I just felt I was never going to be able to solve the situation. And you have to remember this guy was being lapped and I'm hurting my tyres and I'm hurting everything.'

De Cesaris says: 'Dijon? I don't remember at all. What happened at Dijon?'

Rosberg did bang a fist on the steering wheel in frustration and the statistics are an eloquent testament to his anger. He'd been lapping consistently in the 1:09s from early in the race, only going into the 1:10s – and one lap the 1:11s – when in traffic before rapping out 1:09s again. That is what he was doing when he reached de Cesaris and what he was losing, lap by lap, to Prost.

	Lap 47	Lap 48	Lap 49	Lap 50
Rosberg	1:09.9	1:11.0	1:11.5	1:13.6
De Cesaris	1:11.2	1:11.5	1:13.4	1:11.4
Prost	1:09.0	1:08.9	1:09.1	1:09.0

This continued for another three laps, costing Rosberg an estimated ten seconds. Rosberg described de Cesaris at the time as 'crazy ... a madman'. At one point, doing 170mph down the straight, Rosberg banged the side of the Alfa Romeo with his front wheel and he knew this was becoming very dangerous.

Eventually de Cesaris made a mistake and Rosberg went through, de Cesaris off the circuit. Rosberg felt it was the least de Cesaris deserved.

A concertina developed at the front, Arnoux catching Prost ('I would quite happily have gone by him if I could,' Arnoux said) and Rosberg catching Arnoux. On lap 73 Rosberg overtook Arnoux, who pitted imagining he had run out of fuel. Rosberg did not know that Prost's choice of softer tyres was moving against the Renault, nor that Prost had lost a skirt.

On lap 76 of the 80 Rosberg closed ... closed ... closed. You could feel how taut he held the Williams, how hard his demands of it were, how strongly he wielded it through the corners. On lap 77 he flung it through La Bretelle and a gap came up, 2.08 seconds. In the sweepers out the back he drew up to within a couple of car's lengths.

Into lap 78 he held distance with the Renault down the start-finish straight and now at La Bretelle was almost close enough to start threatening. This time out the back Rosberg thrust the snout of the Williams over to the right searching for an opening. Prost countered that. The man with the chequered flag walked towards his position and the Williams team realised he was going to stop the race two laps early. They pointed that out to him in no uncertain terms.

Approaching lap 79, the second last, Rosberg was still those two car's lengths away. 'Don't forget,' Rosberg says, 'they tried to stop the race one lap early. The starter wanted to wave the chequered flag! Peter Collins[2] ran to the start-finish podium, grabbed the bloke's hands and wouldn't let him put the flag up! That's what saved the win. Peter Collins thought: don't you dare.'

Into a downhill left-hander Prost suddenly went wide. It surprised Rosberg although not enough to deflect him from going into the wide open space on the inside and through. He had a couple of corners to fashion a protective gap before they were both on the start-finish straight and the turbo power came at him. He fashioned the gap and it safely delivered him the race.

Prost fell away and Rosberg beat him by 4.4 seconds.

It was an extraordinarily improbable moment for two reasons. Before the race Rosberg said (to Murray Walker and others) that he thought a non-turbo could win it, and this at a turbo track; and a year before he had been out of a drive after an undistinguished career. That evening at Dijon he led the World Championship and that was in his thoughts, not the first victory.

Rosberg 42, Pironi 39, Prost 31, Lauda 30, Watson 30, de Angelis 23.

It left only Italy at Monza and the United States at Las Vegas. A driver could count his best 11 finishes from the 16 rounds but in such a season that was meaningless. Rosberg had nine finishes and could

BELOW *Prost got the Renault to the end of the race, only the fifth time it finished in the points. Even then Rosberg was 4.4 seconds in front.*

therefore keep everything he gained, Pironi was statistically out of it, Prost was favoured by the Renault's unreliability in the sense that he had only scored points in five races, Lauda in six, Watson in six also and de Angelis in seven. We were to be spared mental arithmetic which bedevilled other seasons where drivers were dropping points and the permutations gave proceedings an artificial and sometimes grotesque aspect.

As The Family decamped from Dijon with its customary urgency – you came from the Press Room when you'd filed your story and they were all gone, like a vision dissolved – any of the top five (and excluding Pironi, of course) might take the Championship, although the chances of de Angelis depended on him winning the last two races and Rosberg scoring no points.

That made four, Rosberg, Prost, Lauda and Watson. They were four entirely different personalities, four different nationalities and four different backgrounds although nationalism itself would play no part. As Lauda told me once, 'Forget about flags and anthems and crap like that, in this game they don't matter a damn.'

Rosberg said 'So now I'm 11 points ahead of Prost but he can win Monza and probably I can't. So, let's see ... if Alain wins Monza and I don't finish, then where are we? Yes, only two points difference before Las Vegas – so you've got to be very careful about jumping to conclusions.'

The Finnish tribe decamped to Dijon where that evening they gave the solid streets their rendition of the Keke! Keke! chant and brandished those Finnish flags, but however sturdy the tribe proved to be, however energetically they flourished those blue crosses on white backgrounds, Lauda's Law still applied. Nationalist fervour couldn't help Keke at all.

Never mind. He fully intended to do what he had been doing for the whole of his life, and help himself – in both senses of that term.

Footnote: 1. Grand Prix International; 2. Peter Collins, Australian, was Williams team manager and later held senior posts at Benetton and Lotus.

TOP LEFT *Rosberg, a winner at last. Prost, second, and Lauda, third, look happy enough too – both could still catch Rosberg for the Championship.*

LEFT *Keke's army invade the track and prepare to march on Dijon, just in case anybody there hadn't heard who'd won.*

OPPOSITE TOP *Murray Walker wants an interview – and is going to get it.*

Race Result

WINNING SPEED 196.79kmh/122.28 mph

FASTEST LAP 202.73kmh/125.97mph
(Prost 1m 7.47s on lap 2)

LAP LEADERS Arnoux 1 (1);
Prost 2–78 (77); Rosberg 79–80

Note: The chequered flag was shown a lap late – at the end of the 81st lap – but the results were officially recorded as at the end of the 80th lap.

RACE

	Driver	Team	Engine	Laps	Time
1	K. Rosberg	Williams FW08	Ford Cosworth V8	80	1h 32m 41.08s
2	A. Prost	Renault RE30B	Renault V6t	80	1h 32m 45.52s
3	N. Lauda	McLaren MP4B	Ford Cosworth V8	80	1h 33m 41.43s
4	N. Piquet	Brabham BT50	BMW 4t	79	
5	R. Patrese	Brabham BT50	BMW 4t	79	
6	E. de Angelis	Lotus 91	Cosworth V8	79	
7	M. Alboreto	Tyrrell 011	Cosworth V8	79	
8	N. Mansell	Lotus 91	Cosworth V8	79	
9	D. Daly	Williams FW08	Cosworth V8	79	
10	A. de Cesaris	Alfa Romeo 182	Alfa V12	78	
11	B. Henton	Tyrrell 011	Cosworth V8	78	
12	B. Giacomelli	Alfa Romeo 182	Alfa V12	78	
13	J. Watson	McLaren MP4B	Cosworth V8	77	
14	E. Salazar	ATS D5	Cosworth V8	77	
15	M. Surer	Arrows A5	Cosworth V8	76	
16r	R. Arnoux	Renault RE30B	Renault V6t	75	Fuel injection
nc	E. Cheever	Talbot Ligier JS19	Matra V12	70	
r	M. Winkelhock	ATS D5	Cosworth V8	56	Engine mounting
r	J.-P. Jarier	Osella FA1D	Cosworth V8	44	Engine
r	J. Laffite	Talbot Ligier JS19	Matra V12	33	Skirts/handling
r	T. Fabi	Toleman TG181C	Hart 4t	31	Engine overheating
r	R. Boesel	March 821	Cosworth V8	31	Gearbox oil leak
r	R. Keegan	March 821	Cosworth V8	25	Spin
r	D. Warwick	Toleman TG181C	Hart 4t	24	Engine
r	R. Guerrero	Ensign N181	Cosworth V8	4	Engine
ns	P. Tambay	Ferrari 126C2	Ferrari V6t		Driver unfit (neck injury)
nq	C. Serra	Fittipaldi F9	Cosworth V8		
nq	T. Byrne	Theodore TY02	Cosworth V8		
nq	M. Baldi	Arrows A4	Cosworth V8		

nc = did not complete=; nq = did not qualify; ns = did not start; r = retired

CHAMPIONSHIP

	Driver	Points
1	K. Rosberg	42
2	D. Pironi	39
3	A. Prost	31
4	J. Watson	30
	N. Lauda	30
6	E. de Angelis	23
7	R. Patrese	21
8	N. Piquet	20
9	R. Arnoux	19
	P. Tambay	19
11	M. Alboreto	14
12	E. Cheever	10
13	D. Daly	7
	N. Mansell	7
15	C. Reutemann	6
	G. Villeneuve	6
17	A. de Cesaris	5
	J. Laffite	5
19	J.-P. Jarier	3
	M. Surer	3
21	M. Winkelhock	2
	E. Salazar	2
	B. Giacomelli	2
	M. Baldi	2
25	F. Serra	1

	Team	Points
1	Ferrari	64
2	McLaren	60
3	Williams	55
4	Renault	50
5	Brabham	41
6	Lotus	30
7	Talbot Ligier	15
8	Tyrrell	14
9	Alfa Romeo	7
10	Arrows	5
11	ATS	4
12	Osella	3
13	Fittipaldi	1

PRODIGAL'S RETURN

ITALY, MONZA

Monaco was not the only circuit which coexisted with its own caricature, annually renewed and never questioned. Monza did the same, although mythology is perhaps a better word than caricature. Either way you get the idea.

The Monaco Grand Prix really did (and does) attract a supporting cast of corporate creatures, celebrities, quasi-celebrities, outright poseurs and the well-heeled who want, for whatever reason, to be associated with it. Many came on yachts and decorated them with topless models – so many of them (yachts and models) that they became conventional and your eye would be drawn to the yachts without the bronzed beauties draped over the decks.

The celebs, poseurs and well-heeled did not venture near Monza, and especially their models didn't. There were dark tales of what the teeming, lawless and macho-fuelled Italian hordes did to women, especially in the tunnel towards the paddock in broad daylight. The fact that nobody had ever seen anything like that was definitely not permitted to disturb the mythology.

Lawless? Someone was having dinner near the circuit one year and although he had parked his Mercedes outside and in full view it wasn't there when he emerged. He reported this to the police, who said 'Ah, Saturday today. It will be at the docks at Genoa tomorrow and in the Middle East by Tuesday.' Eoin Young thought this worthy of reproducing in his weekly column, reached into his pocket for his notebook ... and guess what wasn't there?

RIGHT *Mario Andretti comes back to Monza and lays passion on all the passion, by taking pole.*

Italy
Monza

RACE DATE September 12th

CIRCUIT LENGTH
5.80km/3.60 miles

NO. OF LAPS 52

RACE DISTANCE
301.60km/187.40 miles

WEATHER Hot, dry

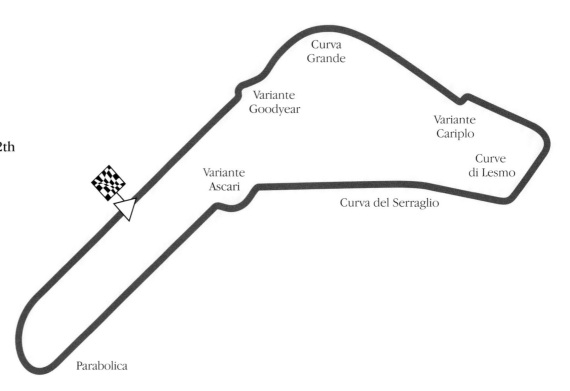

Curva Grande

Variante Goodyear

Variante Cariplo

Curve di Lesmo

Variante Ascari

Curva del Serraglio

Parabolica

DRIVER'S VIEW

'The circuit was the same then as it is today, although the first chicane was a little different [and has been the subject of constant change]. Nevertheless there was a chicane there, a chicane before Lesmo, there was a chicane at the Ascari – so basically Monza was Monza and Monza is Monza. I had raced there before 1982, of course. I won with the Alfa Romeo in the 1,000kms, I won the Grand Prix with Lotus. I enjoyed Monza, it was fine, although it always is a huge compromise because you cannot afford a lot of aerodynamic downforce: you have such a long straight. So I was dealing with that like everyone else.'

— *Mario Andretti*

Then there was the man who showed up with a removal van and a big sign advertising Leave your motorbike here during the race so it will be safe. He charged of course, but in this climate safety was all. Many paid and left their bikes ... and guess what wasn't there after the race...?

Peter Warr, running Lotus, ordered the team's motorhome personnel to 'padlock everything, leave nothing lying anywhere.' He raised an arm to indicate the high metal fencing of the paddock with, outside, dozens of eager-faced spectators pressed inwards. 'They are Italians!'

On this side of the fence police with Alsatians patrolled just in case any of the supporters did come over the top. The police and the canines looked equally fierce and no doubt were.

In spite of all this, or perhaps because of it, Monza was the place where Italy celebrated Grand Prix racing with a great outpouring of passion unapproached anywhere else. That part of the mythology was self-evidently true and therefore, strictly, not mythology at all. To do the outpouring an army came to the parkland north of Milan in their tens of thousands, like a vision from the Middle Ages. At close quarters these footsoldiers with their version of uniform – Ferrari T-shirts, Ferrari caps, Ferrari banners – looked disconcerting because of their numbers and who knew what they might do?

Imola was not the same. Imola was civilisation. Monza attracted near-barbarians and purists who were often the same person. The barbarian used industrial wire cutters to get in and stole whatever he could once he had got in, the purist in him knew about the Osella and the Theodore, knew how fast (or slowly) Guerrero was likely to go in the Ensign and why. The contrast with Monaco was stark enough, the contrast with Detroit total.

Built in 1922, Monza had known virtually every great driver in motor racing history and that created a kind of awe. Murray Walker once told me he walked it every year in a hallowed ritual and once came upon a small flower growing on it. He took it home and pressed it.

Monza was also unlike anywhere else in that once you had joined the immense queues, stuttered stop-start through the town of Monza itself and stammered stop-stop-start through the narrow lanes of Vedano al Lambro – the little, typically Italian place at the circuit entrance – you could hear the crowd as well as the engines in the distance. The Italians

BELOW The immovable object, McLaren designer John Barnard, exchanging views with the irresistible force, McLaren driver Niki Lauda. Tyler Alexander doesn't look poised to step between them.

(known as tifosi, which the dictionary translates as fan and fanatic, making no distinction between the two) could make a truly enormous amount of noise and during the race they could deduce what was happening by the different noises coming at them through the trees from the various grandstands. If a Ferrari took the lead the tifosi gave a primeval shout of such volume and intensity that for a moment you could barely hear the engines.

A beautifully Italian thing happened to overlay the passion. Ferrari had Tambay fit again but Arnoux wouldn't be coming until the following year so they reached across the Atlantic for Mario Andretti to race their second car. Although Italian by birth (and fluent in the language) his family had emigrated to the United States and he was an American citizen. He had been Formula One World Champion in 1978 (with Lotus) and, now in IndyCars and at 42, was one of the most respected figures in all motor sport.

The fact that he had described how as a child[1] he didn't glance back as the ship sailed from Europe, and how the proudest day of his life was when he received his American citizenship, would weigh not at all with the tifosi who any day now would be making sure their wire cutters were in working order. They would reclaim him just as, in the Ferrari, he reclaimed Formula One, and they would decide which facts were facts and which were inconvenient. Mythology works like that.

'I did Formula One for Ferrari in 1971 and 1972 but I drove some sports cars after that,' Andretti says. 'I got to know the Old Man very well. I had direct relationship with him – which was not always the case, by the way, with drivers. He always had a buffer. My relationship was first person.

'I received a call and I said "Yeah, I will do it providing I get a day's test" because I had not driven a turbo Formula One car. I said I needed to familiarise myself. The weekend before Monza I was free and we used that weekend to do the test at Fiorano. They had set up Saturday and Sunday and I arrived of course Friday.'

He flew to Milan and, typically, had thought to get a Ferrari hat before he boarded. He wore it as he emerged from the aeroplane and when the great Italian public glimpsed it he held the whole country in the palm of his hand. A horde of journalists descended on him and he gave a press conference which lasted an hour and a half: 'You don't,' he said, 'turn down a Ferrari drive at Monza.' He had a late lunch with Enzo Ferrari and went out for a few laps of the Fiorano test track. Next day he did 60 laps in extremely hot weather with a best of 1m 07s, fast in that sort of weather.

The prodigal son had come back and was going to pack Monza.

STARTING GRID

1	**1** 1:28.47 M. Andretti	**2** 1:28.50 N. Piquet
2	**3** 1:28.83 P. Tambay	**4** 1:29.89 R. Patrese
3	**5** 1:30.02 A. Prost	**6** 1:30.09 R. Arnoux
4	**7** 1:31.83 K. Rosberg	**8** 1:32.35 B. Giacomelli
5	**9** 1:32.54 A. de Cesaris	**10** 1:32.78 N. Lauda
6	**11** 1:33.13 M. Alboreto	**12** 1:33.18 J. Watson
7	**13** 1:33.33 D. Daly	**14** 1:33.37 E. Cheever
8	**15** 1:33.53 J.-P. Jarier	**16** 1:33.62 D. Warwick
9	**17** 1:33.62 E. de Angelis	**18** 1:34.05 R. Guerrero
10	**19** 1:34.34 M. Surer	**20** 1:34.37 B. Henton
11	**21** 1:34.37 J. Laffite	**22** 1:34.78 T. Fabi
12	**23** 1:34.96 N. Mansell	**24** 1:34.97 M. Baldi
13	**25** 1:34.99 E. Salazar	**26** 1:35.23 C. Serra

FAN'S EYE VIEW

'In the early 1980s I was a busy Oxford solicitor but I always took a few days off to watch a European Grand Prix. The previous year it had been Hockenheim for the German race. In 1982 I opted for Monza, flying from Heathrow to Milan with Alitalia in the days when its usual bumpy landings were always greeted with a polite round of applause from grateful passengers!

'I stayed in Como and was able to explore its impressive architecture, another interest of mine. Friday's practice I watched from out on the track and then located the remaining section of the old disused banked circuit. I was literally staggered, despite being a fit 35-year-old, to find how difficult it was attempting to ascend that banking.

'On race day my ticket was for the stand by the start-finish line opposite the pits and, armed with my Olympus OM 10 camera (now long deceased), I shot several rolls of Kodak's finest. On the return flight Alitalia had its revenge by running out of lunch before reaching my seat to the rear of the plane!'

DAVID HILLEARD
DORCHESTER-ON-THAMES, UK

FROM TOP *Sunday morning warm-up and Piquet's Brabham expires instantly; Piquet breaks into a gallop to get some more horsepower; Monza is a mighty place even when the track's clear and the crowd are waiting; not so many on the grid then as now; Andretti and Piquet and, in a moment, Monza will reverberate to engines and cheering, all for the local hero.*

'The Saturday test was an all-day affair and at the end of it I felt quite familiar with the car. They put a qualifying set-up engine in and I did a new track record. Then they started throwing some stuff on it – things that they had tested. I said "I don't need any donkey miles, I just need to feel good about the car. I am going to give everyone a day off tomorrow. We don't need to run anymore. I'll be ready for Monza." I ran my butt off that day: 87 laps around Fiorano. I'll tell you what – physically I was pretty well beat but it was a good feeling because it was a very productive day. I loved the car, it was all the things that I was hoping for.

'I went to see the Old Man. He sat in a room in Fiorano where they had a camera for every corner. Even in those days he could follow the car on a monitor every inch of the way – which you couldn't do anywhere else – and he sat there in that room all day. We had lunch together.'

Rosberg approached the Grand Prix philosophically and found a single word to encompass that. He would, he felt, be 'struggling'. Qualifying confirmed the judgement. He got the Williams to seventh, the fastest of the non-turbos but a lifetime away from the pole time: 3.4 seconds, a lot even around a circuit measuring more than three and a half miles.

Andretti, Tambay, Ferrari and the new Alfa Romeo turbos proved potent enough in the contemplation to lure a vast crowd for first qualifying on Friday. The stuttering stop-start began at dawn around Monza, gridlocked near the circuit, and some Grand Prix people only just made it in time.

Tambay went fastest on the Friday from Piquet and Prost, Andretti sixth, Rosberg seventh and Watson far down the list. He and Lauda complained that they couldn't find grip.

Other things were happening at McLaren.

Watson had had an unhappy Friday and was close to 'despair' because the Goodyear tyres offered so little grip, especially emerging from the chicanes. He was 19th.

Alan Jenkins 'started in Monza that year when John Barnard fell out with Teddy, shoved him to the back of the garage, ripped the headset off him and gave it to me halfway through practice on Saturday morning. Teddy used to wind JB up just by being there.

'I arrived in Monza with a box full of moulded skirts and bits and pieces which me and Joan Villadelprat[2] had concocted, with varying flexibility from one end to another and God knows what else. John Watson wasn't getting anywhere with Teddy, he was getting frustrated and JB went to speak to Teddy

BELOW *John Barnard (left) and Tyler Alexander watch as Lauda composes himself for a practice run – but, whatever Lauda did, Monza belonged to the turbo cars and not his. He qualified on the fifth row.*

about it because Wattie asked him to and I looked in the back of the garage and suddenly found I was handed a headset.

'Those were the days when you still plugged into the car on the end of a wire. Wattie and I had got quite pally even before that. I think Teddy kept his own council generally but I'd got on reasonably well with him up to then.'

Rosberg could complain of a blown engine and, moving to the spare, had a chilling experience when the fire extinguisher went off and he felt his leg going numb. He parked the Williams and got out faster than a champagne cork out of a bottle.

To disconcert Rosberg would take much more than that and he prepared to do battle again on the Saturday, wringing whatever he could from the car because he had to mix it with the turbos to get points. A combination of circumstances had opened Dijon to him and he'd seized it, but basing expectations or strategy on something similar happening again here was not the way to think and certainly not the way Rosberg thought. His whole career had been grounded in repetitive examples of reality and, eyeing the Championship table, even lowly points might be beyond price.

Saturday was hot and dry and Andretti went out swiftly – after two and a half minutes – to set a 1m 30.3s after three laps. Piquet did a 1m 30.1 and Tambay, out a minute after Andretti, did a 1m 30.0.

Prost was out after four and a half minutes and did a 1m 32.6. These were initial skirmishes because pole was going to be deep into the 1m 28s.

The others – Arnoux, Rosberg, Patrese, Watson – waited.

They came out successively after almost eight minutes (Watson for a 1m 52.8s), 11 minutes (Arnoux for a 2m 03.6), 12 minutes (Rosberg for a 1m 32.6) and 34 minutes (Patrese for a 1m 29.8). By then Mario Andretti had convulsed Monza. His first run ended almost seven minutes into the session and he waited another 20 minutes before trying again. He organised himself and settled with a 1m 55, attacked hard with a 1m 28.7 and finessed that in a great gesture with 1m 28.4.

'In qualifying I was hell for bent because I just really felt up to it,' Andretti says. 'It turned out to be a battle between Nelson and myself and whoever came in last from the run was quickest. I went out and we had so much power in those days, especially in qualifying trim. We were up to maybe 1,100 horsepower. I was actually in fifth gear getting wheelspin in the Lesmos – between the first and second Lesmo. On my quick lap I did the second Lesmo flat and I figured I could not duplicate this. That was it and that time held.

'When I set the time I didn't know if Nelson was out there also, and then all the people were jumping out on the track when they announced it so I figured well, that was good...'

ABOVE *Andretti hadn't forgotten his way round Monza – pole and third place, despite problems.*

ABOVE *Monza in delirium as Tambay leads Arnoux on the opening lap, Piquet trying to stay with them.*

OPPOSITE *The Renault's fuel injection has failed after 27 laps and Prost doesn't look to the crowd for sympathy because he knows he won't get any. Look for yourself.*

Who noticed Watson's first run, peaking at 1m 33.4s? 'The black art in 1982 was the skirts,' Alan Jenkins says. 'When I was given that headset in Monza I could do something with them by keeping the front end from biting in the quick corners. That was all to do with changing the flexibility of the front of the skirt – if, say, you'd thrown the wings away you wouldn't have been able to make the difference we were able to make with it.

'That made Wattie go from the back of the grid to 12th just because all of a sudden as he whipped into the Lesmos and so forth he wasn't getting this pointy feeling which made him worry about the back end.' It happened on Watson's second run.

Nobody could beat Andretti's time and sensible people wondered if there was any point in going back to their hotels at day's end because that lap was going to bring the whole of northern Italy to the circuit on the morrow and you might never get through the queues and in. Vedano al Lambro, so quiet and quaint for the rest of the year, would resemble an enormous car park. The footsoldiers would flow past this and the Vespa riders, exhibiting contempt for their own mortality, would weave improbable paths through it, but The Family, accustomed to hire cars rather than walking or

weaving, prepared for the dawn run: not early doors but the doors before those, even.

And so it happened.

Rosberg had no problems getting to the circuit because he woke at four in the morning, thinking that if he took a single point it would take Watson out of the Championship equation. The thought was so strong that he couldn't get to sleep afterwards.

Contrast that with Andretti. 'Did I get a good night's sleep? Oh, absolutely. I always slept the best when I was on pole and when I had a chance at a good result. To me, that was my life. When things would go well that's when I was the most relaxed. So no problem about sleeping the night before.'

When The Family came in they found messages painted on the grid in white and red letters: Mario and Patrick, win for Gilles. The messages had been painted elsewhere round the circuit too.

Each driver prepares in his own way. 'We used to go all kinds of lengths to try and relax Wattie,' Jenkins says. 'In fact I could see him at breakfast or see him walking into the garage on a Sunday morning – I know bike riders who are like this now – and you could tell if it was a good day or a bad day. However, whatever had happened in qualifying nine times out of ten he'd put it behind him by Sunday

and it didn't matter where he was on the grid: well, that's it, it's down to me now. He'd stopped looking for solutions in the car, whereas people like Alain Prost were still looking till the flag fell. Alain would be saying "No, no, don't drop the flag and start the race, I've still got to change that ride height half a turn." He'd been chewing his nails. Wattie was like that Friday–Saturday. He'd often be blinding in the Sunday warm-up just because he'd put it behind him. The Walkmans had not long been out – the ones you put a little cassette tape in – and I got an electronics buddy of mine to wire one into the radio and we played him Van Morrison tapes on the grid.'

Arnoux, who'd been astonished by the passion of the tifosi as he drove his Renault road car to the circuit – the tifosi making their own dawn run in large numbers and forever ready with an outpouring for Ferrari drivers present and future – made his own contribution to the impending sense of drama by lunching with the Ferrari team and reportedly ignored Renault altogether.

By afternoon and race time Monza palpitated.

From the green lights Piquet pulled ahead on the long drag to the first chicane, Tambay following, then Arnoux, Patrese and Andretti. The 26 starters threaded through the eye of the needle – the first chicane as tight and unforgiving as that, so tight it produced a concertina effect. The cars at the back were reduced to what seemed strolling pace.

Piquet faced a planned pit stop and the imperative, of course, was to establish enough of a lead to do that but his clutch malfunctioned, letting Tambay through as they came round to complete the opening lap – increasing Monza's palpitations – but Arnoux overtook him down the start-finish straight.

On the second lap Patrese overtook Tambay but Prost, eighth, was preparing to make a move. As the race found its rhythm – Arnoux, Patrese, Tambay, Andretti – Prost worked his way up to them. Patrese's clutch failed, Prost powered past Andretti on the start-finish straight and was third. Andretti had had 'the right side turbo expiring on me so I was losing power. When Prost passed me that's when I started losing straight-line speed. I was definitely a lame duck at that point.'

Rosberg ran seventh thinking tactically – that one point – and Watson eighth. A Prost victory would blow the whole thing open. At eight laps:

Arnoux	12m 48.6s
Tambay	@ 7.4s
Prost	@ 16.2s
Andretti	@ 18.7s
De Cesaris	@ 20.3s
Giacomelli	@ 21.7s

BELOW *The crowd watch Mansell on his way to seventh.*

Rosberg came up behind Giacomelli, Watson behind Rosberg. On lap 11 de Cesaris pitted for new tyres, ratcheting Giacomelli, Rosberg and Watson up a place and now Watson made a move, or rather two moves: he overtook Rosberg (who said afterwards it was done under a yellow flag) and then out-braked Giacomelli into the first chicane. It was the sort of thing he did so consummately on street circuits, finding space within the constrictions and asserting himself in one decisive moment.

And whatever happened Arnoux wouldn't be helping Prost.

On lap 22 Prost set fastest lap and was with Tambay, probing into the first chicane, Tambay resisting. The two cars and drivers were beautifully matched and they danced a duet round the parkland while outrageous ill fortune struck at Rosberg. Going flat out down the start-finish straight the rear wing sheered as if a great force had seized it, plucked it from the car and flung it into the air. It happened almost directly in front of where I was sitting and I can still recall the shocking violence of the instant.

Rosberg heard a 'bang' and 'you think you have a flat tyre or something because the car is behaving very strangely.' The mirrors did not show that the wing had gone. Without it the car went much faster on the straight and he sailed past Giacomelli

wondering quite how he could be doing that, a mystery compounded by the fact that Giacomelli kept waving trying to tell him. In the corners, without the downforce, the Williams became a bronco and Rosberg came round to the pits. 'When I stopped I thought they weren't doing anything – because I couldn't see that, either! I was screaming at them to change my "puncture". Finally they told me what had happened.' The repairs cost half a minute and might cost the Championship.

While Rosberg sat impotent Prost made another attempt on Tambay at the first chicane. Next moment his hand raised – I'm in trouble – the fuel injection awry. The crowd adored that: a Frenchman in a French car deserved only their derision, a Frenchman in another French car who'd be driving for Ferrari deserved their veneration. They'd really adore Arnoux winning if it couldn't be Tambay or Andretti.

Rosberg rejoined 15th, Watson running fourth. Rosberg did what he could but ninth was as high as he could get and, across the last third of the race, the four at the front – Arnoux, Tambay, Andretti and Watson – circled with no suggestion the order would change again unless one of them broke down. The maddening aspect of motor racing is precisely that: a car may be in trouble but unless that is in some way visible or audible the spectators don't know.

ABOVE *Arnoux leads Patrese for four laps at the beginning but Patrese's clutch was failing.*

RIGHT *Rosberg before that rear wing flew, taking precious points with it.*

Gran premio d'Italia

PAGINA 23

Colloquio con Mario Andretti, 42 anni, emigrante, nomade per vocazione e destino, per una sola domenica prima guida della Ferrari

'Sono un vecchio pilota felice sull'auto più bella del mondo'

dal nostro inviato CARLO MARINCOVICH

Andretti (Ferrari) ha conquistato la pole position

lo sport □ la Repubblica sabato 11 settembre 1982 PAGINA 20

Rosberg è vicino al titolo mondiale

Quarantamila a Monza per le prime prove; Andretti sesto

Aria di gran premio Tambay velocissimo gira a tempo di record

di CLAUDIO BAGNI

Tambay (Ferrari) a Monza è stato il più veloce

PAGINA 22

Gran premio d'Italia

Come ai tempi del Mundial, l'Italia scende di nuovo compatta in campo: le "sue" auto, i bolidi rossi di Maranello volano a Monza

dal nostro inviato

Ferrari portaci con te
E Andretti è subito davanti a tutti

Il circuito

Così al via

RIGHT *A world in headlines, all about Ferrari, Andretti and Tambay.*

'Monza,' Arnoux will say, 'was a little bit of a miracle for me. Ferrari announced on the Saturday after the official practice that I would be with them: René Arnoux will be a part of the Ferrari team from 1983. The Grand Prix started and I was on the third row. The car was working very, very well but after 20 laps my buttocks were burning me. I felt petrol on them and my legs, everything. I asked myself: what's happening here? And after a couple more laps I said: that's it, I've my buttocks in petrol. The petrol tank, which was in my back, had a little leak and the petrol came out when I braked. I was in the lead and I said to myself: I'll never get to the chequered flag, I'll run out of fuel. I did get to the end, won the race and there was so little fuel left that I couldn't have done another lap, certainly not a fast lap. That was my miracle.'

Prost could no longer win the Championship and the odds favoured Rosberg because Watson had to win Las Vegas and Rosberg get no points: they'd both finish on 42 points but Watson would get it on the most wins tie-break.

At the end, as the leaders moved into the slowing down lap and those behind them were still racing, the tifosi swarmed the track. Like a crowd at a car rally, they melted back when a car approached, came back on again when it had passed. They spread across the start-finish straight by the pits so that Mansell, needing to cross the line to be seventh, suddenly found himself confronted by a wall of people.

Many, many thousands gathered below the podium balcony and Arnoux made it into a stage, worked the crowd from there by gesture – I'm coming soon, I'm coming soon! He took his blue cap off and flung it like a Frisbee down to them and they adored that, all right.

'I went on the podium and I was hypercontent,' Arnoux says, 'but the effects of the fuel burned me for two weeks afterwards. At the time the fuel was special and that burned well...'

Rosberg had different sentiments. 'We were supposed to win the Championship in Monza, we knew what we needed to do and then I lost the rear wing. I lost a rear wing at Fittipaldi, I lost a rear wing at Hockenheim and now at Monza. I consider myself very, very lucky in that it happened in the right era: we had rear-wing cars, so we didn't have a lot of downforce on the front wings. The main downforce came from under the car and that meant it wouldn't swap ends on the straight. A 1983 car would have swapped ends immediately.

'It was one of those occasions when afterwards you don't have to say something. Patrick Head knows and you see that he knows. If you see a guy suffering already, you don't need to "hit" him. Patrick is one of those. You know that it breaks his heart.'

Rosberg 42, Pironi 39, Watson 33, Prost 31, Lauda 30, Arnoux 28.

By an irony, this once Watson didn't escape from the circuit within minutes of the race ending because, presumably, he didn't have a helicopter ride out and he just couldn't face the Vedano al Lambro gridlock. He sat in the Marlboro McLaren motorhome alone, his face both dignified and quizzical as it often was when fate played little games with him. 'It's not easy,' he said wistfully, 'when the others have so many more horses' – the brute horsepower which the turbos delivered at a place like Monza. He'd flogged the McLaren all the way home and still finished 1m 27s behind Arnoux, he'd spent just short of an hour and a half in a hellishly hot cockpit as a prisoner of the possible. He was an artist at that – exploiting the possible – and no mistake, but even he, in his best fighting mood, could do no more. 'So many more horses,' he said again.

Alan Jenkins reflects: 'I think Monza had as much to do with Wattie feeling under pressure and being irritated, in that he wasn't going anywhere, as much as anything else.'

BELOW Alboreto confirms his growing reputation by leading Lauda and finishing fifth.

ABOVE *Monza's traditional post-race chaos before the podium ceremony.*

OPPOSITE *Arnoux leaving Renault for Ferrari, uses the podium as a stage. From it, by gestures like these, he is saying to the Ferrari faithful gathered below, 'I am coming! I am coming!' The prodigal son is partially obscured at right, Jean-Marie Balestre next to him.*

Outside the motorhome someone muttered that one of the drivers had flat-spotted his tyres, an expression I had never heard before. I'd mastered 'keep it on the island', I knew what 'rock apes' were now, and 'banzai laps', and which cars were (and were not) 'straight out of the box' – but this? Eoin Young sat nursing a glass of red wine, as he invariably did, in the Elf motorhome, a sanctuary and food-source for journalists. He was maître d' there, an official capacity supervising and monitoring. He must have thought not him again when I went in.

'What the hell does flat-spotted mean?'

He smiled at my ignorance but respected the fact that I was saying: look, I am ignorant, that's why I've come to ask. Blunt and gruff if he didn't care for you, warm as a log fire if he did, he explained simply and patiently that if a driver brakes hard it can lock all four wheels, slicing rubber off the part of the tyres which happen to be in contact with the

track: the slice making them flat there, and nasty to drive afterwards. We had a glass of wine, and another, and Montreal faded into the distant past.

We've exchanged a lot of words in the 25 years since, but from that moment never a wrong one; nor ever will.

'So' Arnoux says, 'I won, Tambay in the Ferrari was second and Andretti in the Ferrari third. The next day I was going back to France with Gerard Larrousse in the plane and the headline in one of the Italian papers was THREE FERRARI DRIVERS ON THE PODIUM. That was funny. Well, it didn't make Gerard Larrousse, the Sporting Director of Renault, laugh.'

No, I bet it didn't.

Footnote: 1. Mario Andretti World Champion, Andretti with Nigel Roebuck, Hamlyn, London, 1979; 2. Joan Villadelprat from Barcelona got into Grand prix racing as a mechanic and rose to be Tyrrell team manager. He held senior posts with Benetton and the Prost teams.

Race Result

WINNING SPEED 219.53kmh/136.41mph

FASTEST LAP 223.03kmh/138.58mph
(Arnoux 1m 33.61s on lap 25)

LAP LEADERS Arnoux 1–52 (52)

RACE

	Driver	Team	Engine	Laps	Time
1	R. Arnoux	Renault RE30B	Renault V6t	52	1h 22m 25.73s
2	P. Tambay	Ferrari 126C2	Ferrari V6t	52	1h 22m 39.79s
3	M. Andretti	Ferrari 126C2	Ferrari V6t	52	1h 23m 14.18s
4	J. Watson	McLaren MP4B	Cosworth V8	52	1h 23m 53.57s
5	M. Alboreto	Tyrrell 011	Cosworth V8	51	
6	E. Cheever	Talbot Ligier JS19	Matra V12	51	
7	N. Mansell	Lotus 91	Cosworth V8	51	
8	K. Rosberg	Williams FW08	Cosworth V8	50	
9	E. Salazar	ATS D5	Cosworth V8	50	
10	A. de Cesaris	Alfa Romeo 182	Alfa V12	50	
11	C. Serra	Fittipaldi F9	Cosworth V8	49	
12	M. Baldi	Arrows A5	Cosworth V8	49	
nc	R. Guerrero	Ensign N181	Cosworth V8	40	
r	E. de Angelis	Lotus 91	Cosworth V8	34	Throttle jammed
r	B. Giacomelli	Alfa Romeo 182	Alfa V12	33	Side-pod/handling
r	M. Surer	Arrows A4	Cosworth V8	29	Ignition
r	A. Prost	Renault RE30B	Renault V6t	27	Fuel injection
r	N. Lauda	McLaren MP4B	Cosworth V8	22	Brakes/handling
r	J.-P. Jarier	Osella FA1D	Cosworth V8	10	Rear wheel lost
r	N. Piquet	Brabham BT50	BMW 4t	7	Clutch/engine
r	R. Patrese	Brabham BT50	BMW 4t	6	Clutch
r	J. Laffite	Talbot Ligier JS19	Matra V12	5	Gearbox
r	T. Fabi	Toleman TG181C	Hart 4t	2	Engine
r	D. Daly	Williams FW08	Cosworth V8	1	Accident/rear suspension
r	D. Warwick	Toleman TG183	Hart 4t	0	Accident
r	B. Henton	Tyrrell 011	Cosworth V8	0	Accident
nq	R. Keegan	March 821	Cosworth V8		
nq	M. Winkelhock	ATS D5	Cosworth V8		
nq	R. Boesel	March 821	Cosworth V8		
nq	T. Byrne	Theodore TY02	Cosworth V8		

nc = did not complete=; nq = did not qualify; r = retired

CHAMPIONSHIP

	Driver	Points
1	K. Rosberg	42
2	D. Pironi	39
3	J. Watson	33
4	A. Prost	31
5	N. Lauda	30
6	R. Arnoux	28
7	P. Tambay	25
8	E. de Angelis	23
9	R. Patrese	21
10	N. Piquet	20
11	M. Alboreto	16
12	E. Cheever	11
13	D. Daly	7
	N. Mansell	7
15	C. Reutemann	6
	G. Villeneuve	6
17	A. de Cesaris	5
	J. Laffite	5
19	M. Andretti	4
20	J.-P. Jarier	3
	M. Surer	3
22	M. Winkelhock	2
	E. Salazar	2
	B. Giacomelli	2
	M. Baldi	2
26	F. Serra	1

	Team	Points
1	Ferrari	74
2	McLaren	63
3	Renault	59
4	Williams	55
5	Brabham	41
6	Lotus	30
7	Tyrrell	16
	Talbot Ligier	16
9	Alfa Romeo	7
10	Arrows	5
11	ATS	4
12	Osella	3
13	Fittipaldi	1

ROULETTE WHEEL

CAESARS PALACE, LAS VEGAS

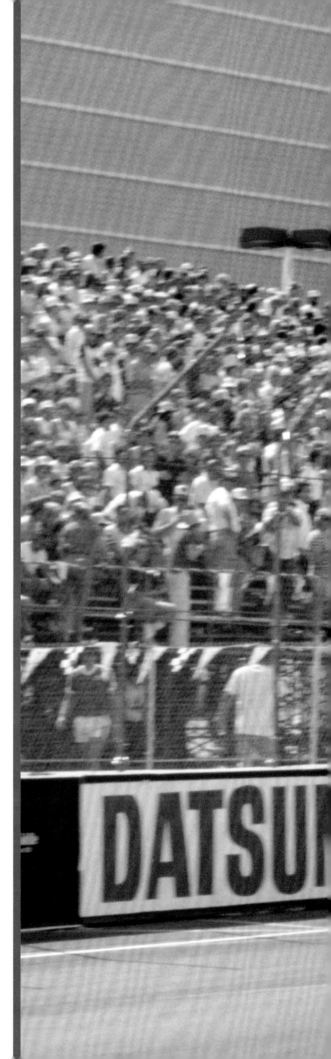

RIGHT *There really was a crowd there to watch Alboreto win the race and Rosberg win the World Championship.*

Keke Rosberg got back to his home in England in the evening after the Italian Grand Prix, which is what everybody always tried to do. During the season every hour at home is precious, almost stolen, and anyway he was playing mind games – with himself. He sensed he must relax mentally to prepare for Las Vegas. He stayed at home until the Friday when he flew to Los Angeles, booked into a hotel, and for a week cleared his mind of everything except aeroplanes. He had a passion for them and went to look some over with a view to possibly buying one. That gave him pleasant mental stimulation, which itself constituted relaxation. To a man of Rosberg's character, doing nothing and thinking nothing must have been an impossibility – remember the Renaissance Center prison? – so he inspected the planes instead. He went to Las Vegas as late as he could, knowing that to take the Championship he had to finish fifth.

These were the points going in: Rosberg 42, Pironi 39, Watson 33, Prost 31, Lauda 30, Arnoux 28. They gave the simplest of permutations.

Rosberg fifth	44
Watson winning	42
Lauda winning, the FIA Appeal	
Court reinstating his third at Zolder	43

The Williams team had appealed Rosberg's disqualification from second place in Brazil but the FIA Court of Appeal rejected that. Williams took action through the French civil courts but, on the

Las Vegas
Caesars Palace

RACE DATE September 25th

CIRCUIT LENGTH 3.65km/2.26 miles

NO. OF LAPS 75

RACE DISTANCE 273.74km/170.10 miles

WEATHER Hot, dry

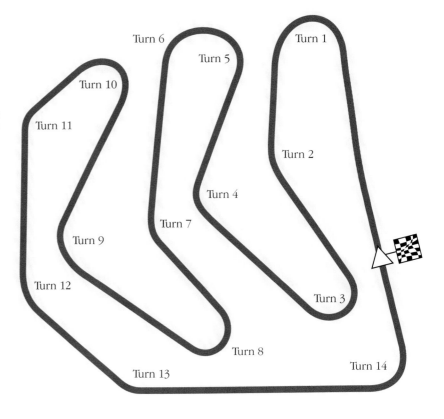

DRIVER'S VIEW

'Racing round a car park is not exactly motor racing. You'd got these totally artificial corners. Once the tarmac and concrete we were racing on got rubber down the grip improved and some of the corners were actually challenging corners. The biggest difficulty was that you were on a racetrack made up of canyons of concrete and in some corners you couldn't see ahead – see if somebody had spun on the exit – because the barriers were higher than the level of the cars. That was a downside. The challenging corners were 4, 8, 9 and then coming through 11, 12 and 13. The quicker corners were the problem in that if you got it wrong you were going to go off very quickly and hit something very hard. The maximum speed was 150mph coming down through 14.'

——————————— *John Watson*

Monday before Las Vegas, received a ruling from them that they would not announce their verdict until 11 October. If they'd found in Rosberg's favour he would have become Champion at that instant (42 now plus 6 from Rio = an uncatchable 48). Rosberg could still settle it in Las Vegas if he got 44, of course, rendering irrelevant whatever the French court subsequently said.

In reality it was Rosberg versus Watson at Las Vegas and, because of their different requirements from the race, neither could do much about the other. More than that, assuming Lauda's appeal failed – as seemed most likely – all Rosberg needed was sixth place, giving him 43, one more than Watson could total.

Fifth, however, took Rosberg clear of all court room machinations, all appeals, all hearings, and clear of all the combinations Watson or Lauda could put together.

Fifth was golden.

Rosberg decided not to concern himself with where Watson was running, and Watson, reminiscing, says: 'I was the principal contender. Knowing you have to win is not a bad way to go into it and I think intellectually it suited me because it wasn't a question of choice, it was a question of circumstance. All I could do was the best I could. I was left with an option and it is as difficult an option as you can get: control the race, win it and somehow try to make sure Keke didn't finish higher than sixth – but you can't control that. If Keke finished lower than sixth, getting

no points, we would have had 42 points each but I'd have won it on a tie-break with most wins.'

Since the abandonment of Watkins Glen in upstate New York in 1980 the United States Grand Prix – and variants of it, like US GP-West and USGP-East – had seemed to settle at Long Beach, had been to Detroit and was now back at Las Vegas for the second year or, more precisely, it was back in the car park of the Caesars Palace hotel.

The residents and visitors hadn't thought much of it in 1981 and hadn't changed their minds. You'd have imagined everyone in Las Vegas might have embraced Grand Prix racing's excesses as a wonderful complement to their own but the two cultures didn't interact: they – high rollers and low rollers and all rollers in between – ain't never heard of these drivers and these cars and, hey, they're doin' it in the car park agen. Same sentiments as Detroit, really. The Las Vegans knew and understood all forms of gambling, they liked world championship boxing bouts and they'd pay whatever money had not yet been stripped from them to watch world famous celebrities perform, but, hey, these cars, man, somethin' else.

If Monaco is (almost) a caricature of itself as a place, Las Vegas is fully a match for it and in a more conscious way. If you are going to have excesses, make them enormous, and Las Vegas had truly made them like that: hotels so big you took a helicopter from the reception along several miles of corridors

ABOVE LEFT *Mario Andretti, very much at home in America, while former team owner Rob Walker, now writing about racing, looks as he always did: benign.*

ABOVE RIGHT *Eddie Cheever seems pretty comfortable too.*

DRIVER'S VIEW

'The track itself was sandy but tracks that were specially built and only used for that were always sandy. I think it was the first time computer analysis was used and it worked unbelievably well. It was a hard circuit on the driver, physically tough. You were constantly turning left. I never had a problem in the race because in my case it was all about mental fitness. I am sure I wasn't the fittest driver but I'm sure I wasn't the unfittest either. I ran every day, I gave the impression that I smoked and drank but I led a very active life in the summer. I was just mentally strong. That's the trick. I used to run at lunchtime, Ibiza, wherever I was. It raises your pain barrier in the heat because heat was the biggest problem in a Formula One car. It wasn't the physical exhaustion, it was the heat. It was so bloody hot at places like Dallas, like Rio, and Vegas was hot. In Dallas I was sunbathing on the pit wall when Elio and Nigel were standing under umbrellas packed in ice. I knew I had them already.'

—————— *Keke Rosberg*

to your room and there you discovered that a slot machine had been placed in the bathroom so that while you attended to your natural functions you wouldn't miss a minute of putting the money in.

Something like that anyway.

The Las Vegans' feelings towards Formula One – indifference – was in no sense matched by Formula One's feelings towards Las Vegas. They were not indifferent.

Gordon Murray remembers 'I locked myself in my room for three days and refused to come out. I hated the place, all the falseness and the gambling. I just couldn't stand it. I left before the end of the race.'

Alex Hawkridge had 'never been there before. What did I make of it? A joke, really. The place was everything I had expected it to be, larger than life as it were, but it just didn't appeal to me in any way at all. I'm not a gambler and I don't like bright lights and it was a glitzy sham of a place, really. And then we got to the circuit – the car park. That was probably the worst venue I have ever visited.'

Chris Witty says 'Las Vegas is a show and we were a four-wheeled circus. I couldn't believe you could create a two-mile track inside a car park – but then

I had never seen the Caesars Palace car park. It was the closest I have ever been to Scalextric in my life. There was no run-off anywhere, it was absolutely flat and all you saw were little heads going around over the concrete blocks. It was very surreal in that sense, very in keeping with the whole Las Vegas, Nevada, thing.'

This is Rosberg's philosophy facing what would be the supreme moment of his career: 'You don't get many chances at the Championship, as was proved afterwards. You don't think about the future, you only think about what's happening now. The opportunity's there and you need to grab it with both hands. So you do everything you can. And don't forget I'd been leading the Championship on and off during the season, it didn't all happen at the end.

'You approach it like any other race. Las Vegas? I don't really care where or what the place is because I don't see what's outside. I don't take much notice and I don't care if it's Detroit or Rio. I go there to race. In Mexico City I even brought my own food and stayed in my room.'

The track measured 2.2 miles (3.6km) and, in outline, resembled something from a geometry class or a giant doodle.

OPPOSITE *Crowning moment. Nothing can stop him now: Rosberg knows fifth place is enough to win the title, and he gets there.*

BELOW *Chapman, at his last Grand Prix, chatting with Peter Warr, the man who would succeed him.*

ABOVE *A world in headlines, and the local press took it seriously.*

The weather was hot, hellishly hot – so hot that some drivers, like Mansell, expressed the view that you couldn't sustain a race distance in it and drivers would be taking it easy until the latter stages. On the first day (the Thursday: it was a Saturday race) Rosberg could barely breathe in the cockpit as he qualified fifth – Arnoux provisional pole, Michele Alboreto dancing the Tyrrell round between the inter-connecting concrete blocks to be second, then Cheever and Prost. Lauda was immediately after Rosberg and Watson tenth. 'The car's not at all as I like it at the moment, because my style is to pitch it into corners and it won't take that. We're going to change it.'[1]

STARTING GRID

Row	Left	Right
1	**1** 1:16.35 **A. Prost**	**2** 1:16.78 **R. Arnoux**
2	**3** 1:17.64 **M. Alboreto**	**4** 1:17.68 **E. Cheever**
3	**5** 1:17.77 **R. Patrese**	**6** 1:17.88 **K. Rosberg**
4	**7** 1:17.92 **M. Andretti**	**8** 1:17.95 **P. Tambay**
5	**9** 1:17.98 **J. Watson**	**10** 1:18.01 **D. Warwick**
6	**11** 1:18.05 **J. Laffite**	**12** 1:18.27 **N. Piquet**
7	**13** 1:18.33 **N. Lauda**	**14** 1:18.41 **D. Daly**
8	**15** 1:18.49 **R. Guerrero**	**16** 1:18.62 **B. Giacomelli**
9	**17** 1:18.73 **M. Surer**	**18** 1:18.76 **A. de Cesaris**
10	**19** 1:18.76 **B. Henton**	**20** 1:19.30 **E. de Angelis**
11	**21** 1:19.43 **N. Mansell**	**22** 1:19.76 **M. Winkelhock**
12	**23** 1:20.27 **M. Baldi**	**24** 1:20.76 **R. Boesel**
13	**25** 1:21.18 **R. Keegan**	**26** 1:21.55 **T. Byrne**

Mind you, Rosberg dismissed all talk of drivers taking it easy by saying that they might say they would but they wouldn't and announced, typically, when he was asked about his own tactics, 'Balls out.'

In second qualifying Prost took pole from Arnoux but Alboreto maintained his pace and Watson's McLaren looked much more responsive to his demands – Rosberg sixth in the 'lightweight' spare, to which Daly says: 'There was a special qualifying car for Keke. I don't know how much underweight it was but I remember all the adjustable cables were taken off it, we had roll-bar adjusters and they were taken off...'

The McLaren team and Ron Dennis confronted a delicate decision. Lauda had global presence and was being paid a fortune – by his own admission he demanded from Marlboro (McLaren's sponsor, who were paying the bills) more than anyone had ever been paid in Grand Prix racing before to return to the sport for 1982.[2] Watson had no global presence and was being paid a great deal less.

'McLaren found itself in a dilemma partly because of the ability of both its drivers [Watson actually leading Lauda on points] but with the added caveat of Niki winning the World Championship on his return – the publicity that he, and therefore Marlboro and McLaren, would have received would have been infinitely greater than me, because as far as the world was concerned I was just a Joe Blow.

'On the Friday night Ron, being the ever-pragmatic man that he is, acknowledged that there was more chance of me doing well than Niki, partly because I had the benefit of three points and partly because really Niki couldn't win it. Ron spoke to Niki and said "Look, these are the circumstances, if you are ahead of John and you're running 1–2, will you step aside and let John take the win?" I think it was the first time in Niki's career that he had ever been asked to do something like that and, in fairness to him, it was not easy to acknowledge that request. Eventually he did acknowledge it. He did it with reluctance but he did it nonetheless. To his credit he said "Yes, I will do it."

'Ron always says "You race for the team, you lose for the team" but equally the team realised that at the last race I was in a better position to win the Championship than Niki was. At the end of the day McLaren winning the Championship was more important than offending Niki Lauda.

ABOVE *The start, Prost away fast from pole, Arnoux after him – but the story of the race ultimately wasn't about either of them.*

'He could have said no, and what would Ron do? Ron would have been annoyed but there was nothing in the contract, as far as I was aware, that stipulated Niki had priority, so Ron wanted to consolidate the situation. He didn't want to have the pair of us racing with the potential that both of us failed to finish. That's where Ron's management and judgement led him, and it was difficult for Niki.'

Alan Jenkins offers this insight: 'Niki's favourite was whingeing about John and he even did it to his face – "You're messing around all through practice then come the bloody race I have to start looking in the mirrors because sure enough you're going to appear." And that was John.'

During the warm-up Tambay pitted and withdrew from the race because he had an injured arm and Guerrero's car blew up. Prost went fastest – from Watson.

Track temperatures were anticipated at 135°, the circuit was like one long corner and offered the drivers no respite, the G-forces would give their necks a beating. Who could, who would, survive it?

Prost brought them prudently round to the grid from the parade lap and as they moved to their bays America spread itself as a backdrop with enormous advertising hoardings. One, proclaiming CAESARS PALACE GRAND PRIX SEPTEMBER 23–26, 1982, captured both America's real interest (the race was on September 25) and the nature of Las Vegas (the hoarding stood atop three ancient, classical stone columns, but were they ancient and were they stone, and who cared?).

The tail of the grid came slowly round the last corner to the grid, probing for their places. The medical car and the wrecker trucks followed, stately, positioned themselves just at the back. At the green light Prost was away fast and the cars behind dug smoke from their tyres so violently that a pall hung like mist full across the track. Prost led Arnoux into Turn One and as they streamed into the track's continuous contortions half a dozen cars jostled for position. By the end of the lap it had settled.

1 Prost
2 Arnoux
3 Alboreto
4 Patrese
5 Cheever
6 Andretti
7 Rosberg
8 Piquet
9 Warwick
10 Daly
11 Watson...

It meant that in the jostling Rosberg had lost one place and Watson two. This was of no concern to Prost and Arnoux, especially Arnoux who intended to leave Renault having made a strong statement. On lap 2 he moved past Prost for the lead. They stretched from Alboreto and Laffite overtook Watson.

The first seven ran unchanged and on lap 4 Watson began to make his move. He dealt with Laffite, dealt with Daly the lap after that, stalked and took Warwick the lap after that. He stalked Piquet now but Piquet was further up the road and Watson didn't deal with him until lap 11. Next: Rosberg.

'Everything,' Watson said at the time, 'seemed to fall into place' and the car felt as good as at Detroit. On lap 15 Prost retook Arnoux and Watson dealt with Rosberg: this was classical and authentic. Watson positioned himself directly behind through a left kink towards a right-hander, pointed the McLaren to the inside and accelerated so strongly he went past in a great surge. Rosberg said: 'When John

came by me I knew there was no way I could stay with him' – Rosberg did stay with him for a handful of corners but then the McLaren moved away – 'and it was clear to me at that stage that he could win the race. If he did that, of course, my points position became crucial. Now I needed those points to be sure of the title and for the first time I concentrated my attention on the Championship rather than the race.'

Watson dealt with Andretti the lap after, Cheever the lap after that. On the same lap Patrese's clutch failed, making Watson fourth and Rosberg seventh. Three laps after that Arnoux's ailing engine expired, making Watson third (and 23 seconds from Alboreto), Rosberg sixth.

An insight into Watson's mentality and technique, which explains what was happening, from Alan Jenkins: 'Wattie had a particular dislike of a car that was in any way nervous at the rear and he used to describe it like this: as long as he could lean upon the rear with some confidence he could beat anybody. He had a very late-braking, very positive turn-in style that he could only manage if the car would let him. If it wouldn't let him, he tended to be hesitant about turning in, which made it appear to understeer.

'It probably did understeer but the fact is it wasn't an understeering car – which people just couldn't understand – it was his tendency to start turning early for fear of the rear biting him. Initially he couldn't really put it into words that well. We hung out a bit socially so in a sense it became possible to talk about it away from the track. I

BELOW Warwick making the Toleman go as far as it could as fast as it could – to lap 32 when a misfire stopped it.

ABOVE *Mid race, and Watson runs third in front of Cheever and Andretti but as long as Rosberg is in the points it doesn't matter.*

remember when I ran Alain Prost after John, all of a sudden there was a guy that called you up every bloody night and wanted to talk about springs, bars and God knows what else. Those were the wonderful days before pit stops and you had to figure out what to do to make the car run for the best part of two hours, and then it was literally up to the driver. This whole juggling act – well, there was so little to adjust on the car. JB [Barnard] was never a great fan of adjustable roll bars. They were all too complicated. We basically plugged in what worked for the balance of the race, certainly on the front of the car. JB reluctantly let us have one on the rear but he wouldn't let us have one at the front.

'That's how Wattie could also pass people so easily and when the car was working he looked like he could pass almost anybody. It wasn't so much he braked later but braked deeper into the corner, because he really needed to turn the car in. It was confusing initially because he'd talk about his understeer and understeer and understeer.'

On lap 27 Piquet retired (a spark plug problem). Patrese was already out, of course, and Gordon Murray headed for the airport.

On lap 27 the Championship moved decisively towards Rosberg because Andretti's Ferrari suddenly skewed sideways in a tight right-hander, the suspension broken.

'Wattie was never going to win the Championship at that stage any more,' Rosberg says. 'I didn't worry where he was, I just had to be in the top five so it wasn't a big job, but, of course, I couldn't afford to have a DNF if he was going well. I was only worried about the DNF really. So you do your own thing and hope the others don't spoil it. Mario drove the Ferrari and he broke the suspension when he was behind me. He could have taken me off. He nearly did. I remember he went across me.'

Andretti remembers it was 'almost identical to the year before when I was in the Alfa Romeo: rear suspension, same side, same spot. When the rear suspension goes you are just a passenger.'

As the Ferrari bumped onto the dusty run-off area there, glimpsed through the dust was Rosberg, fifth.

The race settled again after that but, frustratingly for Watson, he was getting a vibration which affected his vision and the car's handling deteriorated so that

FAN'S EYE VIEW

'I first noticed Formula One in 1970 when, as a teenager, I saw Jochen Rindt's stunning victory in the Monaco Grand Prix on ABC's Wide World of Sports. I became a devoted follower of Grand Prix racing the next year and in 1972 I attended my first major event, the Six Hour sports car and the Can Am race weekend at Watkins Glen.

'With schoolboy fascination I watched as the drivers I had been reading about – Jacky Ickx, Mario Andretti, Ronnie Peterson, Peter Revson and François Cevert – went about their business. I met Cevert briefly in the garage. What a charming and worldly fellow.

'His terrible accident the next year, at the very track at which I had seen him race, dimmed my enthusiasm. I did go to the US Grand Prix in 1974 and witnessed Emerson Fittipaldi's second title but that race also was marred by a fatal accident to Austrian Helmut Koinigg. Afterward, I was walking through the garage – fans could do that in those days – and remember an eerie feeling upon seeing an empty Surtees pit. The announcement came only later after we had left the circuit.

'In 1982 I was a 28-year-old editor at the Denver Post, handling national and world news. I had read reports of an event in Detroit planned for 1982. Having worked briefly for a newspaper in the Motor City, I decided to go. And having never been to Las Vegas, I decided to attend the season finale. I thought the title in that turbulent year might come down to the final race, providing added incentive.'

JAMES PINKELMAN
WASHINGTON DC, USA

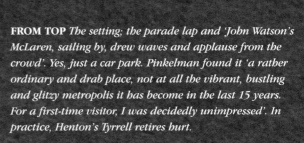

FROM TOP The setting; the parade lap and 'John Watson's McLaren, sailing by, drew waves and applause from the crowd'. Yes, just a car park. Pinkelman found it 'a rather ordinary and drab place, not at all the vibrant, bustling and glitzy metropolis it has become in the last 15 years. For a first-time visitor, I was decidedly unimpressed'. In practice, Henton's Tyrrell retires hurt.

ABOVE *Alboreto moving
to the first of his five
Grand Prix victories
and Tyrrell's first for
four years.*

he got to within ten seconds of Alboreto – who
was ten seconds behind Prost – but no closer.

'It was very much a tyre thing,' Watson says. 'I
drove a bloody good race and the aspect that's
slightly irksome, and I could never prove, were
suggestions that the Tyrrell had something slightly
dodgy in terms of the skirt operation they were
running which gave significant advantage. I got
past everybody except Michele, I drove my heart
out, I was driving flat out and I got to within ten
seconds and I hadn't anything left. I just had
to consolidate.'

Prost's tyres were wearing so badly that 'under

braking I felt as though I would be shaken out of
the cockpit.' Alboreto went past on lap 52, Watson
following four laps later.

Quietly, almost ruefully, Watson says: 'If I wasn't
first it didn't really matter where Keke was. If
Michele had hit the wall I was quids in – but then
Keke would have finished fourth.'

Rosberg knew that if Alboreto did hit a wall and
he – Rosberg – retired for whatever reason, the
Championship had gone. He'd remember the final
20 laps as 'awfully long' although he wasn't tired
and could have pushed hard if he'd needed to do
that. Rosberg knew – every driver does – that if you

270

problem after 53 laps so that, all in the moment, the Championship disappeared – and Ferrari had the Constructors' Championship, not McLaren.

Easy to forget that Daly, who had not been to Las Vegas before, 'caught Keke in the end. I went much better in the races, which was one of the complaints Patrick Head had – if only we could get him to qualify better – because my race lap times were much more comparable to Keke's. Three or four laps from the end I was so physically spent that I was actually getting dizzy in the braking zones. They were also bumpy and they were coming at you the whole time.'

You know the way it is by now, and how they all headed for the airport. Rosberg went to Los Angeles.

'We left Sunday night from Las Vegas to San Francisco to Mansour's Ojeh's 30th birthday party.

LEFT *The world in headlines: big news in Finland, smaller news in Belfast.*

don't push hard you can lose concentration, make mistakes. He sat there thinking: I hope the car holds together, that's all.

It did.

Rosberg 44, Pironi and Watson 39, Prost 34, Lauda 30, Arnoux 28.

Easy to forget that Alboreto drove a race of maturity and without error to win the first Grand Prix of his career. Easy to forget that the Tyrrell team had been winning races since 1971 and would only ever win one more after this, Detroit in 1983, Alboreto the driver again.

Easy to forget that Lauda retired with an engine

OPPOSITE *Rosberg, man of the day, man of the season.*

BELOW *Michele Alboreto gets to kiss Diana Ross, or is it the other way round? The proprieties of the podium are being observed, Watson (second) watching.*

There was Elio, Derek, some other drivers. I was too tired to enjoy it because by the time we got to his house for the party it was 1.00 am and mentally I had had enough. It wasn't one of my better parties.'

Chris Witty, who'd worked for *Autosport* magazine before joining Toleman, 'stayed in America after the race because I wanted to go and see a couple of potential sponsors. I ended up somewhere in Long Beach and Keke was there with Jeff Hutchinson.[3] He was World Champion but we all sat down for something to eat and he said "When I was a SuperVee guy I was struggling but *Autosport* and those magazines helped me through." He didn't say "I dedicate this title to you guys" or anything like that but it was my first experience of a World Champion

being humble. Well, grateful. A lot of people help drivers along the way and drivers can forget about it very quickly.'

To which Keke Rosberg says 'Humble and grateful? I hope I was like that because it was the correct thing to be.'

At the very end a driver exhibited the Olde Worlde courtesy I had met at the very beginning, and now, near the culmination of our tale, you know all the things which happened in between.

Footnote: 1. Autosport; 2. To Hell And Back, Lauda; 3. Jeff Hutchinson, long-time motor sport journalist and photographer, who also made money flying drivers around in his little propeller plane. His journey from London to Mexico for a Grand Prix there was an epic, and his recounting of it much more entertaining than Round The World In 80 Days.

Race Result

WINNING SPEED 161.11kmh/100.11mph

FASTEST LAP 164.99kmh/102.52mph
(Alboreto 1m 19.63s on lap 59)

LAP LEADERS Prost 1, 15–51 (38);
Arnoux 2–14 (13); Alboreto 52–75 (24)

RACE

	Driver	Team	Engine	Laps	Time
1	M. Alboreto	Tyrrell 011	Cosworth V8	75	1h 41m 56.88s
2	J. Watson	McLaren MP4B	Cosworth V8	75	1h 42m 24.18s
3	E. Cheever	Talbot Ligier JS19	Matra V12	75	1h 42m 53.33s
4	A. Prost	Renault RE30B	Renault V6t	75	1h 43m 05.53s
5	K. Rosberg	Williams FW08	Cosworth V8	75	1h 43m 08.26s
6	D. Daly	Williams FW08	Cosworth V8	74	
7	M. Surer	Arrows A5	Cosworth V8	74	
8	B. Henton	Tyrrell 011	Cosworth V8	74	
9	A. de Cesaris	Alfa Romeo 182	Alfa V12	73	
10	B. Giacomelli	Alfa Romeo 182	Alfa V12	73	
11	M. Baldi	Arrows A4	Cosworth V8	73	
12	R. Keegan	March 821	Cosworth V8	73	
13	R. Boesel	March 821	Cosworth V8	69	
nc	M. Winkelhock	ATS D5	Cosworth V8	62	
r	N. Lauda	McLaren MP4B	Cosworth V8	53	Engine
r	T. Byrne	Theodore TY02	Cosworth V8	39	Spin
r	D. Warwick	Toleman TG183	Hart 4t	32	Spark plugs
r	E. de Angelis	Lotus 91	Cosworth V8	28	Engine
r	M. Andretti	Ferrari 126C2	Ferrari V6t	26	Rear suspension
r	N. Piquet	Brabham BT50	BMW 4t	26	Spark plug
r	R. Arnoux	Renault RE30B	Renault V6t	20	Engine
r	R. Patrese	Brabham BT50	BMW 4t	17	Clutch
r	N. Mansell	Lotus 91	Cosworth V8	8	Accident
r	J. Laffite	Talbot Ligier JS19	Matra V12	5	Ignition
ns	P. Tambay	Ferrari 126C2	Ferrari V6t		Driver unfit
ns	R. Guerrero	Ensign N181	Cosworth V8		Engine
ns	J.-P. Jarier	Osella FA1D	Cosworth V8		Accident
nq	T. Fabi	Toleman TG181C	Hart 4t		
nq	E. Salazar	ATS D5	Cosworth V8		
nq	C. Serra	Fittipaldi F9	Cosworth V8		

nc = did not complete=; nq = did not qualify; ns = did not start; r = retired

CHAMPIONSHIP

	Driver	Points
1	K. Rosberg	44
2	D. Pironi	39
	J. Watson	39
4	A. Prost	34
5	N. Lauda	30
6	R. Arnoux	28
7	P. Tambay	25
	M. Alboreto	25
9	E. de Angelis	23
10	R. Patrese	21
11	N. Piquet	20
12	E. Cheever	15
13	D. Daly	8
14	N. Mansell	7
15	C. Reutemann	6
	G. Villeneuve	6
17	A. de Cesaris	5
	J. Laffite	5
19	M. Andretti	4
20	J.-P. Jarier	3
	M. Surer	3
22	M. Winkelhock	2
	E. Salazar	2
	B. Giacomelli	2
	M. Baldi	2
26	F. Serra	1

	Team	Points
1	Ferrari	74
2	McLaren	69
3	Renault	62
4	Williams	58
5	Brabham	41
6	Lotus	30
7	Tyrrell	25
8	Talbot Ligier	20
9	Alfa Romeo	7
10	Arrows	5
11	ATS	4
12	Osella	3
13	Fittipaldi	1

JUST PASSING THROUGH

———— WHERE THEY ARE NOW ————

John Watson reflects that 1982 'was my only chance for the World Championship and there are three or four not unreasonable ifs that would have made me Champion. In fairness, that Championship ought to have been won by a Ferrari driver. From Imola onwards it should have been their championship. If Gilles hadn't crashed, there is a very good chance they would have had a strong finish in Belgium and at that point the Ferrari was stronger than the Renault and had better reliability. I think the Renault was probably a better car but it kept breaking down. At Ferrari you had two hyper drivers, one hyper political [Pironi], the other hyper active [Villeneuve]. Renault had a very strong driver in Alain Prost, and Arnoux, who was a stunningly quick driver as well as good racer, but it should have been Ferrari's.'

This quarter-of-a-century-later Watson remains wise in the many ways of motor sport and a very shrewd judge of that most elusive subject, what it all really means. He has run a driving school and been an informative commentator on Eurosport.

Alan Jenkins offers one of his insights: 'Wattie was completely unable to queue. If you went to an airport and there were even two people in a queue it was two too many. He was the worst traveller ever, nervous and twitchy and just wanted to get it over with. Strangely, he drove fast on the roads too. In those days most of those guys drove like complete madmen. If you drove down with him to his house in Bognor it was like doing the Targa Florio...[1]

'He's a complicated man, Mr Watson, and a lovely bloke.'

These days Watson is an active fisherman ('we must be getting old') and still does television commentaries on the A1GP series.

Echoing Watson, Patrick Tambay still insists that 'if it had not been for a silly expletive physiotherapist who nicked my back I could maybe have had a chance to win the 1982 Championship – with only half a season. It was a year where the Championship was won with very, very few points – it could have been anybody's.' He's still driving in the GP Masters, lives in the south of France and is, as someone observed, the perfect uncle. Of his time in Grand Prix racing, he insists he was like everybody else who's ever been in it.

'We were just passing through.'

Derek Daly knew that during the 'second half of the season it was going away from me. I wasn't driving with the same reckless abandon that I did in Formula 3 and Formula 2, and at Ensign. As that season unfolded, I didn't drive well because I had personal problems and I ended up getting divorced. That's what derailed me. At the end of the year Frank himself called me and said "Derek, I think I am going to have Jacques [Laffite] next year" and I perfectly understood. I said that and "I am going to go to America. I want to clear off out of this lifestyle that I've been in, I want to go race in America. I need a fresh, new life." In a way it was a favour to me because it opened up a completely new chapter to my life. I've been here in America [Indiana] ever since.

'I do a lot of television. My main business focus is a company called Motorvation.

'What I learned in all those years, and what I enjoy passing on to my son – who is 14 and racing go-karts right now – is what I didn't know at the time: that I wasn't invincible. You think you are. You just go do it. It's only when you look back you see your weaknesses.'

Colin Chapman died that December of a heart attack. I came to motor sport too late to know him – we spoke once, briefly, and he was dismissive, but I don't judge him in any way on that. An entirely self-made man, he built a road car company famous

OPPOSITE *Kyalami in all its might and the leaders running in pairs: Arnoux from Prost, Villeneuve from Pironi – a microcosm of the whole season.*

round the world and created a major Grand Prix team. There were shadowy sides to this, some still unresolved. Perhaps two quotations capture the man.

Mario Andretti: 'Working with Chapman wasn't no trip to Paris.'

Peter Warr: 'Colin's genius was that he could look at a difficult problem and find a simple, original solution nobody else had thought of.'

Gordon Murray remembers the immediate aftermath to the 1982 season. 'We got really stymied because we built the BT51. Bernie kept saying to me "We'll keep skirts, don't worry, we'll keep skirts" so I designed a completely new motor car, the BT51, half-tank size, with skirts and sidepods and it was ready so early to run – like October – because I thought the half-tanks was such a good thing to do. We would have been in a fantastic position. And then in October Bernie said "I'm sorry, they are going to get banned" and we scrapped the car. We'd built two already.

'I had to start in October and do a completely new car. The reason the BT52 had no sidepods was because we had no time to go into the wind tunnel. I shoved seven per cent more weight on the back axle because I knew we'd have a lot more horsepower from the engine: shifted the seven per cent, dumped the sidepods, and made the world's simplest pit-stop half-tank car.

'We did a lot of work and we kept developing because I said to Bernie "They're all going to catch up," as they usually do. It was so frustrating because we didn't really get a big advantage from it. Then we had winter and I said to Bernie "Everybody's going to be doing half-tank cars because it's not exactly rocket science to do the mathematics. There are a few equations to work out that it's the thing to do and it gives you all sorts of options in a race.

'We arrived in Brazil, I said to Bernie "All the cars are going to be like that," and nobody had pit-stop cars apart from Williams, who had a kit which they could put on if they thought it was necessary. Nobody had built half-tank cars. I couldn't believe my luck and of course we creamed that year.'

The Toleman team remains in memory as a complete contradiction because, in this flint-hard activity of motor racing where nostalgia is usually treated as weakness, it began as an intimate group of romantics and stayed like that.

I caught an early flavour – long before the Formula One days – because Ted Toleman was a gregarious, Dickensian figure and I went to interview him at the company headquarters in Brentwood, not far from where I live. He took me to his country club and, while we dined exquisitely, he explained that he made his money by delivering cars from ports to dealers.

That was fine but it created a problem. 'You cannot,' he said, 'advertise, because people simply don't care who delivers your car.'

He concluded: 'What we'll do is motor racing as well.'

In those distant days when people drank and drove (the quantity you drank was not a factor, only whether you were in control of the car) we had a lot of port and then a lot more port. I got home slowly and safely, having concluded that if this is how you go motor racing why did nobody tell me before?

The romantic aspect of Toleman is amplified by the fact that they were the last small team to get to the front of the grid. Alex Hawkridge charts that. 'The 1982 season was a big step year for Toleman. The main thing in 1981 was just learning from all the things we'd done wrong but we stuck with it and tried to deal with the problems. The biggest was that we didn't have a suitable turbocharger and the ones we could get were melting, so in an endeavour to stop that happening we mounted the turbocharger on top of the engine, which is high centre of gravity, terrible aerodynamics – but that was what he had to do just to get to run.

'By 1982 we'd some slightly better turbochargers and we were able to put them on the floor. That improved the handling and we were a full second and a half, two seconds quicker than the previous year. In 1982 we started qualifying for races, in 1983

we started to get points and in 1984 we had Ayrton Senna and should have won a race. That was down to the technical team, Rory [Byrne] and Pat Symonds, who are now household names but even then were exceptional individuals. Rory had an incredible aptitude to learn fast, bearing in mind he's not an engineer at all – he's a qualified chemist! But he's very bright and also a tremendous man-manager. People relate to him and enjoy working with him.

'Pat is very clever in an R&D sort of way and he thinks out of the box. We had him working in 1982 on active suspension with a company called Avex Aerospace, and that was well ahead of the dawn of active suspension. We'd have had a powerful package if we'd had the money to develop it.

'We still had the flavour of Formula 2 in the team, really. When I was at March, Adrian Newey was there and now at Toleman we often had fun and games with them – work hard, play hard. They were in a similar position to us – actually a bit better off because they had a Cosworth engine – but we believed in the turbos and had to go our own way. The hardest part was a reliable turbo but for a small team with a small budget what we did was miraculous.'

Chris Witty reinforces that. 'Everything was very different a year later because in 1983 we got the first points, ironically at Zandvoort. We then went into a run of getting cars into the points for four or five

BELOW *Roberto Guerrero had a difficult season but there are always consolations.*

Grands Prix, if not longer. We managed it twice with both cars. So in the space of a year we were able to elevate ourselves and get much greater reliability.

'I look back and Toleman came from absolutely nowhere – no-hopers – with a completely different package, Pirelli tyres that no one had even really considered before, home-brewed engine with Brian Hart, everything like that. I think we were between 30 and 50 personnel and in those days that was enough. The whole thing was fascinating. I enjoyed Alex's idea of taking something from scratch and turning it into a Formula One team and a turbo team.'

Elio de Angelis, his path in life smoothed by family money, was a softly spoken, dignified man of many talents – not least playing the piano to keep morale up during the strike in South Africa. He had a lovely sense of humour and once delighted Allsop with a tale of how he'd been racing in Sicily and on the eve of the race the Mafiosi asked him where he wanted to finish. He tried to explain that he'd come

to compete, the best man to win, but they couldn't grasp that. Tell us where and we arrange it.

He left Lotus at the end of 1985 to join Brabham. Testing at Paul Ricard in May he crashed fatally. He was 28. Many drivers present that day still find talking about it distressing.

No man can be universally popular in Formula One because it isn't that kind of animal but in this era three men came close: de Angelis, Alboreto, and Warwick.

Alboreto moved from Tyrrell to Ferrari for the 1984 season and stayed there until 1989, when he rejoined Tyrrell. He drifted down through Lola, Arrows and Minardi. That didn't trouble him because he needed to drive, and thereby hangs a precious memory.

I'd come across a photograph of him and Senna on a pit wall, both laughing at something. Alboreto was competing at Le Mans for Audi and in their sumptuous hospitality area, he sat chatting quite happily to anyone and everyone. I'd taken the photograph and mentioned to Martyn Pass of the Audi Press service that I was going to approach Alboreto about what had happened.

'Bet he doesn't remember,' Pass said.

'Bet he does.'

He did – and told the tale of how Senna said to him 'What are you still doing here driving a Minardi?' Alboreto said 'Because I love it! – and what are you doing here now you have three World Championships?' To which Senna replied 'Because I love it, too!' That's why they were both laughing.

Another precious memory at the French Grand Prix, Magny-Cours, circa 1991. I mentioned to someone that I was taking my family to Italy on holiday and Alboreto, overhearing, said 'Stay at my place in Portofino. I get the keys now!' Portofino is the chic Italian resort, I was just a face in the Press crowd and his offer, like the man, was totally sincere. I'd already booked a hotel (nowhere near Portofino!) and couldn't take him up.

When news came through that spring day in 2001 that he'd crashed fatally in Germany testing an Audi for Le Mans the whole motor racing community mourned in the way that they had mourned Elio.

Warwick left Toleman for Renault in 1984 and stayed there for two seasons then drifted down through Brabham, Arrows and Lotus. He retired in 1993 and by then he'd won Le Mans in a Peugeot (in 1992) and, that same year, the World Sports Car Championship, to the delight of many, many people who knew a nice bloke when they saw one.

He was one of the most unaffected (and candid) people I've ever met and when he was genuinely famous with Renault he continued to obey the dictum of Rudyard Kipling's poem 'If' about meeting triumph and disaster and treating 'those two impostors just the same'.

The way the Formula One animal is, it rides you hard even as you try to ride it hard. Warwick suffered that and still came close to a major career. If...

He runs a Honda dealership in Jersey these days and his daughters are competitive horsewomen. I wonder wherever they get that from?

Niki Lauda seems to have lived several lives to the full, sometimes simultaneously, and to each he applied the logic, not least winning the Championship in a McLaren in 1984. At the end of 1985 he strode away from Grand Prix racing to run his airline. He is still running it (or a variation of it) today. He had a sharp sense of humour: at the Österreichring in '85 he asked Marlboro publicity lady Agnes Carlier to call a press conference because he had something to say. She wondered what it was. He murmured 'Maybe I'm pregnant.' He was a senior executive at the Jaguar F1 team between 2001 and 2003 and has acted as an adviser to Ferrari.

Tommy Byrne lost his Formula One drive and went to European Formula 3 in 1983, then retreated to the United States. He retreated further, to Mexican Formula 3, and in a phone conversation bubbled over with enthusiasm for it. As a man he was just like that, couldn't help himself. He almost convinced me it was a seriously good career move.

One time I was visiting Road Atlanta and, from nowhere, he sprang out of a saloon car and said in a wondrous mingling of Irish and American accents 'We'll have a beer or two tonight!' He was doing some driving instructing – and we hadn't met since 1982.

The way the Formula One animal is, it can devour even the strong and ambitious and it devoured Tommy Byrne in just a few weeks.

In response to 'What are you doing these days?' Jean-Pierre Jarier says 'That's the big question! I stopped driving in 1983 when I stopped doing Formula One. I had offers to do Indy but I didn't want to do that because I thought it very dangerous. I did touring cars and sports cars, I drove an Alfa Romeo. I stopped altogether in 2003. Now I do TV commentaries and journalism. I'd been editor of *Autohebdo*. All the media have moved to Paris but I wanted to stay on the coast. I have a PR agency which is called Monaco Media and I organise guests on the terraces/balconies during the Monaco Grand Prix. I find them hotels and restaurants.'

Brian Henton drove in the 1983 Race of Champions and then 'walked away from motor sport completely. I had no thoughts of trying to make a living through it and I didn't go to a race for ten years.' What he did do was play cricket for a village second team and 'the first match I broke my finger. I'd been 15 years in motor racing, never had a scratch!' He moved into property in Leicestershire and London and now lives on a country estate. 'D'you know what's strange? Hardly a week goes by when I don't receive fan mail from Germany. It still keeps coming. Let's face it, I wasn't the greatest and it's touching that people remember.'

In 1984 Alain Prost joined McLaren and won three Championships with them. He retired, returned with Williams and won a fourth in 1993. He ran his own

BELOW *Optical illusion: Warwick's Toleman didn't look a challenge to manipulate – but it was. Here in Austria it did seven laps.*

team under his own name between 1997 and 2001, when it folded.

Riccardo Patrese is doing the Grand Prix Masters and 'also some show jumping'. He ended our interview (on his mobile phone) by saying 'I am going to jump in some minutes so I have to finish.' Hilton: 'Horses are very dangerous.' Patrese: 'I know, I know, I know! When you fall down from them it's a big crack on the head.'

Jochen Mass has done extensive work as an expert summariser on German television. He lives in the south of France and when I rang (the week of Schumacher's last Grand Prix, Brazil) he said in his exquisitely modulated English 'Don't tell me you want to talk about him. Everybody else does.' To which I reply 'No, I want to talk about you.' To which he replies 'Oh!' Mass is the most candid of men but he does not discuss Zolder, confining himself only to 'It was one of the darkest times in motor sport and why say more than that?' It is hard not to respect Mass, just as it is hard not to respect his decision to remain silent.

Mario Andretti, softly spoken, is a precise man about his arrangements. I was due to ring him at his office at (his) 10.00 am but he got stuck in traffic and telephoned his assistant, Amy, to apologise to me and give a new time. Not many do that. How do I know? Not many have. And yes, he was there exactly at the new time. He has fathered a dynasty of racers, the latest of which – Marco, son of Michael – is winning. Then there's the Andretti Green racing team in IndyCars, due to contest the American Le Mans series in 2007. And he's a pensioner. Some pensioner.

De Cesaris had been living in the South Seas and when I asked about that he says 'Yes, but I came back!'

Nelson Piquet added a second World Championship in 1987 to the one he'd won in 1981. When he retired he set up his own Formula 3 team. He was frequently spotted at Grands Prix in 2006 keeping an eye on son Nelson Jr in the GP2 series.

René Arnoux is in the Grand Prix Masters and has a karting empire: 'Two tracks in Paris, one at Lyons, one in Aix-en-Provençe. They are indoor and it's going well. And then I am in Switzerland where we make pieces for high-quality watches. I am a happy man.'

ABOVE *Brabham's Gordon Murray invented tyre-warmers. Is this what they did before that? Note in the background behind the mechanic on the right front wheel that Rio's heat did not encourage evening dress...*

Teo Fabi runs 'a construction and development business. I build houses and apartments in Milan.'

Manfred Winkelhock, body of an ox but a surprisingly gentle man, was killed at Mosport in 1985 during a sports car meeting.

Didier Pironi never did drive a Formula One car again and, his motor racing career over, moved to offshore powerboats. He was killed in a race round the Isle of Wight in 1987.

Eddie Cheever replaced Arnoux at Renault in 1983, but despite finishing second in Canada was only joint sixth in the Championship. After that he drove for a further three teams and returned to America to win the Indy 500 in 1998. He then became a team owner.

Jacques Laffite, of the hewn face and smile which detonated at the slightest opportunity, had two nicknames – which tell you a great deal: Jolly Jacques and Jack Lafferty – from the time when he lived in England, determined that his son would speak English, so the F1 fraternity anglicised him! He crashed his Ligier in the 1985 British Grand Prix at Brands Hatch, breaking both legs, but retreated to French touring cars – and kept smiling.

Bruno Giacomelli drove for the Toleman team in 1983 and then, almost mysteriously, his career drifted away. He reappeared for the Life team in 1990 but didn't get near qualifying for a race and drifted away again.

Eliseo Salazar struggled into 1983 with the RAM team but of six Grand Prix meetings only qualified for two. He moved to sports cars and then the United States, enjoying some success in Champ Cars and the Indy Racing League.

Marc Surer lingered with Arrows (plus a season with Brabham) and finally ended his racing career in 1986 when he crashed a rally car and received serious injuries. One time after the British Grand Prix at Silverstone I was in the infield traffic jam trying to get across the *Daily Express* Bridge into the proper traffic jam. The man in the car alongside waved – it was Surer. He made a gesture of resignation with his hands which had two meanings: 'What can you do?' and 'I'm just like everybody else now, aren't I?' They all are when they've passed through.

Nigel Mansell's career subsequent to 1982 has been exhaustively documented. In driving accomplishments, his 1992 World Championship and IndyCar championship the following year make him one of the best of his generation. As a pure, fearless racer he had few equals and even fewer peers. He had big, big balls.

It was the other Nigel Mansell, the one who emerged from the cockpit, who was hard to understand. It was as if he had had to invent himself, complete with an unending struggle against impossible odds: you never sensed the need for such

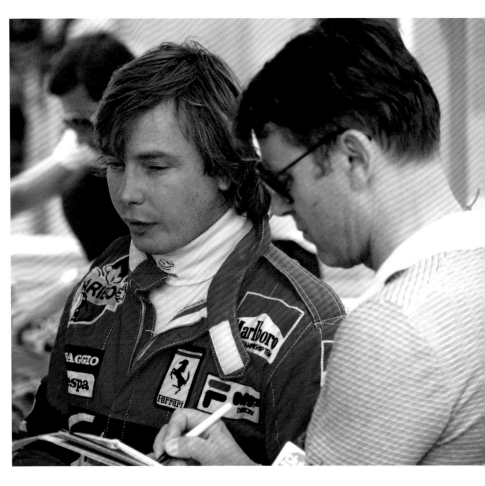

a story inside the cockpit because there never was a need.

In the matter of communicating with a vast British audience at Silverstone and Brands Hatch he had no peers. They looked at him in their thousands and thought they saw themselves.

Keke Rosberg says on the phone he's put on too much weight and so we won't be having lunch when we meet in Monte Carlo, not even salad. I get to his office in a modern tower block and I'm dismayed to discover that he has hardly put any weight on at all. I have...

'The 1983 was going to be my best season but by then the turbos had us. In 1983 I really thought I could walk on water and it's a very dangerous feeling. That was probably a result of 1982 and the World Championship.' His Formula One career ended in 1986 but he competed at Le Mans in a Peugeot, competed in German touring cars, and at one point had his own team. He managed Mika Häkkinen and JJ Lehto and now looks after son Nico.

'Nelson Piquet comes to the races but our relationship is camouflaged because of a huge jealousy that Nico is in Formula One and his son isn't. Nelson isn't one of those people you are going to have important conversations with about deep subjects.

ABOVE *Leading French journalist Renaud de Laborderie gets the inside story from Pironi.*

OPPOSITE *Job specification: Alfa Romeo motor mechanic, Monaco. People of a nervous disposition or suffering from claustrophobia need not apply. The driver is de Cesaris.*

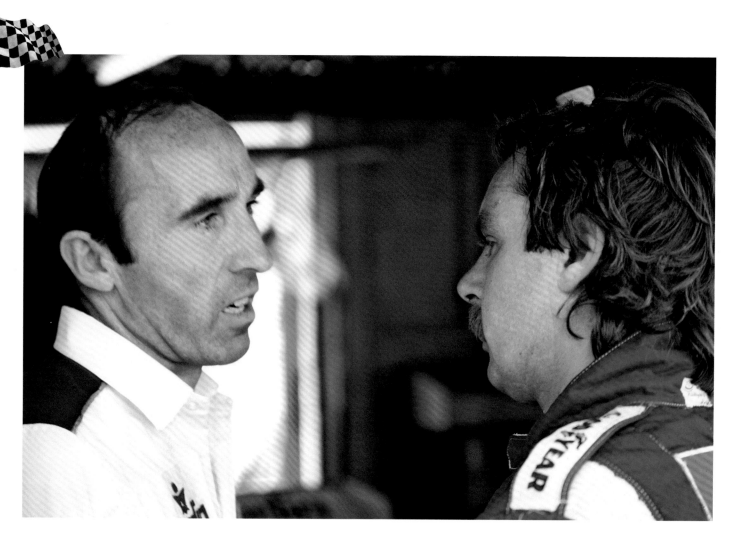

ABOVE *Frank Williams, the driven man who gave Rosberg his chance.*

'Alain Prost I don't ever see. I used to see his kids when Nico was in the lesser formulae. Alain has a very nice and well-educated son. I think Alain spends his life on a bicycle. Not my world. I do nothing without an engine. Patrick Tambay I see, Jean-Pierre Jarier I see because he lives here – we were in the same restaurant last night. I actually forgot to say hello. He hit me in the back at Long Beach in 1983...

'I never see Wattie because I don't go to England, I've got nothing to do with England and basically Wattie never leaves England. I say hello to him at Silverstone, bang, gone.

'Patrick Head always reminded me of a rugby player in those days and it's how people mellow over a period of 20 years. Patrick is a completely different man now.

'When you look at Ron Dennis and Frank today, there aren't many of their generation around anymore – Bernie – and the rest are all newcomers. The drivers are 22-year-olds whereas in our day the team managers were the same age, the journalists were the same age, the drivers were the same age, we were all one generation and so it made it completely different from the way it is today. What is Ron going to talk to Kimi Räikkönen about? Whereas in Rio we'd go to have drinks and a dance.'

The photographers who have contributed to Fan's Eye View through the book have, if I may put it like this, a common sentiment. Fings ain't what they used to be.

James Pinkelman says that 'the Las Vegas of 1982 was a glitzy but drab affair and today's Vegas would be scarcely recognisable to an observer in 1982. When I was last there, on official travel in March 2002, I saw that the Caesars Palace parking lot was now completely filled in by development.

'It's funny: my one subscription racing magazine is *Motor Sport*, which occasionally runs features on "then and now" circuits around Europe. Inevitably, one sees a house or a bridge in the "today" shot that is at least consistent with the look from the "then" historical photo.

'In the United States, no such luck. Riverside in California, the site of many an important race, is today a shopping mall. Langhorne, a deadly oval near Philadelphia, is a condo development or some such thing. I don't think *Motor Sport* would be able to do such features in this country!

'One final note. I found it highly incongruous that, for two years running, the World Championship was decided, not at a traditional circuit such as Monza (Fittipaldi in '72) or even

Watkins Glen (Fittipaldi again in '74), but at this plastic, made up, glorified go-kart track in the Nevada desert. Strange days, indeed, in Formula One back then.

'In 1985, I moved to Washington, DC, where I joined the staff of a Member of Congress. I am now deputy director in an agency of the US Justice Department. I follow Formula One only on TV.'

Gareth Rees says that 'the first Formula One race I ever saw was the British Grand Prix at Brands in 1966 and, looking back, I feel like Formula One just went from strength to strength in that period, before it became so much more professional and exclusive from the mid-80s on. I currently live in Tokyo and never miss a race on TV, but I rarely visit Formula One races these days, partly because I feel frustrated that spectators get such a raw deal with few interesting supporting races and the best views all reserved for corporate guests or at often ridiculous prices.

'Sadly, in the name of progress the Zandvoort of today has a shorter straight and the original Bos Uit is now part of a bungalow park.'

Paul Truswell says that at one stage 'I began to do some public address commentary myself, not only at Brands Hatch but also at other circuits. I am afraid to say that the increasing inaccessibility of the Formula One world to the general public led me to becoming more interested in other forms of racing.'

Charles J. Bough 'retired and moved to Utah in the Rocky Mountains in 1993. I have never lost my love of motor sport. As a point of interest, a local businessman has just opened a new, world class road racing facility just outside of Salt Lake in Toole County. Alan Wilson was the designer and runs the facility. His wife, Desiree Wilson runs the go kart track. We just got together last month – August, 2006 – in Las Vegas with our UK friends.'

David Hilleard says that 'nowadays my interest is only via the television and that not always. The absence of characters and consistent close racing, plus my attitude that "it's not as good as it used to be," accounts for it.'

Not as good as it used to be? A familiar complaint, in motor racing and just about everything else. It's hard to sustain because since 1982 we have had Rosberg as an accomplished front-runner, Prost calculating Championships, Senna driving like a deity and crashing like a devil, Mansell bursting all constraints to murder the 1992 season, Schumacher laying lordly claim to all before him and crashing more than Senna ever did. We have had, brief and bright as comets across our sky, Damon Hill and Jacques Villeneuve in their own right, Mika Häkkinen caressing his way to consecutive Championships, frisky little Fernando Alonso staking out the future as his very birthright.

In spite of what I've just written, and in spite of the normal human inclination to take ownership of a sport at the time you first fell for it ('my era') – which would make me misty-eyed even about the Hungry Tiger in Detroit – I'm going to offer an impartial judgement. No season except 1982 has had 11 winners or so many drivers on the podium (18), beating the 17 of 1968. No other season has had a strike, and few – including ye bad olde days – have brought so much grief. Only one other season – 1958 – has produced a World Champion with a single victory (Mike Hawthorn). Few seasons have had the difference of awesome turbo power on the same tracks as dear old Cosworths, giving two distinct races going on simultaneously but, between them, only one driver taking the race. Then there was Gordon Murray and the Pit Stop Ploy, which changed Grand Prix racing fundamentally. That alone would have made the season important, memorable, historic. Instead, in all this excitement, it stands as a footnote.

Not as good as it used to be?

Somebody said not all ages are golden.

Between 23 January and 25 September 1982, amid the mourning, this one was.

Footnote: 1. The Targa Florio, a rugged road race in Sicily, run between 1906 and 1977, and in its day one of the most important on the European calendar.

BELOW *Truly, now and then. Keke with son Nico – both Williams Formula 1 drivers.*

INDEX